# MIDLAND

*150 years of banking business*

# MIDLAND

## *150 years of banking business*

**A R HOLMES**
**& EDWIN GREEN**

B T BATSFORD LTD · LONDON

**Frontispiece** *Sir Edward Holden, Midland Bank's managing director between 1898 and 1908, and chairman and managing director from 1908 until his death in 1919*

Typeset by CCC, printed and bound in Great Britain by
William Clowes Limited, Beccles and London
for the publishers
B. T. Batsford Ltd
4 Fitzhardinge Street
London W1H 0AH


ISBN 0 7134 4732 X

# CONTENTS

*List of illustrations*   vii
*List of tables*   xi
*Acknowledgements*   xiii

Introduction   1

1   Setting up in banking, 1836–1851   7

2   Midland banking, 1851–1874   35

3   Amber: Birmingham to London, 1874–1891   57

4   Campaigns and conquests, 1891–1908   89

5   Colossus, 1908–1919   121

6   Holden's legacy, 1919–1929   153

7   Opposite the Bank of England, 1929–1939   175

8   Banking on the defensive, 1939–1948   197

9   Burdens of leadership, 1948–1959   213

10   Mixing new ingredients, 1959–1971   231

11   International banking and the 'grand design', 1945–1975   249

12   Will you walk a little faster? The domestic banking scene, 1971–1975   261

13   Under new orders. Midland as a banking group, 1971–1975   281

Midland's modern calendar. Key events in the group, 1976–1986   300

*References*   309
*Appendices*   320
*Index*   343

# LIST OF ILLUSTRATIONS

## Home base: Midland's origins and headquarters

**1.1** Preliminary announcement of Midland's formation

**1.2** Union Street, Birmingham, in the 1830s

**1.3** Midland's office at 20 Union Street, Birmingham, c1860

**1.4** Medallion commemorating Charles Geach, Midland's founder and first manager

**1.5** The Bank of England's branch at Bennetts Hill, Birmingham, c1860

**1.6** Midland's headquarters at New Street, Birmingham, 1867

**1.7** John Dent Goodman, chairman 1880–98

**1.8** Street plan of City of London c1890 showing Central Bank of London and City Bank

**1.9** Midland's board of directors in 1903

**1.10** Head office at Poultry, London, under construction in 1930s

**1.11** The board room at Poultry in 1930

## High street banking: Midland's branch bank tradition

**2.1** Stourbridge 'Old Bank', Midland's first branch office, c1900

**2.2** The manager and staff of Midland's Kenilworth branch in the 1890s

**2.3** Customers at the counter of Midland's Ludgate Hill branch c1901

**2.4** Behind the counter at Peckham branch, c1910

**2.5** The interior of Midland's Watford branch, completed in 1909

**2.6** Machine operators at the bank's Derby branch in 1928

**2.7** Country banking between the wars: Midland's Glastonbury branch

**2.8** City centre banking between the wars: the rebuilt branch at Pall Mall

**2.9** Midland's Liverpool North branch, c1920

**2.10** Liverpool North branch after a direct hit during a bombing raid, May 1941

**2.11** Midland's branch at Queen Street, Cardiff, 1986

**2.12** A preview of the branch banking scene in the late 1980s

## A banking heritage: illustrations from Midland's collection of pictures and archives

**3.1** Charles Geach, founder and first manager of Midland

**3.2** Elevation drawing of the Bank of Westmorland, Kendal, 1833

**3.3** Brass door-plate from the Bank of Westmorland

**3.4** William Purton (by John Constable), c1833

**3.5** Extract from Midland's deed of settlement, August 1836

**3.6** Archives of Midland and its constituent banks

**3.7** The Leicestershire Banking Company's head office, 1874

**3.8** Selection of bank notes issued by country banks which later became part of Midland Bank

**3.9** George Rae

**3.10** Light fittings for a Midland branch before the First World War

**3.11** Design for extension of Midland's Southport branch, 1921

**3.12** Midland's head office, Poultry, 1925

**3.13** Midland's branch at 196a Piccadilly, London

**3.14** Perspective drawing of Midland's branch at Church Stretton, 1913

**3.15** Manchester, King Street branch

**3.16** Perspective drawing of Leadenhall Street branch, London

**3.17** Midland Bank's coat of arms, granted in 1952

## Midland's people: the changing face of staff and management

**4.1** Henry Edmunds, Midland's manager, 1847–67, and managing director, 1867–74

**4.2** John Christie, Midland's general manager, 1887–97

**4.3** Edward Holden, Midland's managing director, 1898–1908, and chairman and managing director, 1908–1919

**4.4** Reginald McKenna, Cassie Holden, Frederick Hyde, Edgar Woolley and Samuel Murray

**4.5** Miss Anne Tulloch, Midland's first woman employee in 1906

**4.6** Cartoon from the *Midland Venture*, 1921

**4.7** The staff of the Ipswich branch in the early 1920s

**4.8** Reginald McKenna, Midland's chairman, 1919–43

**4.9** Cartoon from the *Midland Venture*, 1931

**4.10** Members of the Midland Bank Flying Club shortly before the Second World War

**4.11** Viscount Monckton of Brenchley, chairman, 1957–64

**4.12** Leonard Mather, chief general manager, 1968–72, with Charles Trott, chief general manager, 1972–74

**4.13** Sir Archibald Forbes, chairman, 1964–75, and president, 1975–82

**4.14** Lord Armstrong, chairman, 1975–80, with Stuart Graham and Malcolm Wilcox

**4.15** Group executive committee, 1985

## Foreign affairs: origins and landmarks of Midland's international business

**5.1** The London Joint Stock Bank, Princes Street, in 1850

**5.2** Dinner card celebrating Midland's merger with the City Bank in 1898

**5.3** Caricature of Midland's new foreign banks department, c1902

**5.4** The Fuller 'Flatiron' Building, Broadway and Fifth Avenue, New York, in the early 1900s

**5.5** A £500 bond of the Armavir-Touapsé Railway, 1909

**5.6** A locomotive of the Armavir-Touapsé Railway, 1913

**5.7** Letterhead of Midland's Petrograd office, 1917

**5.8** Advertisement featuring Midland's 'Atlantic Offices' on the Cunard liners in the 1920s

**5.9** The Cunard liner *Aquitania*

**5.10** A foreign exchange dealer's desk, c1930

**5.11** Midland's overseas branch in Gracechurch Street, London, in the 1960s

**5.12** H H Thackstone and E J W Hellmuth with L C Mather

**5.13** Dealing room, Midland Bank group treasury

**5.14** The headquarters of Midland Bank SA, Paris, France

# LIST OF TABLES

**1.1** Midland Bank deposit accounts, 1840 and 1844   29

**3.1** Dividends per £100 invested in paid-up shares of Birmingham banks, 1881–88   73

**3.2** Midland Bank amalgamations, 1883–91   85

**4.1** Midland Bank amalgamations, 1892–99   99

**4.2** Midland Bank amalgamations, 1900–08   107

**4.3** Ratios of advances and bills discounted to deposits in divisions of Midland Bank, 1896–98   114

**4.4** Values and ratios of advances and bills discounted to deposits in divisions of Midland Bank, 1908   116

**5.1** Midland Bank amalgamations, 1910–18   125

**5.2** Midland Bank, value of advances, 1918   130

**6.1** Midland Bank affiliations, 1917–24   163

**6.2** Monthly deposits of the 'Big Five' London clearing banks at half-yearly intervals, 1921–29   167

**10.1** Midland Bank, principal subsidiaries in the United Kingdom, 1909–68   238

**10.2** Clearing banks in mergers in England and Wales, 1968   243

**10.3** Capital position of the major clearing banks after disclosure, 31 December 1969   245

**10.4** Growth of disclosed shareholders' funds of Midland Bank Group, 1950–70   246

**11.1** Midland Bank, consortium links in international banking, 1963–73   255

**11.2** International earnings and facilities of selected banks, 1973   259

**12.1** Inter-bank sterling borrowing and inter-bank borrowing on Certificates of Deposits, 1971–73   264

**12.2** 'Lifeboat' loan support provided by the London clearing banks, 1974–75   272

**12.3** Midland Bank, numbers of current accounts, cheques and cash handled, 1960–75   273

**13.1** Midland Bank Trust Company, 1909–79   296

# ACKNOWLEDGEMENTS

This book was commissioned as one of a series of projects designed to mark Midland Bank's 150th anniversary in 1986. The history project was initiated by the late Lord Armstrong of Sanderstead, then chairman of the bank, and Stuart Graham and Sir Malcolm Wilcox, then Midland's chief general managers. We are greatly in their debt for giving us the opportunity to work on a subject so rich in its history and archives. The steering committee for the bank's anniversary programme has given us support and encouragement in bringing the history to completion, and we are particularly grateful to John Brooks and John Greenwell, the successive chairmen of that committee.

In addition to those who initiated the project, a large number of senior directors, executives and former officials have provided us with lengthy interviews on the modern development of the bank and commented on sections of the text. We are particularly grateful for the contributions of Ken Barber, Hervé de Carmoy, John Cave, Tom Fisher, Sir Archibald Forbes, John Harris, Jack Hendley, Tony Hellmuth, Roger Langdale, Dennis Kitching, Len Mather, Dick Sargent, and Geoffrey Taylor.

Within the bank, a great many departments, branches and individuals have contributed to the preparation of this history. A feature of these contributions is that they have been made willingly and enthusiastically, without the need for official circulars and final demands. This help has been a real encouragement. We are especially grateful to secretary's office, group economics, group communications and public relations, and premises departments. We are also indebted to many individual members and former members of the bank's staff for their positive help. Special mention must be made of the interest and help of Stanley Howard, Ronald Jessup, the late Claude Smith, and Bernard Wesson.

Contacts inside the Midland group have been important in the completion of the book. Even though the focus of this history is on Midland Bank itself rather than the group as a whole, we have had indispensable help from Alex Macmillan and Robin Sim at Clydesdale Bank; Edmund Swinglehurst and Derek Chapman at The Thomas Cook Group; Jack Newland and Noel Simpson at Northern Bank, and Richard Quin at Samuel Montagu & Co Limited.

Outside the bank, we have been privileged in having access to the archives of the Bank of England, by permission of the governor and company and with the kind help of John Keyworth and Henry Gillett. We have also benefited from the cooperation of other banks, notably National Westminster Bank and its archivist, Richard Reed; Lloyds Bank, and John Booker; Barclays Bank, and George Miles; and Baring Brothers & Co Limited, and Dr John Orbell. Like most historians of financial institutions, we have made use of the excellent collections of archives, prints and photographs at the Guildhall Library, London, and we are also grateful to the Leeds Russian Archive and Richard Davies.

Midland's archives were brought together in the 1930s following the publication of the bank's centenary history. Users of these archives in recent years have set a determined and productive example, and their work has proved a marvellous research source in the preparation of this book. The results of investigations by Dr Michael Collins (University of Leeds), Dr Philip Cottrell (University of Leicester), Professor Charles Goodhart (London School of Economics) and, more recently, by Dr Youssef Cassis (University of Geneva) and Drs Forrest Capie and Alan Webber (The City University, London) were especially helpful. Dr Collins also generously allowed us to see the text of his forthcoming book on British banking history. The interest and advice of Professors Leslie Pressnell and the late Sydney Checkland has been an encouragement in this and other recent projects. We are grateful to Professor Theo Barker for the opportunity to give a public airing to the preliminary results of our work at his seminar in modern economic and social history at the Institute of Historical Research, and to Dr William Kennedy, whose seminar on sources and historiography at the London School of Economics has for several years provided a workshop for Midland's history and archives.

Our debt to Wilfrid Crick and John Wadsworth, the bank's first historians, will be obvious almost from the first page of this book, and their recollections of personalities and events have given us a rich source. We have accumulated a number of other special debts. David McKenna gave us fascinating insights and documentation of the career of his father, Reginald McKenna, the bank's chairman between 1919 and 1943. Michael Moss, archivist of the University of Glasgow, generously and constructively commented on the early sections of the book. Our publishers, B T Batsford (and particularly Peter Kemmis Betty, Roger Huggins and Alison Bellhouse), have steered the book on a long and sometimes eventful journey towards production. We have also been very fortunate in the close support given within the bank, particularly from Paul Wyatt, Ian Morison and Frank Pearce; Cyril Finlayson and his staff at the bank's records store at Colindale; Tessa Kendall and Martin Blazejewski, who kept the bank's archives unit operational when it could have been overwhelmed by the history programme; and Evelyn Brown, Winsome Lathrope, Lise Patti and Myra Sharpin, who came to our aid with typing and processing at different stages of the project. The main burden of preparing the typescript for publication has been borne by Julie Mehta, and we are extremely grateful to her for her energy and patience in handling a complex text. Finally we thank our wives and families for their support and congratulate them upon their endurance throughout this project.

In writing this history we have been given free access to Midland's archives and other sources of information. Nevertheless, the treatment and interpretation remain our own rather than that of the bank or of those who have contributed to or commented on the text. As in all joint authorships there has been a division of duties—Edwin Green has been mainly concerned with the first half of the history and Tony Holmes with the second, modern half—but we are, of course, jointly responsible for the end product. We offer it as our own view of Midland's long and fascinating development.

A R Holmes
Edwin Green
*May 1986*

## Company names and other conventions

Midland Bank, since its formation in 1836 and through many changes in its formal name, has always been familiarly known as the 'Midland Bank' or simply 'Midland'. We have used these shortened titles throughout this book.

There are many hundreds of references to individual banks and companies in this history. In order to avoid confusion the description 'the Bank' refers only to the Bank of England, not to Midland or to any other bank. 'Limited' or 'Ltd' has been omitted from the names of banks and companies, and 'Company' has been abbreviated to 'Co' in the names of firms.

Job titles of directors and officials of Midland Bank and all other banks and companies appear in lower case (for example, chairman, governor and manager). We have used upper case only for public appointments (Chancellor of the Exchequer, Mayor). Similarly the names of branches, departments and internal committees of banks and companies have been left in lower case (management committee, overseas branch) whereas official bodies, departments and committees (as in Treasury or Prices and Incomes Board) have been introduced in upper case.

These conventions do not apply to quotations from original documents or publications. All quotations are exact transcriptions from the originals, even where the grammar and punctuation of bankers' diaries and notebooks seem unorthodox or exotic.

# INTRODUCTION

By the mid 1980s, bankers throughout the world were offering their customers an immense range of financial services. The available options included not only the traditional bank functions of handling payments, lending, and receiving deposits; they also included investment and insurance activities on a massive scale, mortgage finance, export and import services, and a multitude of consultancy and advisory services. This diversification of banking business reflected great variations within the marketplace, from the smallest private account to giant corporations or government finance. Many of these customers needed facilities on an international scale, bringing each bank into competition with thousands of other banks and intermediaries.

Midland Bank's modern development is a striking illustration of the diversification of banking since the Second World War. By the 1980s its branch banking network in England and Wales provided a wide range of 'products' to its personal customers. These services were tailored to the saving and borrowing needs of specific sections of its home market and enhanced by initiatives such as 'free-if-in-credit' current accounts in 1984. The bank and its subsidiaries also offered a wide choice of services to British and overseas companies, varying from start-up loans and venture capital for small businesses to corporate finance and money market facilities for major groups and multi-nationals. Not least, in the mid-1980s Midland and its subsidiaries at home and abroad gave access to services in travel, insurance, investment, instalment finance and other support not traditionally linked with banking. The banker had become in effect the supplier of a huge but flexible inventory of financial and related services.

In contrast to this diversified business, banking 150 years ago was narrow in the scope of its activities and local in its reach. When Midland was formally established in Birmingham in August 1836, the first duty of a country bank was to provide its customers with effective and safe means of payment. A bank needed to be able to receive, protect, transfer and pay out cash in the form of Bank of England notes, private bank notes, and coin. On the liabilities side of the business, most (but not all) country banks tackled this task by issuing their own bank notes. Licences to issue notes were necessary after 1808 and denominations of less than £5 were prohibited after 1826, yet notes remained an important channel for small payments. They were also a significant source of bank profits, as they attracted interest-free funds in exchange for notes. Deposit accounts, usually at 30 days notice of withdrawal, were another valuable source of funds, and between 1714 and 1832 the usury laws ensured that these funds did not cost bankers more than 5 per cent per annum. Customers maintaining credit balances on their current accounts, subject to immediate withdrawal, only received interest in certain regions (notably Lancashire) or in periods of severe competition between the banks (in the late 1830s and 1840s, for example). The use of cheques and bankers' drafts to make transfers from current accounts was still relatively rare in the 1830s, leaving current accounts mainly in the role of safe-keeping rather than being fully exploited as a method of payment.

The range of lending services offered by the country bankers was also limited in the early nineteenth century. The discounting of bills of exchange and their many variants remained the dominant form of credit. Bills, which had been a familiar part of the commercial landscape since the fourteenth century, were essentially promises by one manufacturer or trader to pay another supplier or merchant a specified sum at a given date; a payee could obtain immediate cash by selling a bill to a bank at a discount of its full value, leaving the bank either to collect the full value of the bill when it became due or to sell (rediscount) the bill to another bank. Loans and overdrafts, in comparison with this trade in bills, played only a secondary role amongst the assets of early nineteenth-century provincial banks.[1]

In England and Wales in the 1830s, these services were being provided by two main types of bank—private banks and joint stock banks. Since 1708 the formation of banking companies with more than six partners had been prohibited, with the sole exception of the Bank of England. As a result, both in London and the provinces banking business became the preserve of hundreds of small private firms, often linked with their partners' professional and industrial interests. A succession of commercial crises—in 1815–16 and 1825, in particular—exposed the frailty of many of these private banks, and in 1826 the Banking Copartnerships Act ended the Bank of England's exclusive privileges as a banking company. The Act permitted the formation of 'joint stock' banking companies with any number of shareholders and with the right to issue their own notes, provided only that they were not based within 65 miles of London. The 65-mile rule was abandoned in 1833, although joint stock banks formed in London were still not allowed to issue notes.

The immediate result of the 1826 legislation was the launching of joint stock banks throughout England and Wales. By 1836, when Midland was established, over 100 of the new banks had been promoted. Variations emerged in the range of services provided by the different types of bank, and customers could also expect regional contrasts. In Lancashire, for example, payments were traditionally dominated by bills rather than notes, while in London the private banks could provide specialist services in overseas trade or discount business which were outside the range of the provincial banks. With these types of exception, however, the old private banks and the new joint stock banks of the 1820s and 1830s were competing with each other in supplying the same relatively restricted set of banking services.

The transition from the narrowly-based business of the 1830s to the voluminous catalogue of services offered by modern banks provides the setting for this history of Midland. That transition was not always gradual or straightforward. Banks—no less than long-established institutions in government, industry, the Church, the armed services, education and the arts—have undergone periods of sudden marked expansion. They have suffered moments of vulnerability and crisis, and they have felt the decisive influence of changes in leadership, personnel and organization. It is the task of this history to assess the effect of these experiences on Midland since it first opened for business in 1836.

The framework of this book differs from previous work on the bank's archives and history. The centenary study of Midland, *A Hundred Years of Joint Stock Banking* by Wilfrid Crick and John Wadsworth,[2] was a pioneering example of business history in the United Kingdom, particularly in its masterly deployment of original sources. Published in 1936 and reprinted three times between 1938 and 1964, Crick and Wadsworth's book emphasized the bank's diverse regional origins, mainly by examining the scores of country banks which directly and indirectly had become part of the bank by the mid-1920s. This is only one possible approach to the history of a banking business. There is scope for a monetary treatment, for example, setting Midland's history in the broader economic context of financial regulation and the supply of money, or an industrial approach, concentrating on the relationships between the bank and its industrial customers in the very long term.

Historians have already tackled these themes, and studies based on Midland's archives have been published or are in progress.[3] This research, in addition to Crick and Wadsworth's findings, has been invaluable in the preparation of this history and has yielded results which otherwise would have been beyond the scope of the project. Nevertheless, neither the distinctive features of Midland itself nor the exact dimensions and sequence of its growth are easy to trace in the existing published sources. A new history of Midland has been needed, especially in view of the bank's unusually long pedigree as a banking 'company'. With the exception of the Bank of England—an entirely different type of institution—Midland had, by the mid-1980s, a longer unbroken history as a shareholders' company than any of the other major London-based banks.

For these reasons this history focuses on Midland itself as a banking company, in preference to providing detailed histories of individual constituent banks and subsidiaries; histories of several member companies of the group are in any case already published or in preparation.[4] In attempting to disentangle and clarify the bank's identity in this way, we have used a simple chronological framework, taking major changes in Midland's management or structure as the break-points for chapters. The main historical treatment is followed through from 1836 to 1975. This closing date marked the end of a series of unprecedented upheavals in the British financial scene and at the same time introduced Midland's development as a consciously unified group rather than as a bank with an assortment of autonomous subsidiaries and allies (pp 281–99). The key events in the group's development since 1975 are listed for reference purposes in a separate chronology (pp 300–7).

Within this framework, we have concentrated on specific aspects of Midland's development. First, as a priority, we have looked for more exact dimensions of Midland's business. On surveying the early history of the bank, especially in the years before it registered as a limited liability company in 1880, the objective has been a new series of estimates of balance sheet totals (Appendix 1). These estimates indicate that Midland developed at a much faster rate in the mid-nineteenth century than has been assumed previously. As to the more recent past, we have included a profile of the bank's actual profits as well as its published profits in the years before full disclosure of bank profits was introduced in 1970 (Appendix 4). This is the first long run of real profit figures to be published by a major British bank.

Secondly, we have attempted to locate and characterize the sources of Midland's business, particularly in its formative years. Where possible the bank's business and performance has been contrasted with the records of its immediate competitors, initially in Birmingham and subsequently in national and international banking. Thirdly, this history looks at the changing function of a bank such as Midland over 150 years. As part of that task, we have attempted to recognize the banker's perception of his function, as that perception was often a larger influence on the bank's development than the reality of its business. Fourthly, the choices available to Midland at crucial moments in its long history needed clarification. This history identifies some of the moments when Midland faced significant strategic choices and when its changes of direction, although sometimes misjudged or even disapproved of at the time, often proved beneficial to the long-term fortunes of the bank. Fifthly, and by no means least, this history of Midland introduces the individual bankers and businessmen whose backgrounds, attitudes and decisions influenced the long-term survival, growth and reputation of the bank. When an institution has such long experience as Midland, it is the bank's people—directors, managers and staff, shareholders and customers—who deserve to be at centre stage.

❄

# CHAPTER ONE

# SETTING UP IN BANKING
## 1836–1851

> In the district of which Birmingham [is] the great centre of traffic and
> operations, the increase of Banks has been as great, in proportion to the
> business to be transacted in it, as it has been in Yorkshire and
> Lancashire; and we believe the disposition to speculate in new banks
> was never more active than it is at the present moment.
>
> *The Circular to Bankers* (May 1836) p 33

Uncertainties and controversies dominated the British financial scene
in the mid-1830s. Expectations were heightened by the continuing
surge of investment and speculation in railways and steamship
companies, banks and insurance companies. These markets were
hyperactive, and the excitement generated by stock and share trading
was mixed with genuine hopes for structural reforms in the financial
community in both London and the major provincial towns. It was in
these hothouse conditions that the Birmingham and Midland Bank
began business in the summer of 1836.

Public debate about banking in the late 1820s and 1830s was
dominated by the question of which type of company or firm could
offer the most safety and stability to the banking system in England
and Wales. The Banking Copartnerships Act in 1826 had not settled
the dispute (p 3). The Bank of England continued the defence of its
remaining powers even after its privileges in London were curtailed
in 1833. The old private banks in London and the country denied that
the new joint stock banks, with their shares owned by large numbers
of private investors, were intrinsically superior and more secure than
small partnerships.

These differences were the fuel for argument and propaganda
throughout the 1830s. Promoters of joint stock banks needed
shareholders and depositors, and their prospectuses repeatedly stressed
the safety and resources provided by a large and widely-distributed

capital base. The Huddersfield Banking Company, for example, at its formation as one of the first joint stock banks in 1827, pointed to the failure of five local private banks in the financial panic of 1825–26:

> By the failure of these banks a vacuum has been caused which, in all probability, will be filled up by other establishments of a similar nature . . . unless a public company of a more solid description be formed in their place . . . when a bank is managed by a body of directors, who are chosen for their respectability, experience, and fitness for the station, it is always managed without material loss.

Three years later the security of joint stock principles was similarly important to the promoters of the York City and County Bank:

> Joint Stock Companies . . . being on a firm foundation, are entitled to that unlimited confidence which is so essential to the stability of a Bank, and they are consequently free from those panics that have ruined so many English Banks and their connections.

The private bankers retaliated with circulars to their agents and customers, and they proved to be effective lobbyists both in parliament and in government. The *Circular to Bankers*, first published by Henry Burgess in 1827, reflected country bankers' opposition to encroachment by the Bank of England as well as the joint stock banks. Senior partners of private banks such as George Carr Glyn of Glyn Mills and Co of London were persuasive witnesses to parliamentary committees. In giving evidence to the Select Committee on the Bank of England Charter in 1832, Glyn doubted whether directors of a joint stock bank could ever match 'the duty of a private Banker to become acquainted with his customers; his business depends upon it, and his advances must be governed by this knowledge'.[1]

The Bank of England's attitude to the rival types of banking companies was potentially decisive. Although private bankers strongly opposed the opening of its provincial branches, the Bank's more obvious conflict was with joint stock banks which challenged its note-issuing powers or its capability for maintaining branches throughout England and Wales. As a result the Bank of England keenly (but unsuccessfully) resisted the Bank Charter Act of 1833 which permitted the formation of joint stock banks in London. Three years later it refused to discount any bills of exchange endorsed by note-issuing joint stock banks and closed its counter to bills payable at the newly-established London and Westminster Bank.[2] Until the mid-1830s the Bank of England held back from publicly questioning the fitness of joint stock banks, but the promoters of the new companies either in

London or the country were left in little doubt of the Bank's hostility.

Understandably this preoccupation with alternative types of banking units has meant that historians have concentrated on the institutional and structural aspects of English banking in the 1820s and 1830s. The emphasis has fallen on the legislation affecting banks between 1826 and 1844, the role of the Bank of England in government policy, the important influence of the Scottish model on English joint stock banks, and the endurance of joint stock banks in comparison with private banks during the financial crises of the mid-nineteenth century.[3] These contrasts between private banks and early joint stock concerns can be exaggerated. From the point of view of the customer (particularly if he lived outside London) the distinction was probably not obvious. In focusing on the legal and corporate characteristics of early Victorian banks, there is the additional danger that the *business* reasons why banks either survived or died in infancy may be overlooked. The composition of a bank's capital and business and the quality of its management were fundamental influences on a bank's initial progress. This is the more likely explanation of the origins of the four major clearing banks based in London 150 years later. Two of those banks (Barclays and Lloyds) remained private partnerships throughout the upheavals of the 1820s and 1830s and did not choose corporate status until much later in the century; the other two (Midland and National Westminster) were predominantly joint stock banks in origin. Their different pedigrees may have given them distinctive characters but, as far as their initial survival is concerned, the composition of their business was more influential than their original constitution.

Midland Bank's early history gives the appearance of the triumph of joint stock banking over local competition from private banks and other joint stock concerns. With the longest unbroken existence as a shareholders' company amongst the English clearing banks, Midland has a great debt to the pioneers of joint stock formation. Its preference later in the nineteenth century for acquiring other joint stock concerns rather than private banks reflects a strong faith in the principles and traditions of joint stock banking. Yet this consistency may be misleading. Midland began life as a small business, in which the identity of its owners, its management and its customers was crucial; its legal status was bound to be a secondary consideration. In perspective the explanation for Midland's early resilience and its subsequent growth lay in the ways in which its capital and its business were originally put together.

Midland's birthplace was an immediate advantage. A bank claiming

Birmingham origins in the early nineteenth century could expect a relatively healthy childhood and a relatively high life expectancy. Of the four joint stock banks founded in Birmingham between 1826 and 1836, three were still in business by 1856. The survival rate for all England and Wales was lower, with only 79 (or 60 per cent) of the 125 banks founded in the same period still in existence by 1856. Mortality was especially high amongst Midland's exact contemporaries. No less than 59 banks were promoted in England and Wales in 1836, of which only 32 survived for twenty years and only 22 for fifty years. Casualties were particularly heavy in Lancashire and Yorkshire, whereas five of the promotions in Birmingham and the west Midlands (Warwickshire, Worcestershire, Shropshire and Staffordshire) in 1836 were still active and independent in 1856.[4]

Birmingham's business and industrial climate suited the new banks. The guild-based trade restrictions enforced by older incorporated towns did not affect Birmingham, which was not incorporated until 1838. As a result the town had attracted a multitude of small manufacturing firms and one-man workshops. The town's population doubled to 150,000 between 1800 and 1830, with the metal trades providing the main impetus for employment. By the 1830s Birmingham was densely populated with gunmakers, tool shops, small-batch engineering firms, toymakers, copper and silversmiths, jewellers and other craftsmen. With the exception of the Soho engineering firm of Boulton and Watt, the larger employers in the iron and coal industries operated outside the town, leaving most of Birmingham's industrial production in the hands of small businesses with limited capital and low overheads.[5] The owners of these firms, especially when the free trade movement gathered momentum after the Reform Act of 1832, were brimming with political and business confidence.

Birmingham's banks at the beginning of the nineteenth century were closely tethered to the town's distinctive industrial structure. The Lloyds, Attwoods and Spooners were all ironfounders and ironmongers, while Sampson Lloyd's partner John Taylor was a buttonmaker. Samuel Galton, a Quaker, gave up a notoriously successful gunmaking business in favour of banking. Joseph Gibbins senior, also a Quaker, had been a buttonmaker and had later owned a network of interests in the metal trades when he joined Galton in partnership in 1804. The Swiss-born partners of J L Moilliet and Sons, in addition to their banking activities, exported Birmingham's manufactures to the Continent.[6] The partnerships were also closely interwoven, with numerous examples of partners leaving one firm and reappearing in another Birmingham bank. It was this intimacy between Birmingham's business and banking, and between the banks themselves, that in 1827 prompted the Bank of England's agent to describe the town's private bankers as a 'local aristocracy'.[7]

In these examples the partners of private banks were relatives or neighbours of the small manufacturing firms which dominated Birmingham's business. This proximity was characteristic of many hundreds of banking firms throughout England and Wales; country bankers more often than not combined banking services with other trades or professions, most especially in the plentiful examples of attorneys in banking.[8] This 'part-time' element did not mean that businessmen assumed a banking role in order to finance their own capital and stock requirements. In Birmingham's case the adoption of banking was more closely linked with the need for payment systems which were secure and within their control. A small metal firm or workshop in Birmingham needed, firstly, a nearby agent for paying and receiving its bills of exchange and, secondly, a local source of notes or other non-coin currency for cash payments. It was these requirements, inherent in the manufacturing pattern which had developed in Birmingham, to which bankers such as Lloyd and Galton responded. The result was a larger number of private banks than in any other provincial centre in England and Wales. No less than eight private banks were available by 1804, five of which were still in operation after the commercial crisis of 1825.[9] This relatively large supply of banking facilities was typical of the west Midlands as a whole. At the beginning of the nineteenth century the region could claim a greater concentration of banking than any other area in England and Wales. In 1801 each bank office in the west Midlands served an average of 12,000 inhabitants, in comparison with an average of 21,000 for each branch in England and Wales or, at the opposite extreme, 48,000 inhabitants for each bank office in Lancashire and Cheshire.[10]

The opening of the Bank of England's branch and arrival of joint stock banks in Birmingham in the late 1820s was much less of a discontinuity than in other regions of England and Wales. The town's private banks had withstood the 1825–26 crisis more convincingly than many of their contemporaries; a total of 60 private banks failed in the harvest year of the crisis, of which only one (Gibbins, Smith and Goode) was from Birmingham.[11] Almost as an emblem of continuity, it was the old Gibbins office in Union Street which the Bank of England chose for its branch bank in 1827. In the months that followed the private bankers opened accounts at the Bank and otherwise adapted to the new conditions. When the Birmingham bankers did join the agitation against the Bank's privileges in 1827–28, they believed that the threat lay 'not in [the Bank's] operations as a bank, however influential and competitively effective it was, but from its role as an instrument of government policy'.[12]

Continuity was also assured by the direct participation of private bankers in the new joint stock companies, in marked contrast to the feuding which affected several other provincial centres. Birmingham bankers were in any case slow to experiment with the newly-available joint stock legislation. The first initiative was delayed until 1829, when the Manchester and Liverpool District Bank (subsequently the District Bank) attempted to open branches in Birmingham and its neighbourhood. Joseph Gibbins junior and Edward Lovell were authorized to form a local committee and distribute District Bank shares in the area. Gibbins, a son of Galton's original partner (p 10), had escaped from the closure of his own bank Gibbins, Smith and Goode in December 1825, and had eventually paid his creditors 19s 8d in the pound. He had then re-emerged as senior partner in a new bank, Gibbins and Lovell. Rather than accept the District's offer, however, Gibbins chose to reconstruct his own firm as a joint stock bank. This company, the Birmingham Banking Company, was formally established in October 1829. With Paul James, formerly of Galton and James, as manager and Gibbins as a director (from 1831), the new bank was the successor and beneficiary of the private banking business of both Galton and Gibbins.[13] In similar style the Bank of Birmingham was launched in 1832 on the basis of a private bank connection. It was essentially a reconstitution of the firm of Lovell, Goode and Stubbs, which had been formed in 1829 by Gibbins's former partner Edward Lovell. Progress of this bank, despite its note circulation of £30,000, was held back by the local unpopularity of its manager James Pearson. Formerly in partnership with the Moilliet banking firm, Pearson was 'a phlegmatic, heavy man, and his manners were, to say the least, unprepossessing'.[14] The Bank of Birmingham was eventually absorbed by the Birmingham Banking Company in 1838, when its fine building in Bennetts Hill was acquired for the Bank of England's Birmingham branch.

By 1836 the Birmingham Banking Company had emerged as the strongest prospect amongst the local joint stock concerns. Its paid-up capital of £100,000 was nearly double the Bank of Birmingham's resources of £52,680. This total was doubled to £200,000 during 1837, without forcing down the 10 per cent dividends which the bank had paid since its foundation in 1829. The Birmingham Banking Company also seemed untroubled by the entry of non-Birmingham banks into

**Figure 1.1** *Origins of the Birmingham Banking Company, 1829*

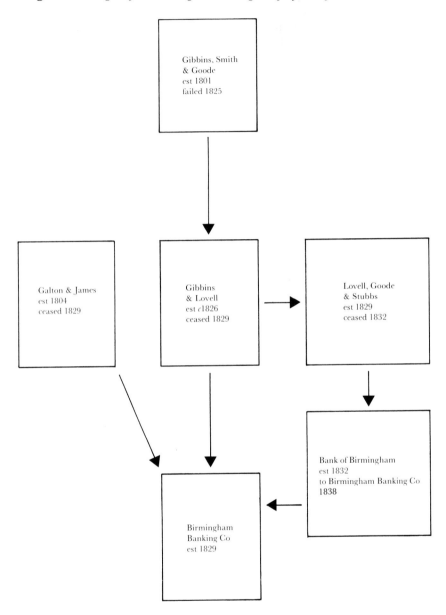

*Sources:* W F Crick and J E Wadsworth, *A Hundred Years of Joint Stock Banking* (Hodder and Stoughton, 1936) pp 51–5; D J Moss, 'The Bank of England and the country banks: Birmingham 1827–33', *Economic History Review*, 2nd series, 34 (1981), pp 540–53

the town. The Commercial Bank of England, the National Provincial Bank and the Northern and Central Bank all opened branches in the town in 1833 but by 1840 only the National Provincial branch survived. This record suggested that the Birmingham Banking Company's initial success was the inheritance of the Galton and Gibbins connections rather than the result of local enthusiasm for joint stock banking. Local pedigree appeared to be more useful to a bank in Birmingham than whether it was a private or joint stock concern.

When two new joint stock banks were launched in Birmingham in 1836, a personal link with the Bank of England's local branch proved to be decisive. Charles Geach of the Bank's Birmingham branch was the lynchpin of both promotions. Tall and heavily-built, this twenty-eight-year-old banker already had a local reputation for outstanding ability and 'singularly agreeable manners'; 'he was entirely free from the "airs" which some self-made men put on. In his appearance there was evidence of power and influence that rendered any assumption superfluous'.[15]

Geach's qualifications were equally impressive. Son of George Geach of St Austell, Cornwall, a distant relative of the banking families of Foster and Bolitho, Geach had been elected to a clerkship at the Bank of England in 1826. This much coveted appointment was probably the result of an introduction by J W Freshfield, solicitor to the Bank and MP for Penryn where Geach's uncle had been Mayor. He had been promoted to a clerkship at the newly-established Birmingham branch in 1828, becoming second inspector in 1831. Although the Bank recognized his 'general excellent conduct', he became dissatisfied with the 'slow course of promotion . . . especially with that policy of the Bank directors which shut out from those of their servants who entered in the subordinate departments all prospects of rising to situations of the highest trust'.[16] This dissatisfaction can only have been increased by the awareness that Bank of England staff were well placed for senior appointments in the new joint stock banks. John Amery, one of Geach's colleagues at the Bank's Birmingham branch, had been appointed the first manager of the Stourbridge and Kidderminster Banking Company when it had been formed in 1834. Geach had immediately applied for 20 shares in the Stourbridge Bank, showing his confidence in the viability of shareholders' banks in the west Midlands; no doubt he was also keen to obtain an inside view of the workings of a new joint stock bank.

Whether Geach volunteered or was recruited is not certain, but by early 1836 he was advising a group of local manufacturers on the formation of a new joint stock bank. Led by George Bacchus, a glass manufacturer from Edgbaston, this group was based in Birmingham and was interested mainly in glassmaking, buttonmaking and ironfounding. On 30 June 1836 Bacchus and his supporters launched the Birmingham Town and District Bank with an initial nominal capital of £500,000. Geach, evidently expecting an appointment in the new business, was overlooked. In his place the directors appointed Bassett Smith, formerly of Gibbins, Smith and Co, in much the same way that the Birmingham Banking Company had relied upon Joseph Gibbins and Paul James seven years earlier.[17]

Charles Geach's work on the Town and District project was not wasted. A second group of businessmen now offered support for a quite separate company and promised the managership to Geach. This remarkable act of faith was pinned upon the skills and personality of one relatively junior banker; there is no evidence that Geach brought either capital or staff into the original enterprise. On the other hand, Geach's new supporters were not adventurers or merely the political and business rivals of the Town and District grouping. They included Robert Webb, then High Bailiff of Birmingham; Thomas Bolton, a metals merchant and manufacturer in New Street; John Francis, a merchant based in Congreve Street; William Lort, 'steel truss and surgical instrument maker'; and William Gammon, a glass manufacturer in Aston. This group, which formed the nucleus of Midland's first board of directors (p 16), obviously believed that Geach's services as a professional banker were valuable enough to use them as the foundations for an entirely new bank.

Geach and his supporters had objectives which were less grandiose than the promises made by many new joint stock banks. When a 'provisional committee' met in the second week of July under the chairmanship of Francis Finch, the promoters devised a prospectus for the 'Birmingham Exchange Bank'. This statement, published in the Birmingham newspapers on 16 July 1836, promised only that the new bank would provide general banking business in Birmingham 'and such other of the neighbouring towns as the Directors shall think proper'. The bank's capital would be £500,000 (in £10 shares), of which £100,000 would be paid up immediately. Apart from rules for voting and the eligibility of directors, no further comment was offered. This contrasted with the verbose and often evangelical tone of contemporary prospectuses for banks and insurance companies, promising security and generous terms to their customers and high yields to their shareholders. The chosen title for the bank showed that the promoters were primarily interested in Birmingham business, and that the 'exchange' aspects of commercial banking (notably the discount of bills) were the first priority. Geach, who was named as manager in the first advertisements, now resigned his Bank of England appointment, admitting that he would have 'gladly remained, if, as a clerk, [he] had been eligible for promotion to a Sub Agency'. He left the Bank on 23 July.[18]

After giving this glimpse of their intentions, the promoters commissioned their solicitor William Wills to prepare a deed of settlement. This document brought the new bank into legally-recognized existence and was signed on 15 August. A late change produced the new title of 'Birmingham and Midland Bank'; from that moment onwards the bank was always known locally as 'the Midland' to distinguish it from the Birmingham Banking Company and the Town and District Bank. The change of name did not necessarily reflect new ambitions for extension far outside Birmingham. The qualifications for directorships, for example, demanded that the bank's directors should live within six miles of Birmingham Town Hall. Certainly the first board of directors was drawn from a relatively small circle of Birmingham-based businessmen. Bolton, Francis, Gammon, Lort and Webb were joined on the board by Thomas Pinches, Jeremiah Ridout and John Taylor. Webb was elected chairman at their first meeting on 16 August 1836.

Other alterations from the advertised plan included a much wider definition of the bank's proper business. Authorization included issuing notes; lending on accounts, real or personal securities, bills of exchange, promissory notes and letters of credit; discounting bills and promissory notes; borrowing on receipts, bills, and investments in government stock or 'stock of this Company or of any chartered Company'. The bank was specifically prevented from investing 'in foreign loans, mining concerns, articles of merchandise, or other adventure, trade or business whatsoever'. As far as capital was concerned, the original nominal target of £500,000 was replaced in the deed of settlement with a maximum capital of £250,000 in £10 shares, of which £2 per share was to be called up immediately. The responses to both the Town and District issue and Midland's own first prospectus had shown £500,000 to be far too ambitious a goal. By 17 August 1836, one month after the advertisement for the Birmingham Exchange Bank, only 7700 shares had been issued, and this relatively slow take-up was surely the biggest factor in the reduction of the target for capital.[19] The share subscriptions were nevertheless sufficient for Geach to rent premises at 30 Union Street and to open the bank at 9.30am on 22 August 1836. Banking hours, in line with the other Birmingham banks, were from 9.30am to 4pm daily between Mondays and

Saturdays. Geach himself was appointed manager. Finch, Lort and Geach's uncle Edward Geach, a lawyer in Liskeard, acted as his sureties, guaranteeing the new bank against any personal default by Geach up to a total of £4000.

In launching the new bank at such speed, the directors and shareholders benefited from the groundwork which Geach had provided for the Town and District Bank project. Their other debt was to Thomas Joplin and the pioneers of joint stock banking in the late 1820s. The earliest joint stock banks in England and Wales had borne the main burden of devising, amending and improving the guidelines for banks owned by shareholders, at considerable cost in legal fees and in terms of delay. The formation of companies such as the Bradford Banking Company and the Huddersfield Banking Company in 1827 had required at least six months of preparation. The advantage to companies being formed in the 1830s was enormous. Instead of carefully constructing their regulations from scratch and painstakingly recruiting investors for the new banks, the promoters of the 1830s relied upon the kit of rules and definitions available in the published deeds of settlement of the earliest joint stock banks. When these precedents were insufficient, there was no great difficulty in writing to or visiting other banks. Pioneers such as Samuel Laycock of the Bradford Banking Company or Hugh Watt, the Scots-trained manager of the Huddersfield Banking Company, were not shy of sharing advice and experience with promoters of other new banks. In Midland's case, the legacy left by the pioneers of joint stock banking allowed the promoters to open a fully-constituted bank only seven weeks after Birmingham heard the first whispers of the new bank.

One drawback to the use of standardized deeds of settlement was the ease with which new joint stock banks exaggerated their business ambitions or understated their need for paid-up capital. Many of the promotions of the 1830s failed to take off or survive precisely because their activities were too diffused or because they were inadequately capitalized. There was even an example of a joint stock bank with 'unlimited power . . . of issuing Shares to any extent', yet as the law stood there was nothing to prevent such a bank from opening with virtually no paid-up capital. These weaknesses, together with the general lack of regulation over new banking companies, were central to the criticisms made by the Secret Committee on Joint Stock Banks in 1836.[20]

Midland's deed of settlement undoubtedly overstated some of its promoters' ambitions. The provision for issuing notes was only briefly considered. No sooner had Robert Webb been instructed to order plates for £5 and £10 notes 'similar to the note adopted by the Bury Banking Co' on 2 September than the order was dropped two weeks later. It is much more likely that the promoters had always preferred the option of using Bank of England notes, on the model of the Birmingham Banking Company (p 19). The formula for the new bank's capital was also unrealistic. The difficulty was not the ratio between the share denomination of £10 and the called-up amount of £2 per share; in the event a call of £3 per share payable in November 1836 improved the ratio from 5:1 to 2:1. A more troublesome weakness was that the deed of settlement, like most similar agreements issued by the new banks, did not control the relationship between the number of shares available and the number actually issued. The result was that by the end of 1836, after the call of £3 per share, less than 50 per cent of the shares were actually issued. With an actual capital liability of £250,000, the infant bank was attempting to operate with available shareholders' funds of less than £30,000.

This predicament was common amongst the joint stock banks of the 1830s and it contributed to the high casualty rate amongst Midland's contemporaries. Inadequate capital was a theme in the failures of the Manchester-based Northern and Central Bank in 1837 and the Yorkshire Agricultural and Commercial Bank in 1842.[21] Midland not only avoided these disasters but also strengthened its long-term expectations. This achievement, against the run of fortune for banks founded in the 1830s, was only possible because the bank clarified its capital and business position more rapidly than did its contemporaries. As a result Midland's directors and managers faced the financial crises of the 1840s with a much surer idea of the bank's resources and its function than if they had attempted to fulfil all the ambitions listed in the deed of settlement.

A key element in this reappraisal was the prolonged negotiation, often bordering upon dispute, with the Bank of England over Midland's own banking arrangements. When the Bank had established its provincial branches in 1826 and 1827 it also experimented with an offer of special discount facilities for banks which agreed to circulate Bank of England notes in place of issuing their own notes. Those banks which came into the scheme were to be allowed to discount their own drafts or rediscount trade bills at preferential rates. The notes or cash drawn from these accounts could then be employed at a higher rate, giving a small but certain profit to the participating banks. The offer was designed to increase the circulation (and profitability) of Bank of England notes and in that way to limit the spread of new country notes. It was also intended to steer the provincial banks away from rediscounting bills with other banks. The experiment was successful. The new Birmingham Banking Company was the first to take up the offer in January 1830, soon followed by Lovell, Goode and Stubbs and by Dixon, Dalton and Co of Dudley. The resulting accounts helped to give the Bank's Birmingham office the largest discount business of any of its provincial branches and the arrangement was subsequently extended to Manchester and Liverpool.[22]

The promoters of the Town and District Bank and the Birmingham and Midland were well aware of the offer, and Geach had probably shared in operating the scheme while he was employed by the Bank. At their first meeting on 16 August 1836, Midland's directors therefore applied for a Bank of England account under the special terms. The Bank's Birmingham branch turned down the application 'in consequence of the smallness of the paid-up capital'. Astonished by this decision, Midland's board sent Webb and Geach to London for an interview with the Bank's governor and directors in early September. The decision was not revoked, but the Bank now cited the imminent report of the Secret Committee on Joint Stock Banks and 'the present extraordinary demand for money and the adverse state of the foreign exchanges' as the reasons for its decision.

Midland's board was understandably puzzled as to the real reason for the Bank's attitude. In October the directors asked the Bank whether the increase of the paid-up capital (in the shape of the £3 per share call) would make any difference to Midland's request for a discount account. The Bank again refused the application, hinting that the size and composition of the paid-up capital was after all the stumbling block. If this was the case, it did not prevent the Bank discounting bills sent by Midland 'to any reasonable extent' at the ordinary market rate of interest. Moreover Geach and his directors were in the odd position of knowing that the Bank was otherwise satisfied with their progress. Charles Tindal, the Bank's agent in Birmingham and Geach's former superior, personally regretted that the account had not been granted, and it was reported that the governor of the Bank 'expressed himself as having a high opinion both of your Bank and of Mr Geach'. For their part Midland's directors were perhaps more aware of the Bank's predicament than many adherents of joint stock banking. They appreciated that 'the Bank of England has a very onerous and difficult duty to perform in curtailing its [note] issues' and realized that this task was influencing the Bank's discount policy.

The main grievance of Midland's board in these first months was the galling knowledge that the Bank of England gave the Birmingham

Banking Company preferential treatment by confirming its special discount facilities. When in March 1837 the Bank asked for a reduction in Midland's *existing* discount account (which incurred ordinary market rates) Geach and his directors complained that the Bank's discount policy in Birmingham was 'favouring the business of one [bank] at the expense of the others'. Their persistence was eventually rewarded at the end of August 1837, when Tindal indicated that the Bank would grant the special discount facilities if Midland's constitution 'were so altered as to meet their views'. More importantly, when Geach met the governor and deputy governor in September, the Bank was for the first time specific in its advice. The special account would be granted if Midland's shares were reduced in number to within 25 per cent of the number issued; Midland would also be required to issue all its shares within a year of opening the account.

This understanding could not have been achieved if Geach and his directors had abandoned their belief in the advantages of a Bank of England account. If they had sought solace—and profit—in issuing their own bank notes, they would have placed themselves firmly in the camp of the Bank of England's principal opponents amongst the joint stock banks. The Bank of England may have had its own reasons for seeking a *rapprochement.* The bank failures of the previous twelve months had confirmed many of its worst fears about the management and financial structure of the new generation of joint stock banks. In 1836 the failure of the Agricultural and Commercial Bank of Ireland, which had been founded only two years' earlier, forced the Bank to make emergency shipments of £2 million in gold to meet panic demand in Ireland. In January 1837 the collapse of the multi-branch Northern and Central Bank not only cost its shareholders approximately £350,000 but also produced a plethora of evidence of legal weaknesses in the constitution of joint stock banks.[23] Under this pressure the Bank may have preferred to strengthen the position of new banks in which it had close knowledge or influence. The alternative was diehard opposition to joint stock banks as a species, but this option was ruled out by the valuable role which some joint stock banks were already filling by circulating the Bank's own notes. The Birmingham Banking Company, for example, was circulating between £150,000 and £190,000 in Bank notes by 1836. This 'circulation account' and the other local discount arrangements helped to make the Bank's Birmingham office the busiest of all its provincial branches. In these circumstances the Birmingham and Midland Bank was a candidate for encouragement and support. It was prepared to circulate the Bank's notes, it was not already overcommitted to an expensive branch network, and it was managed by one of the Bank's own graduates.

The immediate result of Geach's interview at the Bank in September 1837 was Midland's decision to reduce its nominal capital of £250,000 to £120,000. This capital would be represented by 2400 shares of £50 (£25 paid) rather than 25,000 shares of £10 each, with the maximum individual holding increased from 250 to 500 shares. The alteration was approved at a special general meeting of shareholders at Dees Royal Hotel, Birmingham, on 13 November. The Bank of England responded in January 1838 by granting a discount account at the special rate of 3 per cent per annum. Midland was required to keep its total discounts at the Bank between £30,000 and £35,000, with the proviso that it would not rediscount with other banks unless it required facilities of more than £35,000. Any bills presented to the Bank for discount were to be of 'unexceptionable character' with maturity dates of less than 95 days.

These initial negotiations with the Bank of England had been long and at times acrimonious; at one point Midland's directors minuted their belief that the Bank's discount policy towards them had been 'capricious and unjust'. Nevertheless the tension between the two institutions had been creative. Geach and his directors had been persuaded that Midland's capital liability was unrealistic, especially at a time when approximately £6000 had been earmarked for a purpose-built headquarters in Union Street (Plate 1.3). The new capital of £120,000 could be supplemented when the need arose. If there was a drawback to the arrangement, it was the substitution of £50 shares for the original £10 shares. The Bank was anxious for the change, convinced that bank shares should be as free from speculation as possible. A bank such as the Birmingham and Midland, however, temporarily lost the chance to recruit large numbers of small shareholders. This was a considerable disadvantage for a company taking on new business and obviously ran against the instincts of Geach and the bank's original promoters (p 16).

The relationship with the Bank of England remained a central concern of Midland's directors throughout the first decade of the new bank's existence. The arrangements made in 1837 proved durable, and Midland was not affected by the Bank of England's concurrent disputes with the London-based joint stock banks. These disputes again showed the Bank ready to use its role as 'bankers' bank' to intervene in the constitutional and business development of non-issuing banks. At the same time the government was persuaded to introduce its own disciplines into commercial banking. The failure of the Northern and

Central Bank and the evidence presented to the parliamentary committees of 1836–38 and 1840–41 threw suspicion on the 1826 banking legislation; reformers such as William Clay were already advocating limited liability, minimum paid-up capital, minimum share denominations, and the publication of full statements of account.[24]

In response, in 1844 Sir Robert Peel's administration introduced a double-headed programme of banking legislation. Firstly the Bank Charter Act answered the Bank of England's long campaign for control over banknote circulation by restricting each bank's note issue to the amount in circulation in 1844. Issuing powers would be removed from any bank which converted to joint stock status, amalgamated with a joint stock bank, suffered bankruptcy or gave up its banking business. The Bank was entitled to an increase in its own note issue of up to two-thirds of the value of any issue forfeited in these ways. The provisions in effect recognized the Bank as the focus for the future development and control of the note issue. Secondly, later the same year, the Joint Stock Bank Act made it compulsory for new joint stock banks to obtain a charter and to operate with a minimum capital of £100,000 in shares of not less than £100 (all of which was to be subscribed and half paid-up before a bank could open).

The main victims of Peel's brew of reform and restriction were those country joint stock banks which had assumed that they could expand their issue of banknotes. The use of the 1844 deadline introduced all manner of anomalies into the pattern of country bank notes, with some major banks left with tiny note-issuing powers in comparison with much smaller banks. Amongst the banks which later became part of Midland, for example, the multi-branch North and South Wales Bank (founded in 1836) was permitted to issue only £63,951, whereas the Yorkshire Banking Company, reconstructed as recently as 1843 after serious weaknesses had been discovered, was awarded a limit of £122,532. This category of banks was also faced with sudden new responsibilities for paperwork, including weekly summaries of notes in circulation, an annual list of shareholders, and applications for licences for each new branch bank. The obstacles to promoters of new banks were even more daunting. The long and expensive task of obtaining a charter was joined to a legal requirement for annual audits and the monthly publication of balance sheets. In addition any new bank founded under the 1844 legislation would be competing with joint stock banks operating under the less strict 1826 legislation. Many of the country joint stock banks had good reason to resent the way in which they had been treated by the 1844 legislation.

Soundly-managed banks were now being asked to sacrifice their ambitions to make amends for or prevent the recurrence of the failures of the late 1830s. Banks which had issued notes in good faith were now being asked to give up their plans for expanding an effective and profitable banking service.

Banks such as the Birmingham and Midland did not suffer equivalent injuries. Geach and his directors had taken little part in the various meetings and committees formed to lobby for the joint stock banks in the late 1830s and early 1840s. In February 1837, for example, the directors had turned down Joplin's invitation to support a bankers' committee watching over the parliamentary enquiry into joint stock banking. Although the bank is known to have sent representatives to meetings of 'deputies' of joint stock banks in November 1838 and September 1842, Geach and his board were not in the van of lobbyists. At that time their main preoccupation was more pragmatic. Rowland Hill (a customer of the bank) had produced new plans for the reform of the postal system; Midland's directors, aware that methods of payment would be improved, were anxious that Hill's reforms should become law as quickly as possible.

This relatively low political profile was made possible by Midland's decision not to issue its own notes. That choice set Midland apart from many of the banks which were most active in lobbying. When the Bank Charter Act came into force, the decision not to issue notes allowed the bank to escape the main restrictions of the Act. Neither could it complain too vigorously about the slow-turning machinery introduced by the Joint Stock Bank Act. Like all joint stock banks already in existence, it now entered a more sheltered period when the chances of competition from yet another new generation of joint stock banks were remote.

The Bank Charter Act nonetheless represented a major upheaval in the affairs of a relatively inexperienced bank, especially in the management of its relations with the Bank of England. Midland's long negotiations with the Bank in 1836 and 1837 only arose because its decision not to issue notes had earned it the chance of a special account at the Bank. Consequently any change in the rules for note-issuing was bound to influence the terms of Midland's facilities at the Bank's Birmingham branch.

The immediate reaction of Geach and his directors to early rumours of Peel's legislation had been to 'secure to themselves the compensation which they have hitherto received from the Bank' for not issuing their own notes. Geach himself joined the deputation from the joint stock banks which confronted Peel in May 1844, but the sole concern of

Midland's manager was that Peel had promised that any benefit given to the non-issuing banks would be protected by law. The Bank appeared to take the same line. In a private interview with the governor, Geach was told that 'the Bank intended to deal liberally with those Banks [including the Birmingham and Midland] which had fulfilled the engagements which they entered into'. In August the Bank confirmed that Midland would be given a 'circulation allowance' of 1 per cent on the value of its Bank of England notes and that it could continue to borrow notes and coin from the Bank's Birmingham branch on the security of bills (in addition to discounting bills at ordinary rates). The special discount account, however, would be closed at the end of 1844.

These terms removed the important privileges of the discount account, but Geach and his directors were not in a position to argue. Before 1844, a non-issuing country bank had the opportunity to bargain with the Bank of England; if the Bank would not provide facilities, the country bank could reverse its decision and further increase the non-Bank notes in circulation. The 1844 legislation swept away this bargaining position. It was then too late to begin issuing notes, leaving the Bank free to deal with country banks entirely on its own terms.

For a bank such as Midland, which clearly benefited from its links with the Bank, the objective now switched to preserving as many facilities as possible without damaging its business independence. The Bank, fortified by the Bank Charter Act, seemed determined to trim back the privileges which had survived the 1844 legislation. In December 1844 Midland's directors learned that the Bank had imposed a commission of threepence in the pound on all payments on the accounts of the non-issuing banks. Midland and the other non-issuers were asked to sign a 'letter of recognition' which implied that the only exceptions to the commission charge would be payments 'drawn off at the [Birmingham] Branch bona fide for circulation purposes'. Geach, vexed that the restriction had not been fully explained at a meeting with the governor when the first news of the commission scheme had emerged earlier in December, told the Bank that it would be impossible to keep to the terms of the letter of recognition. Tindal, the Bank's Birmingham agent, eventually agreed that the maximum charge for any payment on the Midland's account would be sixpence. On that basis Midland's directors signed the letter of agreement 'to avoid even the appearance of a want of confidence in the Bank of England'.

The affair of the commission charge showed Midland's board that the Bank, despite its formidable bargaining position, would not refuse special terms for its banking customers. Similarly in April 1845 the Bank sought to end Midland's arrangements for borrowing cash at Birmingham on the security of bills. As this appeared to breach the agreement made in August 1844, Geach reopened direct negotiations with the governor during May. The result was that Midland accepted the 'loss and inconvenience' of ending the special borrowing facility, and also agreed to surrender the short-lived 'circulation allowance'. In return, Geach secured a new special discount account of up to £40,000 at 1 per cent below London rate; the account was in addition to a £15,000 facility at normal market rates which the Bank had granted in February. This rationalization and expansion of Midland's account ran for three years and was then renewed on a year-to-year basis.

The Bank of England account was the most intricate and arduous of the responsibilities of Midland's board and management in the first ten years of the bank's existence. Apart from the probable benefits in terms of profitability (p 32), the negotiations also inculcated a sense of independence and identity which was not generated in contemporary banks such as the Bank of Birmingham. This was obvious as early as June 1837, when the directors flatly dismissed a plan for amalgamation with the Birmingham Banking Company. It emerged that Robert Webb, Midland's chairman, had approached the rival bank on his own initiative. Webb was censured by his co-directors and he made no further appearances at board meetings. By January 1838 Webb 'had parted with his Interest in the Company'. Thereafter, until 1880, Midland's directors elected their chairman on an annual basis.

The abhorrence of losing the bank's independence was no doubt influenced by the then unresolved capital position, which would have depressed the value of existing shares in the event of a merger. It was much more important, however, that Midland's business was already developing distinctive strengths in discount banking. Over the following ten years the negotiations with the Bank clarified and brought discipline to this part of its work, placing the emphasis on the quality and security of bill business. Echoing the original plan for a 'Birmingham Exchange Bank', discount arrangements with London agents were given high priority; the original agents, Esdaile and Co, closed in January 1837 and were replaced by Williams Deacon and Co, who in turn were replaced by the Union Bank of London in January 1844. Meanwhile an entry to the important Lancashire market was secured by appointing the Royal Bank of Liverpool and the Manchester Union Bank as agents early in 1837, and by March that year Midland was regularly discounting four-month American bills of exchange. Other bank agencies in these first months included the Stourbridge and Kidderminster Bank (where Geach's former colleague John Amery was manager), the Bank of Whitehaven and, from May 1838, the newly-established Clydesdale Bank in Glasgow. Failures of customers were rare in this period, and bad debts written off in the first year amounted to only £313 on five accounts. Where failures did occur, it was dishonoured bills rather than overdrafts and other loans which were generally the cause.

Midland's dealings with the Bank of England, as well as demonstrating Geach's independent style, left useful clues to the new bank's standing. Full balance sheets for Midland's first ten years have not survived, but between October 1839 and December 1840 the Bank's Birmingham branch was discounting an average of £100,000 per quarter in Midland's special and ordinary discount accounts.[25] The equivalent averages were £244,000 for the Birmingham Banking Company and £96,000 for the Town and District Bank, reflecting the former bank's early start in operating a 'discount account'. An approximate parity between Midland and the Town and District Bank also emerged in their demand for Bank notes. Midland drew off a quarterly average of £104,000 in notes in comparison with the Town and District's usual drawings of £110,000, although both were eclipsed by the Birmingham Banking Company's average note withdrawal of £248,000. As to the character of this business, the Bank of England's agent reported in 1845 that many of the Birmingham Banking Company's bills were for values of less than £100 each; those presented by Midland and the Town and District were apparently for higher amounts, suggesting that the two younger banks had captured the business of some of the town's larger firms and traders.[26] The quality of Midland's bills must have been especially good. The Bank's rules for discounting were stringent (p 21), yet Geach succeeded in placing all Midland's Birmingham rediscounts with the Bank in the 1840s. Geach, according to Tindal, the Bank's Birmingham agent, hoped that 'the assurance that he is discounting nowhere else will satisfy the Governors of his anxiety to keep faith with the Bank'. This exclusive arrangement, persisting even when Geach could obtain better discount rates elsewhere, seems to have created confidence in Midland's operations. Tindal told his head office in 1845 and 1846 that Midland's accounts showed 'favourable results' and were 'most satisfactory'. Geach's insistence on channelling rediscounts through the Bank no doubt contributed to the relatively high rates of discount which Tindal thought Midland was able to charge in the mid-1840s.[27]

Midland's general bill business, of which the rediscount arrangements with the Bank were such a central part, was obviously substantial by the late 1840s. Total bill assets had stood at £144,000 in January 1843; by June 1848, the first year for which internal balance sheets or 'stock accounts' give disaggregated figures, bills were valued at £193,601. By June 1850 the total had reached £209,124. Admittedly 1850 was a year of exceptional business in Birmingham (Tindal could not believe 'that at any period since . . . 1834 the trade of Birmingham was ever more active or more sound . . . every branch of manufacture is in full activity') but Midland's portfolio was by then comparatively large. Although comparisons with other Birmingham banks are not available, the 1850 total was well above average levels for single-office country banks. Amongst the banks which later became part of Midland for which accounts have survived, only three (the Leicestershire, Preston, and Yorkshire Banking Companies) carried larger bill portfolios, and all of these banks were already multi-branch companies.

The relative importance of bills as a part of Midland's assets is not clear-cut, despite the time and attention they had been given throughout the bank's infancy. The difficulty here is the lack of any exact comparison with the bank's loans and overdrafts in the same period. The 'stock accounts' compiled for the directors' use from 1847 onwards did not provide the total debits and credits in the current account ledgers of the bank. Instead they entered a net figure for 'customers accounts', which was the amount by which loans and overdrafts exceeded or undershot the total for current accounts in credit. Any estimate of loans and overdrafts must therefore be linked to an estimate of current accounts in credit.

The re-creation of these sections of the bank's balance sheet is a complex jigsaw puzzle. Of the surviving sources, the year-by-year level of deposit accounts is the only available series which might act as a guide to the size of Midland's current account business. Deposit accounts *were* recorded in the stock accounts but they were listed simply as 'deposits'. (It was these figures which Crick and Wadsworth quoted, and were themselves surprised by, as the main element in the bank's total deposits.)[28] In reality the so-called 'deposits' in the stock accounts were only a part of the total deposit liabilities as they entirely excluded current accounts in credit. In Appendix 1 (p 320) total deposits have been estimated by reckoning that the known returns for deposit accounts were 44 per cent of the bank's deposit liabilities, with current accounts providing the remaining 56 per cent. On this basis it is probable that the bank's total deposits more than doubled from about £122,000 in 1840 to about £316,000 in 1847, followed by a sharp reduction in 1849 and a recovery to as much as £273,000 in 1851. This profile suggests that the volume of the bank's business at this early stage in its development was at least twice as large as previous estimates allowed.

This reconstruction opens the way for an assessment of Midland's total lending. When the estimates of current accounts are coordinated with the entries for 'customers' accounts' in the stock accounts, total loans and overdrafts can be reckoned at an average of over £160,000 between 1847 and 1851, with a low point of only £105,000 in 1849 and a peak of over £196,000 in 1851. These are conservative estimates, as the ratio of current accounts to total deposits used in the reconstruction is below the average for a sample of contemporary banks.[29] At the neighbouring Stourbridge and Kidderminster Banking Company, where John Amery was manager, deposit accounts averaged barely 30 per cent of total deposits in the 1840s and less than 23 per cent in the 1850s. Yet the comparison of estimated advances with the bank's bill business makes it clear that Midland under Geach's management was more heavily involved in discount business than many of its contemporaries. Bill assets averaged 142 per cent of the estimated advances between 1847 and 1851, an appreciably higher ratio than the 100 per cent and 86 per cent ratios of sample groups of banks in the 1840s and 1850s.[30]

The sources of the bank's business in the 1840s are more easily traced than its exact dimensions. From the outset the needs of Midland's shareholders were a powerful influence. The earliest share register was dominated by the names of manufacturers, merchants, shopkeepers and retailers. These groups together supplied 127 of the 199 shareholders in 1837, when they contributed 63.7 per cent of the paid-up capital (Appendix 3, p 327). Each of these groups had a routine use for discount payments in Birmingham, throughout the British Isles, and, in the case of the Oppenheimer brothers of Birmingham and Hamburg, in Europe and the Far East. Shareholders' introductions frequently provided facilities for Birmingham's more substantial firms. Discounts and loans linked to directors and shareholders included Thomas Bolton and Co, the metals merchant and manufacturer; William Hunt and Sons; and Joshua Scholefield and Sons, which obtained a credit limit of £20,000 when William Scholefield was elected to the bank's board in June 1841. William Scholefield, Birmingham's Mayor during the Bull Ring riots of 1839, was a senior and influential member of the town's business and political establishment.[31] His cousin Joshua was signatory to five of Midland's earliest current accounts, including a 'chunk nail account' and partnerships with other Birmingham merchants.

On the liabilities side of the balance sheet, the input of shareholders' business was equally important. The promoters of most new joint stock concerns took it for granted that their share registers were a recruiting ground for customers. In some examples it was a condition of allotting shares that the shareholder should open a banking account in his or her own bank. This rule did not apply in Midland's case, yet by December 1837 the directors were searching the share register 'with a view to influence those who have not already opened accounts to do so'. With less than 200 shareholders at that stage (a total which was steadily reduced when major shareholders consolidated their investments in the 1840s), the scope for new business was limited. In comparison, companies such as the Huddersfield Banking Company, with its 354 shareholders, or the West Riding Union Bank, with 400 shareholders,[32] had large constituencies. Consequently it was essential that Midland's large shareholders used the bank's services to the full. Geach and his directors did not yet envisage opening any branch banks, so that they relied mainly on shareholders to provide business. The result was that one half of the bank's shareholders were amongst the 377 current account customers between 1836 and 1838. Relatively few shareholders opened interest-bearing deposit accounts; they were easily outnumbered, for instance, by the large contingent of accounts in the names of widows, spinsters or their trustees. Nevertheless those shareholders who did bring their deposit accounts to Union Street ran much larger than average balances (Table 1.1). In the case of Thomas

## Table 1.1

Midland Bank deposit accounts, 1840 and 1844

| Category | | Number of accounts | Total balance (£) | Average balance (£) | Percentage of total balance |
|---|---|---|---|---|---|
| All accounts | Dec 1840 | 85 | 53,722 | 632 | 100.0 |
| | Dec 1844 | 141 | 79,702 | 565 | 100.0 |
| Accounts with £1000 + balances | Dec 1840 | 11 | 38,703 | 3518 | 72.0 |
| | Dec 1844 | 19 | 52,815 | 2780 | 66.3 |
| Widows, spinsters or their trustees | Dec 1840 | 21 | 5596 | 266 | 10.4 |
| | Dec 1844 | 31 | 11,508 | 371 | 14.4 |
| Shareholders | Dec 1840 | 9 | 13,805 | 1534 | 25.7 |
| | Dec 1844 | 14 | 21,185 | 1513 | 26.6 |

Adkins the account included no less than £7000 'taken for 5 years certain at 5pc'.

These linkages between a joint stock bank and its principal shareholders were far from unusual in the 1830s and 1840s. Contemporary banks had rapidly provided facilities for their founding directors and shareholders, occasionally at great cost to their narrow resources. The Yorkshire District Bank, founded in 1834, had made 'advances for most incredible amounts' to its own directors and shareholders; losses of £500,000 forced a reconstruction in 1843. More often, however, 'directors' and shareholders' accounts seem to have been operated with much propriety and within the fairly tight bonds of the companies' regulations'.[33] In Midland's case, a striking example was provided by Charles Geach's own industrial interests.

As his departure from the Bank of England had shown, Geach had a strong taste for risk and opportunity. This quality was again to the fore during Birmingham's Bull Ring riots in 1839:

> Mr Geach received private information one afternoon, which induced him to take extra precautions for the safety of the books, securities, and cash. While this was being done, the clerks had collected a number of men and some arms. They also obtained, and took to the roof, a great quantity of stones, bricks and other missiles, which they stored behind the parapets. The men were so placed, that by mounting an inner stair they could ascend to the roof, from which spot, it was proposed, in case of attack, to hurl the missiles upon the mob below. News was soon brought that the mob was congregating in Dale End and that neighbourhood. At the request of some of the magistrates who were present, Mr Geach started off for the barracks, galloping through the mob, who threw showers of stones, brick-ends, and other disagreeable missiles at him, and shouted, 'Stop him', 'Pull him off', 'He's going for the soldiers', and so on. His horse was a spirited one, and took him safely through. He reached the barracks and secured assistance. He then came back by another route to the bank, and the expected attack was averted. There is no doubt that his energetic conduct that day saved the town from violence and spoliation.[34]

Geach's obvious courage and initiative also characterized his forays into industrial business. Two years after the foundation of the Birmingham and Midland Bank, Geach led a group of Birmingham businessmen in purchasing the patents and works of Messrs Hardy and Wright of Wednesbury, who had developed a method of forging heavy-duty iron axles but had exhausted their capital by 1838. The company was reconstructed as the Patent Shaft and Axle Tree Company and its banking arrangements were taken over by Midland. In 1844 Geach bought out his partners and, in the railway mania which followed, the company was producing annual profits of £20,000 by 1846. Under Geach's ownership the company was transformed from a small works of one forge and ten furnaces into a complex of four forges, four mills and 100 furnaces ten years later (the company eventually became part of the Metropolitan Amalgamated Carriage and Wagon Company in 1902).[35] Similarly in 1842 Geach learned of the imminent failure of the Park Gate Iron Manufacturing Company of Rotherham. The company suffered heavily from the fall of iron prices during 1842 and its bills were only discounted on the personal guarantee of the directors. The principal directors and shareholders were all from Birmingham, including Joshua Scholefield and Samuel Goddard, who were both Midland shareholders. The manager was H Wright, formerly of the Patent Shaft concern. Geach 'bought the whole concern for an old song'[36] and when iron prices were driven up by the demand for rails in the 'mania' of 1844–45, Geach's new company benefited. Both the Patent Shaft and Park Gate companies relied heavily upon Midland's discounting services (these outside interests later drew Geach into the promotion of the Manchester Sheffield and Lincolnshire Railway and the Shrewsbury and Birmingham Railway). At the same time Geach was ever-anxious to demonstrate that his ventures would not create a conflict of interests with the bank. In October 1846, for example, he offered to show the Bank of England the books of the Patent Shaft Company as evidence that 'his position at the Midland Bank [was not] subservient to his interests as a trader. . . . He has been equally explicit on this Head with the Directors of his Bank'.[37]

For the bank, the obvious disadvantage to Geach's catholic interest in enterprise was the probability that he would either give up or reduce his managerial work in Union Street. This difficulty was compounded by Geach's enthusiastic entry into public life. He served as an alderman in 1843 and 1844, when his main contribution was the reform of the Borough's book-keeping, and in 1847 he was elected Mayor. As a convinced Liberal, he assisted his business allies William and Joshua Scholefield in their election to Parliament. In 1851 he joined them in the Commons as the member for the City of Coventry, and soon afterwards he was the host for a triumphant visit to Birmingham by Louis Kossuth, the Hungarian patriot. It was not until his election, however, that he gave up his responsibilities at the bank. He continued nominally as managing director, but just three years later, on 1 November 1854, he died in Westminster at the age of only 46. Leaving a wife, four children and an extraordinary legacy of banking and manufacturing enterprise, Geach had imposed on himself an intolerable physical and mental strain over a long period with the result that he could not survive two serious illnesses within a year. Even in a period of prolific entrepreneurial achievement, his death was recognized as an exceptional loss. In the view of *The Times*, for example, 'his habits of business and personal industry were uncommon, and his extensive commercial operations were all conducted with singular regularity and prudence'.[38]

Geach's directors were in no doubt of his contribution. They had devised their own profit-sharing scheme for Geach as early as June 1839. The scheme awarded Geach increases geared to the annual level of the guarantee fund, which was the destination for all the bank's undistributed profits. The basic salary was then £600 but would rise to £700 when the guarantee fund reached £20,000 and to £800 when it reached £30,000. It was an arrangement which recognized Geach personally as the controller of Midland's profitability.

In the event the guarantee fund accumulated rapidly and Geach had reached the salary ceiling of £800 by 1845. Thereafter the bank's undistributed net profit for the year ending June 1848 reached £16,474, a return of 18.3 per cent on the paid-up capital and guarantee or reserve. The equivalent returns for 1849, 1850, and 1851 produced net profits of over £13,000 each year, almost exactly 10 per cent of the total paid-up capital and reserves. The performance was all the more impressive as Midland's board was already making careful provisions for bad debts. Each year's net profit figure excluded £1000 for 'general security of debts' and additional provisions for specific bad debts. The special provisions were as low as £142 in June 1849 but as high as £2155 in June 1851. The use of a 'general provision' was certainly not yet standard practice. The Birmingham Banking Company, for example, whose net profits ranged from £20,000 in 1843 to £40,000 in 1847 (between 8.5 and 15.5 per cent of its capital and reserves), provided only for specific bad debts.

The profit record also enabled the directors to make transfers from the guarantee fund to pay the third and fourth calls on the bank's nominal capital in 1846 and 1850. This arrangement, no doubt to the delight of the shareholders, increased the paid-up capital to the full nominal value of £120,000 without the need for any contributions from the existing shareholders. The board was sufficiently impressed by the achievement to award bonuses to the staff, but their first debt was to Geach himself. In recognition, the remaining 46 original shares in the bank were placed in trust for Geach in 1846 and he was promoted to become managing director. Four years later he was presented with a testimonial and 'costly service of plate'.[39]

Charles Geach had contributed professional skills and business vision to the promotion and early development of the Birmingham and Midland Bank. In the financial turmoil of the 1830s, Geach was one of the very few Bank of England officials to have been recruited by the joint stock banks. It was a choice which proved especially appropriate during Midland's long negotiations with the Bank. Geach's abilities were not simply a matter of training. The survival and subsequent growth of the bank also followed from his alliance with a strongly motivated group of Birmingham businessmen. That group—as directors, shareholders and customers—had encouraged and enabled Geach to develop a single-office bank with a strong deposit base and an especially active bill portfolio. This profile, in marked contrast to that of many contemporary note-issuing country banks, owed much more to banking and business judgment than to Midland's status as a joint stock bank. It is even possible that Geach could have developed a similar type and size of business within the boundaries of a traditional private bank. Crucially, however, a joint stock bank had given him the type of salary and opportunity which would never have been available to a former bank clerk working for a partnership, and, secondly, the support of a group of directors and investors which was too large to have participated in a private banking business.

To have survived the financial crises of the late 1830s and late 1840s was an obvious achievement at a time when even well-run joint stock banks were forced to close. To have also sustained the growth of the business ranked as a major success. Yet in perspective at the time of Geach's retirement from the bank in 1851 Midland remained a comparatively small concern. Its staff was tiny in comparison with London-based banks or neighbouring banks such as the Birmingham Banking Company or Taylor and Lloyds. Apart from Geach, the staff was limited to the new manager, Henry Edmunds (recruited from the National Provincial in 1836), and seven clerks. Midland's paid-up capital of £120,000 was overshadowed by that of the Birmingham Banking Company (£200,000) or the large joint stock banks of London and Liverpool, most of which employed capital of over £500,000. By this measure, Midland ranked as only the thirty-first largest of the joint stock banks in England and Wales. The bank's total deposits, probably exceeding £250,000 in June 1851, were remarkable enough for a single-office bank but they were probably only one half of those held by the Birmingham Banking Company. These total deposits were far outdistanced by those of multi-branch country banks such as the Leicestershire Banking Company (£555,000) or the York

City and County Bank (£753,000) and by London banks such as the
London Joint Stock Bank (£2.9 million). There is little evidence that
bankers in the early Victorian period were much concerned with
questions of ranking, but for Geach's successors there remained a
choice between sustaining a limited role or attempting to build a wider
geographical or business base.

✳

# CHAPTER TWO

# MIDLAND BANKING
# 1851–1874

> The 'Midland', under Mr Edmunds, was pre-eminently a 'lucky bank'. . . the bank was offered more business than it cared for; and his caution and hesitation saved his directors much trouble, and his shareholders considerable loss.
>
> E Edwards, *Personal Recollections of Birmingham and Birmingham Men* (1877), p 63

Even in his own lifetime Charles Geach was deservedly given credit for creating, developing and guarding the Birmingham and Midland Bank's business. His personality and his influence on local business and politics had earned him a place amongst Birmingham's heroes. In contrast his successors in the bank's management seemed to lack the brilliance which contemporaries had recognised in Geach. Edwards, a Birmingham businessman who published his memoirs in the *Birmingham Daily Mail* in the mid-1870s, believed that Geach's 'boldness and vigour' had won a large business for the bank, whereas his successor, Henry Edmunds, managed the bank with 'excessive caution'.

This interpretation was followed by later historians of Birmingham banks, who agreed that after Geach's meteoric career Midland entered a period of conservatism and entrenchment.[1] Midland's own business records suggest that Edwards may have been unjust to Geach's successors. Under almost every heading in the balance sheet the bank advanced at a faster rate in the 1850s and 1860s than it had in the 1840s. While paid-up capital was boosted from £120,000 in 1850 to £300,000 in 1874, the bank's total deposits were lifted from approximately £200,000 in 1850 to over £2.5 million by 1874 (Appendix 2.1, p 323). Published net profits rose from £13,156 in 1850 to £32,021 in 1860 and £63,724 by 1874. Even the guarantee fund, which the directors had used to measure Geach's success, shared in this expansion; the fund grew from £18,450 in December 1850 (immediately after the fourth call on the original capital: see p 32) to £118,398 in 1860 and £240,000 in 1874.

Part of this success was clearly generated by more expansive economic conditions. The anti-protectionist lobby, of which Geach and other Birmingham businessmen were such strong supporters, was at last rewarded. Reintroduction of income tax in 1842 had allowed the government to reduce trade tariffs, leading eventually to the repeal of the Corn Laws in 1846. The free trade conditions which followed brought a massive expansion in British exports, and Birmingham's metalwork goods and precision products were amongst the beneficiaries. This prosperity was not the whole explanation for Midland's rapid advance. The bank's balance sheet compared well not only with the period of Geach's management but also with the progress of other banks. The capital and reserve position was especially strong. Lloyds' paid-up capital was only £143,400 when it became a joint stock company in 1865; the neighbouring Stourbridge and Kidderminster Bank made no increases in its capital of £100,000 between 1850 and 1870, with a reserve of only £50,000 by 1870. Of the Birmingham banks, only Lloyds, with deposits of £4.9 million, had attracted a larger business by 1874.

This performance was not the work of a purely defensive management. Henry Edmunds, who succeeded Geach as manager in 1847 and took sole command in 1851, had been born and bred in Birmingham. He had been a clerk in the bank of Gibbins, Smith and Goode (p 12) and had later joined the National Provincial Bank's Birmingham branch. Geach had recruited him to the Birmingham and Midland one week after the bank opened in August 1836. He had acted as Geach's deputy throughout the excitement of the late 1830s and 1840s, emerging as a key figure in a comparatively small staff. Apart from Geach and William Goode (recruited from the ill-fated Bank of Birmingham in 1837), he was the only member of the original complement with any previous experience of banking. Tindal, the Bank of England's Birmingham agent, admitted in 1849 that 'with respect to Mr Henry Edmunds . . . I do not know a young man in Birmingham of higher personal respectability, or one more attentive to his business; and ample means of judging his character have fallen my way'.[2] Overshadowed as he was by Geach's reputation, throughout the 1840s Edmunds had had the best possible opportunity to assess the bank's directors, shareholders and customers. It was an education which allowed him to transform the bank's business in the 1850s and 1860s and to convert it from a small single-office business in Birmingham into one of the strongest banking institutions in the west Midlands.

The most striking feature of Edmunds' period of command was the enlargement of the bank's deposit base. Deposits were probably below £200,000 in 1850, only one and a half times larger than paid-up capital and reserves. By 1860 estimated total deposits approached £850,000, three times larger than capital and reserves. Within another 15 years the total had trebled to £2,565,054, which was nearly five times as great as the £540,000 liability for capital and reserves. The trend towards a capital to deposits ratio of 1:5 was common amongst English and Welsh banks in the 1870s,[3] but the scale and pace of Midland's transformation was exceptional. Whereas the liabilities of provincial joint stock banks in England and Wales were growing at a rate of about 5.8 per cent per annum between 1850 and 1874,[4] the growth rate for Midland's deposits was probably as high as 11.3 per cent per annum.

The enlargement of deposits was achieved with a mixture of incentives. The traditional device of asking shareholders to open deposit or current accounts was again employed. By 1871, for example, the board was searching the share register to identify any of the numerous female shareholders who were not also customers. In parallel to these efforts the need for new share-owning customers influenced the board in its willingness to enlarge the bank's capital. The process was slow. The shareholders' authorization in June 1851 to issue 600 new shares, raising paid-up capital to £150,000, was not fully used until June 1857. Two years later paid-up capital was lifted to £165,000 by the distribution of bonus shares to existing shareholders. These operations still left the bank's capital in relatively few hands. In 1859 the bank was owned by only 111 shareholders, with an average holding of £1490 in paid-up shares (Appendix 3, p 327). In reality the controlling ownership was even narrower. The 17 shareholders with more than £3000 each in paid-up shares held over 57 per cent of the total. The register was dominated by directors and their families, especially in the examples of Samuel Beale (the largest investor with £9600), William Beale, the Bolton family, John Francis and William Lort. Few shareholders lived away from Birmingham, and examples of small shareholdings were rare.

Edmunds and his directors made greater efforts to broaden the bank's ownership in the mid 1860s. By then new capital was needed to support the growth of assets (pp 47–51), and in August 1864 they obtained shareholders' approval to increase nominal capital to £300,000. This was achieved by creating 2000 new shares in 1865, all of which were issued by 1874 to bring the paid-up capital to £300,000. The original plan in 1864 had been to reduce the nominal value of shares from £50 to £10 (the denomination abandoned in 1837) in order to accelerate the sale and transfer of shares. This sub-division was not carried through but the 1865 issue did have the effect of mobilizing shares and introducing new investors. By 1874 there were 258 names on the register, more than double the 1859 roll-call, with shareholders owning a lower average of £1163 each in paid-up shares. Nearly three-fifths of the shares were still owned by individuals investing more than £3000 each but a greater spread of occupations and addresses was beginning to emerge (Appendix 3, p 327).

Most of the incoming shareholders either were existing customers of the bank or were investors who were prepared to move their bank accounts to the Birmingham and Midland. The identity of customers' and shareholders' interests was taken for granted. Another less common method of attracting deposits from shareholders was introduced in the mid-1860s. From August 1864 Midland's customers were permitted to buy the bank's shares at £120 per share 'in proportion to the size of their accounts'. This offer was equivalent to a 25 per cent discount on the share price and it soon proved persuasive. By the following May 600 shares had been allotted in this way; some customers were allotted shares in more than one batch, implying that they were switching deposits to the bank in response to the offer. The experiment contributed to the expansion of estimated deposits from at least £1.11 million in June 1864 to about £1.56 million two years later.

The acquisition of branch offices and agencies was the more conventional method of extending a bank's business in the mid-nineteenth century. By 1850 the 99 joint stock banks in England and Wales operated 576 branches and agencies, an average of almost five additional offices per bank.[5] In the Midlands several joint stock banks were prolific; the Stourbridge and Kidderminster Bank employed eight branches and agencies by 1850 while the Leicestershire Banking Company already owned six offices. The Birmingham banks showed no such ambition. By the middle of the century neither Midland, Lloyds nor the Town and District had opened a single branch, and the Birmingham Banking Company had limited its extension to branches at Dudley and Walsall. Geach and his directors, concentrating on their Birmingham customers (especially their discount business), showed little interest in establishing or acquiring other offices. Although the deed of settlement had made provision for branch banks, they had unhesitatingly turned down an offer to buy a small bank at Wednesbury when its owner, Samuel Addison, died in 1849. As a result the Birmingham and Midland Bank remained closer to the traditional model for private banks, which rarely had more than one office, than to its contemporaries amongst the joint stock banks.

Immediately before his retirement from the bank in 1851, Geach altered this position. In July that year he opened negotiations with William Robins, sole surviving partner of the Stourbridge banking firm of Bate and Robins, who had been keen to sell the business after the death of Thomas Bate in 1847. Within a month Midland's directors, full of confidence after the fourth call on the bank's shares, authorized Geach to buy the goodwill of the business for £16,000 and the bank premises for £1850. The private firm was then converted to become Midland's 'Stourbridge Old Bank' branch.

The extension to Stourbridge was almost certainly intended to strengthen rather than dilute the bank's involvement in Birmingham business. Stourbridge, ten miles from Birmingham, had been a centre of ironfounding, nailmaking and glassmaking since the eighteenth century. Its strong connections with Birmingham business were given further stimulus by the opening of the Stourbridge Canal in 1779. The town's industries, particularly the iron trades, were closely integrated with Birmingham's metal dealers and manufacturers, and by the mid-nineteenth century there was heavy commercial and financial traffic between the two towns. The firm of Bate and Robins, established before 1770 and ranking as one of the oldest banks in the Midlands, was heavily used for payments to and from Stourbridge. It had not been seriously challenged until 1834, when the Stourbridge and Kidderminster Bank had been promoted by a former customer. The size of the Bate and Robins business was doubtless an attraction to Geach and his directors. By the time of the purchase Bate and Robins controlled over £250,000 of deposits, almost as high a volume as Midland's own; the assets included no less than £114,000 in bills and £22,000 with London bankers. Amongst the major customers were the Rounds Green Colliery, which had been allowed an overdraft of £10,000, and the Eagle Iron and Coal Company, which used an overdraft of £6000 and discount facilities of £7200.

The new acquisition immediately produced a significant expansion in the volume of Midland's business. By 1855 Edmunds was asking the Bank of England's Birmingham agent for increased limits on its discount account to cope with the demands of the new Stourbridge business.[6] The introduction of over £250,000 in deposits after 1851 was equally momentous, probably doubling the bank's deposits to nearly £600,000 after the purchase and pushing the total over £800,000 by 1860. As to profits, in 1851 William Robins had guaranteed a net annual return of £7500, approximately one half of

Midland's own profits at that time. This level was not maintained in the 1850s, although by 1860 it still amounted to £4857 (15.2 per cent of the bank's net profits).

The Stourbridge business was already a going concern with a large and apparently loyal constituency. Edmunds and his directors were not so keen on other opportunities for branch business. They shared Birmingham bankers' reluctance to open entirely new branches, as in their rejection of a petition from local businessmen to establish a branch in Kidderminster in 1855. They also held back from following in the footsteps of failed banks. In 1856, a year which had begun with the Bank of England's agent reporting a run on Lloyds, Midland turned down an offer to 'take up' the business of Farley Turner and Co of Kidderminster after its failure in December.[7] This caution was justified, as the collapse of the Western Bank of Scotland in 1857 soon affected the Midlands. The Dudley and West Bromwich Bank and the Wolverhampton and Staffordshire Bank were both reported to be in difficulties, and in December 1857 Farley Lavender and Co of Worcester was forced to close.[8]

It was not until May 1862 that Edmunds found an opportunity comparable to that at Stourbridge. Nichols, Baker and Crane, bankers at Bewdley in Worcestershire, were the successors to three private banks, of which the earliest, Roberts, Skey and Kenrick, had been founded in 1782. The three banks had been associated with the Skey family's business as drysalters and with a succession of local solicitors. When the town fell into industrial decline in the 1830s and 1840s—its advantages as a river port on the Severn were reduced by the spread of the railways—the surviving firm of Nichols, Baker and Crane became the focus for the district's bank deposits. The bank at Bewdley was supported by a one-day-a-week agency at Cleobury Mortimer in Shropshire, and this combination provided business which the Bank of England's agent described as 'entirely of an *agricultural* nature'.[9] By the early 1860s deposits exceeded £100,000, of which more than one half was held in interest-earning deposit accounts, and the firm made little use of its authorized note issue of £18,597.

Bewdley was over twenty miles west of Birmingham, and the Nichols, Baker and Crane business was quite different in its composition from Midland's operations at Birmingham and Stourbridge. On the other hand the Bewdley bank was in good working order with comfortable profits of about £3000 each year and a deposit-rich balance sheet. Edmunds' offer of £3000 for the goodwill and £1600 for the bank buildings was agreed in June 1862, and the old bank then became Midland's Bewdley branch. The extension made an immediate impact on the deposits controlled at the Union Street head office. The £100,000 contributed by Bewdley probably added more than 10 per cent to Midland's deposits, lifting the estimated total above £1 million in 1862. Within a few months the change was already obvious to the Birmingham branch of the Bank of England; the Bewdley acquisition had 'largely added to their deposits' and as a result Midland had 'a superabundance of cash and large balances with their agents'. No doubt Edmunds and his directors were also pleased with the profitability of the new branch. Net profits averaged £2963 between 1865 and 1872, or about 5.2 per cent of the bank's net profits in those years.

The two new branches altered the routines as well as the composition of the bank's business. Initially Edmunds travelled by carriage or trap to Stourbridge once a week, giving reports on the branch to the weekly board meetings. Both at Stourbridge and Bewdley he was especially anxious to learn and then standardize the procedures which were being used for discounts, overdrafts and the assessment of securities. Surprisingly this attention to the details of working methods did not extend to the overall financial management of the branches. Edmunds and his directors were not yet concerned with the size and shape of each branch's business. The 'stock accounts' which they used in the 1850s and 1860s revealed only the balance of each branch's account with the bank's head office and the value of the branches' net profits; they excluded branch returns for deposits, cash, bills and advances. In other words Edmunds and his board were interested only in the results of their branch operations, leaving their local managers to decide upon and control the composition of the branches' business. This approach, which was also employed by Geach's old colleague John Amery at the Stourbridge and Kidderminster Bank, left the branches with considerable autonomy in the mid-Victorian period. For the time being, they were treated more as subsidiaries than as part of an integrated branch network.

Valuable as the acquisitions at Stourbridge and Bewdley were, they did not and were never likely to affect Midland's long-term viability. A number of contemporary joint stock banks prospered and survived into the twentieth century without ever opening a branch. The Bradford Banking Company, which was amongst the first joint stock inspired banks in 1827 and became part of Midland in 1910, refused to open branches as a matter of principle. Changes in Midland's Birmingham business were much more likely to decide its fate. If the bank had maintained its relatively large bill business it is improbable that it could have survived the successive financial crises of the 1860s and 1870s. Even if it had continued in that form, the scope for a provincial bank with a relatively large bill business was restricted at a time when the money market was increasingly pinned upon London.

It is puzzling both that Henry Edmunds should have been regarded as notably cautious and that the bank should have been labelled as conservative under his management. On the assets side of Midland's balance sheet, a major readjustment was being made in the mid-Victorian period. Inheriting the comparatively large commitment to discount banking which Geach had developed, Edmunds slowly but irreversibly changed the emphasis. In the boom year of 1850 the bill portfolio of £209,124 was equivalent to 135 per cent of estimated advances. Two decades later, in June 1871, bills had quadrupled in value to £829,267, but by then this represented only 78 per cent of actual advances.

The readjustment of the Birmingham and Midland Bank's assets in part reflected the declining importance of bills of exchange in the local and national economy. The bill holdings of a sample of 11 contemporary banks exceeded their combined total of loans and overdrafts in the 1860s, but by 1880 bills represented only 13 per cent of total bank assets in the United Kingdom.[10] This sudden and permanent change in the balance of bank credit demonstrated that customers (especially manufacturers and merchants) were making much greater use of the more flexible credit available through loans and overdrafts. Bills, for so long the obvious device for short-term finance, were not so relevant when improved communications made it easier for manufacturers and merchants to reduce their stocks of materials and goods. Instead customers sought overdraft facilities or renewable loans. Bankers for their part devoted a growing proportion of their training and day-to-day work to the evaluation of securities for loans (pp 67–8).

The relative decline of bill finance from the 1860s onwards was accelerated by damaging banking crises in the middle of the decade. The impact on Birmingham was as severe as in any provincial banking centre. The collapse of Attwood, Spooner and Co on 10 March 1865 was essentially a local failure, apparently the result of the owners draining the firm's resources in property and mining speculations, but the liabilities at the time of its suspension were as high as £1,007,000. Attwood, Spooner and Co, formed in 1791, had been 'thought to be one of the safest banks in the kingdom',[11] and the failure was so much a surprise that the police were called to prevent a riot. A committee of creditors was formed and one week after the failure the committee invited the other Birmingham banks to tender for the assets and property of the partnership. Midland's directors offered to take over the Attwood premises and staff and to contribute £20,000 to the liquidation. The offer was refused, and the assets were eventually transferred to the Birmingham Joint Stock Bank, which had been negotiating to amalgamate with Attwoods immediately before the suspension. In the event most of the Birmingham banks inherited some of the Attwood business. In Midland's case 62 new accounts were opened by former customers of Attwood, leading to a sudden change in the balance of Midland's assets. Loans and overdrafts on current accounts increased by £250,000 between December 1864 and June 1865, no less than 37 per cent of estimated total advances in the previous year.

Although the Attwood creditors were eventually paid 11s 3d in the pound, the failure dealt a heavy blow to business confidence in the west Midlands. In these conditions bankers were forced to reassess the viability of their Birmingham business. Within three weeks of the Attwood failure, Lloyds issued their prospectus for registering as a joint stock bank. The new limited company was to incorporate the business of Moilliet and Sons, the only other surviving private bank in Birmingham. Not all the local banks responded so positively. In May 1865, for example, the European Bank decided to close its Birmingham branch altogether. This ambitious-sounding bank, established only in 1863 and claiming to operate branches in Dublin, Paris, Marseilles, Amsterdam and Rotterdam as well as in London, had recently bought the business of the London Birmingham and South Staffordshire Banking Company. The acquisition was not a success; in the short period since its promotion in 1862 the South Staffordshire bank had become known as the 'clean bank' as so few customers trod across its whitened entrance steps.[12] Midland agreed to take over the business and New Street premises from the European Bank for £3150, but as it was such 'a very small affair'[13] the office was closed and the accounts were transferred to Midland's headquarters in July 1865.

There was little time for recovery from the Attwood collapse before a much larger emergency overtook the local banking community. Signs of stress in the London and provincial money markets began to appear in the spring of 1866, when a number of merchant houses failed or sought special assistance for discounting bills. Then on 10 May 1866 ('Black Friday'), Overend, Gurney and Co of Lombard Street suspended all payments. Overends were easily the largest discount bank in London and at the time of the failure their total liabilities exceeded £10 million. Much of that liability had been created by provincial banks leaving balances with Overends, so that the crisis immediately spread far beyond Lombard Street.

The suddenness of the suspension was as damaging to business confidence as the scale and extent of the Overend liabilities. George Rae, general manager of the North and South Wales Bank, was fortunate in seeing some Overend bills shortly before the suspension and he was exceptionally shrewd in recognizing doubtful names on the bills.[14] For most bankers, however, Overends' reputation was not in any doubt until the moment the failure was announced. The consensus, *The Times* judged, was that Overends were 'the greatest instrument of credit in the kingdom'.[15] Bankers had always given Overends a place of special trust. Six years before the crash, for example, two directors of the Sheffield and Hallamshire Bank had consulted all the discount bankers in London on the question of protection against fraud. Their 'mission' was prompted by the revelation of William Pullinger's frauds, amounting to no less than £263,000, at the Union Bank of London.[16] They were taken aback by the contrasts in the discount market. Some houses were obviously 'respectable and orderly' while others seemed 'singularly mysterious'. Their brokers argued that 'another panic might be a severe, if not a *fatal trial*' for the new joint stock discount houses, and on balance the two Sheffield bankers were more impressed by the older-established firms than by the joint stock discount companies. Certainly there were no doubts about Overends, whom their broker reported to be 'very rich indeed, and the *only* discount House of real wealth'. Their interview with Overends convinced them that 'there is a large amount of business talent in this House', even when Overends offered the grand assurance that

> we now do business on the principle known and acknowledged of *taking care of ourselves*—at all risks to ourselves—formerly we felt bound to discount in times of difficulty for those who traded with us in good times—hereafter we cannot do this—all must take care of themselves in any future Panics.

The size and style of the Overend operation were impressive, and many country bankers had placed deposits or agency business with the firm. As soon as the suspension was announced there was a flood of distress calls from country banks to their London agents and to other banks. Heavy withdrawals were made, even by banks which had done little or no business with Overends. The Sheffield and Hallamshire Bank, which had been so impressed with Overends only a few years earlier, lost no time in sending its manager to London to take up £15,000 in notes and bullion, 'to meet any extraordinary demand which might be made upon this Bank'. These precautions were small in comparison with those taken by the Cumberland Union Bank. The new chairman of this Carlisle-based company, George Head, was married to a sister of Edward Gurney, one of the managing directors of Overends, and consequently the bank feared that it would suffer from 'vague and alarming reports' alleging a financial connection between the bank and Overends. Within a week of the suspension W B Gordon, the general manager of the Cumberland Union, had mobilised a total cash holding of £250,000; the Bank of England provided additional discount and loan facilities, railway investments were prepared for sale, and a Scottish bank agreed to make a special loan of £40,000. The bank's solicitor was despatched to London and on 17 May he returned with £40,000 in gold and £20,000 in notes. In the event the half-yearly Carlisle fair on 18 May (when Gordon had expected a local run) passed 'in perfect quietness and freedom from excitement'.

In these and numerous other cases 'Black Friday' was a severe test for the country banks and for their London agents. Williams Deacons, agents for the Yorkshire Banking Company, told their customers that while 'the greatest excitement prevails' in the aftermath of the suspension, 'we shall be glad if you will be as light with us as you conveniently can'. In these circumstances the government was more than usually ready to listen to the bankers. On the morning after the suspension George Leeman MP, the railway financier and director of the Yorkshire Banking Company, lobbied Gladstone on behalf of the country bankers. Gladstone agreed to allow the Bank of England to waive the restrictions of the Bank Charter Act and extend its note issue. This news was telegraphed to the country banks and the mood of panic was quickly ended. Overends was put into receivership and the country banks were asked to cooperate while the receivers paid off claims by instalments.[17] In the course of a receivership which continued for thirty years, it emerged that Overends had undergone a period of hothouse growth, stimulated by the placing of the country banks' funds on the London money market. These funds had been locked up on speculative ventures outside the money market, notably in property deals in New Zealand.[18]

Although many of the provincial banks absorbed the immediate impact of the crisis, others were not so well placed. The Preston Banking Company, heavily committed to bill finance for the Lancashire cotton industry, suspended payment in July 1866. Its liabilities were over £1 million, although a reconstruction scheme allowed it to escape liquidation (it was eventually absorbed by Midland in 1894).[19] Other victims included the English Joint Stock

Bank, founded only two years earlier but with a large branch network, and the ubiquitous European Bank which had accumulated liabilities of about £2.5 million at the time of its suspension.

At first the crisis appeared to make little impact in Birmingham. Chippindale, the Bank of England's agent, predicted on 11 May that the Overend collapse would not greatly affect Birmingham and its neighbourhood, 'beyond the feeling of alarm created amongst all classes here today as to the future of the Money Market'.[20] Within two months, however, he was reporting the suspension of Charles Harvey and Son, bankers at Longton in Staffordshire.[21]

Worse news soon followed. On 12 July 1866 Chippindale told his directors that the Birmingham Banking Company was in difficulties and warned them of the 'awful consequences' if it failed. A proposal that the other Birmingham banks should provide a guarantee fund of £200,000 was already too late, and by the following day Chippindale was calling for 'a good supply of Treasure and . . . two good clerks'.[22] Suspension of the Birmingham Banking Company was now inevitable, and on 14 July (later known locally as 'Black Saturday') the closure was made public. The directors blamed 'gross past mismanagement' and revealed that much of the bank's resources had been locked up in unrealizable securities. Total liabilities were over £1.8 million, and the creditors were not paid until the original capital had been wiped out and the luckless shareholders had paid out a further £9 per share. Edwards, in his *Personal Recollections*, reported the crisis in almost apocalyptic style:

> the hard-earned life's savings of aged and infirm men, the sole dependence of scores of widows and hundreds of orphans, was utterly gone. No wonder that pious, God-fearing men ground their teeth and uttered curses, or that women, pale and trembling, tore their hair in wild terror, while some poor sorrowing creatures sought refuge in suicide. No wonder that even now, more than eleven years after, the memory of that day still rises, like a hideous dream in the minds of thousands.[23]

Edwards' alarm is understandable. His memoirs were written before the City of Glasgow Bank's collapse in 1878 inflicted even greater and more widespread punishment on bank shareholders. Before 1878, the Birmingham Banking Company's failure was the largest of its kind; no less than 700 shareholders were affected, and the liabilities of over £1.8 million exceeded the penalties incurred by shareholders in the Northern and Central Bank in 1839 or the Western Bank of Scotland in 1857. As with Overends, moreover, the rest of the business community had little public warning of the bank's predicament. The

Birmingham Banking Company was the senior joint stock bank in the west Midlands and it had appeared to sidestep the financial crises of the 1840s and 1850s without difficulty. Its record of profitability and dividends had seemed comparatively healthy. Profits had been maintained at over £30,000 each year in the 1850s and early 1860s, and combined dividends and bonuses had been between 15 and 20 per cent and as high as 25 per cent in 1857. The Birmingham Banking Company was later reconstituted as a limited company and it reopened for business in August 1866. Led by Josiah Mason, the pen manufacturer, the more resilient of the shareholders in the original company paid in a capital of £83,420 for the new concern. The rehabilitation of the bank was completed by the early 1870s, when deposits climbed back over £1 million in comparison with £1.7 million immediately before the crisis.

Courageous as the shareholders of the Birmingham Banking Company were, the financial crises of 1865 and 1866 brought business confidence in Birmingham to a very low ebb. The two major failures were 'enough to break down all faith in banking institutions of any kind'.[24] The Birmingham and Midland Bank escaped this collapse of confidence and even on 'Black Saturday' Edmunds reported to Chippindale that 'the pressure upon them today has been very slight'.[25] Over the following twelve months, large numbers of new accounts were brought to Midland's head office. Deposit accounts at Birmingham nearly doubled to £560,098 between June 1864 and June 1867, and Midland's total deposits are estimated to have increased from about £1.1 million to nearly £1.7 million in the same period. Nevertheless the emergencies of 1865 and 1866 led to a diversification of the bank's assets. The Overend collapse and the subsequent dislocation of the money market put at risk the bank's traditional strength in discount business. This challenge, combined with the countrywide slowing of the demand for bill finance after the 1866 crisis, led to the continuing fall in the proportion of bills amongst Midland's assets (p 42). Although the value of the business was still enormous, with a total of over £1 million under discount between 1873 and 1875, Henry Edmunds and his directors were by then developing the bank's other asset holdings.

The pattern of Midland's assets in the mid-Victorian period was not only a response to the mid-1860s crisis and the general decline of bill finance. It was also the result of efforts to strengthen lending and other categories of assets. Edmunds and his directors were particularly anxious to provide facilities for larger corporate accounts. Charles Geach and directors such as the Scholefields and Samuel Beale had pointed the bank towards this type of business but it was not until Edmunds took Geach's place that the bank attracted many substantial company or institutional accounts. Edmunds himself had applied for and been elected to the treasurership of the Borough of Birmingham in 1850, as 'the Treasurership account . . . is of considerable value'. By 1858 Midland was allowing overdrafts of up to £20,000 on the account. Similarly large lines of credit were made available to the Midland Railway when it transferred its account to Midland's headquarters at Union Street in 1855 (the limit was set at £40,000 initially) and to the Stourbridge Railway Company which borrowed up to £45,000 at Midland's Stourbridge branch in the 1860s. Amongst manufacturing customers, the engineering firm of J G & E Marshall was granted a limit of £51,000 in 1865 on the security of its Britannia works and Bradford Street works. By 1870 the Cochrane group of ironfounding firms had obtained similar facilities totalling £65,000.

Where Midland's own resources were inadequate, Edmunds was anxious to keep a share of the larger accounts by negotiating loans elsewhere. In November 1858 he arranged for Midland's London agent, the Union Bank, to advance £25,000 to the South Staffordshire Water Company, a Midland customer. The more sizeable accounts occasionally required the bank to reorganize or reschedule its facilities in order to rescue or prevent the failure of its accountholders. In the aftermath of the 1866 crisis the tube-making firm of Peyton and Peyton faced serious cash shortages at a time when its overdraft at Union Street was already £36,303. The account had been opened when Abel Peyton, one of the partners, became a Midland director in 1847. Edmunds agreed to reorganize the account by discounting £12,000 in bills and by accepting a promissory note for £18,000, nominally payable in seven days but by agreement not payable for three years. This was a rare case, however, and Midland was not involved in reconstructions such as the North and South Wales Bank's work for the Borough of Birkenhead in the 1840s or the support for the Middlesbrough steel industry provided by two Yorkshire banks in the early 1870s.[26] Neither did the bank incur bad debts frequently or on a large scale. The specific debts are not recorded in any detail, although by 1869 £4468 had been provided for bad debts at the Stourbridge branch. There is no hint of the heavy losses suffered by neighbouring banks. At the time of the Birmingham Banking Company's failure in 1866, for example, that much larger bank had incurred bad debts of nearly £250,000 at its head office and £146,000 at its Dudley branch.

The management of the bank's assets in the mid-Victorian period was not limited to these shifts in the pattern of lending. A new feature of Midland's finances under Edmunds' long period of managership was the creation of an investment portfolio. The joint stock banks formed in the 1820s and 1830s had taken legal powers to buy and sell investments but few of them had developed the advantage. This was especially true of the country banks, whose main contact with the investment world was in the evaluation and sale of stocks or shares offered as securities for loans. Where investments were made they were limited in scale and in scope, with an underlying acceptance that Consols were the only suitable option for banks.

The preference for Consols was usually based on the advice of the London banks. Glyn Mills, in answer to their visitors from the Sheffield and Hallamshire Bank in 1860, argued that 'Consols are the very *best security* that a Bank can hold—and that they have seen three Panics, when for a time all other securities were absolutely unnegotiable, even Exchequer Bills—but—they never knew a time when money could not be borrowed on Consols'. Investments, in other words, should be chosen not for their yield but for their safety, liquidity and their role as securities for special loans from other banks.

This theory was seen in practice immediately after the Overend Gurney suspension, when London bankers such as Williams Deacons told their provincial clients that they 'would have no difficulty in procuring money on your ordinary Consols'. Even after the markets had settled, the orthodoxy was maintained. The London and Westminster Bank, advising the North and South Wales Bank in 1869, reported that the London banks 'employed that portion of its funds not absorbed by discounts and loans, in investments in our own Government Stocks, and to a limited extent in the purchase of first class English Railway Debentures having not more than 12 months to run, but we do not invest in Debenture Stocks'. In contrast the insurance companies were already investing in a wider variety of securities. Mortgages were prominent in insurance portfolios, along with investments in utilities, local authorities and property develop-ment. Railway stocks were attracting approximately 10 per cent of the Royal Exchange Assurance's investments in the mid-nineteenth century, while in the late 1850s the Pelican Life Assurance Company was already investing in a Canadian railway.[27]

Midland's original deed of settlement had empowered the bank's directors to invest any funds not required for ordinary banking business in government stock, Navy and Exchequer bills, Bank of England or East India Company bonds and in properties and annuities. That provision, inspired by similar clauses in Joplin's model rules for the first joint stock banks, was not used until 1862, and seemingly not even considered before that date. The purchase of Nichols Baker and Crane, the Bewdley bankers, had boosted Midland's estimated deposits to over £1 million in June that year. Evidently Edmunds and his directors could not put these extra funds to immediate use, as their holdings of cash and balances with other banks (totalling £131,000) were also at a relatively high level. At Christmas 1862 they therefore authorized the purchase of £30,000 in Consols and shares of the East Suffolk Railway Company worth £10,536, both at cost price. These new items in the balance sheet, although barely 5 per cent of the probable level of advances, proved to be the starting point for the bank's investment history.

Midland's first venture into investment, like the portfolio decisions of most country bankers in the mid-nineteenth century, was probably on the recommendation of the bank's London agent. The directors did not refer to brokers or other intermediaries. This was again the case in 1870 when the board authorized the purchase of £25,000 worth of 3 per cent Consols or 'the new 3 per cent . . . whichever Mr Barton may think preferable'. J A Barton was then general manager of the Union Bank of London, Midland's agent in the City, and it is unlikely that Edmunds and his directors looked any further afield for advice on government securities.

Matching the pace of the growth in the bank's deposits, Midland's investments were enlarged rapidly in the late 1860s and early 1870s. By June 1871 they were valued at £284,000 (comprising over 12 per cent of total assets) and by December 1874 the portfolio was worth £358,235. In making these purchases the board did not slavishly follow the more common preference for Consols. Although they could rely on Barton for advice on gilt-edged stocks, they were ready to make local investments. An example in 1871 was the acquisition of £50,000 worth of mortgage bonds issued by the Birmingham Canal Navigation Company, paying 4 per cent. In August the same year the bank invested £150,000 in the 4 per cent debentures of its customer, the Midland Railway Company.

Buying shares in railways and canal companies was neither expensive nor high in risk. Nonetheless any banker who remembered the investment advice handed out before and during the Overend Gurney affair might not have departed so far from the orthodoxy of investing in Consols. The main theme of investment advice both then and later in the century was the need for liquidity and security. Even an imaginative banker such as George Rae, in his influential *Country Banker*, took it for granted that Consols were the only serious option for a bank's surplus assets.[28] Edmunds and his directors adopted a different approach, with the possibility that they were more concerned with yield and opportunity than with absolute security. The pattern of investment in December 1874 (after which there is a break in the available records until 1880) was far removed from conventional recommendations. Consols valued at £100,000 contributed only 28 per cent of the investment fund. The remainder comprised £33,385 in railways (the Midland Railway and the Irish North Western Railway), £61,850 in utilities (the Birmingham Canal Company and the Birmingham Water Works), £18,000 in an unnamed property at Saltley and no less than £145,000 or 40 per cent of investments in preference shares in the Patent Shaft Company. All these options were likely to provide a higher yield than the uninspiring 3 per cent available from Consols. Not least the directors were prepared to authorize the trading of investments, such as moving £10,000 into United States bonds for a matter of days in August 1871. This manoeuvre was exceptional, however. The more obvious theme of Midland's earliest investments was the preference for good returns from local options rather than unswerving commitment to government stocks.

The deliberate adjustment of the bank's balance sheet produced a strong profit performance throughout Edmunds' tenure as manager. The management of Midland's assets, especially the relative growth of advances and the creation of an investment account, helped to lift interest earnings in the late 1860s and early 1870s. Net profits (before dividends were distributed) were lifted from between £13,000 and £17,000 per annum in mid-century to over £50,000 per annum in the late 1860s and 1870s; a new peak of £63,724 was achieved in June 1874, Edmunds' last full year as managing director. These results were at a high rate of earnings. Representing 12.5 per cent of paid-up capital and 10.8 per cent of capital and reserves in 1851, they were equivalent to no less than 29.2 per cent of paid-up capital and 15.8 per cent of capital and reserves by 1873. Dividends were maintained at between 10 and 20 per cent throughout that period, equalling or outperforming other banks in the west Midlands. The Stourbridge and Kidderminster Bank restricted its dividends at between 7.5 and 12.5 per cent in the same period. The Birmingham Banking Company, which had been generous with dividends and bonuses before its reconstruction, limited its yield to 10 per cent after 1866.

Not the least advantage of this performance was the chance to strengthen the bank's reserves. Transfers from profits helped to rebuild the guarantee fund from only £22,969 in 1851 (after the final call on the original capital) to £231,750 by 1873. In addition a small contingent fund had been created after the financial crisis of 1866 (transfers to the guarantee reserve fund were published in the bank's reports to its shareholders but the new contingent account was treated as an 'inside' fund). This combination brought Midland's reserves close to being a full cover for the paid-up capital—a rare achievement amongst the English and Welsh banks at that time.

Midland's profitability was not solely the outcome of changes in the composition of its business. It also reflected the way in which the bank was relatively sheltered from the fierce competition affecting other parts of the banking community. The banking legislation of 1844 had reduced the promotion of new banks to a trickle, to the obvious advantage of banks already established. When a new wave of banking promotions was initiated by the 1857–62 Companies Acts, few of the 42 new joint stock banks founded between 1860 and 1875 competed directly with the Birmingham banks. As many as 16 of those companies were London-based and London-oriented.[29] Although in England and Wales the total number of joint stock bank offices swelled from only 576 in 1850 to 1364 in 1875,[30] Birmingham and the west Midlands did not share in the new 'banking mania'. The net increase in the number of Birmingham bank offices was only five between 1850 and 1875, a rate of growth which was restrained by the upheavals of the 1860s. The closure of Attwood's, the difficulties of the Birmingham Banking Company, and the merger of Moilliet with Lloyds in 1865 left Midland and the other surviving joint stock banks with a more comfortable market than they would have faced in other provincial banking centres.

The only intrusion which obviously disturbed Midland's directors was the promotion of another 'Midland Bank' during the boom of 1862–63. This London-based concern was originally floated as the Birmingham and Midland Counties Union Banking Company in January 1863, soon afterwards changing its name to the Midland Banking Company. Edmunds immediately protested to the organizers about the similarity of the name, claiming that his bank 'had then for a period of 25 years been uniformly known and spoken of and addressed as the "Midland Banking Company"'. The promoters of the new company promised that they would not open any branches in Birmingham, but the argument was revived in 1874. The Midland Banking Company was then planning to open an office in Stourbridge. Edmunds again protested, pointing out that the similarity of name would lead to even greater confusion over the posting and remittance of bills and cheques. The London-based bank gave way, admitting that they wished to avoid any 'collision' with Midland (the Midland Banking Company's name was altered in 1881 and after a succession of mergers the business was acquired by Barclays Bank).

With the minor exception of this dispute Edmunds and his directors had little difficulty in attracting and then controlling new business. It is likely, as Edwards claimed, that 'the bank was offered more business than it cared for' and that it was the beneficiary of the local crises of the mid-1860s. If competitive pressure on the bank had been greater, a more ambitious attitude towards branch banking could have been expected. As it was, after the acquisition at Bewdley Edmunds and his directors did not chase opportunities for branch extension. In January 1872, for instance, they turned down a new petition to open a branch at Kidderminster.

Free from damaging competitive pressures, the adjustment and growth of business produced perceptible changes in the outlook of the bank's directors, managers and staff. In contrast to the small single-unit bank captained by Geach in the late 1830s and 1840s, Midland under Edmunds' managership took on the appearance and behaviour of a permanent banking institution. This growth of confidence and reputation was already evident in the changes to the bank's capital structure and in its development as an investor. By the early 1870s it had also emerged in the management and in the increasingly public role of the bank.

At Midland's Birmingham headquarters, the growth of business was paralleled by a growth of rules and regulations for the conduct of the bank's activities. These signs of greater formality and institutional practice were obvious to Midland's staff during the 1860s. A Midland clerk who also ran a gunmaking business was the subject of protests by the Gun-Makers' Association in 1862, and the incident persuaded the directors to forbid employees from entering or continuing any non-banking business. Similar rules were being introduced or stiffened throughout the country banks of England and Wales, though not always with conspicuous success. The Lincoln and Lindsey Banking Company had introduced such a regulation in 1843 but twenty-five years later the bank's staff still included an ironmonger and held no less than 26 insurance agents. Midland also suffered transgressions against its new rules. One of the two clerks dismissed in 1867 (the first dismissals for disciplinary reasons in the bank's history) had been discovered attempting to organize a 'Midland Counties Grand Lottery and Jewellery Company'. Other examples of stricter discipline were a closer watch over cash differences during the 1860s and, in 1867, a sharp reminder to the cashiers to show greater efficiency when on duty in the banking hall; customers had complained of the 'want of prompt attention at the counter'.

In these and similar cases the enlargement of the bank's business was raising managers' and customers' expectations of banking staff. The regulations and formality of bureaucratic institutions gradually replaced the more amateurish and sometimes ill-disciplined style of the early years of joint stock banking. After all, jobs in banking were well-paid in comparison with clerical work in civil service departments, local government or the railway companies. Midland's clerks, for example, after completing apprenticeships at between £20 and £50 per annum, could expect to earn over £150 after about ten years and could hope for a branch manager's appointment at a salary of over £350. Other benefits also came their way: the Bank Holidays Act of 1871 ensured that bank staff enjoyed six days' leave in addition to their annual fortnight holiday, and in 1873 Midland's own staff were awarded a bonus of 10 per cent on their salaries. It was inevitable that these levels of reward should be matched to a more professional, rule-bound approach to banking.

This anxiety to raise standards and improve discipline was not only desirable for the internal management of a bank. It was also in keeping with the more public role of bankers in their local community. In the second half of the nineteenth century bank managers began to take their place alongside local clergymen, solicitors and doctors in shouldering voluntary and charitable duties, but this was only possible when a bank had earned the type of solid professional reputation which could inspire trust. Edmunds and his colleagues easily adapted to this role, particularly in taking on a multitude of treasurerships. Edmunds himself served as treasurer of four turnpike roads and collector of duties at the Birmingham Assay Office. The Bewdley branch manager was treasurer of the savings banks at Bewdley and Cleobury Mortimer and also managed the accounts of the Cleobury and Kidderminster Highway Board.

These duties multiplied for Midland's managers and branch managers during the 1870s. In parallel with personal responsibilities, the bank also volunteered for official work. By 1868 Midland was responsible for handling Inland Revenue remittances at Stourbridge, Bewdley and Kidderminster on behalf of the Bank of England. Chippindale, the Bank's Birmingham agent, was naturally grateful for this effort: 'Our esteemed customers the Birmingham and Midland Bank undertake Kidderminster for us, which is a few miles distant from their Branch at Bewdley, and are always most desirous to do anything they can to serve us in any way.' [31] In this, as in other dealings with the Bank of England in the 1860s and 1870s, Midland was being treated as a senior Birmingham bank.

Head office buildings are not an infallible guide to a bank's achievements, but in the nineteenth century they often reflected a change in status and expectations. Midland's office in Union Street had been purpose-built in 1837. Over the next twenty-five years the multiplication of deposits and the increase in staff from three to fourteen made it overcrowded and inconvenient. The need for a new building must have been obvious to the bank's customers, and in August 1865 the local architect Edward Holmes drew the board's attention to an available site in New Street. Midland's directors quickly acquired the leasehold from the governors of King Edward's School and in the following December they commissioned Holmes to design a head office for the site. Holmes produced plans for a substantial neo-classical building in the same palatial style then favoured in the banking and insurance centres of provincial cities. The total final cost of £25,745 (more than twice the figure the directors had envisaged) was probably the reason why Henry Edmunds had unsuccessfully opposed the move.[32] On this issue he underestimated the speed of the bank's expansion. Within only five years of the move to the New Street building in July 1869 the continuing growth of business made it necessary to extend the building.

The new headquarters gave the bank prominence as well as additional space, and it was visible proof to staff and customers that the Birmingham and Midland was no longer a small corner-site banking business. Edwards was especially impressed, contrasting the new head office with the ancient shop of the old Gloucester Bank of James Wood and Co:

> Nowadays we go to a palace to cash a cheque. We pass through a vestibule between polished granite monoliths, or adorned with choice marble sculpture in *alto-relievo* . . . . We stand at counters of the choicest polished mahogany, behind which we see scores of busy clerks, the whole thing having an appearance of absolute splendour. From Jemmy Wood's shop to the noble hall of the Midland, or the Joint Stock, is indeed a long step in advance.[33]

This visible change in status and the increasingly institutional style of the bank was only a fraction of Midland's progress during Edmunds' managership. When he retired at the end of 1874 (he continued as a director until 1880 and received a pension of £1000 until his death in 1888) the basis of the bank's business had been switched to deposit-gathering and the diversification of its assets. Midland had comfortably survived a profound crisis in local banking in the mid-1860s and its capital and reserves had developed an obviously healthy appearance. Shareholders' funds of nearly £500,000 in 1874 promoted the bank to twentieth place amongst the joint stock banks of England and Wales. Of more immediate importance to the directors and shareholders was its improved ranking amongst the Birmingham banks. Measured by capital and by deposits, only Lloyds was larger in 1874; in terms of total shareholders' funds Midland's paid-up capital and reserves of £540,000 had edged ahead of the Lloyds total of £452,060. These were not the achievements of an over-cautious or unimaginative manager. Edmunds' successors faced a sizeable task in maintaining this impetus, particularly in the event of any deterioration in the prosperity of mid-Victorian Birmingham and the west Midlands. The risk remained that the bank was too narrowly based to ensure continual growth in its earning power.

❋

# AMBER: BIRMINGHAM TO LONDON
## 1874–1891

| | |
|---|---|
| Amber | Birmingham and Midland Bank |
| Alum | Birmingham Banking Company |
| Lava | Lloyds Banking Company |
| Sulphur | Union Bank of Birmingham |

(Bank of England's Birmingham codes, 1878)

When the Birmingham and Midland Bank gained a foothold in London in 1891, it was only one of a series of migrations to the capital. Midland's two main local competitors, Lloyds and the Birmingham Banking Company, made the move from Birmingham to London in 1884 and 1889 respectively; the member banks of the Barclays alliance combined to form a single-based London bank in 1898. Contemporaries, historians and even a Treasury committee saw the migration as a deliberate effort to compete through sheer size, leading directly to the creation of a small dominant group of clearing banks. Other factors were important but 'the major form of competition within the increasingly cartel-ridden banking industry was through physical size and the amount of financial resources'.[1] The evidence supporting this view multiplied after 1890, particularly during the second wave of bank amalgamations in the Edwardian period (Chapter Four). The initial moves to London were nonetheless for more specific reasons. Business pressures on the banks and the financial enticements of the capital were at least as influential as their ambitions and competitive position.

In the 1870s, after the retirement of Henry Edmunds as managing director, the Birmingham and Midland Bank continued to develop its local business. Evidently the scope for banking in its home town was still immense. In the period immediately after Edmunds' departure the bank's total deposits exceeded £2.5 million each year between 1874 and 1877 while total advances increased by 40 per cent to

£1,758,201 in the same period. Bill holdings, though contracting to only 43 per cent of advances, were still contributing nearly £750,000 to the assets side of the balance sheet in the pre-crisis year of 1877. The increased lending helped to lift net profits from £63,724 in 1874 to a new peak of £70,994 in June 1877.

The solid progress of Midland's business in the mid-1870s was aided by the overt continuity of the bank's management and staff. Edmunds himself continued as an active member of the board until his increasing deafness forced him to resign in 1880. His place had been taken by William Goode, who was given the full managership at the beginning of 1875. Goode had joined Midland as early as February 1837 (he had previously been a clerk at the Bank of Birmingham), and he had acted as sub-manager since 1855 and as a popular manager under Edmunds since 1867.[2] This continuity was maintained even after Goode's own retirement in September 1878. He was succeeded by G F Bolding, who had been recruited by 1850 at the latest, and neither he nor Goode attempted any radical changes in the pattern of deposit-gathering and lending which they had inherited from Edmunds. Similarly the membership of Midland's board was largely undisturbed, with the directors maintaining their tradition of sharing and alternating the chairmanship. These factors brought consistency both to policy and to banking practice.

The bank's registration as an unlimited company in 1873 also strengthened its local position. By adopting unlimited liability Midland did not add many names to its list of shareholders; the increase in paid-up capital by £25,000 in June 1874 had been dealt with by distributing an additional 500 shares to existing shareholders. On the other hand the recruitment of shareholders was only one means of introducing new customers. Proof of stability and strength was important to the country banks. For any bank which had withstood the crises of the mid-Victorian period, registration under the 1857–62 companies acts provided this type of proof. Oddly, many bankers and businessmen remained sceptical as to the virtues of limited liability, believing that a bank could only keep goodwill as long as its customers trusted in the *unlimited* liability of its partners or shareholders. This suspicion was fed when some of the new limited liability banks fell prey to share price speculation after the 1866 crisis.[3] Even senior country bankers such as George Rae, managing director of the North and South Wales Bank, were strongly advocating unlimited liability until the late 1870s. In a period when this theory of bankers' liability prevailed, banks flying the colours of unlimited liability had a correspondingly higher chance of inspiring confidence and attracting deposits.

The main stimulus to the bank's growth in the mid-1870s came from hectic activity in the local economy. The investment boom of 1871–73 was prolonged in the Birmingham district beyond the turning point for other regions such as Sheffield and Glasgow. The Franco-Prussian war in 1870–71 had put new vigour into Birmingham's gunmaking firms, while the price inflation of the early 1870s led to a spurt in the hardware and metal industries and created a 'feverish and inflated condition of the coal and iron trades of the district'.[4] These were stirring times for Birmingham. With Joseph Chamberlain as Mayor in 1873–75, it was emerging as the pioneer of municipal improvement and social spending. Even as late as 1878 these economic and political signs were sufficiently positive for a group of Birmingham businessmen to launch a new bank, the Union Bank of Birmingham, whose issued capital of £100,000 was more than four times oversubscribed. The new bank's board included tradesmen and local manufacturers, while many of its 654 shareholders were shopkeepers, craftsmen or owners of small workshops; the Bank of England's Birmingham agent described them as 'a large number of good sound men'.[5]

In the meantime the boom had swelled the deposits of the main local banks and allowed them to switch a growing proportion of their assets to loans and overdrafts. Between them Midland, Lloyds, the Birmingham Joint Stock Bank, the Birmingham Dudley and District Bank and the Birmingham Banking Company raised their deposits from £11.2 million to £12.7 million between 1874 and 1877, their total advances increasing by 47 per cent to £7.8 million. Midland shared in this mood of optimism by opening a new branch at Wednesbury in September 1877. It was the bank's first entirely new branch and was apparently a board initiative rather than simply a reply to a petition from local businessmen. Opened at a cost of only £4250 for the freehold premises, the branch was soon operating a number of substantial industrial accounts, including that of Bowater's Bush Farm Iron Works at West Bromwich.

While the Union Bank of Birmingham was still completing its registration the business outlook in Birmingham was already deteriorating. The coal and iron trades in nearby Stourbridge had suffered a downturn as early as 1873 but in Birmingham the end of the boom was delayed until 1877–78. At Midland's head office and branches, a number of major customers were obviously under strain and in October 1877 the Bank of England's agent told his directors that 'the Birmingham and Midland Bank have had some heavy losses of late'.[6] The Bedworth Coal and Iron Company's overdraft had reached £35,000 by April 1878 and £42,000 two months later, and in May the Ivy House and Northwood Colliery was wound up owing the bank £19,000. The exceptional demand for additional overdrafts even forced the bank to arrange separate facilities for its customers in London. In June the Midland Land Corporation obtained a loan of £70,000 for six months from the Union Bank of London; four months later a loan of £14,000 was raised from the same source to enable Thomas Walker, chairman of the Patent Shaft Company and a director of Midland between 1865 and 1881, to pay off a special loan account and so relieve pressure on Midland's loan portfolio.

Signs of local strain were soon overtaken by news of a national banking disaster. Early in October 1878 the City of Glasgow Bank suspended payment, the victim of cumulative frauds by its directors and manager. Modern banking was suddenly exposed in its worst light. This new calamity was not the type of petty personal fraud which occasionally disturbed the banking community, but the wilful corruption of the fourth largest bank in Scotland. Formed in 1839, the City of Glasgow Bank had temporarily closed its doors after the failure of the Western Bank of Scotland in 1857. When it reopened it was systematically raided by its directors for the purpose of speculations in America and New Zealand. The frauds were disguised in falsified accounts throughout the 1860s, yet at the time of its suspension the bank had been able to collect deposits of over £8 million and operate a network of 133 offices. Worse still the bank had maintained its status as an unlimited liability company, with the result that its large roll-call of 1819 shareholders was liable for £700 for each £100 share if they were to meet the total liabilities of nearly £13 million. No less than 599 of these investors could not meet the first call on these shares, and a further 354 shareholders failed to meet the second call. This trail of ruination eventually left the remaining solvent shareholders paying calls of £2750 per share; as the market price of a share had been £225 before the failure, the total loss on each £100 share had reached £2975 when the final meeting of shareholders was held in November 1882.

The trial, conviction and imprisonment of the City of Glasgow Bank's directors and manager offered no consolation to the shareholders or to the rest of the banking community. News of the failure led to a series of bank failures throughout the United Kingdom. Fenton and Sons of Heywood and Rochdale, Lancashire, stopped payment within a few weeks, the Caledonian Bank of Inverness suspended payments in December (eventually re-opening in August 1879), and the West of England and South Wales District Bank failed with losses of over £1.2

million before the end of the year.[7] These alarms rapidly eroded confidence in joint stock banking. Between September and December 1878 the aggregate value of British bank shares was cut back by no less than £23.8 million or 13.5 per cent of the September total. Country banks hurried to call in their cash resources in case of a panic run, reducing the Bank of England's deposits by £1.2 million in the first week of December alone.

The rash of banking failures deepened the recession throughout the economy. In the Birmingham region the signs of strain earlier in 1878 multiplied as soon as local trade and industry felt the effects of the City of Glasgow Bank débâcle. Manufacturers saw their supplies of materials and credit disrupted, and in the six months after the crisis failures in the metal and hardware trades were especially frequent. The severity of the slump was also reflected in numerous reports during the winter that guarantors and companies already in liquidation could not keep up instalment payments on their compositions with creditors.

At the major Birmingham banks there was no sign of the panic withdrawal of deposits which afflicted the North and South Wales Bank in Liverpool immediately after the Glasgow failure. F Barham, the Bank of England's local agent, did not anticipate anything as serious as a bank failure. 'Nor do I think any Bank is in an insecure position, though most of them are getting rather short of cash', he wrote immediately after the Glasgow crash: 'the advances here are on comparatively so small a scale, and the risks so much distributed'.[8] The spread of risk identified by Barham did not prevent serious disturbance to the local banks' balance sheets. Precise accounts of Midland's week-to-week position during the storm have not survived, but the directors' own memoranda show that the decline in bill holdings accelerated from £733,413 in April 1878 down to £580,889 in April 1879, while specific bad debts were high enough to force down published net profits from £67,202 in June 1878 to £60,917 one year later.

For Midland's directors and managers, the events of 1878 forced a sudden shift in their responsibilities. In the mid-1870s board meetings had been concerned mainly with monitoring transfers of shares or approving building work at the bank's properties. Only rarely did Edmunds and Goode trouble their directors with decisions on individual customers' loans or bills. Late in 1878 and throughout 1879, in contrast, the board was overwhelmed with reports of failures, liquidations, compositions and efforts to save or reconstruct all types and sizes of local businesses. Bolding and his managers spent a very high proportion of their working time at meetings of creditors, in interviews with receivers and liquidators, or at inspections and auctions of properties being sold to recover debts.

Some of the most demanding cases were in the heartland of the bank's traditional businesses. Peyton and Peyton, the tube-making concern run by a former bank director and shareholder, sought further help from the bank in November 1878. After six weeks of negotiation the bank's directors agreed to reduce charges on the account and to write off a debt of £18,000. In return the partners agreed to make over to the bank 25 per cent of the annual profits of their Bordesley works until £10,000 of the write-off had been recouped. Even then Midland's directors needed to extend the firm's overdrafts in April 1881, when as part of a reconstruction the bank and the Peytons shared a further write-off of £24,000. These efforts to repair the damage done in the late 1870s were eventually unsuccessful, and Peyton and Peyton was forced into liquidation in December 1883. Other long-standing allies of the bank suffered during the crisis. Samuel Thornton, a director since 1854, resigned in February 1879 after his merchanting business collapsed; his debts to the bank were still as much as £12,000 after his securities had been sold off.

The Birmingham and Midland Bank, like most contemporary joint stock banks, was fully occupied in limiting the damage to its customers in the immediate aftermath of the 1878 crisis. In the two years following the Glasgow disaster the banking community also made concerted efforts to prevent similar shocks to the system. Their principal achievement was lobbying the Chancellor of the Exchequer, Sir Stafford Northcote, over the exact terms of the new Companies Act of 1879. The new legislation removed many of the inadequacies of existing legislation revealed by the City of Glasgow Bank collapse, and its provisions included the publication of audited annual balance sheets by limited liability banks and the adoption of 'reserved liability'. Devised in its final form by George Rae, the principle of reserved liability required registered banks to divide their uncalled capital equally between capital to be called up by the directors and capital which could only be called in the event of liquidation.

The new legislation was valuable to unlimited banks such as Midland. The City of Glasgow Bank case had revealed the full vulnerability of shareholders in unlimited companies, and banks which had registered without limited liability were consequently wrong-footed by the crisis. Whereas the share value of the four limited liability banks in Birmingham fell by only 7.3 per cent between September 1878 and October 1879, the market value of the two unlimited banking companies dropped by 27.6 per cent. Midland's directors responded by joining the queue of country banks registering under the new legislation. The Act came into force in August 1879 and the bank was amongst the first group of 30 banks giving notice of the change in status in December 1879 and January 1880. Limited liability, duly authorized in July 1880, enabled the bank to make radical alterations to its capital structure. As Midland's shares were already fully paid-up, there was the opportunity to add uncalled and reserve capital to the existing paid-up amount of £300,000. The result was an increase in nominal capital to £2,400,000, divided into new shares of £60 with £12 10s paid; only 24,000 of the 40,000 new shares were issued, thereby leaving paid-up capital at £300,000. Apart from the additional protection of reserved liability the conversion halved the minimum paid-up value of a single share and left room for a much larger number of shareholders. The availability of the 16,000 unissued shares also gave the bank the capacity for increasing its paid-up capital without further changes in its legal constitution.

The 1878 crisis and the adoption of limited liability—particularly the need for an annual audit—introduced more formality and professionalism into Midland's banking business. Changes in the managerial structure had emerged even before the City of Glasgow Bank crisis, as for example in the appointment of the bank's first secretary (John Christie) and chief accountant (Joseph Price) in October 1877. At the same time the directors carried increasingly large responsibilities for auditing bills. A 'Bill Committee' was appointed in November 1877, and the directors were also kept busy examining quarterly lists of overdrawn accounts, interviewing customers and visiting branches. The result, once the crisis had broken in the autumn of 1878, was a more explicit control over lending. Goode and Bolding were instructed to report all overdrafts of over £200 to the directors; in making their decision on an application, the directors now ruled that 'in no instance the amount to exceed one tenth of the average yearly returns'.

The assessment of advances against the turnover on current accounts was also supported by managers' visits to their customers' works and the appointment of outside advisers. The first recorded consultancy was on Bolding's recommendation after a customer had built up an overdraft of £5200 and a bill account of £6000 in November 1879. The board approved 'the appointment of an Accountant to report on their business periodically', although that did not prevent the customer's stoppage three months later. Similarly, when failures did occur during the crisis, the bank's solicitor C G Beale handled the growing number of creditors' compositions and bad debt cases (Beale also contributed to the bank's business by introducing new customers). Further afield the bank sought outside advice on credit-worthiness. The exchange of opinions on credit-worthiness was a long established feature of contact between banks but by the late 1870s specialist agencies were also in demand. After the failure of Hibell's Soho wire works in September 1878 Midland was left with a claim on a towage company on the Rhine. Over the next two years the bank used credit agencies in London and Amsterdam and consulates in Germany and Holland in a determined and eventually successful effort to recover the debt.

The more formal and bureaucratic style of Midland's business was fully in tune with the growth of professionalism in banking; the Institute of Bankers in Scotland had been founded in 1875 and the Institute of Bankers, serving England and Wales, had been established four years later. It also reflected the strong pull towards standardization in banking practice, most obviously in the codification of banking law in the 1882 Bills of Exchange Act and the publication of textbooks such as George Rae's *Country Banker* in 1885. Not least, improvements in internal management were essential if the bank was to control its rapidly expanding staff. Whereas Geach and Edmunds had been able to operate with a small close-knit staff, Goode and Bolding needed double the number of clerks to cope with the influx of new business in the 1870s. By 1880, 42 clerks were employed at New Street in addition to three managerial posts. Although ten of these clerks had been in the bank for over fifteen years, 11 had joined less than five years previously; the average length of service was less than ten years and the average age only thirty-three. The staff was not only more youthful but also less familiar with Birmingham banking, with a number of recent recruits joining the bank from Scotland and the West Country.

This larger and less experienced staff needed rules and clear lines of responsibility. Instead of being treated simply as clerks with general duties, the bank's staff were now being allocated specific jobs. These appointments were graded from only £20 salary per annum for new juniors to a basic £1000 for the bank's manager. Their duties usually included the keeping of particular ledgers, registers and keys and sharing in correspondence and counter work. In 1881 Edward Morris, for instance (subsequently Midland's secretary between 1897 and 1916), was performing a prescribed range of duties in the accountant's department:

> To check castings and workings of all Interest and Commission for each half-year.

Keep account of opened and closed accounts.

Investigate weekly totals of customers' accounts and generally assist the Accountant, and on Saturday mornings assist the Cashiers at the counter.

The more professional approach to the demarcation of work also extended to staff benefits. In December 1881 the entire head office and branch staff was insured with the Bankers' Guarantee and Trust Fund. This insurance replaced the old-established *ad hoc* arrangement in which individual members of staff had been required to provide sureties or insurance policies indemnifying the bank against fraud or theft by employees.

Midland's directors were not excluded from the more rigorous approach to the bank's business. The board had carried heavy responsibilities during the crisis and, when limited liability was introduced, they were as ready to reorganize their own duties as they were to introduce new disciplines for the managers and staff. There were obvious incentives. The City of Glasgow Bank case had made plain the legal and criminal position of that bank's directors—even if some directors were less at fault than others. The 1879 Companies Act, especially its provisions for audited accounts, had then given directors a more public duty for the proper management of banks. These pressures doubtless influenced the board when in June 1879 (before the Companies Act came into force) they published a balance sheet and transferred £60,000 from reserves to cover bad debts incurred during the crisis. The directors also formed a new sub-committee in June 1880 to consider 'what improved arrangements can be made for conducting the business of the Board'. The result, evidently at a suggestion by Bolding, was the creation in 1881 of a finance committee of four directors dealing with 'all matters relating to the Bank's investments, unrealized securities and surplus monies, and the general expenditure at the Bank's Head Office and Branches'. Figure 3.1 illustrates the pattern of command which Midland operated as a result of these changes.

Personalities played an important role in these efforts to delegate the main board's work. In place of Thornton, the directors had invited John Dent Goodman to become a director in March 1879. Goodman was a partner in Scholefield Sons and Goodman, an export merchant house specialising in hardware and guns. His partners were Joshua and William Scholefield, who introduced him to the bank. His other interests included J R Cooper and Co, gun manufacturers, who were important shareholders and customers of the Birmingham and Midland. As early as 1855, he also had 'a large contract on his *own*

**Figure 3.1** *Midland Bank board and management structure, 1881–82*

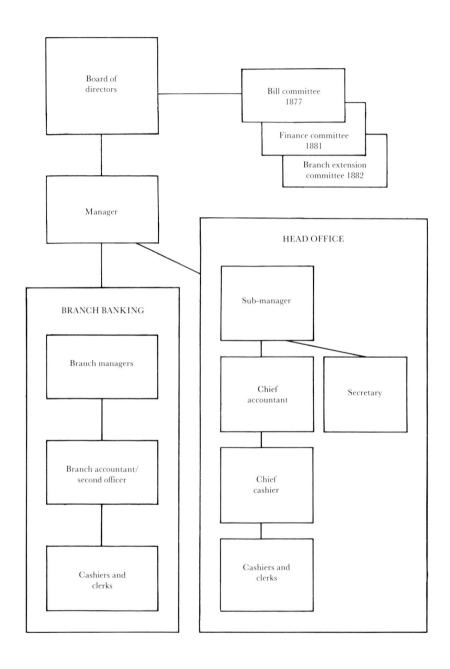

*account* with the Government for the supply of Muskets', and twelve years later the Bank of England's agent described him as 'a man of very superior abilities in Commercial matters, of the strictest honor and integrity, and worth at least £30,000 of his own'.[9] Goodman had become a Midland shareholder in about 1857 and by 1874 his family had invested £7000 in the bank.

Goodman's turn on the chairman's rota came as soon as August 1880. Throwing himself into the task with extraordinary enthusiasm, he was the guiding hand for the new sub-committees of 1880 and 1881; he had also drafted the bank's proposals for adopting limited liability. Arthur Keen, the driving force behind the Patent Nut and Bolt Co of Smethwick and later chairman of Guest Keen and Co, joined Goodman on the board in April 1880 and was a prominent member of the two sub-committees.[10] After 1881 the impact of these changes on the bank's business was strong enough for Goodman to continue as chairman without the usual time limit of one year. This change overthrew a tradition dating back to the departure of Robert Webb in 1837. While the rotation of the chairmanship may have had advantages earlier in the bank's history—notably in keeping an equilibrium between strong groupings of manufacturers and merchants on the bank's board—the regular breaks in continuity were a disadvantage when Midland's first need in the 1880s was to build and fortify its position. The new structure of the board was in contrast to its lower profile while Edmunds and Goode were controlling the bank in the 1870s.

The more deliberate and formalized approach to banking business which emerged from the crisis and from the 1879 legislation was soon obvious in Midland's dealings with its major customers. Initially Goodman and his colleagues were preoccupied with clearing up the affairs of major casualties of the recession. The most pressing cases were Peyton and Peyton, the tube-making concern which was eventually wound up in 1883 (p 62), and the Midland Land and Investment Corporation. Midland Land had been formed in 1874 with F S Bolton (one of the bank's directors) as its chairman. It had invested over £800,000 in freeholds, leaseholds and building development in Birmingham in the late 1870s. Borrowings from the bank had increased to £50,000 by July 1880, secured on a miscellaneous collection of the company's investments. Advised by Beale, the bank attempted to reform these securities but in June 1881 the company was wound up. Its debt to the bank of £46,942 was fully recovered by the slow piecemeal sale of Midland Land's properties, a task which at least gave the bank valuable experience of handling and disposing of mortgage securities. Bolton was able to keep the rest of his family's business interests together, and the Bolton firms remained important customers throughout the 1880s.

By taking a more systematic approach to lending and the evaluation of securities, Midland's directors and managers became closely involved in the financial development of their major customers. The bank, as in the 1870s, employed a mixture of overdraft and bill finance. Previously its requests for proper security had often been tentative and 'unofficial', but after about 1880 securities were investigated thoroughly, even if that meant insisting on changes in a customer's own balance sheet. This was especially apparent in cases where companies wished to issue debentures, by then emerging as a significant part of company finance.[11] The issue of debentures normally demoted a bank's security to a second charge on property, and for that reason Midland's directors and managers would ask for a review of its securities. The Patent Shaft Company, established by Geach and still run by the Walker family, agreed to limit its debentures to £70,000 in return for the bank's conversion of its securities in December 1879. Similar arrangements were considered for the Birmingham Small Arms Company, where Goodman had been chairman since 1861, and Brown Marshall and Co, the Saltley engineering company where Henry Edmunds and F S Bolton were also directors. Both companies ran overdrafts of over £50,000 in 1882 and 1883, but were dissuaded from issuing debentures when the bank (on legal advice) asked for a more exact specification of capital reconstruction. Brown Marshall did not need to issue debentures until five years later, their borrowing being secured in the meantime by six-monthly renewable guarantees.

Closer involvement with company finance was obviously essential if banks such as Midland were to avoid or reduce the bad debts which had been incurred during the slump of the late 1870s. At New Street the legacy of the crisis was all too obvious, not only in unravelling the affairs of customers in difficulties but also in the fall of the bank's profits. Provisions for bad and doubtful debts—£52,000 in 1879, £93,000 in 1880—forced published net profits down from £70,994 in 1877 to £49,360 by 1881. Goodman was acutely conscious of the slippage. His personal notebook was a detailed record of changes in the bank's performance, including the measurement of Midland's prices and yields and the calculation of a 'security' ratio (cash, share investments and bills as a proportion of deposit liabilities). The chairman was also attentive to alterations in the bank's competitive position. He compiled comparative information about Midland's principal rivals in Birmingham (Lloyds, the Birmingham Joint Stock Bank, the Birmingham Dudley and District Bank, and the Birmingham Banking Company). Most of these indicators showed that the bank's business had suffered more erosion than its immediate competitors during the slump. To Goodman the bank's former status as an unlimited company seemed to be the main culprit. He recorded a 30 per cent fall in the value of the bank's shares between September 1878 and 25 October 1879, compared with an average of 9 per cent for the other Birmingham banks and 15.5 per cent for sixteen banks in Manchester, Liverpool and Sheffield.

Goodman and his colleagues believed that the restoration of profitability depended upon bringing new deposits to the bank. With the exception of bills, it was this category of business which was most heavily damaged by the slump. On the basis of Goodman's own figures Midland's deposits had fallen by 25 per cent between 1875 and 1880. The other Birmingham banks had not lost more than 10 per cent in the same interval, except for Lloyds (which actually increased its deposits by 3 per cent) and the unlimited Birmingham Dudley and District Bank (which lost 20 per cent of its deposits). Lloyds' remarkable expansion was already well in its stride and by 1880 its deposits of £5.35 million were more than twice as much as any other Birmingham bank. Midland, having ranked second behind Lloyds throughout the 1870s, was now overtaken by the Birmingham Banking Company with its total deposits of £2.5 million after its merger with the Stourbridge and Kidderminster Bank in 1880. Deposit liabilities of the Birmingham Joint Stock Bank (£1.59 million) and the Birmingham Dudley and District (£1.62 million) were also within reach of Midland's 1880 total of £2 million.

As its first step in recovering deposits, Midland's board considered the opening of new branch offices. It was scarcely an original approach, as the previous twenty years had seen the number of bank branches in England and Wales doubled to over 2200. Midland remained unusual in having so few offices and its three branches were far below the national average of thirteen branches for each joint stock bank.[12] In keeping with the more disciplined style of the board's work, Goodman and his co-directors were anxious to devise a plan for new branches rather than simply take up opportunities such as they had found at Stourbridge and Bewdley. In February 1882 they formed an additional sub-committee to report on 'the general question of the desirability of opening additional branches'. Goodman chaired the new 'Branch Extension Committee' and, reflecting his awareness of the activities of the other Birmingham banks, the committee concentrated on finding new sites within the city. A plan to open an office in Smethwick was dropped but in March 1883 the committee authorized the opening of a new branch in Moseley Road. A week later the new office was the first Midland branch to be connected to New Street by telephone—a striking contrast to Edmunds' long carriage rides to Stourbridge and Bewdley when the bank had bought its first branches.

Ironically the careful planning of new branches was immediately eclipsed by an opportunity which could not be missed. The new Union Bank of Birmingham (p 59) had survived the worst of the recession and had gathered deposits of about £400,000 by 1883. In September that year, however, the manager, John Burgan, absconded after defrauding the bank of some £15,000. With confidence in the banking system still at a low ebb, the Union Bank's directors anticipated a run and sought help from the Bank of England's Birmingham branch. Goodman then intervened with an offer to take over the business, an offer which the Bank of England's agent saw as the preventative to 'a stoppage or disturbance of credit generally'.[13] After a twenty-four-hour search of the Union Bank's books a provisional agreement was reached and then approved by both sets of shareholders. Completed in October, the transfer was financed by issuing 2695 of the 16,000 unissued Midland shares to the Union Bank shareholders and thereby adding £33,687 to the bank's paid-up capital. The effective price, with Midland shares trading at about £32 each, was a mere £86,220 in comparison with the Union Bank's pre-merger market value of £102,386.

The Union Bank merger proved to be a major stroke of fortune for Goodman's new regime at New Street. It brought an immediate increase of some 19 per cent in deposits, recovering the levels achieved in the mid-1870s. It included a fully-functioning office in central Birmingham, which now became Midland's Waterloo Street branch. It was the bank's first amalgamation with another joint stock concern, and it was carried through in the more public arena provided by the new Companies Act. Crucially, it was also the first investigation and amalgamation negotiated by the team of Goodman, Christie (as sub-manager) and Edward Holden, who had joined the bank as accountant in 1881 and had just been appointed secretary. Christie and Holden were each awarded £100 for their efforts in the amalgamation, and another £100 was distributed amongst the bank's clerks.

In contrast to these demonstrations of the success of the Union Bank merger, the long-term significance of the deal lay hidden in Midland's register of shareholders. Before 1883 the bank's shareholders were unusually few in number. Only 284 shareholders owned Midland's paid-up capital of £300,000 in 1879, an average holding of £1056 per shareholder. At that time they were hugely outnumbered by the shareholders of each of the four other major banks in Birmingham. For example Lloyds Bank's paid-up capital of £440,000 was shared by no less than 1528 investors (an average of only £288), and the paid-up capital of the Birmingham Joint Stock, the Birmingham Dudley and District, and the Birmingham Banking Company was distributed amongst 1851 shareholders at an average of £370 per head. The arrival of the Union Bank's shareholders on Midland's register entirely altered the ownership position. The Union Bank had attracted large numbers of shareholders and at the time of the merger the paid-up capital of £107,775 was contributed by no less than 650 shareholders. The effects of this influx were still obvious when Midland compiled its new share register in 1888; there were now 905 investors each owning an average of £369 of the bank's capital. The change was qualitative as well as quantitative. Whereas the 1874 register had been dominated by very large investors (notably the families of directors such as the Beales, Bolton, Francis, Lindner, Phillips and Walker), this category was in retreat by 1888. Shareholders with more than £3000 invested in the bank had contributed 59 per cent of the paid-up capital in 1874 but fifteen years later that share had shrunk to 36 per cent (Appendix 3, p 327). Although partly the outcome of the death or retirement of founding shareholders and partly a reflection of the diversification of private investments in the 1880s, the result was mainly due to the admission of large numbers of small shareholders after the Union Bank merger.

The transformation of the share register was not incidental to the bank's development. Joint stock banks had always recognized the business value of their shareholders. By bringing their own accounts and by recruiting new customers, shareholders were an essential contact between the bank and the local economy. Until the Union Bank merger this linkage had brought Midland the large and valuable accounts of some of Birmingham's senior merchants and industrialists. The Union Bank's shareholders were a quite different proposition. Almost exclusively from Birmingham itself, they included large numbers of craftsmen, jewellers, general merchants, printers, clerks, shopkeepers and shop assistants. These groups were significantly larger contributors to the bank's 1888 share register, with a corresponding decrease since 1874 in the proportion of shares held by manufacturers, widows, spinsters, and 'gentlemen' (many of whom had been retired manufacturers or merchants).

In effect the Union Bank amalgamation took Midland into an

entirely new market. The incoming shareholders brought with them the accounts of several hundred small businesses throughout Birmingham. Commenting on the Bank of England's loss of the Union Bank's discount business after the acquisition, Barham reminded his directors of the 'loss also of healthful exercise to the folk in London who had the job of looking at the lists of small bills we had from them'.[14] Consequently after 1883 the accounts handled by Midland were strikingly varied. Midland's traditional links with manufacturing and merchanting were maintained, led by the great fabricating, metal-working and toolmaking companies such as the Patent Shaft Company and Birmingham Small Arms or, out at Stourbridge, ironfounders and glassmakers. There was also room for large private customers, including landed estates at Bewdley and even Cardinal Newman's account. Alongside such eminent business the bank was now dealing with a host of small firms, ranging from cartridge-makers to 'refreshment contractors', electroplaters to gold pencil makers, and carriage lamp makers to furniture removers. The service industries were well to the fore, with tramways, omnibus companies and, less obviously, 'the London Museum and Union Passage' amongst the bank's customers.

Most of these businesses had only recently begun to use a bank, and their first requirements were for cash and the transmission of payments rather than the sizeable and often complex facilities given to Midland's company customers. It was perhaps this new factor which stimulated and clarified the purpose of further branch expansion after 1883. Three new branches, King's Heath, Smithfield and Small Heath, were opened between November 1883 and the end of 1884, and all three were in the suburban territory occupied by the bank's new shareholders. The Small Heath office was established specifically in answer to a petition from local tradesmen and shopkeepers. New offices at Snow Hill and Aston Street in 1887, Erdington in 1888 and Sparkbrook in 1889 were in the same category, and the only exceptions to the reinforcement of the bank in Birmingham were the opening of a new branch ten miles away at Walsall in 1888 and an agency at Knowle, near Solihull, in 1889.

The progress of the new branches and the results of the Union Bank merger were no doubt closely monitored by Goodman, his co-directors and the long-standing shareholders. At face value the changes helped to lift balance sheet totals to new peaks in the later 1880s. Deposits, from their low point of £1.97 million in 1881, recovered to £2.7 million by 1888. Published net profits climbed back from £49,361 to £56,704 in the same period, allowing the board to recommend dividends of 16 per cent between 1880 and 1887. This was a lower rate of dividend than the 20 per cent paid by Lloyds, the Birmingham Joint Stock, and the Birmingham Banking Company between 1881 and 1884–85. Nevertheless, as a reflection of the relatively high paid-up amount in each Midland share the yield of Midland shares was actually higher than its principal Birmingham competitors after 1884 (Table 3.1).

## Table 3.1

Dividends per £100 invested in paid-up shares of Birmingham banks, 1881–88

| Date | | Midland | BBC | BDDB | BJSB | Lloyds |
|---|---|---|---|---|---|---|
| Dec 1881 | Dividend (%) | 16 | 20 | 12.5 | 20 | 20 |
| | Yield/£100 | 6.25 | 6.25 | 5.88 | 5.59 | 6.51 |
| Dec 1883 | Dividend (%) | 16 | 20 | 12.5 | 20 | 20 |
| | Yield/£100 | 5.90 | 6.20 | 6.06 | 5.51 | 6.33 |
| Dec 1884 | Dividend (%) | 16 | 20 | 12.5 | 20 | 20 |
| | Yield/£100 | 6.40 | 6.25 | 5.33 | 5.33 | 6.27 |
| Dec 1886 | Dividend (%) | 16 | 15 | 10 | 20 | 15 |
| | Yield/£100 | 6.15 | 5.88 | 5.76 | 5.03 | 5.10 |
| Dec 1888 | Dividend (%) | 15 | 15 | 10 | 20 | 15 |
| | Yield/£100 | 5.35 | 4.83 | 5.24 | 4.65 | 4.77 |

*Key*
| Midland | Birmingham and Midland Bank |
|---|---|
| BBC | Birmingham Banking Company |
| BDDB | Birmingham Dudley and District Banking Company |
| BJSB | Birmingham Joint Stock Bank |
| Lloyds | Lloyds Banking Company |

By the later 1880s the reasons for this more cheering performance were being clarified in the bank's internal accounts. These returns, since the appointment of Christie and Holden, were more detailed and systematic than the old 'stock accounts' and they gave a full picture of branch results. They demonstrated that the gains made in the 1880s were largely attributable to the branches rather than to Midland's headquarters. Although deposits at New Street increased from £1,483,580 to £1,681,506 between June 1881 and December 1888, their share of the bank's total deposits declined from 75 per cent to 62 per cent. The branches' contribution of the remaining £878,449 in deposits (32 per cent) in 1888 was dominated by the 'bought in' branches—Stourbridge, Waterloo Street (the old head office of the Union Bank of Birmingham) and Bewdley, in order of importance. Those three branches had been purchased as going concerns rather than built up from scratch, and they now provided 25 per cent of the bank's total deposits. Their profitability was equally impressive. In June 1881 the bank's head office had produced 82 per cent of the unpublished profits of £57,217. That share had shrunk to £44,414 (67 per cent) by December 1888, having fallen as low as £28,891 (55 per cent) in an especially poor year in 1887. Waterloo Street, Stourbridge and Bewdley were the principal profit-makers amongst the branches, leaving the six new branches yielding only 2 per cent of the 1888 profits.

The results from the branches were a clear warning to the directors that the opening of new branches demanded hard work and increasing expenses for relatively little return. The Union Bank deal, in contrast, had produced immediate results despite the blemish in the management of Waterloo Street before the merger. The contrast was not only a matter of patiently waiting for results. The branch at Wednesbury, Midland's first new branch, lifted its deposits from £28,452 in 1881 to £45,111 in 1888 but its profits were never higher than £1208 (in 1883) and were even converted to a loss of £1862 in 1888.

This pattern of earnings suggests that Midland's subsequent rapid growth was not simply a question of 'competition by size'. The progress of Lloyds and other neighbouring banks was certainly an influence on Goodman and his colleagues. Nevertheless by the late 1880s their first concern was to find a profitable means of extending basic banking services for their growing army of shareholders and customers. The bank's results since the adoption of limited liability showed them that New Street's business was relatively static and that the new branches were slow to produce returns. The acquired branches, especially Waterloo Street, were obviously setting a faster pace.

Against this background the search for similar acquisitions in Birmingham and its region became a priority. Midland's previous purchases had all been bargains in the sense that the acquired banks were in a vulnerable position or were otherwise uncertain of their future. The directors' task by the late 1880s was to select candidates for amalgamation and to risk the possibility that its takeover offers would be contested. At the very least they could expect to pay a higher price for expansion. Goodman and his colleagues passed this test of nerve in 1889. In February Christie and Holden negotiated the purchase of the Coventry Union Bank, an unlimited company, which had also been established in 1836. After initial signs of opposition from the Coventry Union's shareholders, the effective price of the deal was £125,020; this was achieved by the issue of 3572 Midland shares at an agreed value of £35 per share.

For this price the bank took control of deposits of approximately £420,000 at Coventry and the branch office at Coleshill, but the Coventry Union's authorized note issue of £16,251 lapsed as required by the Bank Charter Act. Most of these deposits were comparable with Midland's business on its home ground, with the Coventry Union's customers including large numbers of metalworking firms and the forerunners of the cycle-making industry.

This compatibility was not so evident two months later when Midland completed the acquisition of the Leamington Priors and Warwickshire Banking Company. Established in 1835 and with branches in Warwick, Kenilworth and Southam, this bank was dominated by landed and farming interests, agricultural merchants and suppliers. It was not an obvious partner for the Birmingham and Midland Bank. However, when in 1887 the Leamington Bank's business and reputation wobbled after the bankruptcy of Greenway, Smith and Greenway, bankers at Warwick and Leamington, its future seemed bleak.[15] A takeover by the Birmingham Banking Company had been resisted in 1887. Maximilian Lindner, a senior Midland director, suggested that the bank should make a counter offer in January 1888, but the board's attention had then switched to the Coventry Union Bank. As soon as the Coventry amalgamation was complete Christie and Holden reached agreement with the Leamington directors. With an offer of cash and 2533 Midland shares for the business, the deal was worth £102,000 to the Leamington bank's shareholders. The price brought only £204,000 of deposits into Midland's balance sheet but Holden and Christie advised their board that 'while we do not think there is any great bargain in the acquisition of the Bank we are of the opinion that it gives us a good introduction to that end of the County and forms a natural extension of our lately acquired business in Coventry'.

Over the following twelve months Midland's directors and managers looked much farther afield for similar purchases. Banking in Birmingham and its region was by then controlled by only five banks—Lloyds (which took over the neighbouring Worcester City and County Bank in 1889), Midland, the Birmingham Banking Company, the Joint Stock and the District. Of these none of the other local banks was within reach of Midland's existing budget. Assuming that the bank continued to make its purchases by exchanges of shares, its resources were limited by the value of its unissued capital. After the Coventry and Leamington acquisitions, unissued shares worth only about £252,000 (£90,000 paid-up) were still available. For the moment this restricted the choice to smaller banks outside Warwickshire and Worcestershire. At the same time the stiff competition in bidding for takeovers of country banks throughout England and Wales made the search for further amalgamations all the more urgent.

These factors led the bank into new territory in 1889 and 1890. Late in 1889 Christie and Holden outmanoeuvred another bank in making an offer for the Derby Commercial Bank, a twenty-one-year-old company with a single office in Derby. The bid was accepted in December, giving the Derby shareholders a total of 3333 Midland shares valued at £124,987. The effect, rather like the Union Bank merger five years earlier, was to give Midland an additional city-centre branch with a fully-developed business, in this case with £222,000 in deposits. In support of the purchase and to build up the connections of the Derby shareholders and customers, new Midland branches were opened in Leicester and Northampton in 1889 and Sheffield in 1890.

The new grouping of branches in the east Midlands had been well within the bank's capital resources. Extension into the West Riding of Yorkshire, a citadel of joint stock banking, was likely to be much more costly. Goodman and his directors seem to have treated Yorkshire as the natural extension of their investments in the Midlands, following the swing of industrial capital and influence from the ironworks of the west Midlands to the steel and engineering centres of west Yorkshire. Geach, the Scholefields and the Beales all had manufacturing interests in Yorkshire. However, the old joint stock and private banks of Yorkshire were too heavily capitalized to be considered as partners. Alternatively by buying up the Leeds and County Bank and the Exchange and Discount Bank in 1890, Midland selected banks which were too small to sustain development as independent units. The Exchange and Discount Bank had been a conversion of the private bank of Cousins, Allen and Co in 1866. Its offices in Leeds, Bradford and Hull produced a bill business of some £190,000 and deposits of £422,000. Christie and Holden were authorized to offer 5415 Midland shares and cash worth £225,000. James Cousins, the promoter and manager of the bank, was given a seat on Midland's board (offers of directorships were thereafter a common feature of Midland's amalgamations). The Leeds and County Bank was apparently a much larger connection. Founded in 1862, its Leeds headquarters and 12

**Figure 3.2.** *Midland Bank branch locations, 1890*

*Key:* ● locations of new branches
      + locations of branches acquired by amalgamation
*Source:* W F Crick and J E Wadsworth, *A Hundred Years of Joint Stock Banking*
(Hodder and Stoughton, 1936), p 100

branches controlled deposits of just over £1 million by 1890. It had suffered severely during the 1879–80 depression, and it had already considered an amalgamation offer from the York City and County Bank. After these experiences the Leeds and County's shareholders were ready to accept Midland's offer of 4852 shares and cash worth £187,000.

By the end of 1890 the Birmingham and Midland Bank had lifted its deposits to over £5.6 million, a 164 per cent increase since immediately before the Union Bank merger in 1883. Of this total the six amalgamations between 1883 and 1890 had contributed a minimum of £2.7 million in deposits at a cost of issuing Midland shares worth £684,110. Apart from its value in terms of goodwill, the investment had also provided the bank with a network of fully-fitted and properly staffed branch offices in the Midlands and Yorkshire. The network comprised 45 branches at the end of 1890, of which 27 had been bought in. Midland's name now appeared over the doorways and on the cheques and stationery of the branches but in these early stages of the amalgamation movement the bank was careful to cite its connections with the predecessor banks.

Before the two Yorkshire amalgamations, Goodman and his board had been able to finance each new acquisition by the distribution of the 16,000 additional shares created in 1880 but not then issued. This source was insufficient for the two bids in Leeds, however, and the board responded by obtaining shareholders' permission to increase the total capital to £3.6 million. A total of 60,000 new shares was created and as before only £12 10s of the nominal value of £60 per share was

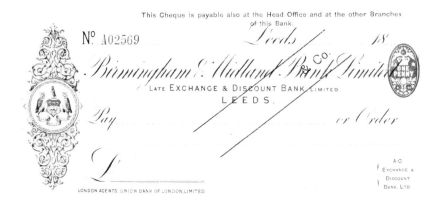

**Figure 3.3.** *Cheque form printed for the Leeds branch of Midland Bank after the acquisition of the Exchange and Discount Bank in 1890*

paid up. The Yorkshire amalgamations swallowed up 6400 of these shares (the remaining 3867 shares coming from the supply created in 1880), and a further 4600 were issued to the public at a premium of £20 per share. These distributions left 9000 shares still available with a value of £360,000 at 1890 prices. This alteration increased the bank's capacity for new purchases. In contrast to the relatively small country banks bought in the 1880s, much larger and more broadly based acquisitions were now brought within Midland's reach.

The migration of banks to London, like many other aspects of the amalgamation movement in banking, was usually publicized as an attempt to match the growing needs of major customers.[16] Other influential factors were the benefits of membership of the London Clearing House in the handling of payments or the agreement of deposit rates and, not least, the need to follow local competitors such as Lloyds and the Birmingham Banking Company into the London market. In Midland's case other influences were also at work. Despite the frequent public references to the needs of large company customers during the amalgamation years, this may have been one of the least powerful motives for the move to London.

Changing patterns in the bank's earnings in the 1880s gave good grounds for the board to look beyond Birmingham. The balance sheets and profit and loss accounts were suggesting that the New Street headquarters were reaching capacity. The branches developed their business at a faster rate, and the main expansion of the business was contributed by the acquired branches (p 74). Although central Birmingham was not saturated with banking facilities, it was better provided with banks per head of population than London. Room for expansion was limited, and in these conditions there was a risk of stagnation in the New Street business. There was the added danger that the head office, its managers and its staff would be ill-prepared for any serious competitive challenge from local or London-based banks.

The relatively sluggish performance of New Street's business in the 1880s warned Goodman and his co-directors that further changes were needed in the management of the bank's assets. The crisis of the late 1870s and early 1880s cast a long shadow, and for much of the decade the bank was entangled in settling the affairs of large customers such as Peyton and Peyton and Midland Land. Large bad debts were incurred as a result, and in the case of Peyton and Peyton over £65,000 was struck off the bank's contingent fund between 1881 and 1884 to cover the losses. The bank had always relied heavily upon a small number of large accounts, especially those linked with directors' interests, but by the 1880s this narrowness had become a matter of concern rather than a mark of strength. The combined overdraft limits of Birmingham Small Arms and Patent Shaft, for example, reached £121,000 in mid 1883, 9 per cent of the bank's total advances. Arthur Keen was particularly troubled by the large accounts, and throughout the 1880s he enlivened the meetings of the new finance committee with severe criticisms of loans to companies connected with directors or former directors. The reliance on key company accounts was not unusual amongst the country banks. The Cumberland Union Bank devoted no less than 8 per cent of its advances to the West Cumberland Iron and Steel Company and another 5 per cent to the Maryport Haematite Iron Company in the early 1880s.[17] Unlike the similarly-sized Cumberland Union Bank, which waded deeper into these commitments in the 1880s and 1890s, Midland was anxious to diversify its assets as soon as it had unravelled the effects of the crisis. This diversification was partly achieved by the enlargement of the bank's investments.

Midland's investment portfolio had been developed from scratch under Henry Edmunds' managership, but between 1874 and 1879, when the bank's resources were redeployed into loans and overdrafts, it had dwindled in value from £431,585 to only £132,831. Tentative efforts were made to rebuild the account in the early 1880s. When a batch of existing advances of £100,000 was to be repaid in July 1884, for example, Bolding recommended switching the money into Consols rather than employing it in new loans and overdrafts. Investments in the major railway companies were well to the fore. In 1881 44 per cent of the total account of £249,376 was committed to debentures issued by the Midland Railway, the London and North Western, the Great Western and the Great Eastern. More extensive buying was delayed until the late 1880s, when the bank experimented with a much wider range of investments. Colonial stocks, in the shape of Canadian and Victorian bonds, were first bought in 1886 and in the same year £9800 was placed in 3½ per cent bonds of the Bombay and Baroda Railway. These types of investment were developed in the next two years. By December 1888 only 27 per cent of the bank's total investments of £472,263 were in government stocks, the recommended haven for surplus bank funds. Indian railways had by then emerged as the largest class of investments, with a 28 per cent share of the total (excluding £10,000 in Indian government bonds). Another 18 per cent was placed in colonial stocks, while British railway stocks had declined to only 16 per cent of the account. Apart from its contribution in fixed interest and dividends, this renewed activity produced useful profits on the sale of investments. These dealings profits exceeded £7500 in 1887 and £4800 in 1888, more than any single branch office produced in net profit in those years.

The bank's assets could also be broadened by placing loans and overdrafts outside Birmingham and its region. In 1883, for instance, a renewable loan of £25,000 was made to Fraser, Kirkpatrick and Smith, Glasgow stockbrokers, and in the following year an overdraft of £10,000 was granted to a Liverpool soap manufacturer. By far the most important of the new connections, however, were the bank's multiplying links with London. In some cases these links reflected the spreading of existing customers' interests, as when Charles Beale borrowed £100,000 in 1884 for the development of property in Cannon Row, Westminster. Yet this category of lending was small in comparison with loans to the London money markets. These loans—essentially money at call and short notice—seem to have developed on the initiative of London stockbrokers and discount houses rather than as a strategy on Midland's part, reflecting the intense competition for new funds for stock dealings and company promotions in the capital since the 1870s.[18] From 1871 onwards Midland was placing up to £130,000 with London discount houses. Ten years later the bank was ready to add stockbrokers' loans to its assets. The earliest example was a six-month loan of £25,000 in January 1881, when the stockbrokers Laurie Milbank approached the bank through the Union Bank of London. Other borrowers later in the year included the brokers Whitehead and Coles and J and A Scrimgeour, and by June 1882 loans to London discount houses and stockbrokers reached £184,431 (6.7 per cent of Midland's assets). In December 1889 lending at call and short notice, which earned a higher rate of interest than other assets, amounted to £257,300 (6.1 per cent of total assets). Weekly returns in the late 1880s and early 1890s frequently included totals of over £400,000 under the same heading.

With London's brokers and finance houses so keen to bring provincial banks within their reach, it was understandable that in return a bank such as Midland should wish to use London's financial services to manage its assets. The bank had been using its London connections for expert advice since the 1870s (pp 50 and 64) and these links were extended and strengthened in the 1880s. In February 1880 the Bank of England actually volunteered 'to transact the whole or a portion of our London business', an offer which Bolding used to extract improved agency terms with the Union Bank of London. The relationship with the London agents was heavily employed in the purchase and sale of investments throughout the 1880s, but Bolding also used other London houses, as when the bank bought Birmingham Corporation stocks through Samuel Montagu and Co in 1882. Contacts with London banks also multiplied when loans to stockbrokers created a heavy traffic in the distribution and collection of securities; this task, in which speed and safety were essential, was obviously easier for London houses than for country banks.

Changes in the allocation of the bank's assets during the 1880s greatly reduced its traditional exposure on a relatively small number of major local accounts. Its amalgamations between 1884 and 1890 increased the spread of risk, and in this sense the mergers were an effort to release the bank from dependence upon very large accounts rather than the advertised attempt to give those accounts increased facilities. Goodman himself made this plain when he spoke to the shareholders after the Yorkshire amalgamations.'Our policy of late', he explained, 'has been to spread our risks as much as we possibly can, avoiding all large and unwieldy accounts.' By moving into the London market, where so much of the bank's new investments and advances were negotiated during the 1880s, this process of diversification could be given permanence.

London had been exerting strong magnetic force within the banking community since the mid-1850s, when the City had attracted a high volume of foreign lending business. The boom in bank formations in the early 1860s had been dominated by new London promotions both for home banking (as for example the Imperial Bank and the Alliance Bank) and for overseas banking (notably the Standard Bank of South Africa). European banks were keen to take a share of the international business which was crowding into London, and branch offices were opened by the Crédit Lyonnais (1871) and the Deutsche Bank (1873). The arrival of the Scottish banks in London mirrored the concentration of payments in the capital. The National Bank of Scotland's London office opened in 1864, followed by the Bank of Scotland in 1867, the Royal Bank in 1874 and the Clydesdale Bank in 1877.[19] As far as English country banks were concerned, the National Provincial's introduction of banking services in London in 1866 pushed the traditional separation of London and country banking towards obsolescence. The entry of the Capital and Counties Bank in 1877, Lloyds (in 1884) and the Birmingham Banking Company (in 1889) to London demonstrated that country banks were as capable of the transition as the London-controlled National Provincial Bank.

Midland's decision to purchase a London bank can only have come from Goodman, the architect of the first series of the bank's mergers. As the first long-term chairman since the 1830s, he had provided not only leadership but also a broader view of the bank's position in the local and national economy. Not the least of his abilities were his close control over the balance sheet, liaison between the board and management, and the selection of the bank's senior men. The entry into London would not have been attempted until all three of these functions had been tackled to Goodman's satisfaction. Changes in the balance sheet and reforms of lending procedures were well under way, and the selection of management and staff made the bank well-equipped for new extensions. Bolding, whose reign as manager had begun in the midst of the Glasgow crisis and ended with the bank showing new levels of fitness, retired in mid-1887 and was given a full directorship. He was replaced by John Alexander Christie, who had joined the bank as secretary in 1877 and acted as sub-manager since 1879. Christie had been trained in the Glasgow branch of the National Bank of Scotland but had moved south as chief cashier to the Birmingham Town and District Bank in 1868. Christie's knowledge of the principal Birmingham customers had been valuable during the difficult period of recovery in the early 1880s, and he had also led the team of Midland officials investigating the books of the Union Bank of Birmingham before the merger in 1883.

Christie's contribution was overshadowed, perhaps unfairly, by the achievements of his immediate subordinate. Edward Hopkinson Holden had joined Midland as accountant in 1881. He had served his apprenticeship with the Manchester and County Bank in his native territory of Bolton, Lancashire. Despite diligent study at Owen's College Manchester, and private tuition in law, by 1880 at the age of thirty-two he ranked as only the fifth of 12 cashiers at the bank's head office in Manchester.[20] He answered Midland's advertisement for an accountant in 1881, when he is reputed to have told the board 'I want to be the manager of a big bank'.[21] Exceptionally ambitious, he was promoted to become secretary as soon as he told his directors that he had applied for the sub-managership of a Bristol bank in 1883. In the role of secretary he shared the credit for the takeover of the Union Bank in the same year and then took Christie's place as sub-manager in 1887. The two men then engineered the amalgamations in the Midlands and Yorkshire in 1889 and 1890.

In Christie and Holden, Goodman had at his disposal two managers who relished hunting out new amalgamations. They were already masters of the rapid review and assessment of other banks' balance sheets, and the negotiations of the 1880s showed that they understood the significance of each bank's provisions for bad and doubtful debts in arriving at a valuation. The selection of targets was nevertheless the responsibility of Goodman, supported by influential directors such as Arthur Keen and Henry Heaton, a Birmingham manufacturer who had joined the board in 1880.

Goodman's choice in London was the Central Bank of London, established as the East London Bank during the promotion boom of 1863. By 1891 it was operating with ten branches and had built up deposits of £1.6 million. Significantly it also owned a city-centre headquarters in Cornhill and had been granted a seat in the London Clearing House, but it was dwarfed by contemporary London banks such as the London and Westminster Bank, the London and County Bank or the London Joint Stock Bank. The Central Bank's directors admitted that they could not compete with these neighbours, and they were also troubled by 'the very large proportion which our working expenses bear to our capital and the business we do'. From Midland's point of view the choice available to Goodman and his directors was restricted by the potential capital then available; after the new issue of 1890 only 9000 shares were still not distributed and any investment in London would demand yet more capital.

Holden had been dispatched to London to open negotiations with the Central Bank as early as 1889. Initially an agreement seemed unlikely, as Midland's first offer of £13 12s for each Central Bank share (a total of £425,000) was far below the Central Bank's first price of £19 10s per share (£609,375). Worse still, Sir John Hollams, solicitor to the Central Bank, objected to the scheme and claimed that there was no provision in Midland's constitution for the merger proposed by Holden. Midland's own solicitors confirmed the point and set about devising a memorandum and articles of association to supplement the original deed of settlement. The new constitition was eventually published and approved in July 1891.

In the meantime Holden had been approached by Sir Frederick Dixon-Hartland, who was keen to sell his banking firm of Lacy, Hartland, Woodbridge and Co. This firm, established in 1809, was based in Smithfield and specialized in banking for the cattle trade. Its six London offices controlled deposits of about £170,000 but it was neither the type nor size of bank which Holden had been commissioned to buy. It then emerged that Dixon-Hartland knew Hollams. Holden promised that if Dixon-Hartland could remove Hollams' opposition to the Central Bank deal, then Midland would buy the Lacy business as well as the Central Bank. According to Holden, Dixon-Hartland breakfasted with Hollams the following day and persuaded him to recommend acceptance of Midland's offer. As a result in August 1891 the Central Bank board and shareholders agreed to the merger at a price of £15 per share, equivalent to £468,750 and slightly more than

## Table 3.2

Midland Bank amalgamations, 1883–91

| Date | Bank acquired | Number of branches | Total deposits (£000) | Paid-up capital (£000) | Price of acquisition* (£000) | Ratio Price paid-up capital |
|------|---------------|-------------------|-----------------------|------------------------|------------------------------|-----------------------------|
| 1883 | Union Bank of Birmingham | 0 | 400 | 108 | 86 | 0.8 |
| 1889 | Coventry Union Banking Co | 1 | 420 | 56 | 125 | 2.2 |
| 1889 | Leamington Priors and Warwickshire Banking Co | 3 | 204 | 40 | 102 | 2.6 |
| 1889 | Derby Commercial Bank | 0 | 222 | 50 | 125 | 2.5 |
| 1890 | Exchange and Discount Bank | 2 | 422 | 100 | 225 | 2.2 |
| 1890 | Leeds and County Bank | 12 | 1079 | 137 | 187 | 1.4 |
| 1890 | Central Bank of London | 10 | 1627 | 156 | 469 | 3.0 |
| 1891 | Lacy Hartland and Woodbridge | 3 | — | — | 36 | — |

*Note\** Agreed value of Midland shares and/or cash paid for acquisition

Holden's first offer. The price was twice as high for Midland as any of its previous acquisitions and, as a measure of its importance, the ratio between the price and the paid-up value of the Central Bank shares was more generous than before (Table 3.2). Four of the Central Bank's directors joined Midland's board and the combined bank altered its name to the London and Midland Bank (a simpler version than the alternatives of the 'London Midland and Counties Bank' or the 'Central of London, Midland and Counties Bank'). The new name had the advantage, Goodman told the bank's shareholders, 'that it will enable us to continue to be known by the name of the Midland'.

Holden's agreement with Dixon-Hartland was not forgotten, and the Smithfield bank was acquired by Midland later in 1891. In addition to the price of £35,850, Dixon-Hartland was rewarded with a seat on the board. The two London acquisitions were then paid for by increasing the nominal capital to £6 million in 100,000 shares, of which nearly 40,000 were still unissued and available after the exchange of shares with the Central Bank. Few shareholders in the

Central Bank refused the offer. As a measure of investors' attitudes to the amalgamations and as a reflection of Midland's success in valuing each acquisition, only 311 of the 32,290 shares offered in exchange between 1883 and 1891 were not taken up.

The enlargement of the bank's capital matched the transformation of its business. In only five years the bank's branch network had been extended from ten offices in 1887 to 65 at the end of 1891, and staff numbers rose to 557 by 1892. By acquiring the Central Bank, Midland increased its deposits from £5.6 million in December 1890 to £8.1 million twelve months later. This progress promoted it to tenth place in the rankings of English joint stock banks. Equally important was the way in which the new deposits did not leave the bank with a weakened balance sheet. The usual measure of safety and comfort in the 1880s and 1890s was the proportion of deposit liabilities covered by the easily-accessible assets of cash, money at call and investments. By this standard, Midland's ratio of 41 per cent after the amalgamation was comparable with the 40 per cent ratio maintained by the Metropolitan Bank (formerly the Birmingham Banking Company) and the London Joint Stock Bank. Higher ratios were already maintained by Lloyds (47 per cent) and the National Provincial (55 per cent). The Central Bank directors, in convincing their shareholders of the wisdom of the amalgamation, also made great play of the relatively lower level of liability on shares in the enlarged bank. The unpaid amount on each Midland share was 79 per cent of the nominal capital value of £60, appreciably less than the equivalent for shares in Lloyds (87 per cent), the National Provincial (86 per cent) or the London Joint Stock Bank (85 per cent).

Towards the end of his life Holden told Ellis Powell, editor of the *Financial News*, that he had been solely responsible for the negotiations with the Central Bank.[22] The details of the amalgamations were undoubtedly his work, as Goodman acknowledged when he announced Holden's promotion to become joint general manager with Christie immediately after the merger. Yet up to and including the Central Bank agreement Holden was still following a course plotted by Goodman. Holden's banking and entrepreneurial skills were of enormous value to Goodman but the pace and direction of Midland's growth remained under the chairman's control. This distinction, which was increasingly blurred as Holden's reputation grew over the next twenty years, is a reminder that the bank was not, and did not yet see itself as, a metropolitan bank let alone an international bank. The new name may have implied that London was now the prime location, but Goodman was clearly determined to keep the Midland name to the fore. He was rightly proud of the Birmingham connection; the bank was the offspring of an exceptionally confident business community, which had acquired all the trappings of municipal development two decades earlier than the capital.

The loyalty to Birmingham was at its most obvious in the bank's new administrative arrangements. The transfer of the head office to Cornhill was at the insistence of the Central Bank, not of Midland; Goodman spoke of it as the London office rather than as the new centre of the bank's business. The Cornhill building was already too small for the Central Bank, so that there was no question of the wholesale transfer of headquarters functions to London. Likewise Christie, the senior manager, remained at New Street rather than Cornhill. Board meetings and shareholders' meetings were to be held alternately in London and Birmingham, a similar arrangement to that already used by Lloyds. In these ways the bank was not yet converted from being a provincial bank to emerging as a metropolitan bank. The Birmingham business and the acquisitions elsewhere in the Midlands and Yorkshire meant that only a small section of the bank's customers was London-based. It was not until the later 1890s, when London became the bank's headquarters in management and business terms as well as in name, that the conversion was complete.

✻

# CHAPTER FOUR

# CAMPAIGNS AND CONQUESTS
## 1891–1908

As everybody about me knows, I have worked day and night and sacrificed everything in order to make this Bank one of the first in the kingdom. . . . I am entitled to say very strong things, and to think very strong thoughts

Edward Holden's letters to shareholders, November 1900

In the 1890s and early 1900s no other British bank could match Midland's expansive development. The rate of growth of its deposits from £8 million in 1891 to £67 million by 1908 outpaced the National Provincial (which produced only a 45 per cent increase to £59 million in the same period) and its old rival Lloyds (which showed a 250 per cent increase to £74 million). The visible evidence in high streets throughout England and Wales was equally striking. By 1908 Midland's name appeared over the doors of 630 branch banks, compared with National Provincial's 247 branches and Lloyd's 554. Military parallels are difficult to avoid. Midland's entry into new territory, whether by amalgamation or by branch extension, gave an impression of belligerence and conquest. Its management and staff operated under an increasingly rigid discipline and were better equipped than most of their competitors. Most obviously, in Edward Holden the bank was led by an autocratic but highly original commander.

Little hint of this achievement was given when the bank acquired its London office and changed its name in 1891. With all its advantages, the new office was a small investment and the bank's main business and commitment remained in Birmingham. The outlook was also clouded by renewed crises in London banking. In November 1890 bankers and investors were appalled by the news that Baring Brothers, the old-established and much-respected merchant bank, was in serious difficulties as a result of the collapse in the value of its South American stocks. A sudden panic was avoided when the Bank of England mobilized a guarantee fund of over £17 million subscribed by commercial banks throughout the country. Successful as this rescue was, the affair was a jolt to bankers' confidence and it was not until 1894 that the guarantee fund was terminated. Throughout that period bankers could not depend upon the stability of interest rates, security values or even the shares of their own banks.

Although a private merchant bank was at the centre of the new crisis, there was no room for complacency amongst the commercial deposit-taking banks. In August 1892 the London and General Bank failed with deposit liabilities of £282,000. The stoppage led to a run on similar small London banks: the Birkbeck Bank, for example, suffered the net withdrawal of over £1.3 million in the first two weeks of August. The 'knock-on' effects of stoppages and rumours of closures also came unpleasantly close when frauds were uncovered at the National Bank of Wales in 1893. Midland had just taken on this bank's London agency and had begun to negotiate for an amalgamation. In February 1893, however, the Welsh bank had accepted a higher offer from the Metropolitan Bank (formerly Midland's neighbours, the Birmingham Banking Company). Disclosure of the frauds—covering a loss of about £500,000—ruined the advantages which the Metropolitan had gained as a result of its move to London.[1] This disastrous experience was thought to have been the cause of the death of James Leigh, the Metropolitan's able general manager, in the following year and it continued to damage the bank's reputation for a decade.

The Metropolitan's entanglement with the National Bank of Wales was a sharp reminder of the continuing fragility of commercial banking. Over the next few years bankers were noticeably more active in efforts to provide better protection against, and earlier warning of, similar misfortunes. At the suggestion of the *Bankers' Magazine*, in 1895 they formed the Central Association of Bankers 'to safeguard the interests of bankers as a whole'.[2] The new Association brought together the representatives of the Committee of the London Clearing House, the West End banks and the Association of English Country Bankers. As the forerunner of the British Bankers' Association, the new body acted as a channel for consultation, information and the defence of the banking industry as a whole. The cohesion of the bankers' community was also evident in the greater use of the Institute of Bankers for uniform legal and educational services, and in the growing numbers of bond and debenture-holders' associations for the protection of investors.

For the directors and managers of Midland, these efforts towards cooperation and greater safety can only have improved the prospects for survival and further development. A number of routes were open. The first option was to remain independent. In the early 1890s, although the pace of amalgamations was at its fastest, there were still over 150 independent banking units in England and Wales. Some of those banks, notably in Manchester and Liverpool, were producing strong results without needing to enter London in their own names. Midland had not closed the option of reserving its efforts for the Birmingham business. Alternatively, the bank could seek a merger with a larger bank in either London or the country, provided that the bank's customers and staff were protected and that the shareholders benefited while the bank's shares were still trading at premiums of about £20 each. Thirdly there was the chance to develop the metropolitan connection and compete with the other London-and-country banks. This category, in order of size, included the National Provincial, the London and County, Lloyds, the Capital and Counties, and the London and South Western Bank. These five banks shared total deposits of £113 million in 1891, nearly one quarter of deposits in England and Wales.[3]

Not until the late 1890s did Midland's choice become clear. In the first seven years after the bank's entry to London, meetings of the directors and the shareholders were held alternately in London and Birmingham. Goodman, Keen and Christie continued to treat New Street as the bank's focal point, and to a great extent the London business was left to the initiative of Bradshaw (the former chairman of the Central Bank) and Holden (who was also responsible for the Yorkshire branches). Rather than consolidate its position in London, the bank seemed more concerned with pushing into new territory in the country. While the Central Bank agreement was being finalised, for example, negotiations with the Manchester Joint Stock Bank were already in hand. An amalgamation was completed in mid-1892, bringing Midland 11 branches in central Manchester and additional deposits of about £520,000. The cost, partly in cash and partly by issue of 4381 Midland shares, was equivalent to £229,000. Only a year later the sixty-year-old Bank of Westmorland, having refused other offers, accepted Midland's outright cash bid of £102,000. In return the bank took over deposits of £323,000, a local headquarters at Kendal and four Lake District branches. As a sign of the intensifying competition for new amalgamations, each £100 paid in shares or cash for the Manchester and Kendal amalgamations brought Midland only £255 in additional deposits, significantly less that the £464 acquired for the same outlay in the amalgamation of the Union Bank of Birmingham ten years earlier.

The excursion into Westmorland took Midland far beyond its traditional boundaries. It suggested that Goodman and his directors were now more interested in a countrywide network. The branches were already spread over more than 250 miles between London and Cumberland. As yet, though, the country banks bought by the Midland were all relatively small or undeveloped; the Leeds and County Bank with its deposits of over £1 million had been easily its largest acquisition in the provinces. An offer for the Preston Banking Company late in 1894 was altogether more ambitious. On one hand the Preston Bank ranked as one of the larger provincial companies. Established in 1844, fifty years later it was working with 26 branches and deposits of £1.8 million (placing it twentieth amongst non-London banks). On the other hand it was a specialist bank with a concentration of business in the cotton industry. This emphasis had cost the Preston Bank a stoppage in 1866 as a result of the 'cotton famine' and the money market crisis of that year, but a reconstruction kept the main lines of credit open and eventually allowed a strong recovery. This return to health (especially the doubling of deposits since the reconstruction) was reflected in Midland's bid in shares and cash equivalent to £636,000. This price excluded a payment of £4000 to the Preston Bank directors and a handsome fee of £20,000 for F W Ponting, the general manager.

Ponting served as 'manager for the Preston district' for the first year after the amalgamation and he subsequently acted as a consultant in handling the new Lancashire business. As part of this consultancy, Ponting was authorized to make an offer for the Carlisle City and District Banking Company. The company was another of the joint stock foundations of 1836, and since the 1878 crisis it had been regularly involved in takeover talks with the other Cumberland banks. Its head office and eight branches held deposits of £742,000, and its business did not overlap with Midland's new interests in Westmorland and north Lancashire. Ponting's bid in shares and cash was equivalent to £290,000, an offer which all the Carlisle shareholders accepted in September 1896.

By early 1897 Midland's shareholders and customers could have been forgiven for believing that the bank's centre of balance had shifted not to London but to Lancashire. All the amalgamations since 1891 had strengthened the bank's presence in the north-west, and some shareholders may have known that since 1895 Holden and Ponting had also been attempting to buy the Liverpool-based North Western Bank (p 95).

In reality the moment had arrived when directions on the future pattern of the bank's growth were badly needed. Several influences were at work. There was an obvious problem of accommodation in London. Although nominally the bank's headquarters since 1891, the Cornhill building was patently inadequate and many of the head office functions had remained in Birmingham. Efforts had been made to find new premises as early as 1893 and an offer for Dimsdale Fowler's neighbouring building at 50 Cornhill had been briefly considered. Temporary relief came in 1894, when a mezzanine floor was installed at Cornhill to provide room for another 44 clerks, but the shortage of space was a practical obstacle to developing the London business.

The bank's capital resources were also being squeezed. The relatively expensive investment in Cumberland had reduced the number of unissued shares to 15,630. This supply would not cover the purchase of any country banks on the same scale as the Preston Bank, and none of the other London, Manchester or Birmingham joint stock banks was within that budget. Even the proposed merger with the North Western Bank would have swallowed most of the remaining shares. Any future growth via amalgamations would make a new issue of capital essential.

Allied to this predicament was evidence that share values of the London-and-country banks were stronger than those of banks based solely in the country or solely in London. Goodman, always a close observer of market performance, noted that shares in the London and County and London and South Western banks moved ahead by 6–7 per cent between 1891 and 1893. Midland and Lloyds saw a 4–5 per cent fall in the same period but this was a small change in comparison with heavy depreciation of shares of London-only banks. The London and Westminster lost 23 per cent of its price in the same period, the Union 20 per cent and the City Bank 13 per cent. These differences implied that investors' confidence was being placed in the larger London-and-country banks, particularly if there was an even balance between their metropolitan and provincial business. They also hinted that the specialist London banks were becoming relatively less expensive as candidates for mergers. For a bank such as Midland, still under-represented in the City, these were incentives to make a heavier investment in London and to adjust its own capital for that task.

Changes in the bank's management during 1897 ensured a decisive reaction to these pressures. The joint command of Christie in Birmingham and Holden in London had gradually placed Holden in a more influential and responsible role. Both by choice and opportunity he won recognition as the dominant partner by the mid-1890s. Goodman and his directors themselves acknowledged the new situation. In 1895, for example, they were so satisfied with the Preston Bank merger that they awarded both general managers a salary increase of £500. Christie was voted a bonus of 1000 guineas for his 'eminent services' but their special thanks were reserved for Holden. Their London general manager received a bonus of 2000 guineas for 'conspicuous ability ... in conducting and completing the recent amalgamations'. When Christie retired in February 1897 there was no delay in appointing Holden sole general manager. In effect the appointment ended the London-Birmingham division in the management and concentrated control in Holden's office in Cornhill. Just over a year later the retirement of Goodman as chairman fortified Holden's new position. Goodman, for so long the source of the bank's initiatives and an outstanding financial controller, had been Holden's chief rather than his instrument. It was the loyalty as much as the enterprise of his general manager that Goodman recommended to the directors when he retired. Holden's relationship with his successor, Arthur Keen, was quite different. Keen was a forceful character, but he had already ended his most creative period in the bank. Having been one of the most outspoken but conscientious board members throughout the 1880s and early 1890s, he was oriented towards his Birmingham interests by the time he took over as Midland's chairman in 1898. He was a rare visitor to London and he relied increasingly upon Holden and Bradshaw, his deputy chairman, during the ten years of his chairmanship.

Holden's promotion in 1897 immediately ended any uncertainties over the bank's capacity for growth. Within a month two new amalgamations were arranged. The first, with the Channel Islands Bank, Jersey, was completed by using only 1333 of the remaining unissued shares (equivalent to a cash price of £60,000). The deal added another £311,000 to Midland's deposits but was essentially an opportunity pursued by Holden when he had been establishing a branch at Southampton, the main sea link with the Channel Islands, at the end of 1896. In contrast during April 1897 Holden was negotiating to buy the Huddersfield Banking Company, one of the oldest and largest of the country joint stock banks. The Huddersfield Bank had been founded in 1827 and was one of the models for the banks of the 1830s. In Sir Charles Sikes, general manager from 1868 to 1882 and also the founding father of the Post Office Savings Bank, it had produced one of the outstanding country bankers of the Victorian period.[4] The Huddersfield Bank's deposits had reached

£3.3 million by 1897. Although the bank also operated 16 branches, the head office at Cloth Hall Street, Huddersfield, was one of the busiest bank offices in the country.

Holden welcomed the Huddersfield acquisition not only because of the exceptionally large amount of new business but also because it gave the chance to rationalize Midland's capital resources. The price agreed was equivalent to £1.08 million and required the issue of no less than 22,582 Midland shares. The exchange took the bank well over its ceiling of issued shares. Midland's board therefore combined the agreement with the doubling of the bank's nominal capital to £12 million. Shareholders' permission was obtained in June 1897 and the bank then became the eighth largest of the banks in England and Wales in terms of capital resources. After the Huddersfield exchange this operation also made 92,299 new shares available for future expansion at a market value of approximately £4.25 million. The price paid for the Huddersfield Bank was 12.5 per cent over the quoted value of that bank's shares. Assuming that a similar bonus would be payable, the creation of this new capital brought some of the other London banks within range of purchase. On the record of their mid-1897 balance sheets and share prices, possible candidates included the City Bank (valued at about £2 million), the London and South Western Bank (£2 million), or the London and Provincial Bank (£2.64 million). These banks would produce only about £250 of deposit business for each £100 paid out in Midland shares (a lower return than any of the bank's previous amalgamations), but on that basis the private bank of Prescott Dimsdale, with £4.4 million in deposits, was another possible acquisition.

Initially the new resources were used to build an even stronger position in Lancashire. The two-year-old negotiations with the North Western Bank finally ended in agreement in June 1897. This bank's business depended largely on the commodity merchants who had banked at its head office in Dale Street, Liverpool, since Moss and Co had opened the original bank in 1807. The head office and eight branches held deposits of £1.5 million by 1897. Nevertheless, after discovering a number of doubtful debts on produce accounts, Holden reduced his offer from £648,000 to £580,500. By comparison a bid for the Oldham Joint Stock Bank early in 1898 was accepted quickly and without dissent. The Oldham Bank had been founded only eighteen years earlier and in the boom years of the 'Oldham Limited' cotton mills it had bought up the Rochdale Joint Stock Bank's three branches, opened seven branches of its own, and accumulated deposits of some £1.4 million.[5] Huge seasonal demands from the cotton industry made amalgamation a more obvious solution for the Oldham Bank than for many country banks, and it was impossible for the mill-owning customers to contemplate a future for the bank without proper representation in Manchester and Liverpool. Ponting was again authorized to negotiate on Midland's behalf, and in February 1898 his offer of cash and shares then worth £600,000 was accepted by the Oldham shareholders.

The Liverpool and Oldham mergers promoted Midland to being the largest bank in Lancashire in terms of branch banks. The total network of 217 branches after the Oldham Bank agreement also placed it amongst the best represented banks in the west Midlands and in west Yorkshire. Its London business seemed thin by comparison, and the need for a practicable London headquarters—rather than a glorified postal address—was now high amongst Holden's priorities. In later life he explained that Midland had been interested in the City Bank for 'some years', possibly since before the acquisition of the Central Bank.[6] According to Holden, talks were only resumed in 1898 as a result of a chance meeting with a City Bank manager. Holden had given help to the same manager on a previous occasion, but when they met again Holden admitted that 'I am so pushed for room that I am myself working right up under the roof, and I don't know which way to turn'. This was enough to give Holden a new introduction to the City Bank's directors.

The City Bank, though overshadowed by long-established banks in the capital such as the London Joint Stock Bank and the London and Westminster Bank, was nevertheless in the first rank of London banks. It had been founded by Royal Charter in 1855 and its deposits of £9 million were distributed amongst 19 branches in the City and West End. Its business with foreign and colonial banks was strong by any standard, with its acceptances of £2.4 million amounting to nearly one fifth of its total assets. From Midland's point of view, the City Bank was extremely well equipped; the grand head office in Threadneedle Street was large and available for expansion, the reserve fund of £500,000 was comparatively large, and the directors had influential connections in the London business community.

Holden's negotiations with the City Bank during the summer of 1898 were the most complex and strenuous in his career. Failure would have cost the bank one of the only remaining opportunities in London banking. Disappointment would also have damaged his standing amongst his directors and in the City within only a few months of taking command of the bank. It was probably for this reason that his first offer was relatively generous, valuing the City Bank at

# HOME BASE:
# MIDLAND'S ORIGINS AND HEADQUARTERS

**PROSPECTUS**

OF THE

**BIRMINGHAM EXCHANGE BANK.**

MANY Gentlemen who are of opinion that the Public accommodation requires the establishment of another Joint Stock Company Bank, in the town of Birmingham, have

*Resolved—*

That a Joint Stock Company Bank shall be established, to be called THE BIRMINGHAM EXCHANGE BANK, for the transaction of the usual business of Bankers in Birmingham, and such other neighbouring towns as the Directors shall think proper, under the following conditions :—

1.—That the Capital shall be £500,000, in 50,000 Shares of £10 each.

2.—That the allotment of shares shall be made by the Provisional Committee.

3.—That within twenty-one days after the allotment of shares each shareholder shall pay down a deposit of £2 per share, but no further call shall be made until after three months' notice.

4.—That the concern shall be under the management of Directors, to be chosen annually by the Shareholders, and that a general meeting be called as early as possible after the allotment of shares, for the purpose of choosing the first Directors. Every holder of a hundred shares to be eligible as a Director.

5.—That no person shall hold fewer than ten shares, and that holders of ten shares shall have one vote, of twenty-five shares two votes, of fifty shares three votes, of 100 shares four votes, of 150 shares five votes, and of 200 shares and upwards six votes.

6.—That a proper deed of settlement shall be prepared under the instructions of the Directors, containing all usual provisions, and especially providing that if one-fourth of the paid-up capital over and above the guarantee fund shall ever be lost, the shareholders, by the resolution of a special meeting, shall have power to dissolve the Company.

Applications for shares to be made to the Provisional Committee, under cover, to Mr. WILLS, solicitor, Cherry-street, Birmingham.

FRANCIS FINCH,
Chairman of the Provisional Committee.

THE Provisional Committee of the Birmingham Exchange Bank are desirous of Renting or Purchasing suitable and commodious Premises for the above Establishment. Persons who have such premises to let or sell are requested to address a communication, stating particulars and price, to Mr. WILLS, Solicitor, Cherry-street.

**1.1** *Preliminary announcement of Midland's formation, from the* Birmingham Journal, *16 July 1836. The proposed title of the* Birmingham Exchange Bank *was changed to the* Birmingham and Midland Bank *immediately before the bank opened in August 1836*

**1.2** *Union Street in the centre of Birmingham in the 1830s, where Midland first opened for business in August 1836*

**1.3** *Midland's office at 20 Union Street, Birmingham, photographed c1860. The building was designed for the bank by Charles Edge and was its headquarters between 1837 and 1869. The original temporary office at 30 Union Street was the second building from the right of the photograph.*

**1.4** *Charles Geach, Midland's founder and first manager. Geach was also a leading figure in the political and industrial life of the west Midlands. This medallion was minted in his memory after his sudden death in 1854*

CHARLES GEACH M.P.
BORN
MAY 1st 1808
ELECTED FOR COVENTRY
APRIL 1851
DIED
NOVEMBER 1st
1854

**1.5** *The Bank of England's branch at Bennetts Hill, Birmingham. Midland's links with the branch (where Geach had been employed before launching Midland) played a key role in the bank's early development.* Photograph, c1860, by permission of the governor and company of the Bank of England

**1.6** *Midland's headquarters at New Street, Birmingham, designed by Edward Holmes in 1867. The building was the bank's main office until 1891*

**1.7** *John Dent Goodman, Midland's chairman between 1881 and 1898. Goodman initiated the expansion of the bank in the 1880s and supervised its move to London in the 1890s.* Portrait by W W Ouless, 1891

**1.8** *Street plan of the City of London in about 1890 showing the Central Bank of London in Cornhill (centre) and the City Bank in Threadneedle Street (top left). The acquisition of these two banks in 1891 and 1898 gave* Midland a London base, and the Threadneedle Steet building was the bank's head office between 1898 and 1930. From Charles E Goad, Insurance Plan of London (1886–92), by permission of the Guildhall Library, London

1.9 *Midland's board of directors in 1903,*
*shortly after the bank's move to Threadneedle*
*Street. The meeting was chaired by Arthur Keen*
*(seated, third from left on the near side) with*
*Edward Holden to his right*

1.10 *The bank's head office at Poultry, London,*
*under construction in the 1930s. This photograph*
*shows the Princes Street extension, opposite the*
*Bank of England*

**1.11** *The board room at Midland's headquarters in Poultry, designed by Sir Edwin Lutyens, shortly after completion in 1930*

£2.625 million by exchange of shares (a bonus of 31 per cent over the market value of the City Bank). For the first and last time, Holden found himself opposed by some of his own bank's directors and shareholders. There was even evidence of Midland shareholders selling their shares in exchange for City Bank certificates in the belief that the City Bank had the better of the bargain. 'This is what I dreaded', Holden admitted in a rare moment of self-doubt: 'Am heartily sick of it, and with Committee and Directors away it is too much for me.'

By this stage, however, Holden had won the confidence of James Vanner who was leading the negotiations on the City Bank's side. Vanner, a silk manufacturer and insurance underwriter as well as director of the City Bank, agreed to reduce the price to £2.556 million. This was to be achieved by the exchange of 48,000 Midland shares, well within the bank's budget of unissued capital. It was the least price that the City Bank board would contemplate, although Vanner carried a letter from Holden threatening to withdraw the offer if the price was not accepted. In return Holden promised to provide six board places for City Bank directors, to alter Midland's name to London City and Midland Bank, and to hold all board and shareholders' meetings in London. The terms were approved in October 1898, with all the City Bank shareholders taking up their options on Midland shares. 'The fusion of these two banks has been a prodigious business', Vanner concluded shortly after he had joined Midland's board, 'and I would say, referring to my friend Mr Holden's share, how glad I am to have him on the same side of the table with myself, for I know what it is to have a table between us'.

The City Bank merger finally converted Midland into a major London bank as well as one of the largest provincial banks. Total deposits of £31.9 million at the end of 1898 ranked behind only those of the National Provincial (£49.3 million), the London and County (£43.5 million) and Lloyds (£37.7 million). The four banks already shared approximately one quarter of bank deposits in England and Wales, a change in distribution which was all the more remarkable in view of the fact that Lloyds and Midland had emigrated from Birmingham so recently.

The Birmingham and Midland Bank's entry to London in 1891 had been influenced by the facilities of the London money markets, the need for improved cash and deposit services for its new customers, and the need to broaden its pattern of lending (Chapter Three, pp 81–3). By the late 1890s, although these factors remained influential, clearly they had become part of much broader ambitions. The marked contrast between the pre-1891 amalgamations and the later acquisitions (up to and including the City Bank merger) implied that the directors and managers were altering their view of the bank's objectives. The change in approach may even have signalled a new attitude to the function of a commercial bank.

To customers and shareholders, the amalgamation movement in banking seemed to offer a more convenient and accessible payments system in exchange for the loss of some local control and identity. Critics of the amalgamations warned that country customers would see their deposits employed in distant parts of the economy while their own borrowing needs would be in the hands of metropolitan bankers unfamiliar with local conditions. The promoters of the City of Birmingham Bank in 1897, for example, believed that the amalgamations had reduced the banks' 'intimate knowledge of local requirements' and promised that their own bank would not be 'dependent for its administration upon London'.

The opponents of the amalgamations of the 1890s were in a minority, however. There were few instances of widespread revolt by shareholders and customers of banks under offer. In Midland's case, since the bank was first quoted on the London Stock Exchange in 1891, very few shareholders in Midland's amalgamated banks preferred cash to shares; only 2955 (2.5 per cent) of the 116,972 Midland shares offered in amalgamation exchanges were not taken up (Table 4.1). Generous bids were doubtless the main reasons for the good response. At the same time the public arguments in favour of amalgamations played a part in conditioning shareholders and customers. The recurring theme of these arguments was the inadequacy of small banks' funds and expertise when faced with the competition of the larger London-and-country banks. In 1890, for instance, the Leeds and County Bank's chairman had acknowledged that 'large and powerful combinations' were 'a necessity to meet the calls now made upon them by mercantile and manufacturing firms'. Eight years later the Oldham Bank chairman agreed their bank could not compete 'with the large institutions which have offices in different parts of the country ... large banks with large resources are able to transact a great deal of business which is both safe and profitable and which is altogether out of the reach of such a small bank as ours'.

Inside the banking community, and especially within the boardrooms of the London-based banks, a wide spread of objectives was making itself felt. Inevitably 'corporate ambition' and the competition for leadership influenced bankers as much as any other business group. Awareness of each bank's performance and ranking was sharpened by

**Table 4.1**

Midland Bank amalgamations, 1892–99

| Date | Bank acquired | Number of branches | Total deposits (£000) | Paid-up capital (£000) | Price of acquisition* (£000) | Ratio Price paid-up capital |
|------|---------------|--------------------|-----------------------|------------------------|------------------------------|------------------------------|
| 1892 | Manchester Joint Stock Bank | 11 | 520 | 103 | 229 | 2.2 |
| 1893 | Bank of Westmorland | 4 | 323 | 26 | 102 | 3.9 |
| 1894 | Preston Banking Co | 26 | 1766 | 200 | 636 | 3.2 |
| 1896 | Carlisle City and District Banking Co | 8 | 742 | 100 | 290 | 2.9 |
| 1897 | Channel Islands Bank | 1 | 311 | 20 | 60 | 3.0 |
| 1897 | Huddersfield Banking Co | 15 | 3335 | 411 | 1084 | 2.6 |
| 1897 | North Western Bank | 8 | 1508 | 405 | 580 | 1.4 |
| 1898 | Oldham Joint Stock Bank | 10 | 1411 | 200 | 600 | 3.0 |
| 1898 | City Bank | 19 | 8996 | 1000 | 2556 | 2.6 |
| 1899 | City of Birmingham Bank | 0 | 245 | 100 | 120 | 1.2 |

*Note** Agreed value of Midland shares and/or cash paid for acquisition

the publication of more detailed financial information. In response to a major statement on banking reserves by Viscount Goschen, Chancellor of the Exchequer, in January 1891, most of the large joint stock banks began to publish monthly statements in July that year. Thereafter the London banks could watch changes in their share of business and measure differences in the balance sheet ratios maintained by most other banks. Contests over acquisitions can only have stimulated each bank's appetite for further expansion, even at the risk of pushing merger prices higher.

At a practical level the striving for leadership amongst a handful of banks was overshadowed by economic pressure on all the banks. A bank's board and management could not ignore the persistence of low interest rates in the 1890s and the resulting depression of banking profits. Midland had not escaped from this predicament despite the expansion of its balance sheet and its net profits (p 118). Dividends were held back at their lowest level of 15 per cent between 1888 and 1896. Under these conditions each bank's attention turned both to the reduction of expenses and to increasing the volume of business which could generate income.

Bankers were more aware of the economies of scale in the 1890s than in the 1870s and 1880s. One of the most obvious advantages of amalgamations between London and country banks was the removal of expensive agency arrangements. In 1896, for example, one of Barclay and Co's partners privately admitted to a Liverpool banker that the Barclays merger with the Gurney banks in East Anglia was 'in order to protect our valuable agency business. We found that the gradual absorption of banks by their larger neighbours was affecting us in this way, and our new departure is therefore to some extent an act of self-defence.' No such considerations had applied earlier in the century, when agency fees had been paid almost indiscriminately. After Midland had acquired Nichols, Baker and Crane in 1862, the Bewdley bank had continued its separate agency arrangements with Barnett Hoare and Co of London. The branch's London business was only moved to the Union Bank of London twenty-two years later, when Barnetts were bought out by Lloyds. By moving to London in 1891, Midland's own agency arrangements became redundant. Over the next seven years the bank's amalgamations allowed the closure of agencies with six separate London banks. As if to underline the new domination of the London-and-country banks, by 1898 Midland's deposits were nearly twice as large as those of the Union Bank of London, its former London agent.

Economies and simplifications were also available in the handling of investments, legal fees and the routine expenses of stationery, printing, postage and telephones. Yet in Midland's case these economies of scale were a secondary objective. The drive to increase the volume of business was as strong as in any of the major banks. 'Our great object in making these additions to our business', Goodman told the shareholders as early as 1891, 'was to build up a strong Bank, one which should command the confidence of the public in every way.' At that time Goodman, like most contemporary bankers, measured the bank's strength in terms of its capital, its reserves, and its support from shareholders. In succeeding years a bank's size and ranking were more often measured in terms of liabilities in general and deposits in particular. It was a distinct shift in attitude, reflecting the greater emphasis upon attracting and competing for new deposits. The negotiation of minimum rates of interest emerged as a time-consuming preoccupation of London bankers during the 1890s.[7] Competition from other types of financial institutions operating on the fringes of banks' traditional markets was already a worry. In 1894, for instance, Midland considered the introduction of 'a scheme for receiving Small Deposits on the lines of the Post Office, the Yorkshire Penny Bank and other similar institutions'. The savings banks, the penny banks, the Post Office Savings Bank, and the cooperative movement continued to take business from the commercial banks throughout the 1890s. By 1898, for example, the trustee savings banks had gathered deposits of over £55 million and the Post Office Savings Bank's total credits exceeded £123 million. Other signs of the high priority of deposit business were the outcries against renewed Bank of England competition in commercial banking.[8] In 1896 Beckett Faber of Beckett and Co, Leeds, complained that the Bank was touting for accounts in Leeds, Hull and Newcastle. R B Martin of Martins Bank, speaking at a meeting of the Central Association of Bankers in June the same year, 'charged the "old lady" with having adopted the role of the "new woman"'.

The emphasis on competing for new deposits was especially strong at Midland. Throughout its years in its home territory of Birmingham, Midland's business had been influenced and often dictated by the borrowing and payment requirements of its own shareholders. Amalgamations in the 1890s diluted that influence. Exceptionally large holdings were already in eclipse by the late 1880s (p 71), and the bank's ownership had then been spread over a wider social and geographical spectrum. Between 1890 and 1897, while the number of shareholders more than doubled from 2049 to 5387, the average paid-up holding fell from £311 to £272. Holden himself 'stipulated that no shareholder should have more than 600 shares' in the bank. Consequently in the takeover of the North Western Bank in 1897 he insisted on paying cash to two very substantial shareholders in the Liverpool bank, rather than allow them to exchange shares.

These changes in the objectives and assumptions of commercial banking meant that, when Holden became Midland's managing director in 1898, the bank's energies were being lavished on the acquisition of new current and deposit accounts. Commentators and contemporary bankers depicted Holden as an aggressive and almost predatory figure in this phase. William Fidgeon, joint general manager of the National Provincial Bank, 'spoke in strong terms of the competition of [Midland] bank' in 1897; in a period when local and national rivalries were at their most intense, Fidgeon apparently saw Midland as an instigator. Beckett Faber, of Beckett and Co, alleged that Holden 'had almost ruined their banking business in Leeds'. Accusations of 'touting' for accounts flew back and forth. Holden warned his managers against 'causing any offence by touting for their accounts', but at the same time he was not sympathetic to the restriction of competition. When the London and South Western Bank proposed a truce in 1906, Midland's board answered 'that it is not in the interest of Bankers to restrain free competition, which would be wrong in principle'.

Much of Holden's reputation for aggression and dynamism was earned through Midland's opening of new branches. In 1892, after a branch had been opened at Brighton, Arthur Keen had asked his co-directors 'what is our Policy? 1st one place then to another', as if to complain that there was no obvious pattern to the extension of branch offices. By the end of the 1890s Holden's answer was to look for representation in every region of England and Wales. This did not yet require blanket coverage of every town and county. It did require branch offices in every major provincial city or town where the bank's customers were likely to need deposit and payments services. Locations not affected by Midland's amalgamations came under review, whether as industrial and commercial centres in their own right, as at Bristol (1899), Southampton (1897), Newcastle (1897) and Cardiff (1898), or in spa towns and resorts such as Cheltenham (1897), Bath (1899), Hastings (1899) and Torquay (1901) or again in expanding London suburbs like Ealing (1898) and Leytonstone (1900).

Not all the new branches fitted this pattern. In cases where amalgamation talks with another bank came to a halt, Midland on occasion responded by opening branches wherever the candidate bank was represented. This had been the result in South Wales in 1893, when negotiations with the National Bank of Wales had broken down (p 90). Similarly a new branch was opened in Nottingham in 1897 when it proved impossible to reach agreement with the Nottingham and Nottinghamshire Banking Company. Conversely, Holden also used public announcements of new branches as 'trailers' for amalgamations. The Huddersfield amalgamation (pp 94–5) was secured when the local bank preferred amalgamation to competing with the incoming bank. There were also examples of rival banks simply giving up a branch office and transferring the business to Midland. This relatively painless method of enlarging the branch network was adopted at Rotherhithe, where the London Joint Stock Bank sold its branch to Midland in 1893, and Aldershot, where Midland took over the Metropolitan Bank's business in 1904.

To open an entirely new branch was to touch rival banks on their most sensitive nerve. In most cases a new arrival was bound to take away deposits and agency business from existing banks. This, and the capture of new business, was reflected in the relatively high level of deposit accounts gathered by Midland's new branches. In December 1898 the average credit value of current accounts in the new branches was only £88 compared with £224 in the bank as a whole. Customers' deposit accounts, in contrast, were worth an average of £473 in the new branches and only £296 in all branches.[9] It was in this competition for deposit business that Holden created so much alarm amongst his contemporaries. When Midland was about to open branches in Bath and Bristol in April 1899, for example, a Lloyds manager admitted that 'we don't trouble about their opening in Bath, they are not class enough, but we fear their going to Bristol'. Soon afterwards, Lloyds were reported to be 'furious' at the opening of the Bristol branches; 'the only Bank that has not succeeded is the London and Provincial'.

It was characteristic of Holden that he should have taken charge of selecting sites and approving designs—even to the tiniest detail of furniture and fittings—for the new branches. He believed that, at a time when the banking community still frowned upon advertising or 'touting' of any kind, the location and appearance of the branches was one of the only means of reaching the market for banking services. With T B Whinney, a professional architect who was commissioned to design and supervise the building of the new branches from about 1900, Holden toured possible sites and encouraged Whinney to design branch buildings of a standardized pattern and quality. Whinney reported directly to Holden, meeting him at least once a month, and by 1905 the architect was dealing with building work at more than ten branches at a time.

Aggressive as Midland's branch extensions may have seemed, they were not the main platform for the bank's growth in the early part of the century. It has been calculated that in the period from 1900 to 1909 only 135 new branches were opened while 247 were added by amalgamation; by 1909 only 40 per cent of the bank's 658 branches had been started from scratch.[10] In terms of deposits (the first business priority for the new offices) only 45 per cent of the increase of £86 million in the bank's deposits between 1892 and 1914 came from new and existing branches. The remainder was attributable to amalgamations in that period.[11] Not least, the new branches were slow to produce profits. In 1897, for example, the most profitable branches were the old head offices of the constituent banks, especially Huddersfield (£25,193 net in the second half), Liverpool (£14,606 in the second half), Leeds Park Row (£24,748) and Preston (£23,023). By contrast branches created by Midland since 1891 incurred total net losses of £622 during 1897. The new branches were proving to be expensive to run. According to Goodman, salary costs in the new branches took 86 per cent of their gross profits in 1894 and 59 per cent the following year, compared to averages of 36 and 34 per cent in the otherwise expensive London branches.

These results confirmed that the primary factor in the bank's growth and earnings continued to be its acquisition of other banks. Specifically, Midland maintained its preference for buying other joint stock banks. For although the bank's shareholders were not so influential in the direction and quality of its business, their role in bringing in new accounts was not forgotten. The purchase of a joint stock bank— especially when it was taken over by exchange of shares—ensured the continuity of several hundred accounts. The takeover of a private bank carried no such promise, especially if the managing partners retired from banking after accepting a bid.

The opportunism which had been so decisive in the Union Bank of Birmingham merger in 1883 was again deployed in the first years of Holden's sole command. An obvious parallel was the acquisition of the City of Birmingham Bank in 1899. This two-year-old bank had been launched in an effort to counteract the amalgamation movement and to revive the concept of a local joint stock bank. This brave initiative had attracted deposits of less than £250,000 and was already making losses by 1899. Its business and single office at Temple Row, Birmingham, were bought by Midland for only £120,000 in cash. Inexpensive deals of this kind were increasingly hard to find however, and in his first two years as managing director Holden was drawn into abortive negotiations with the Lincoln and Lindsey Banking Company (p 124), the Craven Bank, the Nottingham Joint Stock Bank (p 106), the 'BDC' (presumably the Birmingham District and Counties Bank) and the Union Bank of Manchester.

Holden's tactics in each proposed amalgamation justified his reputation for aggressive bargaining. Often sparked off by Midland's proposal to open a competing branch, negotiations with country banks usually opened with hard-talking sessions at one of the major railway hotels in London or the provincial cities. Holden would stress the strengths of the London-and-country banks and the hopelessness of the competitive position of the smaller banks. 'It was the policy of the day to form large institutions', he told 'Mr W' in 1900; 'our bank combined with his would command the best business and destroy active competition.' He was a master of exploiting any differences of opinion within the board and management of a country bank, especially when the chairman or directors showed the slightest inclination towards peaceful retirement from the banking scene. This style risked opposition from the existing management of banks under offer. The general manager of the Union Bank of Manchester, for example, resented the prospect of 'a lecture on banking from Mr Holden'. Others were worried about their own future after an amalgamation. In 1901 a Yorkshire banker was afraid that if Holden 'once got into his Bank as [he] had got into the Halifax [he] should hold him under his finger and thumb' (merger talks with the Halifax Joint Stock Bank had fallen through in 1899). Holden was undoubtedly capable of demolishing the financial statements offered by the country banks. In several cases he 'pitched into' the provisions for bad and doubtful debts. This was a point of special vulnerability in many smaller banks at the turn of the century, at a time when many of their business customers had overextended their borrowing to meet demand during the Boer War. Holden rarely used the calculation of provisions as the excuse for breaking off merger negotiations but it was always valuable in reducing the final price. This factor, and the degree of cooperation shown by the existing regime in a country bank, obviously affected the choice of management after the amalgamation. In most cases the entire management was retained, often with complex and generous service agreements. In exceptional cases either total opposition to an offer or a simple clash of personalities made it impossible for a former chief manager to continue in post after amalgamation. This had occurred in the City Bank takeover, when one of the joint general managers (D G H Pollock) became a general manager of Midland and the other left after 'unsatisfactory' interviews with Holden.

Prominent as these signs of opportunism and aggression may have been, the principal amalgamations after the City Bank merger were more obviously part of a planned expansion. Each of the five banks taken over between 1900 and 1908 fitted a similar financial, structural and geographical pattern. The search for new deposits turned the emphasis towards multi-branch country banks in regions where the bank's representation was thin. Negotiations for small or single-office banks (such as the Whitehaven Joint Stock Bank and Ashby and Co of Staines) were quickly abandoned. Holden's diagnosis of the financial and managerial health of a country bank also became clearer. The five banks acquired in that period were all under-capitalized but with large numbers of shareholders, and relatively 'overlent' but free of serious bad debts.

The first four of the mergers on this model developed and reinforced the bank's network in the east Midlands and Yorkshire. The Leicestershire Banking Company, amalgamated in March 1900, was an efficiently-run bank but its lending to manufacturers of boots, shoes and hosiery was threatening to outrun the growth of its deposits. 'We have now arrived at the position', the Leicester chairman admitted, 'that we must either refuse new business, however good, or increase our resources.' Total advances were within a whisker of total deposits of £3.3 million, and this highly unusual bias helped to keep Midland's price down to £1.33 million, the market value of 25,666 shares given in exchange to the Leicester proprietors. The group of 28 town-and-country branches in Leicestershire and Northamptonshire was a compact and strong network, and, when combined with Midland's existing business in Leicester and Northampton, the merger gave the bank primacy over its immediate competitors in the region. A renewed offer for the Nottingham Joint Stock Bank in the following year built on this position. Again the local bank was overextended by Nottingham's highly-diversified industrial growth. Agreement was delayed for another four years, when Holden forced the pace by threatening to open a larger Nottingham branch in Midland's own name. At the time of the merger in November 1905, the Nottingham bank's 29 offices had accumulated deposits of £2 million. Holden settled for cash payments and an exchange of shares worth £560,000 to the Nottingham shareholders.

In the interval between the Leicester and Nottingham mergers Holden secured two similar agreements in Yorkshire. The 1890 acquisitions had given Midland a strong position in Leeds but it was not yet able to challenge the Yorkshire Banking Company and the York City and County Bank, both of which had branches throughout the north-east. The growth of the Yorkshire Penny Bank and the savings banks added to the urgency of reinforcing the bank's position in the county. Holden commissioned a detailed review of existing bank facilities in Yorkshire in 1899 and 1900. The result, in the summer of 1901, was successive bids for the Sheffield Union Banking Company and the Yorkshire Banking Company. The two banks shared a common ancestry, as the Sheffield Union had been created to take over the Yorkshire's original Sheffield business when it was reconstructed in 1843. Since the 1870s both banks had also been overexposed on large industrial accounts, notably the Sheffield Union's connection with the Naylor Vickers steelworks and the Yorkshire's involvement with Bolckow Vaughan, the Middlesbrough steelmakers. By 1901, however, the Sheffield Union's cultivation of a branch network had brought it deposits of £1.4 million; the Yorkshire Banking Company, with no less than 63 branches, had attracted deposits of nearly £5 million. The Sheffield bank accepted Midland shares worth £450,000. Later that year, after fierce arguments between Holden and the Yorkshire's general manager, the Yorkshire Banking Company's board and shareholders agreed to a price of £1.47 million in shares and cash. Sir James Kitson, the Yorkshire Banking Company's

**Table 4.2**

Midland Bank amalgamations, 1900–08

| Date | Bank acquired | Number of branches | Total deposits (£000) | Paid-up capital (£000) | Price of acquisition* (£000) | Ratio Price / paid-up capital |
|------|---------------|--------------------|----------------------|----------------------|----------------------------|----------------------------|
| 1900 | Leicestershire Banking Co | 28 | 3285 | 490 | 1335 | 2.7 |
| 1901 | Sheffield Union Banking Co | 17 | 1440 | 180 | 450 | 2.5 |
| 1901 | Yorkshire Banking Co | 63 | 4952 | 375 | 1472 | 3.9 |
| 1905 | Nottingham Joint Stock Bank | 28 | 2004 | 200 | 560 | 2.8 |
| 1908 | North and South Wales Bank | 108 | 11,227 | 750 | 2625 | 3.5 |

*Note** Agreed value of Midland shares and/or cash for acquisition

chairman who was also a director of the Kitson locomotive engineering group, joined Midland's board as part of the agreement.

When Midland acquired the North and South Wales Bank in 1908, it was at that time the fullest development of Holden's search for multi-branch country banks in need of capital and diversification. Founded in Liverpool in 1836, the 'Wales Bank' was active mainly in north Wales and the Mersey region, with useful support in Cheshire and Shropshire. For most of the nineteenth century it had been guided by George Rae, doyen of country bankers, and the quality of management and book-keeping systems had comfortably supported a branch network of over 100 offices. In the decade after Rae's retirement in 1898, nevertheless, the Wales Bank was badly hit by the depreciation in security values and by periodic crises in the Liverpool cotton trade. Howard Lloyd of Lloyds Bank sought an amalgamation as early as 1899, and seven years later a merger with the Lancashire and Yorkshire Bank, based at Manchester, was being considered.

The American financial crisis of 1907 eventually persuaded the Wales Bank to accept Midland's offer, worth a total of £2.625 million in shares and cash. Four of the Liverpool bank's directors joined Midland's board. In return Midland added £11 million to its deposits, making the Wales Bank the largest business to have changed hands during the bank amalgamation movement before the London and County and London and Westminster merger in 1909. Midland's nominal capital, which had been raised to £16.2 million to pay for the Yorkshire amalgamations in 1901, was lifted to £22.2 million to provide for the exchange of shares in 1908. This adjustment, raising Midland to second position to Lloyds in terms of nominal and paid-up capital, also created spare capacity of 66,072 shares (worth about £3.3 million) for new acquisitions.

Midland's wider range of objectives in the 1890s and early 1900s could only be achieved with a strong and obvious pattern of command. To contemporaries the bank often appeared to have become a one-man show, with Holden acting all the leading roles as well as directing, moving the scenery and manning the box office. One money market broker admitted in 1901 that his opinion of the bank depended entirely on his opinion of its managing director: 'Holden is able, and his Directors think a lot of him. He is on good terms with himself.' Certainly his own diaries and letters give the impression that most decisions were transmitted through his office. He insisted on dealing with small details of staff discipline or the design of bank furniture as well as with the larger questions of amalgamations or branch extensions. He did not hold any outside directorships and he had few interests outside the bank.[12] In his brief period as Liberal MP for Heywood, Manchester, between 1906 and 1910 'my course was to say nothing' in case any political entanglement damaged the bank's interests.

In reality Holden was extremely reluctant to usurp the authority of his own board of directors. Throughout the 1890s and the Edwardian period Midland's directors were a 'working' board, with a full timetable of committee meetings. The directors' committees dealt with branch extensions, finance, special advances and stock exchange loans. These committees met weekly, in addition to the full board meeting each week. Under a simplified structure introduced in 1906, a London committee of eight directors considered all advances of between £2000 and £5000, bills (except in Yorkshire and Leicestershire), stock exchange loans and share transfers. A parallel country committee of four directors dealt with bills in Yorkshire and Leicestershire and finance or general charges. By then most of Midland's directors were either former bankers or former chairmen of the constituent banks, and they clearly made an essential contribution to the bank's routine work as well as to the larger strategic issues. In this way Midland's board was quite distinct from the other major banks, where directorships were more often dominated by merchant bankers and the representatives of political and non-industrial interests.[13]

Holden himself was keen to maintain a strong and effective board, and he relied upon the help of senior directors such as Bradshaw, Dixon-Hartland, Vanner and W F Wyley (a former director of the Coventry Union Bank). Whereas some other London-and-country banks created local boards of directors in succession to banks taken over, Midland emphasized the recruitment of individual directors to its main board. A number of the bank's amalgamations had been carried through on the understanding that 'advisory boards' would continue to meet at the old head offices of the constituent banks. The board of the Channel Islands Bank, for example, was to continue for five years after the amalgamation in 1897, and a 'joint' board was created at Oldham after the 1898 merger. In the event the advisory boards had brief and shadowy existences, all disappearing within a few months of the relevant amalgamations. The only exception was the 'Liverpool Board' created after the North and South Wales Bank merger in 1908. This committee of seven ex-Wales Bank directors advised the main board on applications of over £2000 from the Liverpool branches. The specialist character of Liverpool business— and the residual strength of Wales Bank traditions—ensured this committee's survival until 1953.

Centralized authority was also a feature of Holden's managerial command. The general managers of the constituent country banks usually continued as local branch managers, and Pollock of the City Bank was the only individual to retain general manager status after an amalgamation by Midland (p 105). Within the bank's head office, however, Holden was increasingly willing to delegate authority. A small circle of ex-New Street bankers was especially important to him. When Holden became managing director in 1898, two other joint general managers were appointed in addition to Pollock. These two, Samuel Murray and John Madders, had both served with Holden at Birmingham in the 1880s. Murray was undoubtedly Holden's key adviser. He had already been involved in the amalgamations, and in the mergers concluded after 1898 he completed each settlement after Holden had opened the negotiations. All three general managers also took responsibility for administration and financial control in their 'divisions'. Before the Wales Bank merger in 1908 these divisions were simply the grouping of branches in geographical 'sections' (Tables 4.3 and 4.4, pp 114 and 116). Murray took charge of the northern sections. Madders was responsible for the Midlands and southern sections and Pollock supervised the London business.

Rather than being sent out into these divisions the general managers controlled them from their London base. Their assistants and inspectors also operated from Threadneedle Street. Consequently for most

**Figure 4.1** *Midland Bank board and management structure, c 1900*

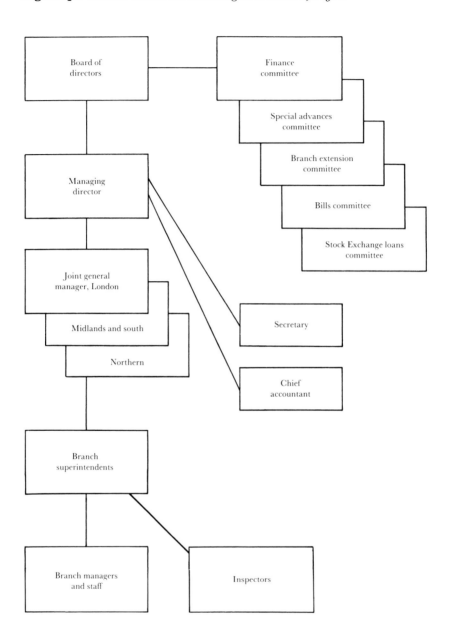

business purposes the main line of contact lay between the divisional general manager with his staff in London and the managers of the branches (Figure 4.1). This type of command was heavily dependent upon, firstly, the loyalty and discipline of the bank's staff (especially at branch manager level) and, secondly, the effectiveness of communications and systems within the bank.

Holden, along with Murray, Madders and Midland's other senior managers, had taken the hard route through branch banking at the beginning of his career. This upbringing made him acutely conscious of the size and performance of the bank's workforce. At Midland, total staff numbers mushroomed from 553 at a salary cost of £77,781 in 1893 to 2887 at a cost of £450,564 in 1908. Centralized disciplines, Holden believed, were essential if the bank was to take the strain of this very rapid expansion. The demarcation of jobs which had become necessary in the late 1870s and early 1880s was now extended to cope with the growing volume of specialist commodity business, stock exchange loans and foreign payments. All these services needed teams of ledger-keepers and securities clerks.

The expansion of staff numbers required uniform division of managerial and clerical duties and full protection against fraud, petty misdemeanours or mere slackness. Some bankers resented this pressure. The profession was already overcrowded and the amalgamation movement had intensified worries about career prospects, pay, and the introduction of labour saving methods during the rationalization of head offices. 'One effect of the modern centralization', the *Bankers' Magazine* argued, 'had been to limit greatly the numbers of those who will in fact rise to well-paid posts.'[14] Others had more personal reasons for grievance. In 1909 Holden instituted a rule that clerks should not marry unless they already received a salary of £150. He explained that 'he had considerable difficulties with young men getting married on insufficient means, and they subsequently got into difficulties out of which they had to be extricated by the bank'.

Protests and dismissals were rare, however, and Holden's striving for loyalty and discipline was largely successful. His preference for personal interviews (or interrogation) earned obvious respect amongst the bank's staff. Above all he never forgot that branch staff were in the front line of modern banking. Branch managers and their staff, although still handling a relatively small armoury of banking services, were competing to establish the bank's reputation as well as to obtain new business. Many of them, especially in new branches, were remote from help and advice. In these outposts, small units of newly-arrived bankers could be thrown up against the prestige of older-established local banks or the intense competition of the other nationwide banks. Holden was always anxious that these new units were given support and reinforcement, even if that meant constant intervention in the working of branches. 'Write to me personally every two days', he told the junior manager of a new branch in 1904; 'report how you are getting on and what progress you are making.'

Short lines of communication with branch bankers were not of course a complete answer to effective staff management. Holden could offer improved pay and prospects; the salaries paid by the constituent banks were brought up to Midland's levels or, if already higher, were allowed to remain. The result was a range of salaries in most branches between about £350 for managers and £40 for new juniors. Clerks' salaries averaged between £100 and £150, with much higher levels for managers and staff in city centre branches. Similarly—contrary to the *Bankers' Magazine*'s gloomy interpretation—the opportunities within Midland were massively increased by the opening of new branches and the enlargement of the head office divisional staff. Branches opened between 1890 and 1909 created no less than 246 managerial and sub-managerial posts, and the number of branch superintendents and inspectors increased from 13 to 21 between 1897 and 1909. These prospects were supported by the bank's own classes and examinations, subscriptions for about 1000 memberships of the Institute of Bankers (higher than any other bank) and, not least, a uniform pension scheme. The 'Officers Pension Fund', introduced in 1897 and rationalized in 1904, was in addition to the Mutual Provident and Widows' Fund which had been inherited from the City Bank and extended to the whole bank in 1901.

The drive towards centralized control coloured Midland's business methods as well as its staff organization. From the late 1890s Midland's branch managers worked to standardized regulations and procedures, continually updated by new instructions and circulars. Each branch's book-keeping and administration were brought into line with the Midland model, and the systems of the constituent banks rapidly disappeared. Liverpool, with special regulations for the accounts of cotton and commodity brokers, was again an exception.

The standardization of branch routines reflected the more systematic approach to commercial banking throughout the country in the late nineteenth century, especially after the foundation of the professional institutes in Scotland and England in the 1870s. To branch managers and to their accountants and clerks, the main adjustments were in the evaluation of securities and bills and in the handling of bad and doubtful debts. Many contemporaries and banking historians nevertheless assumed that the principal alteration was the introduction of a more rule-bound, mechanistic approach to lending. The complaint was that the major London-and-country banks such as Midland, Lloyds and the London and County introduced comparatively low limits on the lending authority of their branch managers, with the result that larger applications needing local knowledge were sent on to head office bankers with little or no appreciation of regional needs. 'The most important part of the business of banking—the lending of the bank's funds—has become centralized in the advance department at the head office', the *Bankers' Magazine* alleged: 'the managers and chief officials at the branches have been relieved of much of their responsibility'.[15] L Joseph, an early commentator on industrial finance, argued in 1911 that overdrafts granted by branches of the clearing banks were 'not of great importance; at any rate they cannot be relied upon at all times, and therefore nobody can count upon them absolutely'.[16]

In Midland's case, advances above £2000 needed board approval from the turn of the century. This approach actually allowed more discretion to branch managers than had been provided by many of the banks which Midland had taken over. In London the City Bank's discretionary limits for its London managers were either £500 or £1000 in the mid-1890s,[17] while at the London Joint Stock Bank (p 129) all unsecured loans of over £300 were referred to the 'Bill Committee' and applications for £1000 and over were reported to the weekly board meetings. In the country the Leicestershire Banking Company required their branch managers to send every single application for head office approval. At the North and South Wales Bank the same rule applied, except for 'temporary overdrafts of moderate amount to regular and useful customers of known means'; even those applications were referred to the bank's head office by 'special letter'.

As far as the bank's customers were concerned, the processing of loan applications was only part of a changed pattern of service. Even though Holden was prepared to allocate many lending decisions to his branch managers, his preference for amalgamation and centralization was bound to effect Midland's business as a whole. The public justification for most of the bank amalgamations and extensions of the 1890s and early 1900s, including those by Midland, was that the enlarged banks could provide a more accessible and efficient service to their customers (pp 100–1). The directors of the Yorkshire Banking Company, for instance, told the Leeds newspapers that they had recognized 'the advantages which could accrue from an alliance with

**Table 4.3**

Ratios of advances and bills discounted to deposits in divisions of Midland Bank, 1896–98

| Division | 1 Dec 1896 | 5 June 1897 | 6 Dec 1897 | 7 June 1898 | 1 Dec 1898 |
|---|---|---|---|---|---|
| **London** | 0.52 | 0.47 | 0.50 | 0.60 | 0.57 |
| **Lancashire** | | | | | |
| Carlisle | 0.91 | 0.87 | 0.85 | 0.80 | 0.68 |
| Liverpool (North Western Bank) | — | — | 0.96 | 0.97 | 0.96 |
| Manchester | 1.12 | 0.94 | 0.90 | 0.87 | 0.83 |
| Oldham | — | — | — | 0.79 | 0.66 |
| Preston | 0.70 | 0.73 | 0.65 | 0.66 | 0.58 |
| Westmorland | 0.26 | 0.29 | 0.24 | 0.26 | 0.26 |
| **Midlands** | 0.57 | 0.56 | 0.59 | 0.60 | 0.55 |
| **Southern** | | | | | |
| Jersey | — | 0.54 | 0.30 | 0.33 | 0.24 |
| **Yorkshire** | | | | | |
| Huddersfield | — | — | 0.67 | 0.70 | 0.74 |
| Yorkshire | 0.74 | 0.67 | 0.60 | 0.66 | 0.65 |
| **New branches** | 1.05 | 1.16 | 1.21 | 0.99 | 0.81 |
| TOTAL | **0.67** | **0.63** | **0.67** | **0.70** | **0.64** |

*Source:* C A E Goodhart, *The Business of Banking, 1891–1914* (Weidenfeld and Nicolson, 1972), p 159

a large bank having a powerful connection in London and all over the country, instead of continuing as a comparatively small institution carrying on business within a limited area and dependent on another bank to transact its business in London'.[18] George Pownall, a future president of the Institute of Bankers, elaborated this theme in 1900:

> the legitimate needs of individual firms or companies are greater, and the small banker is in the nature of things cut off from conducting such business, or, if he does conduct it, he does so by putting too many of his eggs into one basket, and by denying to the bulk of his smaller customers ... the accommodation they naturally look for.[19]

Complex as the real objectives for expansion were, how successful were the banks in meeting their published promises of improved service? Much depended upon the category of customer and the geographical location. Private customers and small traders, particularly if their main needs were a current or deposit account for payments and saving, enjoyed an unprecedented growth of banking facilities in the late Victorian and Edwardian period. The total number of bank branches in England and Wales was lifted from 2075 in 1884 to 4621 in 1904, when Midland's share was 445 branches. All these branch banks were anxious to acquire new business, and personal customers were ideally placed to benefit from inter-bank competition on services, rates, or lending limits. A customer of Midland was especially well-provided for in London, the Midlands, Lancashire and Yorkshire, but did not yet have an easily-accessible service in the Home Counties, East Anglia, the south-west or (before 1908) in Wales.

The type of service to a business customer needing advances or bill finance also varied by region. The creation of a more diversified and balanced branch network enabled the bank to allow higher levels of lending in certain districts. Midland's balance sheets in 1896–98 showed huge variations in the ratio of advances and bills to deposits (Table 4.3).

Except for the new branches, where the ratio was the result of generous accommodation while a new business was being established, the high ratios in Liverpool and Manchester were made possible by relatively low levels of lending in London and the Midlands. The pattern was similar ten years later (Table 4.4).

Variations were also emerging in the treatment of different types and sizes of business account. From the mid-1890s onwards very large corporate accounts won a small but discernible advantage. These were not the type of local industrial customers which had played so big a part in the bank's early history. On the one hand they were customers of a larger and less fragile bank where major corporate loans comprised a smaller proportion of earning assets. On the other hand the new large company customers were themselves operating on a broader national or international scale.

A first advantage for these companies lay in being able to negotiate directly with Holden and his general managers. Prominent examples included Dudley Docker, the rapidly-rising Midlands industrialist, William Pirrie (Lord Pirrie from 1905) of Harland and Wolff, the Belfast shipbuilders, Arthur Keen's own Guest Keen and Nettlefold interests, and Gordon Selfridge, founder of the Oxford Street department store. The leaders of amalgamations in other industries

## Table 4.4

Values and ratios of advances and bills discounted to deposits in divisions of Midland Bank, 1908

| Division | 30 June 1908 Advances & bills (£000) | Ratio: deposits | 31 Dec 1908 Advances & bills (£000) | Ratio: deposits |
|---|---|---|---|---|
| **London** | | | | |
| Head office | 1861 | 9.64 | 1821 | 5.52 |
| London | 2757 | 0.66 | 3508 | 0.61 |
| City Bank | 6913 | 0.71 | 7170 | 0.69 |
| New branches | 620 | 0.49 | — | — |
| **Lancashire** | | | | |
| Carlisle | 663 | 0.42 | 717 | 0.43 |
| Liverpool | 1455 | 0.91 | 1431 | 0.77 |
| Manchester | 1494 | 0.90 | 1483 | 0.86 |
| Oldham | 979 | 0.61 | 928 | 0.66 |
| Preston | 2288 | 0.80 | 1991 | 0.68 |
| **Midlands** | | | | |
| Leicestershire | 2975 | 0.82 | 2907 | 0.72 |
| Midland | 4000 | 0.49 | 3995 | 0.48 |
| Nottingham | 1083 | 0.50 | 1102 | 0.49 |
| **Southern** | 1506 | 0.57 | 1608 | 0.54 |
| **Yorkshire** | | | | |
| Huddersfield | 1861 | 0.67 | 1688 | 0.60 |
| Sheffield | 1531 | 0.70 | 1532 | 0.64 |
| Yorkshire Banking | 3216 | 0.58 | 3387 | 0.59 |
| Yorkshire | 1666 | 0.59 | 1844 | 0.57 |
| TOTAL | **36,868** | **0.68** | 37,112 | 0.64 |

came directly to Holden, as in the case of the Bradford Dyers' Assocation and Scott Lings (promoter of the Cotton Fine Spinners' Association and the Bradford Woolcombers' Association). Their other advantage lay in the wider range of services for which they could use the bank. Midland's multiplying links with overseas banks were one such benefit, especially after the City Bank merger (Chapter Five). Other corporate services now included receiving applications and acting as registrar for new issues. Midland's earliest recorded issue was a $£\frac{1}{4}$ million stock for the Chesterfield Gas and Water Board in 1896, soon followed by tenders for other municipal loans and new issues for the Elswick Cycle Company (1896) and the Bradford Dyers' Association (1898).

These types of service were not normally useful to the small and medium-sized companies using the bank. Customers in this category undoubtedly suffered additional disadvantages from the sheer size of their bank. The problem was not so much the 'bureaucratic' elements in the enlarged banks which some contemporaries complained of, particularly over the discretion allowed to branch managers in their lending decisions (p 113). As a more specific difficulty, the enormous number of business accounts handled by the banks meant that they tended to classify and lump together those accounts for the control of lending. As a result some customers found their applications being judged not on their own security and track record but on the basis of limits on lending to particular sectors. The City Bank had restricted loans on the securities of mining and exploration companies to a total of £250,000 in 1895, and in October 1896 it 'decided that loans on public houses had reached a sufficiently high figure and that it was expedient to discourage an increase of such business'. In 1896 Midland itself compiled an analysis of the accounts of customers in the 'cycle, cycle fittings, cycle tubes and other accessory trades'. The return showed advances of £196,000 against credits of £580,000 but the board decided that the balances for the industry as a whole should be 'revised from time to time'. Colliery accounts were managed in the same way, although Holden admitted in January 1900 that 'our Board is very prejudiced against collieries. They refused an account the other day with a credit balance of £20/30,000.' This style of categorization was largely dictated by the bank's bad debt experience in particular industries, so that the facilities given to the relevant customers obviously fluctuated with the fortunes of other accounts in the same category. Yet it is doubtful whether these customers would have had better service from the remaining country banks. Some, like the Leicestershire Banking Company or the Cumberland Union Bank, were so overlent to single industries that their accommodation may have aggravated the problems of the local economy; others, such as the small or single-office joint stock banks, had no capacity to balance lending between sectors or regions.

When Holden was elected Midland's chairman in 1908 the bank's concentration on deposit-taking had given it second place amongst the banks of England and Wales in terms of total current and deposit accounts. For a bank which was not fully committed to a London headquarters until 1898, Midland's rapid promotion in the rankings underlined the fundamental and continuing importance of provincial banking business. The position of Lloyds, whose deposits of £73 million were the only business larger than Midland's deposits of £67 million, was further proof of the extraordinary strength of the Birmingham tradition; the London banks seemed limited and unambitious by comparison. Although they were now fully 'metropolitan' in character, the two largest banks in England and Wales were emphatically not dominated by London business or London bankers. Midland itself was highly centralized under Holden's management but at this stage centralization reflected a managerial outlook rather than a business bias towards London.

Midland's conquest of new territory in the 1890s and early 1900s brought with it formidable extra responsibilities. In 1898 the bank was already liable for some 95,000 separate current and deposit accounts and by 1908 the total had reached 245,192.[20] The bank had also emerged as a major employer, with 2887 staff in 1908. Meanwhile, as the oldest of its responsibilities, the number of shareholders had increased nearly threefold from 5387 in 1893 to 14,200 in 1908.

If there was a single factor which brought the interests of these groups together, it was the stability and security of the bank rather than spectacular profitability. The 1890s had in any case reduced expectations of banking profits, and the attention had switched to steady returns. In July 1899, for example, in one of his last letters to Holden, John Goodman advised against fluctuations in the half-yearly dividends of more than one per cent:

> I know you don't care about following other Banks. . . . I feel sure the shareholders would prefer a regular dividend—it would, further, have the advantage of being less bothering to the market. By regular dividend I don't want to bind you to a strictly uniform dividend, but let it follow the profits making use of your reserves to secure as much uniformity as would be prudent.

Goodman's successors responded by keeping the bank's dividends at between 18 and 18.5 per cent for the first decade of the century. These returns compared closely with those of Lloyds Bank (18.12 to 18.75 per cent) but were rather higher than those of Barclays (at 15 per cent) or the Union of London and Smiths Bank (11 to 12 per cent).[21]

It was equally important that the bank should show no sign of stress or instability in the face of crisis. The nineteenth-century crises—in 1857, 1866 and 1878—had seriously tested each bank and the commercial banking system as a whole. In the banking community after the Baring crisis, however, few banks showed fragility during a succession of potentially damaging incidents. Midland and the other London-and-country banks were especially resilient. The difficulties of Dumbell's Banking Company on the Isle of Man throughout the 1890s (leading to its closure in 1900), the Hooley frauds, and cotton frauds in the Liverpool-American trade in 1907 made no great impact on the business profile of the major banks. Remarkably Midland and its chief rivals were also largely unaffected by the financial crises in Australia in 1893 and the United States in 1907. Certainly the Bank of England bore the brunt of managing the effects of these international crises, releasing the commercial banks from serious strain. The lack of disturbance in Midland's business was nevertheless a measure of the successful diversification of its risks. Emergencies which would have once threatened the life of dozens of country banks were now absorbed quickly and without panic. From this perspective Midland's uninterrupted progress had secured it a strong defensive position as well as a reputation for aggressive expansion.

❋

# CHAPTER FIVE

# COLOSSUS
## 1908–1919

The first two decades of the twentieth century were a new heyday for amalgamations, alliances and reorganizations in British business. Giant combines were created in the steel and armaments industries, in engineering, textiles and transport. Even more consolidation was needed to meet the extraordinary economic demands of the 1914–18 war, and by then very large-scale finance and management were an essential part of government industrial activity as well as of the private sector. Few industries underwent such transformation and concentration as banking. The largest ten banks in England and Wales, having captured 46 per cent of deposits by 1900, increased that share to 97 per cent by 1920.[1] Soon after the end of the First World War, Midland, Barclays, Lloyds, National Provincial and Westminster had already emerged as the 'Big Five' group of banks which was to dominate British commercial banking for the next fifty years.

The sheer size and spread of these banks' interests forced a change in the perception of banking business, particularly in the climactic period immediately before and after the 1914–18 war. Until then, bankers themselves had shared with their customers and shareholders the assumption that the main duty of the banks was to provide a payments and deposit service on a commercial basis. That service might be local, regional or national, but it would not normally extend outside England and Wales. In the Edwardian period, in contrast, the scale and range of banking services quickly expanded and the major banks began to behave and to be treated as organizations with a much larger and more public role. They emerged as institutions which held expectations and responsibilities stretching far beyond their traditional business functions.

The transition was at its most obvious in the relationships between the banks and public policy. Throughout the history of commercial banking, especially since the arrival of the joint stock banks in the 1820s, bankers' contacts with government had centred on questions of the banks' legal status, the protection of bank customers and share-holders, and the control of banknote issues. Under these conditions bankers were cast in the role of petitioners 'against the shackles of restrictive and discriminatory legislation'; interventions on broader public concerns—as in the bankruptcy law reforms of 1883—had been rare.[2] Successive governments had for their part made little effort to involve the banks in economic affairs. Even during the Baring crisis the contribution of the commercial banks had been orchestrated on the independent initiative of the Bank of England rather than by Whitehall. The pattern altered significantly after the turn of the century. Both on their own initiative and by invitation the banks were acknowledged to have a role in economic policy and even foreign policy. This was partly the outcome of the change of government; the election of the Liberal administration in 1905, with its programme of ambitious social and economic reforms, immediately brought the City within closer reach of government. At the same time the banks themselves were ready to broaden their economic responsibilities and in some cases to influence policy.

Edward Holden, as Midland's chairman and managing director between 1908 and 1919, epitomized this change. His activities and well-reported statements impinged upon government as well as upon the other banks and the rest of the financial sector. In that way he was fashioning the public view of not only his own bank but the major clearing banks as a whole. In this decisive phase in banking, he could not be left out of the calculations of bankers or government ministers. A W Kiddy, a leading contemporary financial journalist, saw him as 'a kind of superman in the banking world'. *The Times* agreed that 'no man has done more to mould the tendencies of modern British banking'.[3] Banking historians have generally accepted this view of Holden's importance. He was 'a colossus in the banking world'; if Felix Schuster of the Union of London and Smiths Bank was the 'intellectual and theoretical leader among contemporary bankers', Holden was 'probably responsible for the greatest changes in the structure of banking' between 1891 and 1914.[4]

Holden's reputation was based first and foremost upon the way in which Midland enlarged and diversified its business under his leadership. No amount of economic sophistication would have made up in public influence for the size and content of the bank's balance sheet. In most eyes, Midland's graduation from relative obscurity in the early 1890s to being the largest bank in the world in 1919 was

Holden's personal, autocratic achievement. To Sir John Clapham, historian of the Bank of England, Holden was 'the dominant and aggressive leader of the London City and Midland Bank'.[5] Certainly his directors were in no doubt of his value to the bank. Effusive tributes to general managers at shareholders' meetings were one of the oldest traditions in British banking, but the praise heaped on Holden in the early 1900s was exceptional. 'The administrative genius and strong controlling hand of our able Managing Director', the deputy chairman told the shareholders in 1901, 'make themselves felt in every department of the Bank, and it is not too much to say that his indomitable energy inspires and animates the whole staff from Carlisle and Newcastle in the north to Brighton and Southampton in the south.' A more exact valuation was attempted in 1907, shortly before Holden added the chairmanship to his duties as managing director. He was already unusual amongst bankers in being granted a service agreement: originally negotiated in 1899, the contract was revised in 1907 to give him a salary of £6000, a special bonus of £15,000, a pension of £3000, and an additional death benefit of £5000.

While the impression of personal rule was to be sustained throughout Holden's chairmanship, in reality he was increasingly prepared to delegate managerial responsibility. The three joint general managers appointed in 1898 took the main burden. Samuel Murray and John Madders had been especially close to Holden since their recruitment in Birmingham (p 109). D G H Pollock, the third new general manager after the City Bank merger in 1898, retired in 1907. His successor, W H Hillman, was also a product of the City Bank at Threadneedle Street, but he in turn retired in 1909. The choice of a replacement looked further forward. Only thirty-nine at the time of his appointment, Frederick Hyde had begun his career in 1885 with the Derby Commercial Bank shortly before its amalgamation with Midland in 1890. Holden evidently selected him for rapid promotion, and by 1907 he was a joint manager at Threadneedle Street. There Holden instructed him in his own personal view of banking:

> You have had to be the bull-terrier . . . . I am getting toned down as I get older, and I want you to profit by my experience. Your policy therefore must be to go gently and quietly. Whatever you have to do with your customers, let it be the gentle and the quiet policy. Wherever you can, play up to these London gentlemen.

Much of the groundwork of Midland's expansion under Holden's chairmanship was left to this team of general managers. Preparations for the amalgamation of the Bradford Banking Company, for instance, were handled by Murray and his colleagues while Holden was on a long convalescent leave at Eastbourne in the autumn of 1909. As before, Murray was also trusted with the legal and staff-work for each new acquisition.

Senior managerial support of this kind was essential at a time when amalgamations continued to be the fastest route to expansion within the United Kingdom. Skills and experience in mergers were badly needed, as the concentration in banking over the previous twenty years had severely restricted the choice of candidate banks. The banks which had survived were more likely to have established their own large branch networks and to have become relatively more expensive in terms of capital. The emergence of a leading group of about ten commercial banks also ensured that few bids would not be contested by rival banks or by shareholders dissatisfied with bid prices.

Small well-established country banks were in particularly short supply by the end of the first decade of the century. Murray's offer for the Bradford Banking Company in 1909 was therefore against the run of large, multi-branch amalgamations. Although it had been amongst the earliest half-dozen joint stock banks when it was launched in 1827, it had not attempted to set out from its Bradford headquarters. The result, Murray and his colleagues were well aware, was a decline in its deposits from £2.3 million in 1899 to £1.7 million by 1909. This size of enterprise was outnumbered and inadequately resourced to compete with Midland and the other recent arrivals in the city. An agreement was carried through early in 1910 at an effective price of £792,880. The cost to Midland was covered by an exchange of shares, without needing to increase the existing nominal capital of £22.2 million.

Two acquisitions in 1913 were much more typical of the dwindling population of English country banks. The Lincoln and Lindsey Banking Company and the Sheffield and Hallamshire Bank were both Midland's contemporaries as joint stock banks founded in the 1830s. These two banks had developed strong local branch networks—the Lincoln bank with 31 offices and the Sheffield and Hallamshire with 14—and both had attracted deposits of nearly £2 million by 1913. Both banks agreed to an exchange of shares with Midland, valuing the Lincoln bank at £569,952 in current share prices and the Sheffield bank at £757,727. Once again the offers were possible within Midland's existing nominal capital of £22.2 million (p 108). Holden was especially delighted with the Lincoln deal, both because it gave control of the largest bank in the county and because he had been interested in a merger since 1899. It was, he believed, the 'cleanest little bank he had taken over' and its quality was reflected in the

**Table 5.1**

Midland Bank amalgamations, 1910–18

| Date | Bank acquired | Number of branches | Total deposits (£000) | Paid-up capital (£000) | Price of acquisition* (£000) | Ratio Price paid-up capital |
|------|---------------|--------------------|-----------------------|------------------------|-------------------------------|------------------------------|
| 1910 | Bradford Banking Co | 0 | 1714 | 408 | 793 | 1.9 |
| 1913 | Sheffield and Hallamshire Banking Co | 14 | 1875 | 300 | 758 | 2.6 |
| 1913 | Lincoln and Lindsey Banking Co | 31 | 1788 | 163 | 570 | 3.5 |
| 1914 | Metropolitan Bank (of England and Wales) | 165 | 11,761 | 550 | 1685 | 3.1 |
| 1918 | London Joint Stock Bank | 310 | 58,567 | 2970 | 6334 | 2.1 |

*Note\** Agreed value of Midland shares and/or cash paid for acquisition

relatively high price paid for the Lincoln shares (Table 5.1).

Not all negotiations with the remaining country banks were so successful. Midland's relative weakness in the West Country was slowly being repaired by the opening of new, purpose-built branches, but this programme had not yet compensated for the bank's lack of success in finding a merger partner in the south-west. Sporadic discussions with Stuckey's Bank of Langport (the oldest and largest of the Somerset banks) had failed to produce agreement and were eventually overtaken by a bid from Parr's Bank in 1909. The Wilts and Dorset Bank, itself an amalgamation of two western banks with 100 branches and deposits of nearly £13 million by 1914, was an even more promising prize. It was a chance which Midland missed, however, and Lloyds produced a successful bid early in 1914. Holden's immediate response was to open new branches in 21 West Country towns where branches of Lloyds and its new acquisitions overlapped. From experience he judged that Midland could take the business of any Wilts and Dorset customers and shareholders who were dissatisfied with the merger.

The process of branch extension was not often the result of such aggressive tactics. More usually it was the systematic filling of gaps in regional representation. The emphasis in the first years of Holden's chairmanship remained the south and west, East Anglia and the suburbs of London and the major provincial cities, with the difference that Murray and Madders took a larger share of the planning and detailed management which Holden had once dealt with singlehanded. A total of 274 entirely new branches were added in this way between 1910 and 1919, over 41 per cent of the number of branches operating in 1909. Costs of building and fitting out branches pushed up the quoted value of the bank's premises from £1.78 million to £3.62 million between 1909 and 1919. This investment, coupled with the high overhead costs always incurred by the opening of new branches, helped to restrict the bank's published profits to about £700,000 annually between 1907 and 1911. This was a relatively high income from shareholders' funds of over £7 million, and it was still above that of contemporary banks (Appendix 4).

Ambitious as the branch extensions were, they were overshadowed by two massive amalgamations in 1914 and 1918. The Edwardian period had seen the rapid transformation of bank amalgamations from the simple acquisition of relatively small banks by large London or provincial banks to much more complex purchases of important, multi-branch banks by the London-based giants of the industry. The latter model had in turn been developed to enable mergers between high-ranking London-and-country banks, probably as the most effective means of matching the new ascendancy of banks such as Midland and Lloyds. By about 1910 this style of merger was responsible for renewed acceleration in the rate of concentration. The outstanding example was the 1909 marriage of the London and County and the London and Westminster, bringing together banks with deposits of £46 million and £27 million respectively and a total of 304 branches. Their combined deposits of over £72 million exceeded Midland's £70 million and were within reach of the Lloyds total of £76 million.

This enterprising merger directly challenged the two Birmingham-born banks. A response was delayed for five years, until Lloyds made its offer for the Wilts and Dorset Bank. Midland's directors and managers were equally keen to follow the pattern established by the London County and Westminster. There is evidence that in 1913 Holden opened negotiations with the London Joint Stock Bank, a company whose £37 million in deposits made it comparable with the Capital and Counties, Parr's Bank and the Union of London and Smiths. The talks collapsed when the two banks failed to agree upon a price. Holden turned instead to the Metropolitan Bank, which as the Birmingham Banking Company had been Midland's neighbour and rival throughout its early history. Although the Metropolitan had recovered from the damage done by the purchase of the National Bank of Wales in 1893, the experience cast a long shadow over the bank's balance sheet and limited its resources for growth. Consequently its deposits were less than £12 million by 1914 (making it the smallest of the London-and-country banks), and there remained nearly £500,000 in dormant accounts. Nevertheless it had a network of 165 branches (mostly in the west Midlands and Wales), and its financial control systems were very well constructed, perhaps embodying the lessons of the bank's succession of disasters in the nineteenth century. The Metropolitan accepted Midland's offer, which was worth £1,685,357 by exchange of shares, and the amalgamation was completed in July 1914. As a result Midland's total deposits of over £125 million at the end of 1914 were larger than those of any other British bank.

Too large a cost to absorb within the bank's existing capital, the merger with the Metropolitan made it necessary to issue extra nominal capital of £6 million, equivalent to £1.25 million in paid-up capital. The addition raised total nominal capital to £28.2 million. Ownership of this capital was by now widely distributed in comparison with most of the other major banks. This characteristic, in stark contrast to the relatively narrow ownership of the bank fifty years earlier, had been achieved by an almost exclusive preference for amalgamating with other joint stock banks rather than with private banks. Since the merger with the Union Bank of Birmingham in 1883, Midland's directors and managers had been keenly aware of the business value of large numbers of shareholders. Holden kept faith with that tradition, and after the Metropolitan amalgamation the bank had 26,130 names on its register. In January 1914 he had also accelerated the distribution of shares by splitting the denomination of each £60 share into five new shares. The effect was to reduce the nominal value of a new certificate to £12 and its paid-up value to £2 10s. 'By this division' Holden explained, 'we shall extend our market, thus giving to those who desire a less liability, greater facility to distribute their shares.' The outbreak of war in August 1914 led to much heavier sales than Holden had envisaged, largely because executors and trustees were prepared to unload their shares at a loss, but by the end of 1914 the market for the bank's shares had recovered.

The emergencies and disruptions of the wartime economy brought the expansion of the branch network practically to a halt. Senior bankers' attention was switched to the demands of national finance and the manpower problems created by mobilization. In the first years of the Great War, the opening of new branches was rare. Those that were opened were more often than not established to service military camps or munitions factories. Some branches were temporarily closed for the duration of the war and arrangements were made to share facilities with other local banks; others, including Midland and Metropolitan branches in places where the two banks overlapped, were permanently closed. Meantime the existing branch network was faced with handling a surge in the volume of business. The bank's deposits nearly doubled in the first three years of the war (ahead of the rate of inflation), and the bank's town and city branches were frantically busy dealing with payments and lending for industrial customers involved in government contracts.

Wartime necessities entirely altered the composition of the bank's staff. The amalgamations and the opening of new branches had lifted the total of Midland's employees to over 5000 by 1914. After the outbreak of war recruitment to the armed forces rapidly depleted this workforce, and by the end of the war over 4000 Midland staff had joined up. Of these 717 were killed on active service, and many hundreds were wounded. Midland, along with the other banks, ensured that appointments were kept open for those who joined up and paid supplements to keep their total incomes at bank salary levels. Meanwhile at the head office and branches the gaps in staff were being filled by female staff. Midland had recruited its first female employee, Miss Anne Tulloch, in 1907, and small numbers of typists and stenographers had then been introduced at the bank's principal London offices. Not until January 1914 did the appointment of women and girls for clerical duties begin in earnest, and as soon as war broke out recruitment and training was accelerated. By the beginning of 1915 the bank was employing 350 female clerks, and that total had increased to 3600 early in 1918. Their duties included key-holding, counter service, and, in smaller branches, acting as second officers to the managers. Holden and his general managers were delighted with the quality of the whole staff's work during the war, and it was clear that their female staff had earned themselves a larger and more permanent role in banking.

The challenges and complexities of wartime conditions did not prevent senior bankers from planning new channels for expansion. Holden's initiatives in Ireland and Scotland were to take Midland into entirely new territory (Chapter Six). In England and Wales the emphasis remained on unions between major London-based banks, on the pattern of the London County and Westminster agreement. By February 1918 two such schemes had been made public: the National Provincial's merger with the Union of London and Smiths, and the London County and Westminster's acquisition of Parr's Bank. The two mergers created banks holding total deposits of £170 million and £215 million respectively. Lloyds followed with an offer for the

# HIGH STREET BANKING:
# MIDLAND'S BRANCH BANK TRADITION

**2.1** *Stourbridge 'Old Bank', Midland's first branch office. In 1851 Midland acquired Bate and Robins, a Stourbridge bank established in* *1770, and carried on the business in the same building at 38 High Street, Stourbridge. This photograph shows the branch in about 1900*

**2.2** *The manager and staff of Midland's Kenilworth branch in the 1890s. The branch was formerly an office of the Leamington Priors and Warwickshire Bank, which became part of Midland in 1889*

**2.3** *A rare view behind the counter at a branch bank before the First World War. This photograph shows the staff of the London Joint Stock Bank's Peckham branch, with their ledgers, scales and coin shovels, in about 1910*

**2.4** *Customers at the counter of Midland's Ludgate Hill branch, London, in about 1903*

**2.5** *The splendid interior of Midland's Watford branch, photographed soon after completion in 1909. The building was designed by T B Whinney, who was responsible for scores of Midland's new branches before the 1914–18 war*

**2.6** *Machine operators at the bank's Derby branch in 1928. Mechanized accounting was introduced throughout the branches from the late 1920s onwards. These operators are using early examples of electrically-powered ledger-posting machines*

**2.7** *Country banking between the wars: Midland's Glastonbury branch, designed by Woolfall and Eccles in 1921, was typical of the large number of high street branches opened after the First World War*

**2.8** *City centre banking between the wars: the bank's branch at Pall Mall, in London's West End, is the successor to the old private bank of Wright and Co (established 1759). The* *photograph shows the branch after complete rebuilding to designs by Whinney and Austen Hall in 1927*

**2.9** *Midland's Liverpool North branch in Great Nelson Street in about 1920. The branch was built in the 1860s as an office of the North and South Wales Bank, which became part of Midland in 1908*

**2.10** *Liverpool North branch, after a direct hit during a bombing raid in Liverpool in May 1941. The branch was one of 31 Midland branches totally destroyed by enemy action during the Second World War. Nearly 600 other branches were damaged*

**2.11** *Exterior and interior of Midland's branch at Queen Street, Cardiff. The branch was originally opened in 1921 and it was entirely refurbished in open-plan style in 1986*

**2.12** *A preview of the branch banking scene in the late 1980s, based on designs prepared for Midland by Fitch and Co plc in 1986*

Capital and Counties Bank, while Barclays took over the smaller London Provincial and South and Western Bank. Simultaneously Holden had reopened negotiations with the London Joint Stock Bank in February 1918. Although terms were agreed in principle, the deal had not been concluded four months later when Holden told his board that 'the Chancellor of the Exchequer was preparing to appoint Lord Colwyn and Lord Inchcape as a special committee to consider the amalgamation of the London Joint Stock Bank with this Bank'. In the event the 'Colwyn Committee' was appointed to investigate bank amalgamations in general and to recommend legislation or supervision. Midland was left in a particularly difficult position. Its merger proposal had not been completed, whereas the new amalgamations of the National Provincial and the London County and Westminster were effectively beyond the reach of legislation or interference.

Irritated as Holden and his directors were, the Chancellor's intervention cannot have come as a complete surprise. Objections to the 1917–18 wave of bank mergers had been raised in Parliament and in the press. The main theme of those protests was that the banks were already creating a monopoly or 'money trust'.[6] Here, in Midland's proposed amalgamation with the London Joint Stock Bank, was the largest concentration yet attempted: it would create a bank controlling about £350 million in deposits, a branch network of more than 1300 offices, and, not least, nearly 1000 agencies of foreign banks. The combined bank would be the largest in Britain and in all likelihood the largest in the world. The Colwyn Committee took up the call for legislation to control such massive units. Reporting in July 1918, it argued that there was a real threat of monopoly and that the Bank of England's position in the money market would be undermined. 'Experience shows that ... the larger English banks consider it necessary to meet each important amalgamation, sooner or later, by another.'[7] According to the Committee, even the Stock Exchange and money markets were being squeezed and restricted by each new merger. The Committee was also alarmed that the interests of small customers and shareholders were being damaged.

Holden's evidence to the Committee and his public statements throughout 1918 vigorously denied these claims. He was particularly scornful of the charge that amalgamations were detrimental to the customers with small accounts. In Midland's experience, the balance had actually altered in favour of small businessmen and private customers. The general level of advances had risen at branches acquired through amalgamation, and by 1918 a significant proportion of the bank's advances was devoted to small loans and overdrafts (Table 5.2).

**Table 5.2**

Midland Bank, value of advances of £500 and under, 1918

| Size of advance (£) | Number of accounts | Total value (£) |
|---|---|---|
| 100 and under | 21,073 | 959,508 |
| 101–200 | 8873 | 1,302,599 |
| 201–300 | 4903 | 1,241,968 |
| 301–400 | 3091 | 1,085,774 |
| 401–500 | 2719 | 1,238,504 |
| TOTAL £500 and under | 40,659 | 5,828,353 |

*Source:* E H Holden's evidence to the Treasury Committee on Bank Amalgamations, 1918

As far as local services were concerned, Holden replied that the banking system had created over 5000 entirely new branches in England and Wales between 1877 and 1915 and that in comparison with the late nineteenth century there had been 'no bank failures of importance' between 1900 and 1913. In the same period small shareholdings had actually increased their importance in the ownership of British banks. Midland's subdivision of its shares in 1914 had accelerated a process already well under way, and by 1918 the average paid-up value of each of the 42,000 shareholders' investments in the bank had declined to £171. Later investigations confirmed that the banks' distribution of ownership was far wider than that of other major corporations. A newspaper survey in 1926, for example, revealed that the average individual shareholding in the four 'grouped' railway companies exceeded £1000 (£1644 in the case of the Southern Railway) and that average investments in the great shipping companies had reached £663 (Peninsular and Oriental) and £404 (Cunard). Banks were the home for more modest investments, ranging from averages of £130 and £209 for the Westminster and for Midland to £306 for Barclays.[8]

Although the Colwyn Committee's recommendations for anti-trust legislation were taken as far as the preparation of a parliamentary bill, the Treasury eventually agreed to drop the bill in return for a private arrangement with the bankers. The undertaking required the banks to submit any proposed amalgamation for Treasury and Board of Trade approval. This 'gentlemen's agreement' proved remarkably durable and was still an influence on the structure of British banking fifty years later. The immediate result, however, was that the Chancellor gave Holden permission for the London Joint Stock Bank merger. The support of Lord Inchcape, who was a past-president of the Institute of Bankers, was no doubt an influence on the Treasury's decision. Midland's offer, worth approximately £6.3 million by exchange of shares, was accepted in August 1918. Additional capital worth £13.25 million nominally and £2.76 million in paid-up shares was issued to cover this price. The issue lifted Midland's capital to £41.45 million, of which £7.17 million was paid-up. The enlarged bank was then renamed the London Joint City and Midland Bank and, in recognition of the largest amalgamation in British banking at that date, all 15 of the London Joint Stock Bank's directors joined Midland's existing board of 18 directors.

The debate over bank amalgamations in 1918 had produced striking differences of approach to the future development of British banking. The Colwyn Committee and sections of the government and press were primarily concerned with the effect of concentration on the domestic economy. Holden by contrast took the widest international view of the operations of the banks, envisaging the London-based banks locked in a long-term rivalry with the American and German banks. It was a theme which he had pursued throughout his chairmanship at Midland but by the time he gave evidence to Colwyn and Inchcape he was passionately advocating commercial banking on a scale which could compete for the largest corporate and sovereign bank accounts in the world:

> Foreign countries were compelled in settling their transactions here to keep large resources with us and these resources have been used, I believe, to some extent in financing our own industries . . . . If we lose our position and with it this foreign money, our financial resources will be much reduced, and it will be less possible for us to face the competition of the big Banks and Institutions in Germany and America. In my opinion the right policy to enable us to face the competition of the future is to concentrate the banking resources of our country so that we may be more powerful to assist our own industries, and more powerful to meet the competition of other countries.

This wide horizon was far removed from the tactical battles which Holden had mastered in the 1890s and in his first years as Midland's managing director. By 1918 his pronouncements were being given full public and official attention. The scale of Midland's banking business in England and Wales, particularly after the Metropolitan and London Joint Stock Bank mergers, demanded no less. With the

'Big Five' London banks controlling about four-fifths of deposit banking in England and Wales,[9] it was impossible to ignore senior bankers' views on the international financial outlook as well as the domestic economy. Holden's qualifications for influencing opinion or policy were especially strong. In addition to the extraordinary expansion of Midland's traditional commercial banking business, he was increasingly ready to diversify the bank's earning assets. That diversification included innovations outside traditional banking as well as a growing commitment to foreign banking operations.

The Colwyn Committee were not unfair when they criticized the major banks for matching one amalgamation with another. This feature of competition was and remained as common in banking as any other business sector. On the other hand the Committee was too quick to dismiss some of the business reasons for the expansion of the largest units. The banks' initiatives, including many amalgamations, were more likely to have been determined by 'considerations peculiar to the banking sector'[10] rather than the pursuit of size for size's sake. This was certainly the case in Holden's efforts to extend Midland's involvement in foreign banking.

At the beginning of the twentieth century Midland's foreign business was largely inherited from the City Bank, which had been amalgamated with the bank in 1898. The City Bank had been an exponent of foreign acceptance business, and its bequest to Midland included approximately 40 agencies of overseas 'correspondent' banks. These agencies were arrangements for the City Bank to act as the London bank for foreign and colonial banks, which in return had acted for the City Bank in their own countries. In about 1902 these accounts were drawn together with a smaller number of Midland's own foreign agencies in a central 'Foreign Banks Department' at the Threadneedle Street head office. There the number of accounts and the value of credits dealt with rapidly multiplied to keep pace with the growth of world trade and British foreign investment in the decade before the First World War. By 1908 the bank's correspondent links numbered 132 and by 1918 (even before the London Joint Stock Bank merger) that total had increased to 850.

The new commitment to acting as banker to overseas banks was partly an answer to demand from the bank's own customers. Many existing or potential new customers in the export and import trades needed a fluctuating amount of international facilities, and the flexibility of correspondent banking arrangements was often more suitable than opening accounts directly with overseas banks. This was particularly relevant to textile and machinery exporters in the

Midlands and north of England, where country banks were increasingly inadequate for large foreign payments. It was also relevant to the great variety of corporate customers seeking help in London in the late 1890s and early 1900s. Holden himself dealt with applications for services which would have been beyond the scope of country banks; at the turn of the century this remarkable graduate of Manchester and Birmingham banking was being consulted by a railway wagon company exporting to Japan, an American cereal food producer setting up a British factory, and a London piano manufacturer with most of his business in New York and Hamburg.

The expanding needs of corporate customers were already a well-worn theme in bankers' explanations for the growth and concentration of their business (pp 98, 117). Conversely there were opportunities for British bankers to set the pace and point the direction for their customers' business development. This was Holden's choice following his first visit to the United States and Canada in 1904. The expedition profoundly influenced Holden's attitude not only to foreign business but also to the managerial options available to a major bank. He was enthusiastic about the scale and style of the business corporations which he saw in North America, and in return he made an immediate impression on his guests. 'Mr Holden is no dreamer', one journalist reported. 'He moves quickly, thinks rapidly and speaks with amazingly emphatic precision. Grey-moustached and ruddy, he had an almost Willardian mobility of face and a pair of decidedly electric eyes . . . . And he talks political economy as easily as some men talk horses.'[11] The practical outcome of the visit included the lengthening of Midland's list of correspondent banks in North America and the overhaul of office systems at Midland's head office. The bank's staff also felt the impact of Holden's American adventure. After 1904 the bank made greater use of incentives and training for its staff, as for example new classes in modern languages and a voluntary examination on the Companies Act of 1907. Both experiments were oversubscribed.[12] Holden also urged the British universities to offer courses in international finance, pointing out in 1905 that the American banks were recruiting from the American and German universities.

Some of Holden's American-inspired initiatives made little headway. A proposal to open Midland branches in New York and Chicago was abandoned even before he returned to England on the grounds that the plan risked breaching the restrictive American banking laws. In contrast, his decision that Midland should offer foreign exchange services was a spectacular success. This, perhaps the most significant result of his American visit, was prompted by the capture of an increasing volume of London's foreign business by European banks. The merchant banks had traditionally dominated that market but they now appeared powerless to defend their position against the London branches of banks such as the Crédit Lyonnais and Dresdner Bank. The clearing banks, meanwhile, did not deal in non-sterling currencies and were forced to obtain drafts in foreign currencies from other banks. Holden feared that the overseas banks might use their foreign exchange services to invade the ordinary business of the major commercial banks. 'You find them touting all over the country amongst the manufacturers for foreign bill business', he wrote later, 'and you also find them conducting what are practically current accounts.' Holden's visit to America in 1904 offered a possible solution. First, the American banks were already operating departments for specialist services, including foreign exchange. Secondly, his discussions with American bankers suggested that a new British force in the London currency markets would attract the foreign exchange business of the American banks.

On this basis Holden formed a foreign exchange department early in 1905. It was the first of its kind in British commercial banking. The new department (together with the shipping department for handling shipowners' international payments, established later the same year) was quite separate from the foreign banks department dealing with correspondent arrangements. Holden, rather than attempt to train his own men for this specialist work, recruited experienced dealers from the successful European banks. Herman Van Beek was brought from the International Banking Corporation, and David Miller and David Lorsignol from the Crédit Lyonnais—rare examples of 'head-hunting' by British banks before the First World War. Lines of communication to the new department were also kept deliberately short. 'The chances of making money in Foreign Exchange, as a rule, do not wait until a committee has had time to consider the matter', Van Beek wrote in 1907: 'I have only to mention it to Mr Holden and it receives a decision within a matter of a few seconds.'

Initially the new department was criticized in the City as being outside the scope of a clearing bank. Edward Fontaine, Holden's secretary, later remembered that the bank was publicly rebuked by the governor of the Bank of England for its 'unorthodox behaviour' in setting up the new department.[13] Holden was not to be dissuaded, however, particularly as he was then joining the bankers' dispute with the Bank of England over gold reserves (pp 142–3). In due course the other major banks followed by establishing their own foreign currency departments and the innovation was the forerunner of the massive foreign exchange operations of the modern clearing banks.

Aggressive as it may have appeared to fellow bankers, the initiative in foreign exchange was influenced by a defensive theory. Holden saw the foreign banks in London as a threat not only to Midland but to British banking as a whole. If the introduction of such a specialist service helped to concentrate business at Threadneedle Street, then it had the double virtue of depriving European banks of further advantage. This factor, with its international political and economic overtones, affected the bank's attitude to other services outside traditional banking. The underwriting and issuing of loans on behalf of foreign and colonial governments and railways was already a well-established part of the London financial picture. The prime movers had always been the merchant banks, as in the example of Barings' links with South America. After the decline of Paris as the centre of international finance as a result of the Franco-Prussian war of 1871, London-based commercial banks were able to share the market. The London Joint Stock Bank's issue of the £15 million North German Confederation Treasury Bonds in 1870–71 was an example.[14] Similarly Glyn Mills issued loans for the Canadian government, its railways and its municipalities; the London and Westminster dominated the loan business of the Australian and South African states in the 1890s and early 1900s; and Parr's Bank, through the efforts of the remarkable missionary banker Allan Shand, handled many Japanese and some Chinese loans in the same period.[15]

The marketing of foreign loans was by no means universal amongst the major London banks. As the flotation of foreign loans multiplied in the Edwardian period, there was every chance that the non-colonial loans would be diverted to European banks or to newcomers to the London market. Midland itself had not been involved in any such issues when Holden became chairman in 1908. The protection of the bank's business, and an understandable anxiety not to lose ground in expertise to the London and Westminster and Parr's, were therefore the mainspring for Midland's entry into the foreign loan market in 1909. It was a development which led the bank into entirely new territory and into unpredictable commitments.

In 1909 the London City and Midland Bank was named as the issuing bank for the £3.4 million 4½ per cent bonds of the Armavir-Touapsé Railway, guaranteed by the Russian Government. The issue was to finance the building and operations of a 168-mile railway between Touapsé on the Black Sea to Armavir, on the line between Rostov and the Caucasus. Additional lines were planned to extend the railway to Astrakhan on the Caspian Sea. The issue was nearly four times oversubscribed when it was launched on the London market in June 1909.

The contrast with Midland's traditional business could not have been greater. At the time that the Russian loan was being issued, for example, Holden and Murray were treading the more familiar ground of preparing a bid for the Bradford Banking Company. Yet senior bankers could not ignore new international alignments, especially if their European competitors put British banks and their customers at a disadvantage. The Triple Entente between Britain, France and Russia in 1907 was one such realignment. The Russian economy, after a long slump and the disastrous war with Japan in 1905, was suddenly the focus of intense financial activity. St Petersburg was the scene of fierce competition between French, German and British financiers and industrialists. The prizes included agencies for major loans for municipal and reconstruction projects, contracts for railways, and rearmament work in munitions and shipbuilding. In the three years after the entente the Russian capital was thronged with agents for foreign banks, contractors and manufacturers.

David Miller, who had been recruited by Holden for the new foreign exchange department, made a series of visits to Russia between 1907 and 1909. It is probable that his first duty was to ensure that correspondent links with Russian banks were in good enough repair to bring business to the bank's industrial and trading customers. By 1909, however, he had persuaded Holden to tender for the Armavir-Touapsé issue. For handling the Russian end of the business, Midland was represented by Birch Crisp, a London stockbroker and company promoter connected with the Russo-Chinese Bank.[16]

The success of the Armavir-Touapsé loan encouraged Holden and his colleagues to build up the bank's position in Russia. Their first obstacle was Crisp's activities. In the early summer of 1909 reports reached London that Crisp was claiming to represent the bank (and other London banks) in bidding for a series of municipal loans. The bank promptly denied this connection and refused to be linked with Crisp's new Anglo-Russian Trust, formed early in 1910. Instead Miller was sent back to St Petersburg in July to investigate the forthcoming loan issues for St Petersburg, Kharkov, Odessa and Baku. There he reported that the city was '*full* of all sorts of people nibbling after the municipal business', and he was inundated by offers to watch over Midland's interests in Russia. Remarkably, even in this atmosphere of rumour and intrigue, Miller was reporting to Holden on a much more ambitious proposal. That plan was nothing less than the ownership or part-ownership of a Russian bank.

Direct foreign investment in the Russian economy had for long been dominated by the French. This pattern was followed in the banking sector after about 1908. By 1916, for instance, foreign investment in the ten largest Russian commercial banks had reached 45 per cent of their total capital, and French interests were responsible for half that investment; majority shares in both the Russo-Asiatic Bank and the St Petersburg Private Commercial Bank were held in France.[17] Meanwhile in London in 1909 Sir Henry Burdett was canvassing proposals for a new British-financed bank in Russia, and Crisp's Anglo-Russian Trust was eventually formed on that model. The legal difficulties in establishing a bank from scratch were nevertheless formidable, and the acquisition of an existing bank was a possible alternative.

As early as June 1908 Andrew Haes, senior partner in the London stockbrokers Haes and Co, was considering the prospects for an English investment in the Union Bank of Moscow. This bank had been formed a month earlier by a three-way merger of the Moscow International Commercial Bank, the Orel Commercial Bank and the South of Russia Commercial Bank. All three companies had been launched in 1871–72 and were inextricably linked with the miscellaneous industrial interests of their promoter, L Poliakoff. This was still the case after the merger, although the Russian State Bank had then intervened by taking a 33 per cent share and by placing its nominee, Count Tatischeff, in the presidency of the combined bank. The Union Bank was operating through 68 branches after the merger but its first priority was to rebuild its written down capital of 7.5 million roubles (about £750,000).

Haes opened negotiations with the Union Bank in late 1908 or early 1909. Initially Alexander Watt, his agent in Moscow, was instructed to sound out the Russian bank and the Russian government on the question of 'a British syndicate' sharing the ownership with the State Bank and the existing shareholders. In the meantime the plan was introduced to Holden, presumably by his son Norman Holden, a partner in Haes and Co. By the summer of 1909, on the basis of reports from Watt in Moscow and David Miller in St Petersburg, Holden was prepared for Midland to act independently without the help of a syndicate. He was also ready to buy out the State Bank's shareholding and to double the Union Bank's capital to 15 million roubles (£1.5 million). The main difficulty now, according to Watt, was the opposition of the Russian Credit Chancery; the Chancellor, L Davidoff, was thought to lean towards rival German interests in Russia.

Holden was not easily put off. In September Murray and Norman Holden were sent to Russia to investigate the Union Bank's balance sheet and to put Midland's case to the Russian government. It was an arduous mission, as intermediaries such as Watt had given the Russians little idea of the scale and ramifications of the British commercial banks. Consequently Murray's task was to stress the quality of the investment being offered. 'It was essential to get English capital on first class lines', he told the governor of the State Bank. A successful deal would be possible if 'first class English names were associated . . . . a good English banker should become a Manager and have with him several fully trained smart English officials who could bring English organization into the business.' The rationale of this approach was the proliferation of the Russian connections through a nationwide British bank rather than through the narrow agency of a London merchant bank or stockbroker. Murray explained to Sir Arthur Nicholson, the British Ambassador (who had also been much involved in the negotiation of new Russian loans since the entente) that 'what was wanted was to interest the Commercial and Manufacturing England as well as the London Money Market, and this could only be done through a large bank like ours'.

Although a majority of the Union Bank's board favoured an agreement with Midland, early in October Davidoff persuaded the State Bank not to give an option on its shares. Russian ministers now claimed that the Union Bank's capital was adequate and attempted to interest Murray in the purchase of 'the Private Bank' (presumably the St Petersburg Private Commercial Bank). At the same time Murray's investigation of the Union Bank's balance sheet produced growing evidence of a damaging overcommitment to Poliakoff's industrial interests. In Murray's view bad and doubtful debts were already more than double the existing capital of 7.5 million roubles. Although Edward Holden, Murray and Haes were still considering an offer in February 1910, the change in the Russian attitude and the worrying information about the Union Bank's loans effectively ended one of banking's most unusual and original merger plans.

The return of Murray's mission from Russia in October 1909 did not extinguish the bank's ambitions in Russia. These ambitions needed alternative channels. Miller remained in St Petersburg throughout October and November in the hope of capturing some of the municipal loan business. It had been obvious to Murray, nevertheless, that Davidoff and other Russian ministers would look more favourably on an alliance of British banks. As a result, in November 1909 an informal syndicate was brought together consisting of Barings (traditionally the main London agent for Russian loans), Midland, Lloyds and Parr's. The three clearing banks each took a 10 per cent share, and C J Hambro and Son (5 per cent), Panmure Gordon and Co and L Messel and Co (both with 2.5 per cent) also participated. The arrangement 'would include the St Petersburg Loan', Holden told Miller; 'Lord Revelstoke [senior partner in Barings] himself will take charge of the negotiations, and there will therefore be no necessity for you to remain in Russia'. The arrangement enabled Midland and its partners to join forces with Barings in tendering for Russian loan business. In effect the syndicate members agreed not to act singly or in their own names. Lloyds left the syndicate in 1910, but Midland and the other members (later joined by J Henry Schroder and Co) maintained the agreement until 1914.[18]

The events of 1909–10 had narrowed the bank's choices for a presence in Russia. Although the correspondent linkages were not affected, ownership or part-ownership of a bank was now ruled out, and Holden was not prepared to join in Crisp's efforts to promote a new Anglo-Russian bank. There remained the option of establishing overseas offices in the bank's own name. This possibility had been mentioned to Murray by Sir Arthur Nicholson in 1909. Two years later Lloyds set a precedent elsewhere in Europe by acquiring the bank agents Armstrong and Co of Paris, renaming it Lloyds Bank (France). The London County and Westminster Bank then established a French subsidiary in its own name in 1913.[19] Initially, Holden was not enthusiastic. In 1911, for instance, when an official of the Banque Française told Holden that 'the French banks were now desirous that English banks should go to Paris', Midland's chairman replied that it would be impossible. Later plans for Midland branches overseas included Paris in 1915 and Madrid in 1917, but both proposals were dropped when it seemed unlikely that the legal and capital requirements for incoming banks would be relaxed. In the case of Russia, however, agency links with Russian banks might not be enough to handle the multiplicity of business opportunity. Companies such as Pearsons, the contractors, and International Harvester were heavily committed to Russian development. Customers in the textile industries of Yorkshire and Lancashire carried on a large and expanding trade with Russia. Clearly there was an argument for specialist expertise or even a permanent office. Holden (perhaps prompted by David Miller) acknowledged that the circumstances were unusual. In 1913 he seconded to the Azov-Don Bank in St Petersburg Frederick Bunker, who was a member of the foreign banks department and who was married to a Russian. Bunker was soon urging Midland's chairman to open an office in the bank's name. Holden agreed and in 1916 Bunker was appointed Midland's 'representative'. An office was opened in the Moika, St Petersburg (by then renamed Petrograd) in February 1917 'for the purpose of facilitating the business of this bank between Russia and the United Kingdom'.

Even after the profound disruption of the Russian economy during the First World War and the Revolution of March 1917, Bunker handled a formidable workload of international payments and even recruited new customers for Midland's London offices. It was miraculous that he continued for so long, for as early as August 1917 it was clear to him 'that things were drifting nearer and nearer to a complete State debacle'. Over the following six months Bunker faced the risks of 'murder or plunder', especially after the Bolsheviks gained the ascendancy in November 1917. He remained in Petrograd after the British Embassy had evacuated and he finally left in 1918. 'Actual banking business had come practically to a standstill, and could only be done at the best in fear and trepidation, as being subject to "illegality" from the bolsheviks standpoint.' After a hazardous rail journey through the Red and White Russian lines and after being caught up in the Whites' siege of Tammerfors in Finland, Bunker escaped to Sweden. His assistant was not so lucky and was taken prisoner by the Germans when attempting to cross the ice from Finland to Sweden. Bunker, with great aplomb, then turned to the systematic overhaul of Midland's correspondent links in Sweden, Norway and Denmark. He eventually returned to the bank's new overseas branch and became the chief manager in 1934.

The retreat from Petrograd influenced Midland's overseas banking business for generations to come. This was not simply a negative reaction to overseas representation. After 1918 Holden and his successors consistently advocated the extension of correspondent banking, acting as 'bankers' bank' in London rather than competing with foreign banks on their own territory. This, combined with the specialist services in foreign exchange and shipping, was the guiding principle of the overseas branch after its formation in 1918. The new department was primarily a clearing house for the existing agencies and the additional correspondent arrangements inherited from the London Joint Stock Bank. This rationalization of objectives also brought an organizational gain. Before 1918 the bank's overseas activities were 'conducted by several separate and quite distinct departments and offices within the organization'. The creation of the overseas branch thereby reduced duplication and stiffened central control. As to Russia, the ten-year involvement was not wasted. After 1918 the experience gained by Murray, Miller and their staff and the courage shown by Bunker enabled the bank to resume a larger Russian business than any other British bank in the 1920s. All thought of a direct presence had been abandoned, however, and the relationship was put on the same agency footing as the bank's links with other nations.

Holden's cultivation of foreign banking business, developing from the series of adventures which had followed his 1904 American tour to the consolidation of the overseas branch in 1918, was his largest and most complex effort to broaden the bank's business. This change did not prevent Holden from embarking on other forms of diversification. On the assets side of the balance sheet Midland's investments (like those of the other major banks) had been switched further away from government securities after 1899 and towards Indian railway and colonial government stocks, American railroad bonds, municipal bonds, and—especially after 1911—Canadian railway bonds. Midland's ratio of investments to deposits was amongst the lowest of the London-based commercial banks. The average of 16.19 per cent between 1891 and 1914 was barely half that maintained by the National Provincial, for example. The portfolio was nonetheless one of the more ambitious in its spread of interests. By December 1908 British railway and corporation stocks provided 29 per cent and colonial and government stocks 13 per cent of Midland's investments of £9.58 million. 'Sundry' investments of £881,000 included British railway ordinary shares, United States and South American railway shares, holdings in telegraph, telephone and navigation companies, and shares in Titus Salt and Co and the Queensland National Bank. If British banks were truly moving 'towards a more aggressive, earnings-oriented, enterprising, outward-looking investment policy',[20] then Midland under Holden's regime was more than keeping pace.

A more public form of diversification was the bank's entry into trustee and executorship services. Since 1901, when the Royal Exchange Assurance was the first institution to act as a corporate trustee, a number of banks and insurance companies had obtained authorization to operate as executors and trustees. As with foreign exchange business Holden recognized that this type of service could syphon off conventional banking business. In 1907 he produced a plan for similar services so as to 'preserve the business of our customers and not send them to other banks'. Unlike the other newcomers to the business, Midland formed an independent company rather than a trustee department within the bank. This innovation overcame the legal and moral objections to mingling trust moneys with bank liabilities and gave protection both to the trustee company's clients and to the bank's customers. Incorporated in December 1909 as the London City and Midland Executor and Trustee Company (now the Midland Bank Trust Company), the new company was wholly-owned by the bank and was the first functional subsidiary to be launched by a clearing bank.

Initiatives such as Midland's foreign exchange department and the new Executor and Trustee Company added to Holden's public standing. He was not only the outstanding exponent of bank amalgamations but he was also visibly pushing back some of the conventional boundaries of commercial banking. It was with these achievements that throughout his chairmanship he behaved and was treated as a financial authority in a way which would have been inconceivable to John Goodman and his predecessors. In the previous generation of bankers, only Sir John Lubbock (partner in Robarts Lubbock and Co and the founding president of the Institute of Bankers) had maintained such a high profile. Unlike Holden, however, Lubbock owed some of his reputation to his interests and achievements outside banking. Midland's chairman caught attention solely as a banker.

Holden's increasingly public role was particularly obvious in his speeches to shareholders and to members of the banking institutes. He used these occasions as the platform for strong and sometimes quarrelsome views on financial policy. The speeches were 'eagerly awaited events'[21] in the City and financial journalists could confidently expect Holden to produce new policy proposals or challenges to the Treasury or the Bank of England. He urged the creation of a national war-chest based on gold payments as early as 1909. He advocated a British parallel to the United States' Federal Reserve system. Above all he repeatedly argued that the clearing banks should keep their own gold reserves rather than deposit them with the Bank of England. It was iniquitous, he believed, that the gold placed by the banks with the Bank of England should be indirectly employed in competing with the banks themselves in the discount market. After the American financial crisis of 1907 he was convinced that the Bank of England's reserves were in any case far too small to operate as a 'last resort'.

These views were shared by many other senior bankers, notably those involved in the gold committees appointed by the London clearing banks in 1907 and 1912.[22] Yet Holden was less patient than some of his contemporaries. He was prepared to ship gold bullion back and forth to America and France according to his assessment of the reserve position as well as the state of the exchange in London. These shipments of up to £1 million at a time brought further rebukes from the governor, but to Holden they were serious attempts at remedying deficiencies in banking reserves. Demonstrating that his gold operations were not mere gestures he went to the trouble of building new bullion safes at Threadneedle Street in 1909. When the gold controversy was renewed four years later it was alleged that he even contemplated coining gold on Midland's behalf, only to be told that the Mint was fully occupied with work for 'the prior and very old customer'.[23] More certainly he exhorted his fellow bankers to publish details of their holdings of gold. He sought public assurance that gold reserves in the banks' own custody were close to 5 per cent of their liabilities. If they would not do so, he would publish Midland's position in an attempt to force an inter-bank agreement. He kept his promise in the bank's balance sheet for June 1914, when Midland was reported to hold £8 million in gold, 7.3 per cent of total liabilities of £109 million. Although Lloyds had stated that its gold reserves were in at least as high a ratio as Holden's guideline, the outbreak of war prevented the other major banks from answering Holden's challenge with detailed statistics of their gold positions. The sheer size of the country's gold transactions appeared to make these issues increasingly relevant. In 1913 the Bank of England reported gold imports of £31 million and exports of £17 million; in the following year, under the shadow of war, gold imports of £77 million were notified, £48 million more than gold exports.

On the gold question Holden was publicly intervening on matters of public policy. Both in his speeches and in his dealings in gold Holden notified the government and the City that the clearing banks were large enough to affect and be affected by the management of the economy. As his statements on gold had shown, he did not accept that the stability of the banking system should or could depend upon the Bank of England alone, especially at a time when the Bank was still competing with the commercial banks. If the Bank of England could not provide the necessary safety mechanisms, then it was now the responsibility of the clearing banks to strengthen their own reserves and to coordinate their efforts at moments of financial crisis. The viability of this independent role was demonstrated when the Yorkshire Penny Bank was endangered in 1911.

The objectives of the Yorkshire Penny Bank, established in Halifax in about 1857, were originally those of a friendly society and savings bank, 'to encourage thrift among the working classes of Yorkshire'. Minimum deposits were one penny per customer, but in order to protect this minimum from the Savings Bank Act of 1863 (which required minimum deposits of one shilling) the bank had registered as a limited company. A network of 'village branches' and 'school branches' had been established throughout the West Riding, cheque-book facilities were introduced in 1872, and total deposits grew at a remarkable rate from £229,000 in 1870 to over £5 million in 1890 and £13 million in 1900. By the Edwardian period commercial banks in Yorkshire (including Midland) saw the bank as a major competitor. While the Yorkshire Penny Bank's deposits were mushrooming, however, the bank's directors and managers paid little attention to the management of its reserves and investment portfolio. As a result by 1900 it was in the difficult position of holding nearly £13 million in deposits but without any capital and with a reserve fund of less than £300,000. This predicament became serious when in the Boer War period security prices began their long decline. The bank's reserves could not keep pace with the dwindling margin between the book and market values of its investments and by 1910, when the bank's depositors were owed over £18.5 million, only £468,000 was allocated to the reserve fund.

By 1911 the financial stability of savings banks was already a sensitive issue. After the collapse of Jabez Balfour's London and General Bank and the Liberator Building Society in 1892, small savings had again been raided by the failures of the fraudulent Charing Cross Bank in 1910 and the Birkbeck Bank (largely as a result of not depreciating its investments) in 1911. In contrast the Yorkshire Penny Bank was a much larger institution with a more prominent role in the banking industry. It was closely identified with Yorkshire business life, and with more than 500,000 customers it had a broader social and political significance. The government had special reasons for anxiety as Lloyd George's proposals on Increment Duty and Leasehold Reversion Duty were then being canvassed. According to Ellis Powell of the *Financial News*, Asquith and Lloyd George feared that 'any extended bank trouble would be attributed to the undermining of public confidence resulting from these attacks on property owners and builders'.[24]

While security prices continued to fall, rumours of the Yorkshire Penny Bank's vulnerability reached Holden in July 1911. Murray was dispatched to Leeds to make an investigation and Holden broke off his holiday to review the position with Lord Cunliffe, governor of the Bank of England. Holden and Cunliffe agreed that a rescue attempt was essential if confidence in the banking system was to be maintained. As to how the rescue was to be achieved, 'Holden set the pace'.[25]

Within days he arranged for other banks with Yorkshire branches ('the subscribing banks') to contribute capital for a reconstruction scheme. This was on the understanding that non-Yorkshire banks ('the guaranteeing banks') would guarantee the Yorkshire Penny Bank's investments against further depreciation.

Murray's investigation of the Yorkshire Penny Bank's books indicated a deficiency of £600,000 in the reserve account. He and his chief recommended the formation of a new limited company to take over the old business, the creation of paid-up capital of £750,000 and reserves of £750,000 (all contributed by the subscribing banks) and a cover of £900,000 for depreciation (provided by the guaranteeing banks). Any depreciation of investments above £900,000 would be shared by the subscribing and guaranteeing banks up to a maximum of £1 million. These proposals were accepted by the Yorkshire Penny Bank board at a meeting at the Great Central Hotel, Marylebone, on 29 and 30 July 1911 and were announced to the press on 3 August. A panic was avoided and the new Yorkshire Penny Bank was able to resume business without interruption.

Holden had not only taken the initiative in devising a rescue scheme and recruiting the other banks in support; Midland was also the largest contributor to the capital and reserves of the new bank. Of the subscribing banks, Midland provided £375,000 while Barclays, Lloyds, the London Joint Stock Bank and the Union of London and Smiths Bank each contributed £187,000. Each subscribing bank nominated a director to the board of the new bank but two places were reserved for Midland. As one of these representatives Holden continued to provide benefits to the new bank. He instructed Midland's Yorkshire branches not to compete with the Yorkshire Penny Bank, and it is probable that the other subscribing banks issued similar directions; the only evidence of touting for Penny Bank business came from Ilkley, where the West Yorkshire Bank had not joined the reconstruction agreement. Holden and his senior Midland managers devoted much time and effort to monitoring the progress of the new bank over the next five years. Care and secrecy were needed when the reputation of savings banks was so fragile. A month after the outbreak of war, for example, a news film reporting 'Runs on Savings Banks in Belgium' was being shown in British cinemas. Holden and Murray persuaded the Board of Film Censors to suppress the film on the grounds that it might create a panic in Yorkshire. Similarly, when newspapers reported the failure of the National Penny Bank in the same month, Murray feared that the placards carrying the slogan PENNY BANK-SPECIAL would be construed as a reference to the Yorkshire

Penny Bank 'and might, in the present crisis, be very damaging'. The Home Secretary, Reginald McKenna, duly asked the police to remove the placards.

Valuable as this attention to detail may have been to the business of the new bank, the continuing worry was the falling value of its investments. By mid-1913 the guaranteeing banks were already carrying a liability and the subscribing banks had added £128,000 to the bank's reserves. Three years later another £183,000 had been needed to top up the reserve fund. In 1916 Holden urged the Treasury to join the guarantee, blaming the depreciation of securities partly on the rise in income tax from 1s 2d to 5s in the pound. After a series of stormy meetings at which Holden threatened 'to call together the Members of Parliament for Yorkshire and the Lord Lieutenant if the Government would not give the support that was necessary', the Treasury agreed. Reginald McKenna, by then Chancellor of the Exchequer in the Asquith government, nevertheless believed that a Treasury guarantee without further commitment from the banks would be 'impossible to defend either to Parliament or to the public'. The directors of the Yorkshire Penny Bank (that is, the nominees of the subscribing banks) vigorously defended their position:

> In wishing to avoid a national catastrophe now and after the war, we are actuated by the same spirit as that by which we were moved in 1911 when we and the guarantors subscribed 3 millions sterling to prevent it. Upon that occasion the object was not to make profit neither was it to save loss ... it was purely for the purpose of preventing a national crisis.

As a result of a private meeting between McKenna and Holden, the eventual form of the agreement put a limit to the Treasury's participation. The agreement in August 1916 was a guarantee against further deficiencies above the £1 million covered by the subscribing and guaranteeing banks. This Treasury guarantee was unconditional for ten years. If after ten years the Treasury was not satisfied that the Penny Bank had secured its independence, then the bank would be wound up. Profits would not be distributed to the subscribing banks as long as the guarantee continued and any funds available for investment would be in British government securities. In the event the recovery of the bank's business permitted the cancellation of the Treasury guarantee and the release of the guaranteeing banks in 1922. The subscribing banks, which had borne the brunt of the liability since 1911, chose to remain shareholders.

The ending of the guarantee in effect completed the rescue of the Yorkshire Penny Bank. The operation had been carried out without creating any serious panic or loss of confidence amongst the banking public, while the negotiations between the government and the bankers were valuable precedents for later corporate reconstructions. These were largely Holden's achievements. By taking the initiative in 1911 and then by ensuring that the damage was properly repaired, he had demonstrated that the major banks were as capable of crisis management and as aware of the political and social consequences of banking failures as the Bank of England had been during the Baring crisis. By giving up so much management time and by foregoing the advantages available to his own bank, Holden was in no doubt that the major banks' responsibilities now extended well beyond their own balance sheets and loan portfolios.

The rescue of the Yorkshire Penny Bank was necessarily carried through in secrecy. Holden's key contribution was not widely known until after his death, yet his involvement in this and other policy questions was understood by the Asquith government. He was knighted in 1909 and his strong Liberal pedigree gave him a place on the list of nominees for peerages during the constitutional crisis of 1911. He had decided to leave the House of Commons in 1910 but he continued to be treated as one of the government's senior allies in the City. In 1910 or 1911, as Ellis Powell reported some years later, Asquith actually recommended Holden for the Chancellorship of the Exchequer. 'But according to Sir Edward's own statement, ... Mr Lloyd George intervened with a veto, saying that he would not remain in the Administration if Sir Edward Holden were admitted.'[26]

Holden did not tell Powell whether he would have accepted Asquith's offer. Both Midland's chairman and the Prime Minister were more likely to have recognized that his influence in the City was at least as necessary to the development of policy. If that was the case, the Yorkshire Penny Bank episode illustrated his wider public role. Even that contribution was overshadowed by the responsibilities which bankers carried in the early stages of the First World War. Few bankers had spoken so openly about the imminence of war and the need for financial armour; few bankers had been so aware of the power and resources of the German banking. He could not easily be excluded from any discussion or action to meet the financial emergencies of war.

The rapid deterioration of the international political situation in July 1914 had paralysed London's bill market and had already brought some of the merchant banks close to ruin. The major banks, preoccupied with the status of their gold reserves, protected their positions by paying out notes rather than gold; as a result queues formed for gold withdrawals at the Bank of England. At the Stock Exchange, prices were falling rapidly towards the end of July, several jobbers' firms were 'hammered' and the Stock Exchange itself was forced to close on 31 July. Some banks (particularly foreign banks) had called in their loans to brokers, thereby accelerating the sale and the fall in prices of securities. In these conditions cooperation between the Treasury, the Bank of England and the clearing banks was desperately needed if the panic was to be arrested and then eliminated.

Holden and his colleagues on the bankers' gold committee—notably Sir Felix Schuster of the Union of London and Smiths Bank and Lord St Aldwyn of the London Joint Stock Bank—carried the main burden of the bankers' policy-making in the days immediately before and after the outbreak of war on 4 August 1914. In line with a proposal he had made to the gold committee, on 31 July the banks offered to transfer gold to the Bank of England in exchange for notes (at the same time Holden moved £500,000 in gold to one of the Manchester banks as a precaution against a run). Two days later the offer was turned down but the Treasury did grant a moratorium on bill payments to halt the drain on the merchant banks and discount houses. This freeze of a large proportion of the commercial banks' assets immediately created a need for additional currency. Holden, Schuster and St Aldwyn advocated a system of 'Treasury notes' in which the government advanced to the banks £1 and 10 shilling notes up to the value of 20 per cent of their deposits. The notes would then be put into circulation to relieve the pressure on the existing currency. The plan was adopted at a renowned meeting organized by Lloyd George in Whitehall on 4 August.[27] The bankers, Holden recalled later:

> decided that while in their opinion a Moratorium was advisable, they would only partially take advantage of it, and they accordingly agreed to pay all cheques passing through the Clearing House, however large or however small. They further agreed that on the first Friday they would pay all wages in gold.

When the banks finally reopened on Friday 7 August the moratorium and Treasury note arrangements were equal to the extra demand for currency. The absence of panic surprised even Holden, who paid tribute to the way in which the press had presented the measures and the way in which bank customers had accepted the position. Only £13 million Treasury notes were issued initially (the ceiling was actually £225 million, or 20 per cent of bank liabilities), but by the end of the year £38 million notes were in circulation. The involvement of the major banks was critical in this phase. Murray, for example, recorded a number of examples where other banks refused to cash cheques but Midland managers had made payment within the terms of the moratorium. Lloyd George also complained that 'some bankers were not doing their duty', although the Treasury hastened to assure Holden that the criticism was not aimed at Midland or Midland branches. Holden's instructions were quite clear:

> be liberal in your lending and meet every legitimate demand if you can. We have over 1000 Branches, and the Managers of those Branches were instructed to refuse nothing to their Clients without referring to Head Office and Head Office gave every assistance that it possibly could.

This approach enabled the bank to release assets frozen by the moratorium fully one month before the arrangement was formally and officially brought to an end on 4 November 1914.

Along with the other major banks Midland's new commitments after the 1914 crisis included investment in the new war loans and the provision of foreign credits to support Britain's allies or to secure food supplies. An allotment of £10.5 million in war loans was made to the bank in November 1914 and four years later the bank's war loans were valued at £57.5 million (excluding £14 million in advances secured by customers' holdings of war loans). Meanwhile Holden was closely involved in the government's efforts to raise funds in the American market. The need for a dollar loan had become urgent when in the summer of 1915 the value of sterling in New York was sliding rapidly. By the beginning of August Holden was sounding out his American contacts (notably J B Forgan, president of the First National Bank of Chicago) about the prospects for a loan to the allies. Later that month the London clearing bankers (prompted by Asquith and McKenna) nominated Holden to join an Anglo-French loan mission to the United States. The mission was led by Lord Reading, the Lord Chief Justice, and the result was the issue of a $500 million (£100 million) loan to the allies in October 1915. Rated at 5 per cent and maturing in 1920, the issue differed from later war loans in that the Americans agreed to waive collateral.

Holden's special contribution to the Anglo-French loan mission was to ensure that the underwriting of the loan was widely spread amongst the American banks, many of which he had been in contact with since his first visit to the United States in 1904. It was probably in this role that he incurred the displeasure of J P Morgan and Co, the British government's main financial agent in the United States earlier in the war.[28] His old contacts were also valuable when in November 1915 it was arranged that the main British banks could borrow $50 million from the American banks on the security of war loan investments. The purpose of this multi-bank agreement, which Holden had suggested before returning from America in October, was to create a fund for short-term intervention in the Anglo-American exchange market. Holden and Schuster negotiated the loan contributions from individual American banks, and the management of the fund was entrusted to a 'London Exchange Committee' comprising the governor of the Bank of England, Brien Cokeyne (the deputy governor), Holden and Schuster. The committee acted as an advisory body while its sweeping powers over exchange operations were delegated mainly to Treasury officials.[29] Holden attended regularly until the end of February 1916. He also continued to advise successive Treasury ministers on the management of war loans, although after 1917 he was increasingly alarmed by the financial strategies of the Lloyd George government. 'They mean mischief to the bankers', he confided to an old colleague in Manchester in 1917, and within a year he was in conflict with the Treasury over the question of amalgamations (p 129). Without large banking units at the government's side, he contended, the apparatus of war finance would have been impossible to construct; without the amalgamations, he might have added, the government could not have turned to acknowledged banking leaders such as Holden and Schuster.

Midland's emergence as the largest bank in the world at the end of the First World War was the achievement of the shareholders who had then contributed over £40 million in capital, the customers who had deposited nearly £350 million, and the 10,000 members of staff who were operating a network of over 1400 branches. By 1919 few commentators could separate the scale of the bank's expansion from the quality of its leadership over the previous twenty years. In the United States, where he had learned and apparently taught so many lessons, Holden was taken to be a rarity:

> Calling men by their qualities rather than nationalities . . . there are three Yanks in London from whom their cousins in the States can learn much . . . they are all Yanks in enterprise and business daring . . . . They are Holden, Leverhulme and Selfridge and they drift as naturally together as ships on a pond.[30]

To Arthur Kitson, a financial journalist often taken into Holden's confidence, 'Sir Edward stood head and shoulders above all the bankers of his time, not only in this country but throughout the world'.[31] On Holden's death in July 1919 it was his public profile and his contribution to policy which distinguished the obituary notices from those of most of his contemporaries.

His motives were mainly patriotic [Kitson continued]; while he enjoyed all the elation that comes to the successful man who outdistances his rivals, his greatest pride was in being able to point to the scores of industries that had been built up with the financial aid he had supplied. 'My policy', he once told me, 'is to increase rather than diminish banking facilities ... during financial crises.'

This commitment beyond the walls of his own bank took commercial bankers into new territories of management and responsibility and at the same time raised public expectations of the leaders of the major banks. For Midland, that transition was made possible by Holden's personal brand of leadership. Samuel Murray was better placed than anyone to evaluate that personal factor. The bank, he had told a group of Russian bankers at St Petersburg in 1909,

> have a Chairman who is actually & really the Managing Director & daily in direct attention to the business & a man who is a Banker and with a name in the City to make matters good & with the power and more than that the energy & ability to work matters to a success.

Murray owed his career to Holden and he had good business reasons for extolling the virtues of Midland's management, yet his eulogy did not seem any exaggeration ten years later, when Murray and his lieutenants were bequeathed the largest responsibility in commercial banking.

# CHAPTER SIX

# HOLDEN'S LEGACY
## 1919–1929

In the years immediately before and after the First World War, the rapid growth of large-scale corporations was making unprecedented demands upon the direction and management of British companies. In some cases the sheer determination and force of character of the men who had created the largest amalgamations carried them through the first phases of managing their extended empires.[1] This dependence upon an individual's leadership in both building and maintaining a large company could not be prolonged indefinitely. Policy-making and managerial capacity would be more seriously tested when the next generation of directors and managers took up their responsibilities. In this sense the loss of a guiding hand was a moment of vulnerability in the life of the new enlarged companies.

The prospects of these giants of the business world depended upon the responsibilities which had been carried by the previous chairman or managing director, the effectiveness of plans for a management succession, and the clarity of the company's business development. In Midland Bank's case, Sir Edward Holden's individual authority had never been in real doubt from the date of his appointment as managing director in 1898 until his death in 1919. In management and policy matters his reserves of energy and ideas appeared to be inexhaustible, with the capacity to handle decisions from the most trivial point of detail to the largest questions of international policy. His absence was bound to stretch the bank's management resources. This predicament was accentuated by the death of Samuel Murray, Holden's lieutenant for nearly thirty years, less than three years after the death of his old chief.

Murray was twenty years younger than Holden and he had been expected to give continuity to policy and administration, particularly in the integration of Midland's constituent banks. If Murray had been designated sole chief executive in 1919, his death would have left the leadership of the bank dangerously weakened; it was crucial that Holden's choice of successors should serve the bank for at least a decade. After a period of rapid concentration within the banking business, a period of stable and resilient leadership was essential.

Holden had always been reluctant to combine the duties of chairman and managing director. In choosing his successors he made it clear that the two roles should be separated. Providentially he also insisted upon the sharing of the general management duties between Murray and two other joint managing directors, Frederick Hyde and John Darling. Darling, the former general manager of the London Joint Stock Bank, retired after an illness in 1920,[2] and he was replaced as joint managing director by Edgar Woolley.

The succession of Hyde and Woolley immediately improved the outlook for the future leadership of the bank. Hyde (at the age of only forty-nine in 1919) and Woolley (just fifty-two when he joined Murray and Hyde in 1920) were clearly long-term appointments at a time when most of the general managers of the clearing banks were in their sixties. Both men had been selected and carefully trained by Holden. They had been given a series of senior head office appointments in the late 1890s and 1900s, and, although there was rivalry between Holden's protégés, it had always been made clear to them that they would be expected to succeed Murray. As early as April 1907 Holden had told Woolley that 'we have represented both of you to our Directors. We have held up both of you as young men who have an all round experience and said they would do well to look to you in future. Now it will depend upon both of you from now as to the future.'

While Holden's support for Hyde and Woolley was part of a long-term succession plan, that strategy could only be secured by an authoritative chairman. Holden's own preferences were made clear in April 1917, when he had invited Reginald McKenna to join the board. McKenna was apparently astonished by the invitation, but, when he accepted in January 1918, the board agreed that he should become a full-time director 'with a view to his acquiring a thorough knowledge of the bank's working'. Few former cabinet ministers can ever have been asked to take their non-political duties so seriously. For the next year McKenna shared the chairman's room with Holden, learning the daily routine of a senior banker, meeting Midland's major customers, and working with Murray and the other general managers. 'During that time', McKenna later told Wilfrid Crick, 'Sir Edward did nothing without informing Mr McKenna, even to the last detail, so that the training was most intensive.' The clear implication was that McKenna was to take over Sir Edward's duties 'in the event of his relinquishing the position which he now held'. This arrangement was eventually put into effect eighteen months later when the board elected McKenna to the chairmanship. The only condition attached to the appointment was McKenna's agreement to give the whole of his time to the bank's service and not to engage in any other business or political work.

The choice of McKenna was partly the outcome of close political contacts and partly a reflection of Holden's view of the role of the bank chairmanship towards the end of the long run of amalgamations. McKenna had been a central figure in Liberal politics since the turn of the century. Until the resignation of the Asquith government in 1916 he had held a series of senior posts in the Liberal government which came into power in 1905, leading to his appointment as First Lord of the Admiralty in 1908, Home Secretary in 1911, and Chancellor of the Exchequer in 1915. As Chancellor McKenna found himself in regular contact with Holden, although the two men had been well known to each other since Holden had entered the Commons in 1906. Holden was a key figure in McKenna's response to the exchange crisis of 1915, and in the following year their cooperation was decisive in the second reconstruction of the Yorkshire Penny Bank. In these two emergencies McKenna and Holden could work together, despite the great differences in their backgrounds and the ancient gulf between Whitehall and the commercial banks. When McKenna's 'unflinching loyalty'[3] to Asquith took him out of office in 1916, Holden had quickly recognized that McKenna's abilities would be wasted on the backbenches.

The selection of McKenna was not solely a matter of opportunity. Holden's preference for an outsider was also influenced by the lack of an obvious successor on the existing board. A number of directors, notably Lord Pirrie of Harland and Wolff, Sir Percy Bates and Sir Thomas Royden of Cunard, and Dudley Docker of Metropolitan Carriage and Birmingham Small Arms, were so committed to their companies' contributions to the war effort that they could not be treated as candidates while the war continued. Others could not be considered as very long-term appointments: Robert Beazley, Lord Carnock, Simpson Gee, John Glasbrook, Frederick Nash, Sir Guy Fleetwood Wilson, and William Wyley were all over sixty-five years of age when McKenna was invited to become a director.

A more positive factor in favour of an outsider of McKenna's stature was the fast-growing awareness that Midland's affairs were now a matter of much greater public concern. As one of the largest of the clearing banks (and the largest in the world as a result of the amalgamation of the London Joint Stock Bank in 1918),[4] Midland could never again expect the relative privacy and lack of public attention which it had enjoyed in the years immediately after its arrival in London. Public anxiety over business conduct had in any case been sharpened by the controversy over war-profiteering and, although the banks had not been involved in that debate, they were already feeling the weight of press and public opinion against major banking amalgamations.[5] Official intervention added to these pressures, especially as a result of the Colwyn Committee's investigations (pp 129–31). In these changed circumstances Holden foresaw the advantages of a chairman who would be familiar with the workings of Westminster, Whitehall and Fleet Street.

Reginald McKenna's long experience in government and politics well suited him to this role. It was important that McKenna himself saw the chairmanship as an opportunity to contribute to public affairs in post-war Britain. Almost as soon as he took the chairmanship he was able to use it as a platform for the discussion of monetary policy and the expansion of trade, setting the bank firmly in the context of the economy as a whole. In his own view, it was a task which carried as much responsibility and influence as a senior post in government. He was often consulted by his former colleagues and opponents but he continued to maintain that he would not return to political life. Sir Maurice Hankey, Secretary to the Cabinet, writing to Lloyd George in March 1921 after a luncheon with Midland's directors, reported that McKenna 'declared that he had absolutely abandoned politics and intended to stick to the City'.[6] This commitment was tested in May 1923 when Stanley Baldwin, Prime Minister in the new Conservative Government, invited McKenna to return to the Cabinet as Chancellor of the Exchequer. At that time it was widely reported that McKenna would only agree to become Chancellor if he could represent the City of London as an independent MP; when the sitting member did not give way McKenna refused Baldwin's invitation. In fact, a few days after his meeting with Baldwin on 25 May, he told his fellow directors at the bank that 'in view of his recent illness, he had consulted his doctor, who had forbidden him to take upon himself the responsibilities of Chancellor of the Exchequer until the expiration of two and a half to three months'. The offer from Baldwin remained open but by the autumn McKenna had chosen to remain at the bank.

McKenna's decision to join Midland's board and then to remain as chairman was indispensable both to the making of policy and to the morale of the bank's management in the decade after Holden's death.

The sense of continuity was especially valuable in the bank's efforts to find new ways of maintaining its growth after the Great War. Within Midland, that task was seen in terms of finding yet more channels for attracting and employing ordinary bank deposits. This perception of Midland's function, much as Holden and McKenna enjoyed speaking and intervening on the international scene, was rooted in the development of the clearing banks' home market in the United Kingdom. The assumption was that growth at home would be coupled with centralization and the adoption of uniform Midland procedures in place of the old country banks; the simplification of the bank's registered name to Midland Bank Limited in 1923 was a visible sign of this philosophy. Certainly McKenna (presumably with the concurrence of the joint managing directors) never questioned the need to continue the expansion and centralization of the bank's domestic business, arguing that 'the policy of extending . . . into areas likely to produce a future profit has been justified by past experience'. After the publication of the Colwyn Committee's report in 1918, however, the opportunities for growth were much more limited than they had been in the heyday of the amalgamation movement. The need for Treasury approval for future amalgamations challenged the assumption that mergers would produce improved facilities and forced the largest banks to find other ways of extending their business.

One ready-made answer to this challenge was the deployment of the type of affiliation arrangement which Holden had just completed in Ireland. Ireland, like Scotland, had enjoyed a long and distinctive banking tradition. In the period up to and including the First World War, however, Irish-based companies were increasingly drawn into the mainland's financial markets. The £6 million flotation of Guinness in 1886 was a spectacular example of the value of London connections.[7] The demands of major corporate customers were certainly a strong influence on Midland's initial involvement in Ireland. Lord Pirrie, a valued customer of Midland since the 1890s and a director since 1906, controlled one of the United Kingdom's largest shipping groups in the early part of the century, and his interests included the chairmanship of Harland and Wolff, the Belfast shipbuilders. Pirrie was keen to obtain improved banking facilities in Belfast, and in 1916 he persuaded Holden that it was necessary for Midland to have direct representation in Belfast. Despite the turmoil caused by the Easter Rising, Midland chose to enter Ireland by establishing branch offices in Belfast and Dublin.[8] Premises were bought 'with a view of commencing business in Ireland immediately after the War', but in early 1917 the plan for direct representation was shelved in favour of a scheme for absorbing the Belfast Banking Company. The Belfast Bank had been established in 1827 and had emerged as one of the three major banks in the north of Ireland, with a big participation in public corporation business. At first Holden appeared to favour approaching the Belfast Bank with a proposal for outright purchase and amalgamation. Between January and March 1917 Alexander McDowell, a Belfast solicitor and friend of Lord Pirrie, negotiated a provisional agreement which required the liquidation of the Belfast Bank and the transfer of its shares to Midland. The Belfast Bank viewed the prospect of direct competition with Midland 'with grave apprehension' and duly fell into line with the McDowell proposals. William Patterson, the Belfast Bank's solicitor, took a different position. Noticing that McDowell's scheme did not fully distinguish between the two classes of Belfast Bank shares, which carried different dividend rights and held different prices in the market, Patterson warned that 'there will be legal luminaries, and foremost among them the legal departments of the other banks, who will be eager to find some loophole or opportunity of challenging the amalgamation'. If this should happen, and if only one shareholder chose to go to law, Midland might find itself paying an overinflated price for the amalgamation. Patterson later recalled that 'it was a tense time for the Belfast Bank—life or death. Our death had been decreed and the order gone forth for our liquidation when I was brought on the scene. The great McDowell ... was very wroth and resented my opinion, and it was only after my third attack that I shook him and he rushed to London to consult Clauson.' A C Clauson, a King's Counsel, confirmed that Patterson's analysis was correct and McDowell's initial scheme was dropped.

In place of a direct amalgamation Clauson and Cassie Holden (son of Sir Edward and one of Midland's legal advisers) proposed an entirely new form of banking union. Their plan, presented in May 1917, argued that it was not necessary to liquidate the Belfast Banking Company; the business could be carried on by converting the existing bank from an independent company to a wholly-owned subsidiary. The shares of the Belfast Bank (and hence much of its goodwill) could remain intact by a simple exchange of shares between Midland and the Belfast Bank. Ownership of the Belfast Bank would pass to Midland and the Belfast Bank's shareholders would be given an equivalent shareholding in Midland. As part of the arrangement the business and management of Midland's Belfast subsidiary would remain a separate entity. According to McDowell 'the idea was that except in exceptional matters their [the Belfast Bank management's] decisions would not be interfered with'. The plan was approved by the shareholders of both banks in June 1917. The 'affiliation' agreement of 20 September 1917, which was the first of its kind in British banking, brought Midland an indirect representation of over 80 offices in Ireland, a note circulation of nearly £1.75 million, and deposits of about £9.25 million. The effective cost of this package was £1.24 million, about 12.5 per cent more than the market value of the Belfast Bank before rumours of the deal had begun to circulate. The resulting exchange of shares was completed without any increase in Midland's existing nominal capital of £28.2 million.

The agreement with the Belfast Banking Company had in no way been designed as a means of heading off criticisms of the traditional forms of bank amalgamation but it now became a model for the London banks' alliances in Ireland and Scotland. Because the agreement had protected the managerial autonomy of the Belfast Bank, and because it did not subtract from the local banking facilities available in Ireland, any similar agreements would not breach the undertakings which the banks had given to the Treasury. McKenna and his colleagues, anxious to extend the Midland's interests in Scotland, now moved quickly to secure an affiliation agreement with the Clydesdale Bank. For the shareholders, customers and staff of Midland, the bank's interest in Scotland was a reassuring continuation of Holden's expansionist style. Rumours that Midland had bought premises in Glasgow had circulated as early as the spring of 1917, and in June that year it was confirmed that the bank 'at an early date will commence business in Glasgow, opening two branches in prominent parts of that city'.[9] The other London-based banks were disconcerted by the announcement: Henry Bell, general manager of Lloyds Bank, admitted that 'if the rumours were correct it would probably be considered necessary to follow suit'. In the event Lloyds adopted an affiliation arrangement with the National Bank of Scotland in 1918, and Barclays formed a similar link with the British Linen Bank in 1919.[10]

Initially Midland's acquisition of premises at 91 and 93 Buchanan Street, Glasgow, in 1917 had indicated that Holden planned a new Scottish branch network under the bank's own name. These plans had been postponed when the purchase of the Belfast Bank and the London Joint Stock Bank proved more complex and drawn-out than had been anticipated. By the autumn of 1919, however, encouraged by the success of the Irish affiliation, McKenna and his managing directors altered the original plan for direct representation and made a formal offer for the affiliation of the Clydesdale Bank.

In presenting the fusion to Midland's shareholders, McKenna

stressed that the Clydesdale Bank already had 'a very wide connection in Glasgow and throughout the industrial areas of Scotland'. This emphasis was especially attractive to Midland. The Clydesdale, established in 1838, ranked as the third largest bank in Scotland at the time of the offer, with deposits of about £35 million and over 150 branch offices. For Midland the advantages of an alliance also included the Clydesdale's valuable London business and its representation in Cumberland. The Clydesdale's Cumberland branches were the only Scottish banks in the English regions and, since their opening in 1874, they had been intermediaries between the heavy industries of the Clyde and the Cumberland iron and steel industry.[11] The Clydesdale's customers also included many of the west of Scotland's busiest exporters, especially contracting firms and engineering companies, and these accounts were compatible with Midland's own spread of interests. In some cases, the two banks were already handling the business of major companies with bases both in England and Scotland, notably in the shipping, shipbuilding and engineering industries. Harland and Wolff, with interests on the Clyde as well as in Belfast and London, was a particularly important example, and it is probable that Lord Pirrie was again an influence on the affiliation negotiations. For customer and banker alike, the new alliance was the opportunity to simplify and reduce duplication in dealing with these accounts.

The affiliation with the Clydesdale was adopted in November 1919, broadly following the lines of the Belfast Bank agreement. John Darling, one of the Midland's joint managing directors, and David Young, the Clydesdale's London manager, agreed upon a scheme which enabled the Clydesdale 'to retain its name and continue its existence as a separate entity in all respects. Mr Darling also wished our directors clearly to understand that their powers would be in no way diminished.' McKenna, authoritative even at this early stage of his chairmanship, concluded the detailed negotiations with John Henderson, general manager of the Clydesdale, and signed a draft agreement on 21 November. McKenna then undertook to approach the Treasury's Advisory Committee on Bank Amalgamations, who informed him that there was 'nothing to fear so far as the Treasury is concerned'. When the Committee's consent was obtained Midland's shareholders voted in favour of the affiliation on New Year's Eve to take effect on 1 January 1920.

By valuing each of the 100,000 Clydesdale Bank shares at £42 10s, Midland paid £4.25 million for the affiliation. This price could not be met without increasing the bank's capital, as the number of unissued Midland shares available for exchange was relatively small after the

# A BANKING HERITAGE:
# ILLUSTRATIONS FROM
# MIDLAND'S COLLECTION OF
# PICTURES AND ARCHIVES

**3.1** *Portrait of Charles Geach by J Partridge in about 1850. Geach, a Cornishman who began his career with the Bank of England, was the founder and first manager of Midland in 1836 and was later the bank's managing director until his death in 1854*

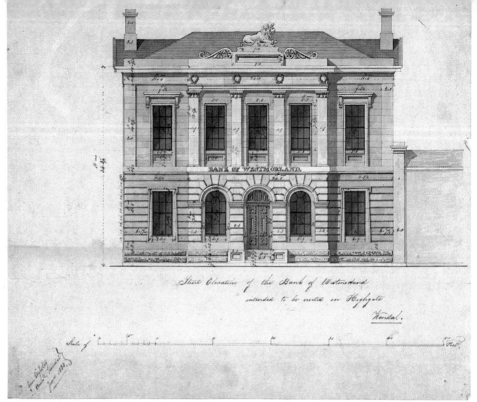

**3.2** *Elevation drawing of the Bank of Westmorland, Kendal, by the architect George Webster in 1833. This bank, which became part of Midland in 1893 and is now its Kendal branch, is one of the oldest purpose-built banking offices in England and Wales*

**3.3** *Brass door-plate from the Bank of Westmorland, now Midland's Kendal branch*

**3.4** *Portrait of William Purton by John Constable in about 1833 (after a portrait probably by Robert Home). Purton was a partner in the old country bank of Cooper and Purton, the predecessor of Midland's branch at Bridgnorth, Shropshire*

**3.5** *Extract from Midland's deed of settlement, 22 August 1836. This document, signed by Charles Geach and the other founders of the bank, marked the beginning of Midland's unbroken record as a shareholders' company*

**3.6** *Midland's archives include the records of scores of constituent banks as well as the parent bank*

3.4

3.5

3.6

Head Office of The Leicestershire Banking Company, 1st October, 1874

Architect Joseph Goddard. The building was built by
T.H. Herbert at a cost of £7,349 and took 18 months to complete.
Costs for interior heating were £150, gas lighting £72.18s.

This Bank was amalgamated with the London & Midland Bank in 1900

**3.7** *The banking hall of the Leicestershire Banking Company's head office. This fine watercolour perspective was based on Joseph Goddard's design for the building in 1874. The Leicestershire Banking Company amalgamated with Midland in 1900, and the building is now the bank's Granby Street office, Leicester*

3.8  *Bank notes: a selection of notes issued by country banks which later became part of Midland Bank*

**3.9** *Portrait of George Rae by Frank Holl, 1884. Rae was one of the outstanding bankers of his generation. Between 1865 and 1890 he was managing director of the North and South Wales* Bank *(which became part of Midland in 1908) and he was the author of* The Country Banker, *a standard work on banking first published in 1885*

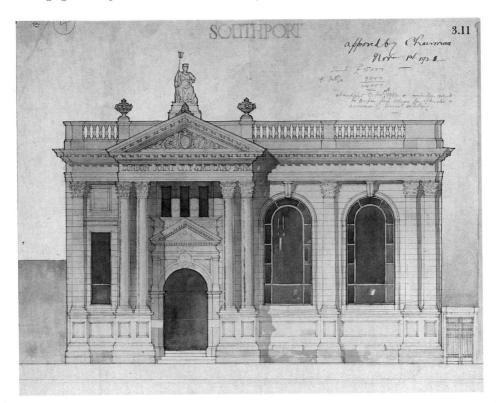

**3.10** *Detail drawing of light fittings for a Midland branch before the First World War*

**3.11** *Design for extension of Midland's Southport branch by the architects Woolfall and Eccles in 1921 (the branch was originally built for the Preston Banking Company in 1888; the architect was E Johnson of Southport)*

**3.12** *Midland's head office, Poultry, from the designs of Sir Edwin Lutyens in association with Gotch and Saunders. This perspective by Cyril Farey was signed by Lutyens in 1925. Building work began the same year and in 1930 the bank occupied the Poultry section of the new headquarters*

**3.13** *Midland's branch at 196a Piccadilly, the first of a series of buildings for the bank by Sir Edwin Lutyens. The branch, shown here in Cyril Farey's perspective, was designed by Lutyens in association with Whinney Son and Austen Hall and completed in 1925*

**3.14** *Perspective drawing by Frank Rimmington of Midland's branch at Church Stretton, Shropshire, based on designs by Woolfall and Eccles in 1919. Many hundreds of elaborate plans and drawings were produced (usually for personal approval by the bank's chairman) while the branch network was expanding quickly early in this century*

**3.15** *Manchester, King Street branch, designed for Midland by Lutyens and Whinney Son and Austen Hall and completed in 1933 (perspective by Cyril Farey)*

**3.16** *The bank's branch at Leadenhall Street in the City of London, by Lutyens and Whinney Son and Austen Hall (1928-31). The branch is shown here in a perspective drawing by Cyril Farey*

**3.17** *Midland Bank's coat of arms, granted in 1952. The coat of arms and badge were the inspiration for the bank's griffin symbol: in heraldic terms the griffin represents the guardian of treasure*

London Joint Stock Bank merger in 1918. The solution was the issue of a new class of Midland shares (fully paid at £2 10s), which lifted the bank's capital to £45.2 million in December 1919. From the point of view of Clydesdale's shareholders, the settlement awarded them a premium of approximately £12 10s per share over the current market price of Clydesdale shares.[12] This allowance of 42 per cent compared favourably with the premiums of 19 and 29 per cent of market price offered in the two other Anglo-Scottish bank affiliation agreements of 1918 and 1919. This premium acted as an incentive for the Clydesdale shareholders and the formal arrangements were completed during the early part of 1920 by the exchange of shares and the election of Midland and Clydesdale directors to join the ranks of their opposite numbers. 'There is in commerce a steady growth of great combinations', Sir James Bell, the Clydesdale's chairman, reported to his shareholders in February 1920, but unlike conventional amalgamations the affiliation arrangement provided for the Clydesdale's independence and expertise. 'There will be no question of consulting with London and consequent delays.'

Throughout the early part of 1920 senior officials of both banks were kept busy with the details of the affiliation. Standardization of practice was an important part of their work, as for example in the control of lending in response to the heavy demand for credit after the First World War. The two managements advised each other of the criteria which they were then using; 'in view of the pressure all round for trade purposes', Hyde pointed out, the Midland 'were discouraging all large advances for Stock Exchange or speculative purposes'. Arrangements for the working of particularly large accounts were also settled. The main administrative changes following the affiliation were the Clydesdale's adoption of Midland's staff pension scheme and, by March 1921, the admission of the Clydesdale staff to Midland's Staff Association.

Affiliation with the Clydesdale, as McKenna had pointed out to Midland's shareholders in November 1919, was a much more rapid and effective means of developing the bank's Scottish connections than building a network of new branches. The drawback was that the Clydesdale did not provide the comprehensive representation which Midland sought. At the time of the affiliation the Clydesdale Bank's main strength was in central Scotland. Although this region contributed most of the business of the Scottish banks, the Clydesdale was poorly represented in the Highlands and along the north-east coast. The setting up of entirely new branches in these regions was not really an option—there were already more banks per head of population than anywhere else in the United Kingdom, and the overhead costs of buildings, staff and communications would have been formidable. As direct amalgamations were so frowned upon by the Treasury, another affiliation agreement offered the best opportunity for a more coherent representation in Scotland. By 1924 the most obvious candidate for such an alliance was the North of Scotland Bank.

Established at Aberdeen in 1834, the North of Scotland Bank had won the lion's share of banking business in north-east Scotland in the nineteenth century. The bank's influential promoters had included Alexander Anderson, the driving force behind the North of Scotland Insurance Company, the Great North of Scotland Railway and many other Aberdeen concerns.[13] This strong leadership brought valuable connections to the North of Scotland Bank and by 1908 it was able to acquire the rival Aberdeen Town and County Bank. The combined branch system of the two banks, with a total of over 150 offices and deposits of over £20 million in 1924 had especially strong links with agriculture and the fishing industry. This set of interests offered Midland a much stronger all-round representation in Scotland when balanced against the Clydesdale's business and industrial accounts. From the North Bank's point of view, moreover, the link with an English institution was increasingly attractive. By 1924 deposits had fallen by 20 per cent since the high point of £22.6 million in 1920, while in 1923 the withdrawal of promised government aid was a serious blow to the bank's customers in agriculture and the fishing industry. In this sense the greatly increased resources of Midland appeared to provide both safety and a greater opportunity for growth.[14]

The North of Scotland Bank's affiliation to Midland broadly followed the model of the arrangements with the Belfast Bank and the Clydesdale Bank. The alliance was completed in 1924. Valuing the North Bank's 163,000 shares at £24 each, Midland paid an effective price of £4.03 million (without needing to increase its nominal capital). This gave the Scottish shareholders a premium of £9 15s per share, equivalent to about 65 per cent of the market price of the shares before the offer became public and the largest bonus on paid-up capital which Midland had yet offered for the ownership of another bank (Table 6.1). Midland was also prepared to write off a liability of no less than £16 per share. All but 60 shares had been transferred by September 1924, despite the efforts of some commentators to discourage any 'attack on Scottish financial independence'.[15] The North Bank's amply-rewarded shareholders were clearly aware that the English

**Table 6.1**

Midland Bank affiliations, 1917–24

| Date | Bank affiliated | Number of branches | Total deposits (£000) | Paid-up capital (£000) | Price of affiliation* (£000) | Ratio Price paid-up capital |
|------|-----------------|--------------------|-----------------------|------------------------|------------------------------|-----------------------------|
| 1917 | Belfast Banking Co | 84 | 9258 | 500 | 1237 | 2.5 |
| 1920 | Clydesdale Bank | 158 | 34,814 | 1000 | 4250 | 4.2 |
| 1924 | North of Scotland Bank | 156 | 20,528 | 652 | 4034 | 6.2 |

*Note** Agreed value of Midland shares and/or cash paid for affiliation

affiliations of the National Bank of Scotland, British Linen Bank and Clydesdale Bank had not seriously interfered with the operational autonomy of the Scottish banks.

By the mid-1920s Midland's affiliations in Scotland and Ireland gave a significantly larger representation than the alliances adopted by the other English banks. The Westminster's investment in the Ulster Bank brought deposits of £21.6 million by 1924; the deposits of the Lloyds-affiliated National Bank of Scotland had reached £31 million, while the business of the British Linen Bank, wholly owned by Barclays, was valued at £26.6 million in deposits. With combined deposits of over £66.7 million (£15.4 million in Ireland and £51.3 million in Scotland), the business of Midland's subsidiaries was more than twice as large as any of the other Anglo-Irish and Anglo-Scottish affiliations. In earnings, too, Midland's investment produced a comparatively good result. In the five years between 1925 and 1929, the published net profits of the bank's Scottish and Irish affiliations added up to an average of £720,000 each year in comparison with the average £216,000 accruing to the Westminster Bank, £286,000 to Lloyds Bank, and £323,000 to Barclays from their Irish and Scottish subsidiaries.[16]

Given the Treasury Committee's close watch over banking amalgamations at home, the success of the new affiliation agreements in Ireland and Scotland was an incentive for similar alliances with banks operating outside the United Kingdom. There were some attractions to this strategy. Throughout the period of amalgamations the banks had rehearsed the argument that rapid growth in new markets was essential if the needs of their major corporate customers were to be met. These customers' requirements were massively extended during the Great War and in its immediate aftermath. The number of substantial international companies trading from and with the United Kingdom had continued to increase, particularly in the chemical and heavy engineering sectors. In the postwar boom of 1920 the combined value of imports, domestic exports and re-exports had reached a peak of over £3490 million, nearly three times as great as the values being recorded ten years earlier and ahead of the rate of inflation.[17]

External factors also favoured some form of affiliation or direct representation abroad. In 1916 Walter Runciman, President of the Board of Trade and a colleague of McKenna's in the Asquith administration, had argued that British banks should be 'a little more venturesome' in their overseas strategies. The Faringdon Committee on Financial Facilities for Trade, reporting later that year, had declared that 'it is essential that British products should be pushed, and manufacturers, merchants and banks must combine to push them'.[18] The British Trade Corporation, set up as a result of the Faringdon recommendations, was only a short-lived experiment but the banks themselves were willing to answer the case by acquiring or establishing overseas subsidiaries. Lloyds and the London County and Westminster had already launched French subsidiaries before the Great War, and the National Provincial and Barclays followed them into Europe after 1917, notably through the Paris-based Cox and Co (France), acquired by Barclays in 1922 and renamed Barclays Bank (Overseas). Barclays was also eager to extend its network of subsidiaries outside Europe, and in 1925 the fusion of three overseas banks under the banner of Barclays Bank (Dominion, Colonial and Overseas) was then the most ambitious experiment in overseas representation yet attempted by the British banks.[19]

Powerful as these influences and examples were, Holden's successors at Midland made no moves to secure a direct presence overseas. The fate of the Petrograd initiative in 1917–18 was bound to be a psychological barrier to further adventures, but at the same time it was emerging that the closure of the Russian office had not permanently damaged the bank's strong correspondent links in Russia. In the 1920s this business staged a remarkable recovery, with Midland maintaining large balances on behalf of its Russian correspondents and supporting its own customers in the manufacturing and commodity trades. Direct representation was evidently not yet essential to an effective overseas business. This appeared to be confirmed when the subsidiaries and foreign branches of the other clearing banks were not the successes which had been anticipated. The Westminster Foreign Bank's Spanish branches were all closed by 1923, while the Zurich branch of Lloyds and National Provincial Bank was shut in 1922. In the relatively small business community of the City of London, Midland's senior managers probably knew that both the Westminster Foreign Bank and Cox and Co (France) were trading at a loss in the early 1920s. They would certainly have been aware of the Bank of England's disapproval of further overseas adventures. The Bank was worried by the prospect of exchange losses and incurring large bad debts in international markets; the confusion in the European exchanges, especially the undervaluation of the French and Belgian francs, made this a real risk. In 1923 the Bank of England closed the accounts of all the overseas banks controlled by the clearers, seriously inconveniencing both Barclays and Lloyds.[20]

By the mid-1920s the unconvincing performance of the foreign subsidiaries and branches of the other banks helped to persuade Midland's senior management that direct overseas representation was unnecessary and undesirable. Holden had laid the foundations of this orthodoxy in the last months of his chairmanship, and McKenna then elaborated this non-interventionist policy in public: 'Very naturally you may wonder why this bank holds a privileged position in its business relations with foreign and colonial bankers', he told shareholders in 1921. 'We have refrained from competing with our foreign friends in their own country and I cannot help thinking that we have gained favour in consequence.' It was an argument which other British bankers may already have accepted, as there is evidence that both Lloyds and National Provincial actually lost ground in France and Belgium after the launching of their joint Continental subsidiary.[21] In practice McKenna could demonstrate that the strategy was rigorously applied in the early 1920s. Explaining the Belfast Bank's sale of its branches in Eire in 1924, McKenna assured shareholders that 'it is not the policy of the Midland Bank to own branches in territories outside the United Kingdom'.

This approach was the platform for the growth of Midland's international earnings in the 1920s. As McKenna had argued, it remained possible to win more business by non-intervention and by acting as a banker's bank rather than by advancing into new territories under the bank's own name. The annual net profits of Midland's overseas branch, for example, averaged £259,000 between 1920 and 1929, with a peak of £467,000 in 1920 and a low point of £159,000 in 1922. In comparison Lloyds and National Provincial Foreign Bank, representing two other large clearers, earned average net profits of only £12,660 between 1919 and 1930.[22]

At the heart of this expansion was the further development of the bank's network of overseas correspondent banks. Throughout the 1920s Midland was providing credits to foreign governments and guaranteeing the finance of exports of electrical goods, textiles and other manufacturers. This type of business did not need the support of foreign branches or subsidiaries when it could be transmitted through the bank's overseas branch and its correspondents. To this end the number of agreements with overseas correspondents was raised from about 650 in 1919 to nearly 1200 by 1929; the new links were particularly numerous in central Europe, the Middle East and the Far East. The volume of foreign transactions multiplied at a similar rate with total acceptances (mostly on behalf of overseas banks) advancing from less than £9 million in 1917 to over £29 million in 1919 and nearly £40 million (38 per cent of the 'Big Five's' combined acceptances) by 1924. Much of this growth was achieved without Midland's managers setting foot outside the overseas branch in Old Broad Street, where senior officials such as L D Anderson and A Moreno were hosts to bankers from all over the world. At the same time the correspondent network was maintained and extended by an arduous programme of travel and direct negotiation with overseas banks. Bunker and C A Wurth (the bank's 'overseas representative' between 1920 and 1929) toured Europe and South America reporting on local financial and political conditions. In the topmost reaches of the bank this network of overseas contacts was supervised by J G Buchanan, a joint general manager who had been recruited on contract by the London Joint Stock Bank from the Crédit Lyonnais, and A T Jackson, a joint general manager with special responsibilities for dealings with the American and Canadian banks. McKenna also contributed to this work. In a business where prestige and personal contacts were warmly appreciated, the chairman made a series of visits to Midland's overseas partners, notably in a long and well-publicized expedition to the United States and Canada with Jackson in 1927.

Midland's postwar affiliations and overseas activities owed much to the ideas and style of management of Sir Edward Holden. They emphasized the importance of the United Kingdom market and the value of a London base. The same influences were at work in branch banking, the bank's dominant source of earnings throughout the 1920s. Even so, a different approach was called for. The compulsory ending of major amalgamations in 1918 in effect cut away the main prop of Holden's plans for growth in the home market. Had it not been for the intervention of the Treasury Committee, it is probable that Holden would have considered further acquisitions amongst the remaining clearing banks. When that opportunity was removed, his successors were forced to seek alternative means of growth. This predicament was shared by each of the 'Big Five' clearing banks, and their efforts were rewarded with stability in the level of their deposits rather than with any sizeable growth (Table 6.2).

Throughout the 1920s Midland was able to hold the largest single share of bank deposits in England and Wales. While unable to stretch its lead, the bank defended its position in its home market both by introducing new services and increasing its branch representation. Some of its new services were vehicles for goodwill and publicity rather than for attracting large slices of new business. The 'Atlantic offices', for instance, were installed aboard the Cunard liners *Berengaria*, *Mauretania* and *Aquitania* in 1920–21 in an effort to introduce and advertise the bank to the growing numbers of ocean travellers. Their income was limited to profits from currency exchange as the three offices did not accept deposits. Other initiatives reflected a more direct

## Table 6.2

Monthly deposits of the 'Big Five' London clearing banks at half-yearly intervals, 1921–29

| Date | A Midland (£ million) | Barclays | Lloyds | National Provincial | West-minster | B 9 London clearing banks | Column A as % of Column B |
|---|---|---|---|---|---|---|---|
| June 1921 | 371 | 332 | 342 | 266 | 309 | 1779 | 20.8 |
| Dec 1921 | 377 | 331 | 349 | 274 | 319 | 1813 | 20.8 |
| June 1922 | 368 | 321 | 342 | 269 | 299 | 1750 | 21.0 |
| Dec 1922 | 356 | 303 | 332 | 264 | 282 | 1688 | 21.1 |
| June 1923 | 348 | 296 | 336 | 259 | 266 | 1647 | 21.1 |
| Dec 1923 | 362 | 302 | 342 | 265 | 271 | 1685 | 21.5 |
| June 1924 | 358 | 296 | 336 | 258 | 270 | 1663 | 21.5 |
| Dec 1924 | 357 | 301 | 341 | 256 | 274 | 1674 | 21.3 |
| June 1925 | 348 | 299 | 338 | 254 | 269 | 1646 | 21.1 |
| Dec 1925 | 350 | 306 | 339 | 254 | 273 | 1663 | 21.0 |
| June 1926 | 349 | 304 | 337 | 255 | 270 | 1650 | 21.1 |
| Dec 1926 | 368 | 310 | 348 | 260 | 287 | 1713 | 21.5 |
| June 1927 | 376 | 309 | 354 | 259 | 272 | 1711 | 22.0 |
| Dec 1927 | 376 | 318 | 359 | 274 | 282 | 1757 | 21.4 |
| June 1928 | 383 | 318 | 348 | 268 | 278 | 1755 | 21.8 |
| Dec 1928 | 396 | 335 | 354 | 291 | 295 | 1841 | 21.5 |
| June 1929 | 384 | 331 | 351 | 273 | 288 | 1790 | 21.4 |
| Dec 1929 | 381 | 337 | 353 | 273 | 286 | 1805 | 21.1 |

*Source:* London clearing banks monthly returns

attempt to broaden the availability of the bank's services and to attract funds which might otherwise move into the enlarged market occupied by government savings, building societies and savings banks. A 'small deposit scheme' was introduced through the branches in December 1920, allowing customers to open interest-bearing deposit accounts for as little as £1. Though not unique amongst the clearing banks, the announcement of the scheme was followed by feverish efforts by the other clearers to publicize their own small deposit facilities. Similarly, in 1926 the bank launched its 'Home Safe Account' scheme. Designed for small savers, the service provided account-holders with locked money-boxes which only the bank could open. The idea was borrowed and adapted from American and British savings institutions (including the Yorkshire Penny Bank), but it was the first venture by a leading clearing bank into this area of small savings. It was thrift at its simplest and most secure, and hundreds of thousands of accounts were opened, often by people who had had no previous contact with a clearing bank. From the point of view of the branch offices, it was also an opportunity to promote Midland's services more vigorously than had been permissible in routine banking duties. Branches were encouraged to compete for the highest number of home safes issued each month, anticipating the type of competition which was used to market new services in the 1960s and 1970s.

Not all these efforts to broaden the bank's business were successful. McKenna and his colleagues suffered a reverse when in May 1927 Midland was disqualified from introducing a scheme for small draft payments without incurring the stamp duty on cheques. The bank had planned the distribution of receipt forms, known as 'chequelets', to customers for the payment of sums under £2. When the receipt form had been filled in, it could be presented for cash payment at the branch on which it was drawn, either by the drawer or a tradesman or other creditor. In this way the 'chequelets' had the advantages of cheques but, according to advice from the Inland Revenue, they were not subject to the two penny stamp duty. The scheme was generally welcomed, with the *Bankers' Magazine* predicting that it would probably lead to 'an increase in the opening of banking accounts by very small depositors'.[23] The Chancellor of the Exchequer (then Winston Churchill) and the Treasury took a different view and challenged the legality of issuing receipt forms without stamp duty; their interpretation was later upheld in a test case. The bank, hearing the Treasury acknowledge that Midland had been given incorrect advice by Somerset House, duly suspended the issue of the chequelets.

These attempts to enlarge the bank's business constituency were paralleled by a serious effort to broaden its ownership. Even in the bank's infancy Midland's founders had been keen that shares should be in small denominations, available to the largest possible number of investors. The tradition was founded on the belief that shareholders gave the bank access to new business both by bringing their own accounts to the bank and by introducing their own customers, friends and relatives. This link was a factor in Midland's introduction of low-denomination shares in the 1920s; if the bank wished to recruit and keep customers with small accounts, it needed to widen the availability of shares. The process was begun with the creation of the fully-paid £2 10s shares in 1919, most of which were used in exchange for Clydesdale and North of Scotland shares. Then in 1925 an entirely new class of fully-paid £1 shares was issued. No increase in capital was needed (the £1 shares were created by cancelling unissued £12 shares), and the new certificates were offered both to shareholders and to members of staff. Within five years over £2.25 million of the new shares had been issued, about 17 per cent of the bank's total paid-up capital.

The short-term financial impact of the alterations to the bank's services cannot have been great, especially after the withdrawal of the 'chequelets' initiative. The most useful feature of the home safe account service, for example, was the introduction of customers who would pass on the connection with Midland to their children and relatives. Ultimately the stability of the deposits of Midland (together with the other clearing banks) relied most heavily upon raising the numbers and improving the distribution of new branches.

The first ten years after Holden's death saw Midland open more new branches and sub-branches than at any other time in its history, reaching a total of 2044 offices by 1929. No less than 638 new offices were established between 1920 and 1929, excluding the 315 branches which were introduced through the new Scottish subsidiaries. The net increase was somewhat less, as 91 branches were closed as a result of the duplication of Midland, Metropolitan or London Joint Stock Bank offices in the London area and the west Midlands. The addition of 547 branches was nevertheless a larger numerical increase than that attempted by the other clearing banks. With the important exception of the National Provincial Bank (which extended its branch representation by no less than 58 per cent to 1308 branches in the same period) the increase of over 36 per cent in the numbers of Midland's branches between 1920 and 1929 was more ambitious than its other main competitors. Barclays had lifted the number of its offices to 2042 by 1929 (an increase of 31 per cent since 1920), Lloyds had advanced to 1853 (a 21 per cent increase), while the Westminster Bank had moved cautiously to a total of 1050 branches, only 5 per cent more than in 1920.[24] This was nevertheless a massive expansion in branch banking as a whole, and by the end of the 1920s few towns and large villages in England and Wales were without one or more branches of the major banks.

In their plans for Midland's new generation of branch banks, Hyde, Woolley and their general managers were bound to follow the obvious geographical and social shifts within the economy. The traditional heavy industries of the north of England and South Wales, overcapitalized during the Great War and in the postwar boom, were feeling the effects of recession throughout the 1920s. In contrast, in the Midlands and the fast-spreading suburban areas of London, industry and trade was soon on the upturn; a wide range of new materials and industrial techniques became available, and the growth of 'new' industries was distinctly biased towards the south.[25]

Midland's branch extensions were broadly in line with these trends. Matching the growth of population and industry in the Greater London area, 119 of the new branches (19 per cent of the total) were opened in that region, mostly in outer London. As many as 65, or 10 per cent of the new branches, were located within about seventy-five miles of London. The profitability of the new branches reflected a similar pattern. Conspicuous amongst the successes were branches in the West End of London, in Kent, Surrey and Hampshire and in seaside towns throughout the country. At the other extreme new offices in Lancashire and industrial Wales were unable to offer any significant profit throughout the 1920s. Very few offices were likely to turn in profits for their first year or two, but by 1929 the distribution in favour of London and the south-east had allowed Midland to show an overall profit on its formidable extension programme since the Great War. This contribution helped to keep Midland's published profits between £2 million and £3 million each year, allowing the bank to maintain the 18 per cent dividend which it had paid since 1904. Actual profits (before payments to the bank's internal contingency funds) were as much as 27 per cent higher than these totals.[26] Nevertheless the overall trend of profitability was beginning to move down in the 1920s. Midland's published net profits declined from 13 per cent of its capital and reserves in 1920 to 10 per cent in 1929. This was in line with the returns from the other major banks, reflecting the high cost of their new branches and the increased competition for deposits.

The unprecedented addition to the bank's representation also placed a strain upon the administrative resources of the bank. The selection of premises, the recruitment of additional staff and the creation of control and accounting systems were all tasks which affected the long-term business prospects of new branches. The bank's premises account, despite strenuous efforts to write down values, had nearly doubled from £5.3 million in 1920 to £10.2 million in 1929 (easily the largest premises account published by the clearing banks). Apart from the sheer numbers of new branches, the sharp rise was the result of Hyde and Woolley's insistence that the new offices should be built and fitted out to the standards laid down by Holden. This was a question on which Holden had held strong, dogmatic views, and it was always unlikely that his successors would venture far from his instructions. Consequently the bank's architects—principally Whinney Son and Austen Hall and Gotch and Saunders in the south and Woolfall and Eccles in the north—continued to be briefed for high-specification new branches.

The 1920s was a period of lively competition between the banks and other financial institutions for a dominant architectural image, and the quality of design and fitting for new and rebuilt branches was part of that contest. This factor was at its most obvious in a series of prestige buildings which Sir Edwin Lutyens designed for the bank in the 1920s: the new head office at Poultry, in association with Gotch and Saunders (1924–30), the Princes Street extension to the head office, in association with Laurence Gotch (1930–39), and the branches at 196a Piccadilly (1921–25) and Leadenhall Street (1928–31) in London and King Street, Manchester (1928–35), in association with Whinney Son and Austen Hall. The chairman's intervention was especially important in the history of these highly praised examples of Lutyens' commercial architecture. McKenna had already been one of Lutyens' most enthusiastic clients when he joined the Midland's board. His wife Pamela was the niece of Lutyens' mentor, the garden designer Gertrude Jekyll, and Lutyens had already built a house in Smith Square, Westminster, for the McKennas. Sir Edwin was later responsible for two more houses for the family. As a consequence McKenna strongly supported his architect's credentials when the bank came to commission the branch at 196a Piccadilly and the much-needed new head office.[27] Over and above this personal link, the close attention which both McKenna and Hyde gave to the Lutyens commissions was a reminder that Sir Edwin's buildings were the largest new commitments in the bank's premises account throughout the interwar period. 'We are confident', McKenna assured shareholders in 1927, 'that the necessarily large expenditure recently incurred will justify itself by contributing to the greater efficiency and ever-

widening scope of the bank's activities.' This was a theme echoed by
F L Bland, president of the Institute of Bankers in 1933, when
defending the banks' recent heavy expenditure on new buildings: 'the
rebuilding which has taken place generally at headquarters was
rendered absolutely necessary by expansion of staff to meet extended
services, and it would have been very false economy not to have done
that providently and well'.[28]

The branch extensions and rebuildings of the 1920s made a
significant difference to Midland's balance sheet, but this growth was
achieved without any substantial additions to staff numbers. In the
banking system as a whole, total staff numbers actually fell from about
65,000 in 1922 to 60,000 in 1929, confirming Holden's warning that
the industry was carrying 'a surplus of labour'. The high level in the
immediate postwar period was a temporary phenomenon. 'Most of
the large banks faced the post-war rush of business whilst still in the
throes of one or more half-digested schemes of amalgamation', the
Institute's *Journal* reported in 1920:

> Consequently a part of the staff was engaged in routine work with which
> they were unfamiliar, and this difficulty was enormously aggravated by
> the return from active service of large numbers of men who had lost touch
> with their old work and with business habits. . . . The banks are, in fact,
> face to face with those difficulties inherent in institutions above a certain
> size.[29]

In these circumstances it was inevitable that some 'wastage' would
occur as the effects of the amalgamations were overcome and the
numbers of temporary women staff and juniors were reduced. This
pressure, combined with anxieties over opportunities for promotion in
a crowded profession, was an important stimulus to the formation of
the Bank Officers' Guild in 1919. The Guild's membership had reached
30,000 by 1922 and in response all the clearing banks fostered their
own internally elected staff associations; Midland's Staff Association,
for example, was launched in 1919 with the active support of Holden
and the bank's directors. After 1919 the Guild and the Association
were in keen and often hostile competition for new members. While
England and Wales did not suffer the strikes or disruption which
affected the United States, Ireland, and Scotland in 1920, employee
representation was now a much larger factor in the planning of the
major banks' operations.

At Midland, one result of the formation of the Staff Association was
a rationalization of salary scales. Traditionally, bank staff had
benefited from bonus payments, and in the early years of the century

these awards had become routine. Then in the postwar slump of 1920 to 1922 the level of bonus had been cut, to the obvious disappointment of clerical staff. After consulting the Staff Association the bank agreed to end the old bonus payments and to supplement salaries instead. Consequently, in 1924 minimum salary scales were increased by about 10 per cent to a range of £85 minimum for junior clerks in London with annual increments of £15 up to £370 (the equivalent range for branches in small towns was £65 to £350). As to promotion prospects, the expansion of branch banking in the 1920s answered many of the anxieties of bank staff. Midland's own numbers steadied at approximately 12,000 in the 1920s but the addition of over 400 new managerships and another 150 sub-managerships increased promotion prospects. Parallel to this change the bank could place much greater stress upon the quality of its existing staff and new recruits; in 1929 some 500 candidates from Midland were successful in the Institute of Bankers' associateship examinations, in comparison with only 197 in 1920. With this wide choice of Midland staff coming forward in search of professional status, there was no danger of a serious shortage of managerial and appointed staff to support the branch extension programme.

By the end of the 1920s, perhaps the major question affecting the future of Midland's enlarged branch network was the capacity of its central accounting and control systems. In the years immediately after the Great War, for instance, the outstanding task had been the standardization of methods in the territories of the old constituent banks. Some of the banks which Midland had absorbed had themselves failed to integrate fully the different systems of their own constituent companies, notably in the case of the London Joint Stock Bank's acquisition of the York City and County Bank.[30] These variations could handicap bankers being promoted from one region to another. As late as 1936 a manager of one of the Sheffield branches 'admitted that he was at a disadvantage, being an outsider as far as the Sheffield Union Bank was concerned'. This was nearly forty years after the Sheffield merger, a remarkable tribute to the persistence of local banking traditions.

In overcoming these difficulties, the most significant breakthrough was the introduction to the branches of a fully mechanized book-keeping system. Ledger-posting machines had been installed at the overseas branch and Threadneedle Street in the mid-1920s, and in July 1927 Hyde and Jackson began to discuss 'the possible use of the machines for listing large credits and ledger trials'. H L Rouse, who had worked on the installation of the bank's first machines, was asked to draw up plans for using the machines throughout the branch system. After trials in 1928, the bank's inspectors reported that 'the system was pretty well watertight in large offices' and arrangements were made for implementing Rouse's plans throughout England and Wales. This progress was matched by standardizing the non-mechanized accounting tasks and documentation throughout head office departments and the branches. In support, the bank's inspectorate was rationalized and strengthened in the same period. Although a thorough appraisal of lending methods was delayed until Hyde's emergence as sole managing director in 1929, these changes in the bank's systems brought the kind of discipline and structure which was needed if the extended branch system was to operate efficiently and offer the bank a source of long-term growth.

Between 1919 and 1929 Midland had been able almost to double its branch representation. Without contravening the Treasury Committee's requirements, the affiliations in Scotland and the new branches in England and Wales had more than maintained the bank's place as the largest of the British clearing banks. Yet for the directors surveying the bank's balance sheet at the end of the 1920s, there were signs that the search for growth of deposits was being eclipsed by worries over the lending position. The bad debts incurred by all the banks in the early 1920s had been greatly reduced in the mid 1920s but by 1929 the level of bad and doubtful debts and unproductive advances was again rising. In Midland's case, bad and doubtful debts had increased from £428,000 in 1924 to £1.86 million in 1928 and £2.03 million by the end of 1929; the troubles in the Lancashire cotton industry and in the South Wales coal and steel industry already accounted for more than half of these provisions. It was these developments which were of most obvious concern when Frederick Hyde took over as sole managing director after Woolley's retirement in 1929. This preoccupation with controls over corporate loans, and the more general problem of the banks' relations with industry, were now to emerge as the major challenges not only to the skills of McKenna, Hyde and their colleagues but also to the assumptions and strategies which had been inherited from the period of Holden's chairmanship.

✦

# CHAPTER SEVEN

# OPPOSITE
# THE BANK OF ENGLAND
# 1929–1939

The small patch of land around the Bank of England was the scene of continuous building work throughout the 1920s and 1930s. Ambitious new head offices were being built for all the main clearing banks, and the Bank of England itself was extended and adapted to the designs of Sir Herbert Baker. In the midst of this noisy festival of building, Midland became an immediate neighbour of the Bank of England. Midland's move into its new head office at Poultry was formalized in April 1930, when it became the bank's registered address. Nine years later the Princes Street section of the new building was also completed, bringing all Midland's principal head office departments under one roof. From this site Lutyens' 'palace of finance'[1] looked across Princes Street at the Bank of England; the Portland stone elevations and high domes of the new building were an unmistakable sign of Midland's place at the centre of the banking community. They were also a symbol of the bank's massive responsibilities in a period of great economic upheaval.

Most of the City's splendid banking halls had been planned early in the 1920s, when hopes for the future of the domestic economy were still running high. By the time the builders and engineers allowed the bankers to occupy their new offices in the late 1920s and early 1930s, conditions had changed dramatically. The magnificence of the bankers' surroundings was in contrast to the depression which gripped most of Britain's basic heavy industries. Financial crises at home and abroad—the Wall Street crash of 1929, the central European banking crisis of 1931, Britain's abandonment of the gold standard in 1931, and the conversion of war loans in 1932—transformed the character of banking business at the highest level in those years. The new headquarters of the banks, instead of serving as tranquil surroundings for hospitality for customers and international bankers, were the scene

of emergency meetings, attempts to rescue major customers, and fierce
arguments over reconstruction agreements.

In these conditions Midland often appeared to be at odds with the
financial policies of the Bank of England. The feeling grew that
Midland was 'opposite' the Bank in spirit as well as in its location. The
responsibilities of the central bank and the largest of the clearing
banks were entirely different but contemporaries and then historians
were quick to point out unneighbourly differences between the two
banks. The public statements and the personality of Reginald
McKenna, Midland's chairman since 1919, contributed to this picture.
In the 1920s McKenna's rapport with John Maynard Keynes,
especially in their campaign against the return to the gold standard in
1925,[2] had set him apart from the other leading bankers of the day.
Financial commentators emphasized this difference of approach, and
it is doubtful whether McKenna actively discouraged them. 'He is not
very popular with his fellow bankers', 'Rhadamanthus' had written in
a syndicated article in August 1928:

> Personally they find him charming, but they murmer against his policy
> and his speeches ... he has stated his belief that the Bank of England
> exercises a pernicious effect on industry by its artificial control of the bank
> rate; that its policy is directed from political and diplomatic considerations
> rather than with the welfare of British commerce and industry at heart.[3]

Fifty years later the Bank of England's historian agreed that
McKenna's opinions and intellectual weight placed him in a special
position. Midland's chairman 'had been Chancellor of the Exchequer
and could have become so again, and was probably the most ambitious
as well as the most intelligent of all the clearing bank chairmen in
these decades'.[4]

The moment at which McKenna's views were most obviously
opposed to those of the central bank was in his treatment of the Bank
of England's witnesses to the Committee on Finance and Industry
(otherwise known as the Macmillan Committee after its chairman
H P Macmillan) in 1929 and 1930. The Committee had been formed
by the incoming Labour government in November 1929, largely in
response to a long-standing demand from Labour politicians and from
some leading industrialists for a full enquiry into monetary policy.
The case for an enquiry was also argued by McKenna himself.[5] In the
event both McKenna and Keynes joined the Committee, whose other
influential members included Professor T E Gregory, Ernest Bevin,
R H Brand of Lazard Brothers and J Frater Taylor, then serving as
the Bank of England's nominated chairman of Beardmore and Co.[6]

Both on the government's instructions and by choice, the Committee concentrated its attention upon the relationships between the financial institutions and industry, trade and employment. Montagu Norman, governor of the Bank of England, had always suspected that such an enquiry would be the excuse for an assault upon the policies which he had been pursuing since the return to the gold standard in 1925. He was not easily persuaded to give evidence to the Committee. When he eventually attended on 26 March 1930, his suspicions appeared to be confirmed. He reported to his colleagues that McKenna had 'attacked him in a rather aggressive manner in regard to facts and figures which he had not in his mind' and complained that he (Norman) understood very little of Keynes' remarks during the session. Keynes for his part felt that the Committee was 'bewildered' by the governor's evidence.[7] The published evidence certainly suggests that the Committee (Keynes and McKenna in particular) and the governor were talking different languages. Keynes was in an ebullient and challenging mood, confronting the governor with opposing interpretations of the management of Bank Rate, while McKenna was armed to the teeth with statistical and analytical questions which he would not always allow Norman to answer. The following exchange was typical of the *impasse* which resulted:

*McKenna:* I want to have this perfectly clear. Am I right in understanding from you that you do not consider industry requires more credit unless the market borrows from you?

*Norman:* No, I do not say that; I think industry now requires a great deal of long credit subject to—

*McKenna:* That is, a particular borrower requires a long credit instead of a short credit. I am dealing now with the total quantity of money. You do not conceive that you need create a larger base for credit unless the market first borrows from you?

*Norman:* No, not exactly that; I said the indication I have that there is a need of credit comes from the market and the market is mainly the buffer between the Bank and—

*McKenna:* The indication to which you pay attention, may I put it that way?

*Norman:* One of the indications to which I pay most attention.

*McKenna:* What are the other indications to which you pay attention?

*Norman:* I cannot tell you in general terms as they may vary in different circumstances.[8]

This lack of communication and lack of progress in the Committee suggested a deep-seated antipathy between Norman on the one hand and Keynes and McKenna on the other. One of Norman's biographers took this view, certainly as far as the personalities were concerned. While McKenna 'pestered Norman with his regular sermons on the correct ways of managing currency and generally running the Bank', Norman was guilty of 'gravely underestimating' the influence and polemical skills of Keynes and McKenna.[9]

Undoubtedly there was always an edge to the Norman–McKenna relationship. In reckoning up the abilities, outlooks and ambitions of the two, it would have been surprising if McKenna had bowed to the almost feudal mastery which Norman adopted in other sections of the business community. Yet the differences in personality magnified their differences over banking and monetary affairs. Norman's brilliance and devotion to duty were obscured by his secretiveness and his obvious discomfort in presenting arguments or entering public controversies.[10] McKenna, for all his experience and his coherence in argument, conducted his campaigns in a style which was quite unfamiliar to the City. There was a grandeur and authority about his public statements which was widely respected, but his manner in meetings and interviews was more reminiscent of a courtroom than a banking parlour. His cross-examinations of witnesses to the Macmillan Committee were perhaps extreme examples but even those who worked with McKenna remember that his ideas and public statements were hammered out in a fierce heat of argument and counter-argument. While Hyde and his senior colleagues obviously acclimatized themselves to this style of leadership, Norman was rarely at his ease in his dealings with Midland's chairman.

In reality cooperation in banking matters between the Bank and Midland was becoming much closer than public interpretation of the relationship between Norman and McKenna would suggest. In confidential evidence to the Macmillan Committee on 21 March 1930, for example, McKenna stressed that 'in my own personal very strong view I wish the Bank of England to retain this responsibility [for variation in the quantity of money], and of all the people . . . whom I should regard as competent to exercise authority I think Mr Norman is the best'. This was especially true of the banks' relationships with industry. By the late 1920s the complaint that the clearing banks were insufficiently courageous in their lending to manufacturing industry had become almost compulsory to any discussion of the economy. It was a view which was canvassed by senior figures in politics and industry, including Sir Basil Blackett, a former controller of finance at the Treasury and a director of the Bank of England from 1929 until his death in 1935, and Sir Arthur Salter, director of the Economic Section of the League of Nations. Blackett argued that the clearers held huge deposits which, in contrast to the mobilization of bank finance in Europe, were of little use in the repair of British industry. 'Only rationalisation can save us', he declared in 1929; 'it means for us essentially the getting rid of individualism in industry, co-operation, amalgamation, ruthless scrapping of out-of-date plant and out-of-date directors, and it can only be done if the banks come out boldly and face it.'[11] The banks were also taken as the scapegoats by critics on both sides of the House of Commons and even in the Cabinet. Sir Arthur Steel-Maitland, Minister of Labour in the Conservative government from 1924 to 1929, denounced the timidity of bankers; in his scheme for industrial reorganization in 1928–29 he favoured by-passing the banks altogether in favour of government loans.[12]

In private the banks could refute these criticisms by counting the cost of support for industrial customers during the 1920s. There was no shortage of examples of intervention and reconstruction, and in these efforts Montagu Norman was as active as anyone. In Midland's case, large doses of extended credit and management time had been prescribed for major customers in the cotton industry, in heavy engineering (notably Vickers, where McKenna was a member of the advisory committee which played an influential part in the reorganization of the company between 1925 and 1927), and in the motor industry (at Austin, Belsize Motors and Rover, for example).[13] The clearest reflection of Midland's commitment was the level of its advances to business and industrial customers. Its total advances of over £210 million in 1929 were larger than those of any other clearing bank, representing 22 per cent of the total advances of the London clearing banks. More significantly over 50 per cent of the bank's advances were in the category of industry and trade (Appendix 5, p 338). This allocation, far from being timid, was larger than the industrial and commercial lending undertaken by the other banks. Of those banks whose advances were classified in the late 1920s, Martins Bank put on loan to trade and industry only about 43 per cent of its advances and Lloyds Bank's allocation was perhaps even less. The average figure for the clearing banks given in evidence to the Macmillan Committee in 1929 was only about 49 per cent.[14]

Although published information about the banks' advances was increasingly detailed by 1930, much of the qualitative information about the relationship with industry could not be used as a defence against criticism. Any attempt to publicize a bank's support for its customers would have been viewed both as a breach of confidentiality and as an open invitation to competitors to take advantage of information about interest rates, securities and the assets and market position of each customer. As a result criticisms of the banks' role in industry could not easily be answered, even if those criticisms were being made at the highest levels of government. This same concern for confidentiality remained a serious obstacle to discussion or cooperation between the major banks. Even where individual banks may have done their utmost to support or rescue a customer, their reluctance to collaborate may have prevented them from recognizing either the imminence of a bankruptcy or the broad potential for development of some categories of business.[15] The distinguished accountant Sir William McLintock, for instance, believed that the major industrial reorganizations could not succeed until the 'individualism run riot' of the main clearing banks could be reined in.[16]

By 1930 there were signs that senior bankers recognized the need for greater cooperation between the banks in their relations with industry and commerce. The formation of the Macmillan Committee was a persuasive factor. Far from concentrating its questions exclusively on the Bank of England's role in the banking community, as Montagu Norman had feared, the committee grabbed the opportunity to dispel some of the mysteries surrounding the clearing banks' dealings with industry and trade. The chairmen and senior general managers of the clearing banks found themselves cross-examined in great detail. Frederick Hyde, on Midland's behalf, was given a thorough questioning, although the published minutes suggest that with McKenna providing moral support from the other side of the table the atmosphere was rather more good-humoured than it was for some other leading bankers. The questions ranged widely over the duration of advances, the extent of the banks' control over industries, the role of directors nominated by the banks, the special problems of the cotton industry, and the operation of fixed ratios for the control of lending.[17] In all these areas, Hyde and his opposite numbers in the other banks were caught up in a process of self-criticism which was much more complex and far-reaching than their evidence to the Colwyn and Cunliffe committees in 1918.

When it was eventually published in 1931, the Macmillan Committee's report did not make radical new proposals for the clearing banks' conduct of their industrial business. Admittedly there was a half-hearted recommendation that relations between the Bank of England and the clearers 'might with advantage be somewhat closer than they are now', but the overall conclusion was that the existing banking system was adequate for 'the normal short credits to industry'. The report's only major reservation was that the existing apparatus left a gap (later labelled 'the Macmillan Gap') in the supply of long- and medium-term finance for small business. The report recommended the launching of an agency which might fill this gap by lending in small amounts up to £200,000, but no firm guidance on this initiative was offered.[18] As with other enquiries of this kind, however, the committee's investigations produced results in anticipation of its conclusions. Senior bankers, after undergoing such detailed questioning, were already conditioned to the possibility of new initiatives. Cooperation and the creation of a united front was a much more desirable objective than it had been when McLintock had spoken of the banks' 'individualism run riot' in 1928.

It was in these changed circumstances that Montagu Norman and his advisers suggested that the banking community should join a cooperative venture to assist in industrial reorganization. In November 1929 Norman had established Securities Management Trust as a subsidiary of the Bank of England, and this new agency was given the task of advising on all the industrial reorganization schemes in which the Bank had an interest. Then in June 1930, while the Macmillan Committee was still sitting, the governor was able to persuade all the clearing banks and other financial institutions to establish the Bankers Industrial Development Company (BIDC). The Bank subscribed a quarter of the nominal share capital, with the remainder provided by the other institutions (including Midland). The objective of the new company was to consider schemes for industrial reorganization and, 'if approved, to procure the necessary financial support for carrying out the scheme'. The priority was consultation and advice, and direct finance was only available for new investment schemes in exceptional circumstances.

In practice the activities of BIDC were dominated by the same group of experts whom Norman had recruited to Securities Management Trust: Sir Guy Granet (a partner in Higginson and Co), Frater Taylor, Frank Hodges (a member of the Central Electricity Board), Charles Bruce-Gardner, and Professor Henry Clay, from Manchester University.[19] Midland and the other clearing banks were nevertheless kept closely informed of the work of this high-powered group, who demonstrated that the new initiative did not deserve its name tag of 'Brought in Dead'. BIDC's output included major projects for Stewarts and Lloyds (where BIDC helped to finance the new Bessemer steel works at Corby), Guest Keen and Nettlefolds and the Woolcombers' Association. Its support for the Lancashire Cotton Corporation was perhaps the most demanding of its projects. This Corporation had been founded in 1929 in an attempt to rationalize the finance and production of Lancashire's cotton mills. Montagu Norman had supported the venture by authorizing the Bank of England to advance nearly £1 million on the Corporation's debentures. Midland was closely involved in the new venture, both as banker to large numbers of mills and, at its Oldham branch, as one of the bankers to the new Corporation. In the long negotiations which followed, the affairs of the Corporation drew heavily upon the time and expertise of E T Parkes, a joint general manager with special knowledge of the cotton industry, and his successor G P A Lederer. Parkes and Lederer maintained the position that 'reform must come from within the trade and that we had all along been opposed to dictating to our customers what they should do' but the involvement of the Bank and BIDC meant that there was more cooperation and sharing of information between the banks than in many other sectors of industry. The result was that 'the Corporation was undoubtedly larger and the operation more swiftly executed than would have been the case if the matter had been left to the directors of the individual companies'.[20]

The formation of BIDC, combined with the influence of the Macmillan Committee hearings, was now an incentive for regular consultations between the major banks. The impetus was maintained in the early 1930s with a series of new proposals for industrial finance. Montagu Norman was particularly anxious to meet the Macmillan Report's call for new sources of finance for small business, and in February 1934 he suggested an entirely new project to the London clearing banks. He invited the clearers to participate in an 'Industrial Mortgage Corporation' which would provide advances of up to £50,000 for periods of two to ten years. These loans were aimed at companies which would not normally obtain a bank loan or contemplate a public issue. Norman believed that a capital of £500,000 would be sufficient for the proposed corporation, reckoning that the Bank would provide £200,000 if the major clearers would invest £50,000 each. At this point McKenna intervened. Midland had just been approached by the Charterhouse Investment Trust, which was looking for subscribers for a similar scheme. Midland's chairman wondered whether a commercial proposition might be preferable in the long run, as it would 'relieve the Bank of England from any participation'. Norman replied that the Bank would not make any move if the objective could be met by a *bona fide* company. As a result the Charterhouse Industrial Development Company was founded in June 1934 by the Charterhouse Investment Trust, with the Prudential Assurance Company, Lloyds Bank and Midland subscribing the remaining capital in November 1935.[21] In June 1934 the Committee of London Clearing Bankers also welcomed the formation of Credit for Industry by John Gibson-Jarvie of United Dominions Trust. Although the clearers decided not to nominate a director to this company, they agreed with Norman that 'the recommendations of the Macmillan Committee in this respect will be adequately met' by the two new companies.

Both Charterhouse Industrial Development Corporation and Credit for Industry soon found themselves competing with other agencies for industrial finance. New entrants included Leadenhall Securities Incorporation (launched by J Henry Schroder and Co in 1935) and the New Trading Company (founded in 1934 and later renamed S G Warburg and Co). Although there was a flood of applications to these new agencies, very few of the proposals offered the type of security or credit-worthiness which were needed as an absolute minimum. By July 1935 Credit for Industry's outstanding loans were less than £400,000; similarly Nutcombe Hume of Charterhouse Industrial Development Corporation told one of Midland's general managers in February 1940 that the new company had examined over 7000 proposals but had been able to finance only seventeen. He concluded that 'where there was any credit-worthiness either in capital or character, the banks covered the position'.[22]

This new group of intermediaries, while not operating on a scale large enough to solve the problems identified by the Macmillan Committee, increased the level of cooperation between the Bank of England and the clearing banks and between individual clearing banks. The banking community had presented a united front on many previous occasions, but (as for example in the Baring crisis of 1890 and the rescue of the Yorkshire Penny Bank in 1911) unanimity had been the temporary response to desperate financial emergencies. In the case of the cooperative experiments of the 1930s, in contrast, there was a new willingness to collaborate and share information as a contribution to the reorganization schemes which played so prominent a part in the interwar industrial scene.

This more positive approach also showed itself in a series of rescues and reconstructions affecting major bank customers. Partly as a reflection of Montagu Norman's own individualistic approach, the Bank of England was already intervening to prevent the collapse of strategically important companies such as Sir W G Armstrong, Whitworth and Co, Beardmore and Co, and the Lancashire Steel Corporation. In the examples of Beardmore and Lancashire Steel the efforts to rationalize existing methods of production and finance were only possible in an alliance with other banks and institutions.[23] For the City as a whole, however, the largest and most complex example of intervention was the reconstruction of the Royal Mail group of shipping companies between 1931 and 1936. This was a task which demanded the cooperation of most of the London clearing banks, the Scottish and Irish banks, the Bank of England, and, for the first time in an operation of this kind, the Treasury. Midland, as banker to one of the largest companies of the group, carried an especially great responsibility, and the efforts to save the group from liquidation emerged as one of the main preoccupations of McKenna, Hyde and their colleagues in the early 1930s.[24]

The root of the problem was the government's guarantee under the Trade Facilities Acts of bank loans of nearly £7 million to the Royal Mail group from 1923 onwards. In 1930 member companies of the group included the Royal Mail Steam Packet Co, Elder Dempster and Co, the Pacific Steam Navigation Co and the Oceanic Steam Navigation Co (or White Star Line). These lines and their sister companies controlled 15 per cent of the British merchant fleet at a time when nearly half the world's tonnage was in British hands. Lord Kylsant, chairman and overlord of the group, had also inherited from Lord Pirrie control of Harland and Wolff, the Belfast shipbuilding concern, and through that connection, the Scottish steel firm of David Colville and Sons. This gigantic group of interests became seriously overextended in 1929 with gross total liabilities of over £120 million, and by 1930 it was apparent that the government's guarantees would be called in. Unless a settlement could be engineered the City faced the collapse of a key section of the British shipping industry and—in view of the prestige and connections of the Royal Mail companies— the devastation of share prices in the shipping sector. The importance of the group as an employer, particularly in the shipyards of Belfast and Glasgow, also introduced sensitive political and social considerations and both the King and the Cabinet made repeated enquiries to the Treasury as to the progress of the case.

As soon as the difficulties of the group became known to the Treasury and the banking community, it was clear that the valuable shipping and shipbuilding assets could only be protected by cooperation on an unprecedented scale. Accordingly the Treasury insisted that Lord Kylsant should call a conference of the group's creditors on 19 May 1930. Representatives of all the leading banks attended the conference, which quickly agreed to appoint its own committee of enquiry, comprising Frederick Hyde, Sir William McLintock and Brigadier-General Arthur Maxwell, senior partner in

Glyn, Mills and Co. Within two weeks this high-powered committee had adopted the principle that the group's shipping lines should, so far as possible, be carried on as going concerns. They also recommended a six-month moratorium on the group's loans and the appointment of a voting control committee to supervise the management of the constituent companies. These suggestions were adopted by the creditors, and by November 1930 Kylsant had little option but to withdraw from active duty as the group's chairman. Nine months later he was convicted on a charge of issuing a false prospectus and sent to prison for twelve months.

Kylsant's departure left the way clear for the voting trustees (Walter Runciman, McLintock and Maxwell) to begin the long and arduous task of reconstructing the group's finances. This was only achieved by urging the forbearance of the group's bankers, and Frederick Hyde played an influential part in this demanding experiment. Midland's participation was in any case essential—no less than £2.8 million of the Trade Facilities Act loans were due to Midland and its affiliated Belfast Bank, with another £600,000 on overdraft—but along with McLintock and Maxwell, Hyde had been quick to recognize the importance of preserving the prestigious shipping lines of the group. Their extinction would have permanently damaged the shipping industry's competitive position and hastened the break-up of the shipbuilding industry. After five years of complex manoeuvring the main constituent parts of the group had been reconstituted as Royal Mail Lines and Elder Dempster Lines. The White Star Line, after nerve-racking negotiations which gave great anxiety to the Bank of England and the clearing banks, was eventually merged with Cunard in 1934. While most of the credit for this achievement belongs to McLintock and Maxwell, Hyde was a key ally in the less glamorous tasks of winning fellow-bankers around to the reconstruction arrangements and, in the case of Harland and Wolff, ensuring that shipbuilding capacity was not irreparably damaged.

The rumble of the Royal Mail crisis could be heard throughout the City in the 1930s. Yet it was by no means the only reconstruction which brought the banks together to untangle the affairs of major customers. The diaries of Hyde and his colleagues record an increasing level of cooperation between the major banks in the running of large industrial and shipping accounts. The financial affairs of the department stores and the commodity markets (notably in the tin market and in the 'pepper crisis' of 1935) were also a high priority for London's senior bankers. Not least, McKenna, Hyde and their opposite numbers in the other banks were able to take concerted action in a series of problems in overseas banking. The main clearing banks retained their separate approaches to foreign business but in the 1930s, with Montagu Norman's encouragement, they could be persuaded to put aside these differences. When the Anglo-South American Bank neared collapse in September 1931 as a result of its overcommitment to nitrate producers in Chile, the Bank of England was asked for loans or discounts of £3 million. Norman was willing to help but he was keen that the risk should be spread. Midland, along with Barclays, National Provincial, and Westminster, agreed to join the Bank in a consortium to cover the Anglo-South American Bank's acceptances. By May 1932 the consortium (now joined by the smaller clearing banks and four merchant banks) had taken over liabilities of no less than £8.5 million with Midland and Barclays each contributing £1 million. This concerted action headed off a complete collapse of the Anglo-South American Bank. Although the Bank of England and the other members of the consortium recovered only half of the value of their support, the remnants of the Anglo-South American Bank's business were saved from liquidation when the Bank of London and South America took over its liabilities in 1936. In these desperate circumstances the idea which Holden had once mooted for the merger of all the British banks in South America finally became a reality.[25]

The external situation in Europe was also a continuing source of anxiety after the events of 1929–31. The failure of the Osterreichische Creditanstalt of Vienna and the subsequent collapse of the German banking system in the summer of 1931 imposed a threatening strain on the London banks.[26] Over £350 million of foreign-owned funds was pulled out of the London market between June 1930 and December 1931 and, at the height of the rush in the summer of 1931, the country's own deteriorating liquidity position was encouraging the outward flow of funds.

London's merchant banks were more seriously and more immediately affected by the crisis than the major clearing banks. The outstanding German commitments of the accepting houses were over £35 million in 1931, in comparison with the clearers' combined credit lines of about £15 million. The arrangements for sorting out the confusion nonetheless leaned heavily on the time and resources of the British clearing banks. At a seven-power conference in July 1931 the British government had joined an international agreement 'to arrest the further withdrawal from Germany of banking facilities of all kinds and thus avert complete financial breakdown'. The government in turn requested all the major British banks (including Midland) to maintain a 'standstill agreement' not to collect their claims on

Germany. Operating through the Joint Committee of British Short-term Creditors, the banks accepted these conditions and for the next eight years allowed the renewal of the agreement.

Midland's German commitments in July 1931 were £3.3 million (channelled mostly through its old correspondent links with the Deutsche Bank and the Dresdner Bank). This was less than 7 per cent of the London total, but McKenna and Hyde were increasingly alarmed by the extension of the standstill later in the 1930s. They were particularly troubled that the effective rate of interest on loans made under the agreement was significantly lower than the rate allowed to British industrialists and traders. However the vulnerable position of British business in Germany left little room for manoeuvre. Writing to Hyde in February 1933, R H Brand (a director of Lazard Brothers and a leading member of the Joint Committee) warned that 'very powerful interests in the new German government have opinions about interest rates and foreign debts decidedly different from those of bankers and there seemed a considerable risk for the future in adopting a completely uncompromising attitude'. McKenna and Hyde were soon alerted to these risks. In 1933 they received a comprehensive report on German conditions by Wilfrid Crick, manager of Midland's intelligence department. Crick had described the type of economic regime which the Nazi party was imposing and he made it clear that there was little hope of an early end to the standstill as long as Hitler's government kept such a stranglehold over the German banking system. McKenna and Hyde accordingly joined other senior bankers in pressing for reductions in the level of standstill commitments. As late as February 1939 the credit line remained as high as £36 million with Midland's own commitment only slightly reduced to £2.75 million. The German banks, encouraged by their government, resisted by negotiating yet further extensions, with the result that the standstill agreement was not formally terminated until the outbreak of war in September 1939. The payments were resumed under a new agreement in 1952 and it was not until 1961 that the last standstill debt had been repaid to British creditors.[27]

The growing cohesiveness at the centre of the banking community ensured that the Committee of London Clearing Bankers, which had discreetly watched over the interests of members of the Clearing House since the mid-nineteenth century, now played a much more prominent role as a forum for senior bankers. Consequently by the end of the 1930s the Committee, together with the British Bankers' Association, rapidly won the banks' cooperation in preparing emergency plans for controlling the banking system in the event of war (Chapter Eight).

On a more personal level the sharing of information and responsibilities was also helping to break down some of the prejudices and rivalries which had afflicted the period immediately after the First World War. McKenna's ideas for enlarging the banks' credit base, for example, which had either been ignored or treated as heresy in 1929–30, were influencing the Bank of England's own attitude to the supply of credit at the end of the 1930s. McKenna himself enjoyed a much warmer relationship with the Bank of England as he and Norman neared the ends of their careers; as a sign of this greater understanding, McKenna was the governor's original choice to negotiate the sale of British-owned American securities in New York in August 1939.[28]

The changing relationship between the Bank of England and the major banks and between the banks themselves had been hinted at as early as 1930 in Sir Ernest Harvey's evidence to the Macmillan Committee. It was a theme which was taken up in an appreciation of Norman on his retirement in 1944:

> Down to the financial crisis of '31, there was virtually no liaison between the 'big five' and the Bank. The formal quarterly Bank lunches were the only occasions when Norman met the chairmen. During the thirties, however, though actual meetings were still infrequent, a spirit of co-operation gained ground on both sides.[29]

In the example of Midland, this journey towards the centre could only be attempted after a deep-seated change in its outlook. In the period before and immediately after the First World War, the bank's stance and reputation had been that of an ambitious and acquisitive organization, dominated by the ideas and personality of Holden and ever-anxious to take an independent line on issues of banking policy. Twenty years later the assertive spirit of 1913–14 appeared to have diminished. At Midland the change of approach was not so much exhaustion as a distinct development in the personality of the bank and its leadership. The extrovert and somewhat insensitive attitudes of Holden now gave way to a much more self-conscious and self-critical style of banking. Superficially the change in attitude was not obvious. Midland's advertising and public relations activities were at least as outward-looking as those of its competitors. Reginald McKenna's speeches to the bank's shareholders continued to be one of the City's set-pieces of analysis and discussion. In the celebration of the bank's centenary in 1936, the national and local publicity efforts were a remarkable example of professionalism at a time when the banks found it difficult or demeaning to advertise their services in any meaningful way. The bank's publications were also winning respect.

The *Midland Bank Monthly Review*, first published in 1916, had become perhaps the most authoritative of bankers' commentaries on the economy and economic policy, while specialist publications offered financial advice to exporters, travellers, and new customers.

This readiness to publicize the bank's activities and maintain its reputation would doubtless have seemed unnecessary to Holden and his contemporaries. They had rarely discussed their business in public and always assumed that a strong balance sheet and a firm annual statement to shareholders were sufficient to secure confidence. This was no longer possible after the banks had come under close scrutiny in the later stages of the amalgamation movement. The Colwyn Committee and the Macmillan Committee had both asked for explanations of the clearing banks' operations and policies, and in the 1920s and 1930s the performance and decisions of the banks continuously featured in political debate and in the financial press. In this environment Midland's publicity efforts between the wars were reflections of an awareness and an anxiety about the public standing of the major banks.

If senior bankers were increasingly uneasy over public exposure and criticism, then they found little comfort in the performance and profitability of their companies in the deep recession of the late 1920s and early 1930s. The deposits of the London clearing banks had slipped from over £1800 million in December 1921 to just over £1700 million ten years later. Although the volume of deposits began to recover in the aftermath of the slump, the London clearers' advances fell away from £978 million in 1929 to only £730 million in 1933. The heavy accumulation of bad and doubtful debts as a result of business failures during and immediately after the slump was an additional burden. In Midland's case, internal provision for bad and doubtful debts exceeded £2 million in December 1929, with a particularly heavy concentration in the textile industry, coal, iron and steel, and in stockbroking and the commodity trades. Three years later the position had further deteriorated; provisions for bad debts reached £722,897 and doubtful debts were rated at £4.8 million. While the total provisions still did not exceed 3.25 per cent of total advances, they damaged confidence as well as performance. Profit levels certainly suffered. Published profits were just £2.3 million in 1930, and for the only time between the wars this figure included a net payment (£264,039) from the bank's internal contingent funds. Dividends were reduced to 16 per cent, the lowest return since 1896, and it was not until 1954 that the rate was restored to 18 per cent. Most of the other clearing banks made similar cuts in dividend, but for others the predicament was more serious; in the case of Williams Deacon's the situation was only saved by affiliation with the Royal Bank of Scotland in 1930.[30] Midland's own annual published profits then recovered to about £2.5 million in the late 1930s. Actual profits—in effect net profits before any transfers to contingency reserves—averaged nearly £3.4 million between 1935 and 1938. Even so, profitability had been eroded since the 1920s. The bank's published profits, at 8.7 per cent of capital and reserves between 1931 and 1939, were about one per cent ahead of the average for the English banks but they were still below the levels maintained in the 1920s. They were also below the levels of industrial profits in the 1930s.[31]

Under these external and internal pressures, McKenna, Hyde and their colleagues took a markedly more cautious and inward-looking attitude to the development of the bank. In 1929 Hyde had formed an executive committee (later known as the management committee), which brought a much greater degree of formal centralization to the management of advances and money market activities. The daily committee meetings, which were attended by all the joint general managers, were a highly effective channel for important banking decisions, and they were to dominate the routine domestic business of the bank for another forty years. At the same time Hyde's initiative surrendered much of the personal power which he and Woolley had inherited from Holden and Murray. Major business decisions were thereafter a matter of collective responsibility, leaving less room for the type of speedy and authoritative decision making which had been possible in the early years of the century. The basic management structure had changed little since the beginning of the century (p 109), but several new layers of command had been added since the First World War (Figure 7.1). These new ranks of management were badly needed to cope with the volume of head office work in the aftermath of the amalgamations but inevitably the processing of decisions was not as rapid as it had been under Holden.

In parallel to these changes in management, accounting controls were tightened throughout the bank, aided by the gradual introduction of mechanized accounting in the branches after 1928. The auditing of bad and doubtful debts was also overhauled, with Hyde insisting that his general managers had much more detailed information about each case. Other innovations in the control of systems included the use of microfilm in the cheque clearing departments (from 1934). With the direct encouragement of the Macmillan Committee, after 1932 much greater attention was given to the classification and analysis of the banks' advances, enabling the general managers to keep a closer check

**Figure 7.1.** *Midland Bank board and management structure, 1929*

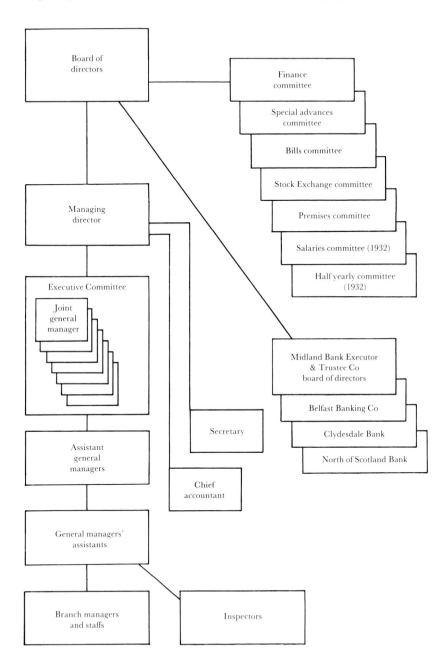

on lending to particular industries or particular regions (Appendix 5, p 338).

The increasingly introspective approach was most evident in the bank's handling of its branch network. In the 1930s the pace of expansion slowed dramatically. The net increase in the number of new offices dwindled to only 96 between 1930 and 1939, an addition of under 5 per cent of the total number operating in 1929 (Appendix 6, p 339); as most of these branches were opened in the period 1930–34, the slowing down appeared to be a real loss of impetus rather than the direct result of the recession. It was the least ambitious phase in the history of the branches since the 1880s and was entirely overshadowed by the adventurous planning of the 1920s. Also in contrast to the early 1920s, when new branches had followed the old pattern of high street banks in towns and villages throughout the country, many of the new branches opened in the 1930s were on new fringes of the banking market: they included offices at universities (Leeds University branch was the earliest example in 1931), industrial sites (for example Slough Trading Estate in 1928 and Filton, Bristol in 1936) and at special events (a branch was operated at the British Industries Fair from 1932). These initiatives showed a much greater flexibility of approach and a recognition of the need for a much wider social and geographical distribution of banking services. On the other hand there was no attempt to follow up these initiatives in any systematic way. Whereas Holden had virtually saturated certain sections of the market where Midland was poorly represented, his successors in the 1930s were reluctant to commit the bank to more than token experiments. This nervousness, especially in the case of industrial site offices, was to place the bank at a disadvantage when branch expansion was held in check in the years after the Second World War.

Although the declining rate of expansion did not in any way threaten Midland's position as the largest of the clearing banks, the less confident attitude to planning soon had an effect on the prospects of the bank's staff. In the early 1930s the pressure on profits was already holding down the level of salaries throughout the banking industry. The Bank Officers' Guild warned that at least one of the 'Big Five' was cancelling its bonus payments by up to £150 per head and trimming its salary scales, while even the Bank of England's staff suffered a 10 per cent cut in their salaries in 1933. At Midland limits on annual increments and overtime pay were in force between 1931 and 1934.[32]

When salary scales were revised in 1935 the range of minimum clerical salaries (£70 to £360 in London, £50 to £340 in small

# MIDLAND'S PEOPLE:
# THE CHANGING FACE OF STAFF AND
# MANAGEMENT

*4.1 Henry Edmunds, who succeeded Charles Geach as Midland's manager (1847–67) and then as managing director (1867–74). The bank more than doubled the size of its business under his management.* Portrait by H T Munns, 1872

*4.2 John Christie, general manager of Midland Bank between 1887 and 1897. In this period Midland's amalgamations converted it from being a country bank into one of the largest London-based clearing banks*

*4.3 Edward Holden in about 1881. Holden, who had begun his career with a Lancashire bank, was appointed Midland's accountant in 1881. His rise to the top of the banking world was meteoric: he became the bank's managing director in 1898 and chairman and managing director in 1908*

**4.4** *Reginald McKenna (seated), Midland's chairman in succession to Edward Holden, with (left to right) Cassie Holden, deputy chairman; Frederick Hyde, Edgar Woolley, and Samuel Murray, the joint general managers*

**4.5** *Miss Anne Tulloch, who was Midland's first woman employee in 1906. In the First World War she was responsible for supervising the bank's entire female staff, which numbered 3600 by 1918*

**4.6** *Cartoon from the* Midland Venture, *the bank's staff association magazine in 1921*

**4.7** *A branch group in the early 1920s: a portrait of the staff of Ipswich branch—then typical in size and manpower—soon after the First World War*

"For Tomorrow - is Friday."

E.S. Howell

& is also the last day of the month;
an All-in Return & looks like being
a wet week-end !!!

**4.8** *Reginald McKenna, a former Home Secretary and Chancellor of the Exchequer, was Midland's longest-serving chairman from 1919 to 1943.* Portrait by James Gunn, 1934

**4.9** *Cartoon from the* Midland Venture, *1931. Since the mid-nineteenth century inspectors have been responsible for enforcing all banking rules and regulations; their unannounced visits to branches were always a moment of great nervousness for bank staff*

- THE INSPECTORS' ANNUAL DINNER -

**4.10** *Midland's staff share a great range of interests and enthusiasms. This photograph shows members of the Midland Bank Flying Club shortly before the Second World War. Many members of the Club served with the RAF during the war, and the Club remained active until 1949*

**4.11** *Viscount Monckton of Brenchley, chairman from 1957 to 1964*

**4.12** *Leonard Mather* (right), *the bank's chief general manager between 1968 and 1972 with Charles Trott, chief general manager from 1972 to 1974*

**4.13** *Sir Archibald Forbes, chairman of Midland Bank from 1964 to 1975 and president from 1975 to 1982*

4.12

4.13

**4.14** *Lord Armstrong* (centre), *chairman from 1975 until 1980, with* (left) *Stuart Graham (chief general manager 1974–80 and group chief executive 1980–81) and Malcolm Wilcox (chief general manager, 1974–80)*

**4.15** *Group executive committee, 1985*
Back row, left to right
*Michael Julien, group finance director; Ian Paterson, chief executive, Midland Bank domestic division; John Thackway, group personnel director; Hervé de Carmoy, chief executive (international division); Frank Cahouet, chairman, Crocker National Bank; Ernst Brutsche, chief executive, group treasury*
Front row, left to right
*Robert Logan, deputy chairman and group chief executive, Samuel Montagu Holdings; John Brooks, deputy group chief executive; Geoffrey Taylor, group chief executive; John Greenwell, chief executive (United Kingdom business); Brian Goldthorpe, chief executive (group risk management), (not present, John Harris, executive director)*

country branches) was actually below the levels operating in the 1920s. This result was typical in banking and in other service industries, but as an additional discipline the bank insisted that its clerks should pass Part I of the Institute of Bankers' examination before they crossed the salary 'bar' of £160 per annum. Part II of the Institute's qualifications was required before a Midland clerk could earn more than £260 each year. Under this more rigorous regime, from 1936 the bank's staff were also required to meet their own income tax liabilities for the first time, and the revision of salary scales which followed did not fully cover the additional cost for individual members of staff.

These changes were a small price in comparison with the upheavals in employment in other parts of the economy. In banking, perhaps for the first time since the City of Glasgow Bank crisis in 1878, it was no longer possible to rely upon job security. Midland's staff appeared to be unscathed by redundancies, though the events of the early 1930s did not allow room for complacency. The Banking Unemployment Insurance Board reported that the cost of unemployment benefits exceeded the agreed contributions from the banks for the first time in the Board's history. A total of £29,318 was paid to unemployed bank officials eligible under the scheme in the year 1932–33.[33]

The area of greatest anxiety for Midland's own staff was the question of promotion prospects. The slowing down of the branch expansion programme, combined with the economies achieved through mechanization, was undoubtedly a brake upon recruitment and promotion. H L Rouse, who had masterminded the bank's mechanization plans, confirmed in 1933 that 'two ledger-posting machines should enable two male clerks to be released and should only necessitate the engagement of one new female operator'.[34] One immediate effect of these changes was a change in the numbers of female staff. In the clearing banks as a whole, the number of female employees rose by 2000 between 1929 and 1935 (reaching a total of 13,000 by 1939) while the number of male clerks fell by 4000. Male clerks who had been recruited or promoted to staff the new branches of the 1920s now found themselves marking time. Much tighter control was also applied to recruitment. Candidates for appointments were expected to have reached school matriculation standard and to pass the bank's own internal qualifying examinations. In 1930 Midland and four other banks also recognized a 'common entrance' banking examination supervised by the City of London College. In response to these more competitive conditions banking staff were noticeably more anxious to support the local centre activities of the Institute of Bankers.[35]

By the end of the 1930s the new element of caution and selfconsciousness in Midland's approach to its business was accentuated by uncertainty over the future leadership of the bank. Frederick Hyde's influence and reputation in the City of London, combined with the no-nonsense approach of a practical banker, had kept intact many of the managerial traditions built up by Sir Edward Holden. But Hyde's health deteriorated in 1935 and 1936 and, although he resumed work with undiminished energy and concentration, illness forced him to retire in June 1938. He died only seven months later. He was succeeded by Herbert Astbury, who was given the new title of chief general manager. Astbury had already taken on many key responsibilities in the period since Hyde's first illness in 1935, but he came to office with a rather narrower experience than his predecessors. His loyalties and interests had been greatly influenced by his early banking background and connections in Birmingham, and he was not groomed for the senior appointment in the way that Hyde and Woolley had been. Moreover, as the extinction of the title of managing director implied, the nature of the job had altered. Whereas Holden, Hyde and his colleagues had obviously carried the type of personal authority which placed them on a higher rung than the general managers of the old constituent banks, Astbury's appointment placed him first among equals. Astbury, like Hyde, was given a seat on the board but the formation of the executive committee in 1929 had replaced personal rule with a collective leadership. This development (combined with the knowledge that Astbury himself was less than five years away from retirement) left the question of the succession full of uncertainties. The promotion of G P A Lederer as 'assistant chief general manager' appeared to clear his path after Astbury's departure, but what was the significance of Clarence Sadd's promotion to the new, ponderously-named appointment of 'deputy assistant chief general manager'? Lederer had been promoted ahead of A T Jackson (who was within less than four years of retirement) but Sadd could offer only two years' experience as a joint general manager. Inevitably the question of these rankings was an unsettling influence on the bank's senior management in the late 1930s. The composure and breadth of approach which had characterized Hyde's own period of office could not easily be recaptured.

The retirement and death of Frederick Hyde left Reginald McKenna as the only surviving member of the small group which Holden had selected in 1919. Even the chairman's authority was less persuasive than it had been in the 1920s and early 1930s. After reaching the age of seventy in 1933, he could not be expected to maintain the pace which he had set himself in forty years of public life. More crucially, his own confidence suffered when in 1935 his name was mentioned during the furore over the London commodity trades. In February 1935 the failure of James and Shakspeare Ltd, commodity brokers, had led to a major collapse in the London pepper trade. The firm's failure was the result of an unsuccessful attempt to corner the market in pepper and shellac, and it led to the trial and conviction of the organisers of the speculation on charges of publishing a false prospectus. The clearing banks, with Montagu Norman's persuasive encouragement, quickly intervened to protect the London produce brokers from the worst effects of the crisis. The banks also provided guarantees for the Mincing Lane brokers while surplus stocks of pepper were sold off between 1935 and 1941.[36] In the meantime it had emerged that McKenna was a shareholder in James and Shakspeare and that the Dean Finance Company (a subsidiary of Tobacco Securities Trust, of which McKenna was also chairman) had invested in the firm. McKenna himself was able to show the Official Receiver that 'he was not informed and never contemplated that the proceeds of the issue [of James and Shakspeare] were required or would be used for the purpose of financing shellac. . . . Pepper was never even mentioned to him'.[37] Nevertheless, because he had given his support to the firm without enquiring closely into its circumstances, it was essential that he should sever his connections with the Dean Finance Company. In March 1936, immediately after the trial, he resigned as chairman of the Tobacco Securities Trust.

The episode affected Midland in two important respects. First the bank had made loans to James and Shakspeare, and it was now clear that both the bank and its chairman had acted without sufficiently detailed information about the firm's commitments. A review of lending procedures was surely needed and, as a result of the James and Shakspeare case, methods for dealing with loan applications were investigated and overhauled at Midland and its banking subsidiaries between 1937 and 1938. Secondly, the chairman's own position was affected. McKenna, worried that references to him during the case made the bank vulnerable to criticism, offered to resign but was firmly dissuaded by the senior directors of the bank, who believed that resignation would be far more damaging both to McKenna and to Midland. In the aftermath of the case the chairman was more reluctant to play a major part in the bank's routine business; in the remaining years of his chairmanship he increasingly relied upon the help and advice of senior directors (notably Sir Thomas Royden, Dudley Docker and Cassie Holden) who had supported him in 1935 and 1936.

By 1939 the experiences of the early 1930s and the more recent anxieties over the leadership of the bank had dented the confidence and authoritativeness with which it had tackled its business in the 1920s. The assertive style of Holden had given way to a more self-critical and cautious approach. As the counterpart to this reorientation Midland was unable to stretch its lead over the other major banks in its share of deposit and lending business. Deposits, fluctuating between a low point of £360 million in 1931 and a peak of £496 million in 1937, represented 21 per cent of the deposits of the nine London clearing banks. Advances, between a low level of £164 million in 1933 and a high point of £221 million in 1939, regularly amounted to 22 per cent of the clearing banks' lending. This record was by no means poor but it confirmed that the expansionary impetus had been halted for the first time in fifty years. In contrast, and alone among the 'Big Five', Barclays Bank was able to improve its share of deposits from 18.5 per cent in 1929–30 to over 19.5 per cent by 1938–39; its share of advances showed a rather sharper increase, from about 18 per cent in 1929–30 to about 21 per cent by the end of the decade.[38]

The challenge posed by Barclays' expansion was postponed by the threat of war in 1939. The banks now turned to the task of preparing for wartime emergencies and coordinating their efforts to protect the routine machinery of banking business. In facing these demands they were better-placed than they might have been ten years earlier. Whereas at the end of the 1920s there were few signs of cooperation and concerted action in the banking world, by 1939 the banks could adopt a much more cohesive approach to major questions of practice and policy. It was a change which owed much to their common efforts to tackle the problems of industrial finance in the aftermath of the Macmillan Report, and, not least, to the improvement in the relations between the clearing banks and the Bank of England.

✳

# CHAPTER EIGHT

# BANKING ON THE DEFENSIVE 1939–1948

In 1938, when Germany occupied Austria and Czechoslovakia almost unopposed, it became clear that the Chamberlain government's policy of appeasement would do no more than buy time in which to prepare for war in Europe. For British bankers and businessmen as well as for the armed forces the experiences of the 1914–18 conflict were of only limited help in drawing up plans to meet the emergency; aerial power had been in its infancy during the Great War and invasion had never seemed a real threat. By 1938, occupation of mainland Britain was at least a possibility and the devastation caused by bombing from the air had been all too clearly demonstrated during the civil war in Spain. Within the banking sector there was an obvious need for coordination and as early as May 1938 the Bank of England was inviting the clearing banks to cooperate 'in the study and preparation of measures necessary in the event of this country being involved in a major war'. The banks therefore began to plan on the basis of probabilities, taking into account the conscription of a large part of their staffs, the safety of records, securities and premises, the provision of additional cash for wartime needs and the maintenance of their sophisticated system for clearing cheques and other forms of money transmission. An additional burden was also to be placed upon them: the task of operating complicated and ever-changing exchange control regulations to ensure that the United Kingdom's foreign assets and earnings would be deployed in paying for the war effort.

This contingency planning had an immediate impact on the operation of branch banks throughout the United Kingdom. Along with the other clearers, Midland faced the problem that the records of customers at each branch were kept solely within that branch, and if enemy action caused them to be destroyed it was necessary to find a way in which they could be reconstructed. As a guard against this type of loss, a system was devised whereby each branch was allotted another as custodian where duplicate records would be maintained and kept up to date by the daily despatch of coded information about the day's transactions. Duplicate signatures and records of items held in security and safe custody would also be maintained there. These precautions could only be made workable by safeguarding the clearing system. Consequently, the clearing banks agreed that the Clearing House would be moved to a less vulnerable site at Trentham Park, on the former estates of the Duke of Sutherland near Stoke-on-Trent. This Central Clearing House, which became operational on 28 August 1939, was far more ambitious in its scope than the prewar arrangements. In addition to the clearers' cheque payments, it dealt with 'London Sundries', such as cheques drawn on non-clearing banks, drafts on shipping firms and interest on government stock payable at the Bank of England.[1]

Midland Bank's long tradition of centralized control, created by the need to bring together the accounting and administrative functions of the many banks absorbed in the Holden era, left it specially vulnerable to the problems which would arise if the new head office in Poultry were to be damaged or destroyed. It was therefore agreed that on the outbreak of war the general managers and their support teams would move out to the new district head offices at Birkdale, Leamington, Bath and Weybridge, each situated centrally within the division under control. It was also planned that extra cash reserves would be held at strategically placed centres throughout the country. Banking hours were to be reduced so that the branches could operate the more complex clearing and duplication arrangements. Instead of opening from 10 am (9 am in London) until 3.30 pm as they had since 1922, the branches were to open only between 10 am and 2 pm; on Saturdays banking hours were to be reduced from three hours to two-and-a-half hours. These plans were complete by early 1939 and each branch manager was issued with a sealed envelope to be opened only on receipt of a specific instruction from head office. When war was declared on 3 September, the sealed orders were opened and the bank's managers learned for the first time of the new wartime systems of control and duplication.

Just as 1938 provided a breathing space in which to anticipate the troubles ahead, the relative inaction of the first months of the war gave the banks a period of calm in which to test the efficiency of their planning. By the summer of 1940, which saw the heavy defeat of the allies in France and led to the expectation of an imminent invasion, the new systems had already been tested and become operational. It was also a period in which the banks could adjust to the new climate of inter-bank cooperation on interest rates, priorities in lending and exchange control regulations. The Committee of London Clearing Bankers and the British Bankers' Association were the main channels for this consultation, enabling both bodies to develop a degree of organization and influence which would have been inconceivable thirty or even twenty years earlier.[2]

The expected aerial assault began in earnest in April 1940, when London was the target. At the same time the south coast towns had to endure constant shelling from guns across the Channel in occupied France. Bombing raids on the major ports of Hull, Newcastle, Bristol, Liverpool, Cardiff and Swansea soon followed, and industrial cities such as Coventry and Sheffield suffered serious damage and loss of life. Despite the mounting losses of German aircraft as a result of the increasingly skilled operations of RAF Fighter Command, it was not until mid-1941, when Germany turned on her former allies in Russia, that there was any abatement in the intensity of the raids. Midland's branch banks suffered severely from bombing in that period and later. Over the six years to 1945 there were some 1350 reports of damage and 31 instances of total destruction, but, as a reflection of the courage and endurance of the staff as well as to the efficiency of the precautions taken, the business of the bank and its customers continued almost without interruption. With an ever-increasing flow of experienced men to the armed forces, much of the routine work was carried out by temporary staff, both male and female, and a heavy burden fell on managers and other senior men in directing their efforts.

Almost every branch bank in the target areas had its story to tell. London staff suffered worst of all. As well as the hazards of working in damaged premises, often without heat or light, they faced the problem of getting to and from their places of work, sometimes after having suffered damage to their own homes. Many preferred to sleep in the basements of the branches rather than travel, and the men took their turn in firewatching duty at night and in other forms of Civil Defence. In the special defence areas along the coast, wives and children were evacuated leaving bank staff, classified as essential workers, to carry on providing services throughout the bombardment. In these conditions of hardship and danger, it was remarkable that only seven members of the staff lost their lives whilst actually on duty at their branches.

The onslaught on life and property clearly called for a sustained level of rapid decision-making on questions affecting the practical administration of the banks. In Midland's case, mobile teams of inspectors were organized to deal with the branches damaged and temporarily put out of action during the bombing. The inspectors' reports gave a graphic account of the hardships suffered in those early war years of 1940 and 1941. In August 1940, for example, during a raid on Portsmouth, the bank's branch at Southsea, Palmerston Road, had the unenviable distinction of being the first to be completely destroyed. The business was almost immediately restarted in alternative premises which were in turn burned out in the following January. Throughout this series of disasters, customers' accounts continued to be serviced from help provided by adjacent branches. London suffered grievously in that same August and September. Peckham, the Monument and Grays Inn, Chiswick, Norbury and Camden Town branches were either destroyed or very badly damaged and in the following month, three more were totally destroyed.[3] In each case business continued, if not quite as usual, with nevertheless a lapse of only a few days before records were reconstructed and new homes found in which to provide customer services. The attitude of the staff to prevailing conditions could be measured by the laconic comments of a hard pressed south coast branch manager who reported that his branch was suffering 'three air raids and two Defence (Finance) Regulations circulars a day, and it was the latter which gave most trouble'.

Midland's northern strongholds also suffered major disruption. In particular Liverpool experienced a series of heavy raids on eight successive nights in May 1941 which completely destroyed six of the bank's branches. The total losses included King Street branch, formerly the head office of Leyland and Bullins which was one of the oldest of the private banks indirectly absorbed by Midland via the North and South Wales Bank. This was a great loss as the building had been preserved in its original style, and like many of the other former head offices of the constituent banks it had carried on a prestigious and profitable business.[4] Sheffield was a similarly important centre in the bank's network which was the target of heavy raids. Colin Cooper, one of the bank's Sheffield managers, recalled the mood of resolution with which the branches faced raids on the city during December 1940:

> On the morning of Friday the 13th Bank Street was a raging inferno, Church Street Branch had all its windows blown out but was structurally undamaged and Market Place Branch was presenting an unyielding front to a wall of flame . . . . That evening the situation deteriorated. Quite by accident an unexploded time-bomb was discovered at the rear of Church Street premises. The office was cleared at 3 pm and within a couple of hours an explosion wrecked the whole of the back premises . . . .

Later the same evening, the Market Place branch was cordoned off owing to the dangerous condition of nearby buildings, with the result that on the Saturday morning the three principal Sheffield branches (with a total staff of 105) were out of action. The bank (together with the Westminster and District Banks) hurriedly arranged to use Cutlers' Hall, next door to the Church Street branch. Over the weekend, the branch staff and the bank's contractors converted the dance floor of Cutlers' Hall for temporary use as a bank, and banking services were resumed there on the Monday morning:

> When the customers streamed in on that morning they saw a line of cashiers standing behind trestle tables with odd lots of tills spaced out on the polished dance floor behind them—'Between this pillar and that pillar is Church Street, between that pillar and the further pillar is Bank Street and from there to the orchestra stands is Market Place.'

In these odd circumstances, the customers of Church Street and Market Place branches were able to obtain a complete service almost immediately. At Bank Street, however, it was another seventeen days before the bombed-out building had cooled down sufficiently to enable the staff to open the fire-proof safes. Incredibly, the branch records were intact, but the incident led to the overhaul of the custodian system through Midland's branch network. Until then, the bank's inspectors had reckoned that the destruction of more than one city-centre branch in the same raid was unlikely. Hence the custodians for many branches in large cities such as Liverpool and Manchester had been located in the same neighbourhoods. Their first year's experience of heavy bombing, and the Sheffield raid in particular, forced them to change their minds, and from January 1941 onwards the records of city-centre branches were much more widely dispersed.[5]

If the circumstances in which the bank kept its mainland branches operating under wartime conditions were unusual, those affecting the Channel Islands branches were extraordinary. Midland had been represented in the islands since 1897, and at the outbreak of war it operated nine offices on Jersey, Guernsey and Sark. When German troops occupied France, all available British forces were needed to concentrate on the defence of the mainland, and on 19 June 1940, it was made known that the islands would not be defended. The Germans arrived on the islands on 30 June but not before the combined banks had organized an improvised withdrawal of all bearer bonds and any securities which could have proved to be of value to the enemy. With all security records, these were shipped to England in 80 sacks. Of Midland's total Channel Islands staff of 53 it was arranged that eight bank men of military age and two women would be evacuated. The remainder stayed and awaited their fate. The German forces took control and from then on, nothing was heard from Midland's branches in Jersey, Guernsey and Sark.

Meanwhile in London the bank had established a special Channel Islands department where customers who had reached the mainland could continue to use their accounts, painstakingly reconstructed from duplicate records. Not until the islands were freed in May 1945 was it revealed that all banks had been placed under the nominal control of the Reichsbank Directorate in Paris. Although there had been agreement to maintain customers' accounts in sterling, the currency in circulation had largely been substituted by Reichsmarks at an artificially high rate of exchange. It was not long before the States authorities, deprived of normal sources of income, were obliged to turn to the banks to supply their needs. The banks had little option, and over the five years of occupation, advances by Midland branches rose from £774,000 to £2,733,000, mainly to meet demands by the authorities. On the other side of the balance sheet, deposits rose from £2,613,000 to £4,376,000, reflecting the inevitable inflation caused by shortages and an artificial currency situation. Small change became scarce, and currency notes were issued for sums as low as sixpence, adding to the problems of the hard pressed staff of the banks.

After the Allies landed in France in 1944, conditions on the islands became desperate both for the Germans and the islanders. Shortages of food and fuel intensified the general discomforts of occupation, and in May 1945 the German garrison was forced to surrender. The bank's chairman immediately wrote to the three managers and their replies give some indication of the hardships endured under enemy occupation. A E Le Masurier, manager of Guernsey branch, reported that:

> Since 1940 we have carried on under trying conditions which did not improve with time. In the first case we were compelled to advance money to the States of Guernsey without any security being deposited and on which any interest charge was refused until communication with the mainland became possible. Then, properties were taken over by the occupying forces and in some cases entirely demolished. We saw our security gradually taken from us and were unable to do anything. We never knew when the Germans would call on us or what they would do. They visited us on several occasions and opened all boxes and parcels left for safe custody. They took out 187 items from these, including one gold 10/- coin and left these with us on a blocked account. The food situation became really critical and our thanks are most certainly due to the Red

Cross for parcels of food received this year and without which we could not have survived. The bank premises received considerable damage during a raid on the harbour last year. We had to remove to temporary premises for ten days while rubble was cleared and all windows barricaded. We are asking the Machines Department to send us a few parts and, if possible, a mechanic as one of our two ledger posting machines broke down some time ago and we have had to repair the other with parts taken from this one. In spite of the very trying conditions prevailing and lack of contact with Head Office, I can assure you that the prestige of the bank had been upheld and that we will get our full share of post-war business.

It was perhaps characteristic of the banking profession that in Mr Le Masurier's first communication after five years in enemy hands, he showed a greater abhorrence of the enforced breaches of banking principles and practice than of personal hardships endured. From Library Place, Jersey, W T Desreaux wrote in similar vein, adding:

As could be expected, conditions have at times been very trying. The activities of collaborators, informers and black marketeers have done much to add to the general troubles, the activities of the last mentioned group being especially aggravating and our ledgers show many swollen balances, due to their insatiable greed.

The staff at Hill Street, Jersey, had been faced with an even more unpleasant predicament. The manager, P H Renouf, reported:

As will be seen by the returns made by us, the occupying forces ordered the surrender of all English notes held by the banks. I was chosen to act as the bank managers' representative to protest against this requisition, and I also acted as spokesman when the bank managers refused to accept Reichsmarks in exchange. I am sorry to say that one of my cashiers, Mr H M Fish, was deported in September 1942 and sent to Germany under an order by which 1400 British subjects were deported. I trust that he is now back in England and in good health.

(Happily Mr Fish survived his ordeal in Germany and was able to resume his career in the bank.)

On the mainland, the bombing had abated by the summer of 1941 and, although sporadic attacks continued, there were none of the concentrated raids which had marked the previous twelve months. It was not until June 1944, when the Germans launched the flying bomb and V2 rocket attacks, that the anxieties and hardships returned in full measure, this time without even the possibility of any warning. Yet between the two periods of concentrated attack other problems had intensified. In October 1942, a committee under Lord Kennet's chairmanship investigated the manpower position in the banks and discovered that over 50 per cent of the prewar male staff had by then been called up for the forces and replaced by women, youths of under call-up age and older men unfit for military service. This factor had already led to major shifts in the pattern of employment at Midland. By the summer of 1942, over 6200 Midland staff were serving with the forces, while no less than 38 per cent of the 12,700 staff remaining with the bank were temporary staff. The influx of temporary staff had more than doubled the number of female staff from 2400 before the war to 5200 in August 1942, and these trends were maintained for the remainder of the war. By August 1945 the contingent of Midland employees with the forces had risen to over 8400, and the bank's own staff was restricted to less than 12,000. Of those maintaining the bank's services, 44 per cent were temporary staff and the proportion of female staff to male staff had also risen to 44 per cent. By the end of 1945 the loss of 420 members of staff killed on active service and 25 civilian staff killed in air raids meant that at least some of the temporary staff would be needed as replacements or as relief staff during the period of demobilization.[6]

Valiant as the efforts of the temporary staff were, the departure of such large numbers of trained bankers on war service placed an enormous burden on those who remained. Managers undertook cashiering duties, long hours were commonplace (particularly when it became necessary for custodian branches to reconstruct the records of knocked-out branches), and long queues were as familiar at till positions as they were at rationing points. The strain was slightly reduced, as the Kennet Committee noted in October 1942, by the closure of 20 per cent of the 8469 banking offices which had been operating in the United Kingdom at the outbreak of war.[7] The Committee strongly recommended more closures of sub-branches in order to prevent further dilution of experienced banking staff. By mutual arrangement between the clearing banks, the Committee's suggestion was implemented and by 1945 the total population of branch banks had fallen to 7000. Of these, Midland's share had decreased from 2138 offices in August 1939 to 1790 at the end of 1944, a shrinkage of 17 per cent; by far the larger proportion of the 348 closures were voluntary economies rather than the result of enemy action.

By 1943, when the news from the battle fronts had turned decisively in favour of the Allies, the British clearing banks could admit that the emergencies of war had taught invaluable lessons on the running of their business. They had learned that the vast army of temporary staff was capable of handling a wide range of tasks which had previously been reserved for trained bankers. They had discovered that mechanized banking depended upon a good supply of replacement machines and parts (the war had grossly overextended the life of machines originally introduced in the 1920s and 1930s). The banks had also entirely lost their nervousness over inter-bank cooperation. At all levels, whether in the higher reaches of the Committee of London Clearing Bankers or in branch banks sharing facilities after bombing raids, the banking industry had been able to act with a greater sense of identity and common purpose than ever before. The use of the custodian system and the rationalization of the clearing system had made contingency planning a much more respected commodity in the banking world. This was especially true for Midland, where the successful use of regional headquarters outside London showed that orderly management was not the prerogative of highly centralized systems of control.

There was clearly a distinction between a bank's plans for meeting wartime emergencies and its plans for longer-term development, but in Midland's case the success of the emergency measures produced a more positive attitude to the bank's future business development. Under the leadership of Alexander Woods, a joint general manager, and Wilfrid Crick, then the bank's economic adviser, a 'Post-War Planning Committee' was established in 1943 to recommend specific business initiatives. Managers and other members of the staff were invited to make suggestions, and the committee also took into consideration the lessons to be learned from experience of operating under emergency conditions. One of the major problems lay in the need to retrain the 8000 men returning from the forces and to train members of the temporary staff recruited during the war years. The concept of training branches for new entrants (which had arisen from the need to provide induction courses for wartime staff) was expanded and eventually became a permanent feature of the postwar years. By 1946, nine such branches were in operation for refresher and induction courses and in 1948 Midland opened its first residential college at Oxted for senior pre-management training.[8]

The postwar planning committee also produced a number of reports which were remarkable in the way in which they forecast changes in banking attitudes. The committee foresaw the many advantages of the decentralized control of branches which had been forced on the bank by the emergency. It forecast the need for longer-term lending, managers' discretionary lending powers, closer contact between managers and head office officials and the possibility of competing with other lending institutions such as building societies.

As a reflection of these views, the chairman's statement in January 1946 emphasized bankers' responsibility for 'looking beyond balance sheets, technical borrowing arrangements and the figures on a customer's account to the reality of economic effort and achievement that lies behind them'. The subsequent acceptance of all these ideas, often many years afterwards, was an eloquent tribute to the work of the committee.

In the final years of the war and in its immediate aftermath, many of the opportunities identified by the postwar planning committee were not fully grasped. The reasons for this lack of commitment were complex. Changes in the leadership of the bank were ultimately an inhibiting factor. The death of Reginald McKenna in September 1943, after an unequalled period of twenty-four years as chairman, was more of a shock to the leadership of the bank than might have been expected. Although he had reached the age of eighty, he had remained an influence in the City with a continuing flair for pronouncements on economic affairs. Many of the obituary notices and tributes emphasised the way in which he, like Norman, had become one of the unchanging features of the financial landscape, while Keynes reminded *The Times*' readers that McKenna 'in a way that no other banker has ever attempted, made the chairmanship of his great institution a pulpit from which to instruct and educate public opinion .... he was the one powerful champion of the new ideas speaking from an unchallengeable position in the City itself.'[9]

Until he was taken ill in June 1943, McKenna had been a firm supporter of the bank's efforts to map out its postwar business ambitions. Ironically his liking for analysis and planning did not extend to the question of his own successors. Before the war he had been keen to nominate Sir John Anderson (a former permanent secretary at the Home Office and later a member of Churchill's War Cabinet) as his successor. The proposal had been blocked by Dudley Docker, who 'did not want "The Policeman" as Chairman'. Anderson moved to the Treasury in 1938 and the question of the succession was left in abeyance. McKenna himself appears to have assumed that Sir Thomas Royden would be prepared to take over. 'All my anxiety about the Bank', he told Royden in July 1943, 'has been relieved when I thought of you there, senior director, ready to take charge .... It is not a commercial mind that is wanted but a statesman's, and you have statesmanship in a high degree.' In the event, Royden was not prepared to forfeit his influential position as senior director, and the board elected instead Stanley Christopherson. Christopherson, who had been elected a director of the London Joint Stock Bank in 1907 and had become Midland's deputy chairman in 1922, was obviously not a permanent replacement; at the age of eighty-two, his role was that of caretaker.

Doubling the uncertainty over the future leadership of the bank, Herbert Astbury had been forced to retire as chief general manager as a result of ill-health in January 1943. He had been succeeded by two chief general managers, G P A Lederer and C T A Sadd. The two men presented a remarkable contrast in management styles. Lederer, with extensive experience of the troubled economy of Lancashire and the north-west, was regarded as an excellent and conscientious technical banker. Sadd's temperament was more flamboyant. Notwithstanding his solid banking background in the east Midlands and London, the financial press repeatedly circulated rumours that he harboured political ambitions. To Lederer's great disappointment (and possibly because he had never treated Sadd as a serious rival), the board promoted Sadd to the new position of chief executive when Christopherson took on the chairmanship in the autumn of 1943. Sadd was given the additional appointment of vice-chairman in 1944; he was knighted in 1945.[10]

Clarence Sadd brought to his new roles a keen interest in the bank's relations with the public at large, an interest which was still unusual amongst senior bankers. As part of this emphasis, he treated the welfare of banking staff and the role of the Institute of Bankers (of which he was president between 1946 and 1948) as essential components of the postwar development of banking. As The Times later recognized, 'he was an early exponent of the need for cultivating personal relations within banking and in presenting a favourable impression of the banking service to the country at large'.[11] This approach was probably influential in the selection of a successor to McKenna and Christopherson. With an obvious nod in the direction of the 'statesmanship' which McKenna had prescribed, the bank's directors announced that Christopherson would be succeeded by the Marquess of Linlithgow in February 1945. Linlithgow had given distinguished service as Viceroy of India in the difficult period from 1936 until 1943, and at the age of only fifty-seven when he joined Midland he could be expected to enjoy a long chairmanship. Unlike McKenna, however, Linlithgow had not been offered the intensive period of familiarization with banking business which Holden had provided for his successor (p 154). This relative lack of experience obviously strengthened the decision-making position of his vice-chairman, Sir Clarence Sadd.

The uncertainty over the future leadership of the bank between

1943 and 1945, coupled with the new emphasis upon the public face of banking, inevitably distracted attention away from some of the opportunities which had been identified by the postwar planning committee. There were also powerful factors outside the bank's control which prevented Linlithgow, Sadd, Lederer and their contemporaries from adopting a more positive strategy. For the banks and the business community in general, the harsh economic and political environment after 1945 made it difficult to distinguish between war and postwar conditions; in many aspects of their work, bankers found themselves maintaining wartime routine long after they might have expected recovery and prosperity.

The effects of war finance meant that Linlithgow and Sadd inherited control of a banking business which was entirely different from the prewar model. The government's massive and ever-increasing expenditure on the war effort could not be met from current revenue. Even allowing for lease-lend and other help from abroad, the government had borrowed by channelling savings into its own hands and by bringing pressure to bear on the clearing banks to turn over to official sources all available funds and to restrict advances for non-essential purposes. The British public had become accustomed to cheap money as Bank Rate had stood at 2 per cent since 1932 (except for a brief period in 1939). For the private investor, the National Savings movement had become the vehicle for patriotic appeals, with National Savings Certificates and Defence Bonds offering returns of around 2.5 to 3 per cent; Midland and the other clearing banks played a full and active part in the marketing of those investments. At the same time firms were encouraged to anticipate tax payable by the purchase of Tax Reserve Certificates. Midland's deposits had risen steadily from £496 million at the end of 1939 to £1060 million—nearly 22 per cent of the clearers' total—at the end of 1945, whereas advances fell from £221 million to £176 million (Appendix 2.2, p 325). The rise in deposits found its way into government hands through increasing investments, Treasury deposits receipts and Treasury bills which totalled over £800 million in 1945. By August 1945 government paper and cash amounted to over 82 per cent of the deposits of the London clearing banks.

This dramatic change in the balance and destination of financial resources was reflected in routine banking as well as official statistics. The government and the Bank of England were able to demand, and obtain, a continuation of the regulations affecting foreign exchange and capital transfers. At Midland's overseas branch this arrangement meant that the much-reduced staff could not be released from the unrewarding task of filing the hundreds of thousands of exchange control documents required by the authorities. This was a handicap at a time when the first priority was the restoration of international contacts. The growing strength of the American banks was an obvious challenge, and British bankers recognized the probability that the dollar would replace sterling as the principal international trading medium. The massive loan of $3.75 billion in 1947, for example, showed that the US authorities were prepared to exact trading advantages by imposing onerous conditions on the conversion of foreign-held sterling balances.[12] Tied down by the exchange regulations, Midland's overseas branch was left with little room for manoeuvre. Lord Linlithgow's international standing was certainly an asset, and in the first year of his chairmanship he toured the Middle East and the Americas on the bank's behalf. He was greatly impressed with 'the high esteem in which the name and service of the Midland Bank are held', but it remained clear that there could be few opportunities for new business initiatives until the burdensome legacy of war finance could be thrown off.

The continuation of wartime official controls was similarly frustrating for those in command of the branch network. Midland, like the other clearing banks, was keen to rebuild branches damaged or destroyed during the war. The bank's postwar planning committee had also anticipated major shifts in the geography of industry after the war, and it had argued that new branches would be needed in government-assisted development areas and industrial estates. Hopes of a rapid restoration of the branch network were dashed by official building restrictions and the continuing shortage of materials. A serious arrears of rebuilding and improvement work accumulated, and it was not until 1956 that the total number of operational branches had been restored to its prewar level.

In the austerity of the immediate postwar period bankers accepted official supervision of foreign exchange business and building controls as the essential conditions of an emergency. Frustrating as they may have been, these conditions reflected the government's absolute responsibility for war finance. In the first years of peace, however, bankers were alarmed at the prospect of continuing and increasing official intervention in the banking system. Indirectly there were signs that the government, acting through the Bank of England, was prepared to support specialist lending agencies outside the clearing bank system. There were important precedents. The Agricultural Mortgage Corporation had been established by the Bank of England and a number of other banks in 1928, but it was not until the

Agricultural Act of 1946 that the Corporation was given larger grant-making powers; Midland became a shareholder of the Corporation in 1946.[13] Similarly the Bank of England and the London banks had established the Bankers' Industrial Development Company (BIDC) in July 1930 to provide finance for industrial reorganization (pp 181–2). Following a recommendation by the Committee on Post War Employment in January 1944, Lord Catto (Norman's successor as governor of the Bank of England) laid plans for a greatly strengthened agency. Although the proposals were 'embraced with some reluctance by the English and Scottish banks', Catto piloted the formation of the Industrial and Commercial Finance Corporation (ICFC) in July 1945. A nominal capital of £15 million was subscribed by the clearing banks and the Bank of England, and the new agency was introduced to the business world as an institution which would fill the 'Macmillan Gap' by 'devoting itself particularly to small industrial and commercial issues'.[14]

This much more ambitious scheme left the banks with the uncomfortable knowledge that the new Corporation could capture their business in a period when their own plans for expansion had been shelved. For this reason, although they were the main shareholders, the clearing banks did not welcome the opening of ICFC branch offices. W G Edington (then Midland's chief general manager) pointed out to John Kinross, ICFC's general manager, that the new company seemed to be 'going out of their way to explore new avenues of lending, eg financing shares in private companies to provide for prospective death duties and the formation of a ship mortgage company'.

While some bankers worried that the new initiatives might damage their business when there was no opportunity to respond, the nationalization of the Bank of England in 1946 was a much more direct form of official intervention. The effect on the banking system was nevertheless not so profound as might have been expected, as the change of ownership simply gave legal effect to the dominant influence of the Treasury both in central banking and in the control of the nation's deposits. This nominal transition was acknowledged by Linlithgow in his statement to shareholders in January 1946:

> I think we may legitimately take it as a silent tribute to the banks, as well as to the intentions of the government, that no untoward reactions have been seen from so delicate a legislation project.

Likewise, in their day-to-day dealings, the clearing banks were not compelled into following the Bank of England's advice simply as a result of its change of ownership. In the autumn of 1947, for example, the Bank of England's discount office warned the banks against making loans for property investments: 'Such advances were inflationary . . . and tended to force the hand of the Capital Issues Committee when customers applied for permission to issue mortgages to repay bank overdrafts.' Midland replied that such advances seemed reasonable, and the other clearers were in agreement.

Even if the nationalization of the central bank did relatively little to disturb the working relationship between the clearing banks and the Bank of England, the legislation carried political overtones. The Labour Party's proposals to take part of the insurance industry into public ownership in 1946 appeared to intensify the threat to the financial community. The proposals to nationalize industrial life assurance companies were eventually dropped in 1947, partly as a result of persuasive counter-arguments from the Co-operative Insurance Society.[15] Yet the possibility of greater government intervention created anxiety and concern amongst the clearing banks, particularly as to the public presentation of the banking industry. Midland's position (at least until 1948) was often out of line with its neighbours. Its view of government policy was distinctly more optimistic than that of the other banks'. In August 1946, for example, the *Midland Bank Review* gave wholehearted support to the international monetary agreements negotiated at Bretton Woods and the associated loan agreements at a time when the City was sceptical. A more controversial view, given in Lord Linlithgow's statement on the 1947 accounts, was the support for the government's industrial and financial policy:

> We are seeing our problems more clearly . . . . Important steps have been taken towards equilibrium between total demands (and) material, labour and productive capacity . . . the financial side of the nation's business, both public and private, is being brought into closer conformity with productive realities.

This attitude was in stark contrast to that of other bank chairmen, and the difference was widely commented upon in the financial press. It was also at odds with Linlithgow's personal views. The source of the discrepancy, some commentators argued, was that there were differences of opinion within the bank, notably between Linlithgow and Sir Clarence Sadd. This explanation is plausible, but only in the context of a continuing uncertainty over the leadership of the bank. Linlithgow and Sadd were operating in a quite different relationship from that between McKenna and his chief general managers. The relationship between board and executive had become blurred, largely as a result of Sadd's ambiguous position as both vice-chairman and chief executive. This difficulty, which had arisen through no fault of either Sadd or Linlithgow, made it extremely difficult for Midland to recapture the authoritative style (both in its public statements and in its business) which it had adopted in the first quarter of the century.

By 1948, when Sadd retired, it was evident that responsibilities at the highest levels of the bank needed clarification. The leadership problem, when combined with the inhospitable economic conditions after the war, had already delayed the type of initiatives envisaged by the postwar planning committee. Consequently by 1948 it was essential that the bank's decision-making structure should be re-examined before Midland could face the challenge of economic recovery and renewed competition between the banks.

※

# CHAPTER NINE

# BURDENS OF LEADERSHIP
# 1948–1959

> I do not know which makes a man more conservative—to know nothing but the present or nothing but the past.
>
> J M Keynes, *The End of Laissez-Faire* (1926), p 16

The years between 1948 and 1957 were not happy ones for Midland Bank. It lost its long-established position as the largest of the United Kingdom's clearing banks, fell behind in the restoration of its branch network, and suffered a major disagreement with its staff which led to the dissolution of the Staff Association. At a time when new thinking and planning were necessary if the bank was to take advantage of postwar opportunities, it seemed that the senior management was looking over its shoulder to the past for guidance, with an over-reliance on traditional policies of central control of branches at home and correspondent relationships abroad. Banking methods as well as the structure of the organization were in stagnation; lending policy was consistently conservative, with few attempts to assess the going-concern potential of customers with new ideas. It was not until 1957 and 1958 that a new spirit of enterprise was in evidence but by then momentum had been lost and the task of trying to climb back to the bank's former pre-eminence was a formidable one, demanding changes in management attitudes and the commitment of substantial resources to a programme of expansion.

Structural problems within the bank played a large part in the loss of momentum. At the most senior level, it might have been expected that Sir Clarence Sadd's unique position as vice-chairman and chief executive would create a strong bridge between the board and the general managers. The advantages of this type of link were obvious. From the chairman's point of view, particularly if he was relatively inexperienced in the ways of banking, he could call on his vice-chairman for professional advice. From the banker's viewpoint, the vice-chairman could be expected to understand, explain and defend the decisions of his general managers.

In practice the bridge between the board and the executive had proved to be weak. After Sadd's retirement in 1948, Linlithgow invited W G Edington and H L Rouse (the two chief general managers) 'to consider and make recommendations on the future relationship between the Board and Executive and on the management of the Bank in general'. They disclosed that the board's recent practice had been to convene their fortnightly meetings at 12.30, leaving time to carry out little more than certain essential statutory duties before the directors retired for lunch. At a time when no less than 12 of the 31 directors were over seventy years of age, it was not surprising that board meetings were neither creative nor controversial. This was also the case in the directors' committees, which were much less active than in the second half of McKenna's chairmanship. Moreover, Edington and Rouse could show that the management committee (established by Frederick Hyde in 1929 and hitherto the supreme executive authority in the bank) felt that the vice-chairman's additional role as chief executive was an abrogation rather than a reinforcement of their powers. Undoubtedly this attitude was a matter of personalities as well as job descriptions and it may have been inherited from the disappointment which many line bankers had felt when the more extrovert Sadd had been promoted ahead of G P A Lederer (p 207). This difficulty was compounded by a sense of disorientation at the higher levels of management; if the management committee was to lose its authority in this way, the framework of decision-making would begin to dissolve. Inevitably, general managers who had been brought up to treat membership of the committee as the summit of a banker's authority were made uncomfortable by the prospect of a single director holding a veto over that authority.

Under these pressures Edington and Rouse urged a return to the position which had existed in the 1930s (Figure 7.1, p 191). They dutifully pointed out the need for more frequent board meetings at which much better information would be made available to directors on topics of general interest, such as the progress of advances, investment policy and premises matters. This type of briefing had been available during McKenna's chairmanship, but the exigencies of wartime management had led to a significant reduction in the paperwork presented to directors. The main burden of the Rouse/ Edington recommendations concerned the bank's management structure, and here they left no room for doubt: 'The functions of the Management Committee and the Board are entirely different and should be kept distinct; ie the members of the Management Committee should not be directors and vice versa.' These recommendations were fully accepted by the board (probably with some relief) and had two important consequences. The opportunity to build a really effective liaison between the two sides was lost in that no current chief executive was offered a seat on the board again until 1966. Secondly, the authority of the management committee was considerably enhanced by the recognition of its absolute power to take decisions, subject only to the requirement to keep the chairman advised daily of its operations. In both these results, the Edington/Rouse report introduced a note of inflexibility which was to characterize both the structure and the business of the bank for nearly a decade.

For the chairman and for the board, the Edington/Rouse recommendations carried considerable practical advantages. The management of the bank could be left in the hands of the two current chief general managers (Edington and Rouse), while at board level the bank could revert to the practice of appointing deputy chairmen from among the ranks of the directors. Accordingly in June 1948 no less than three deputy chairmen (Sir Alexander Roger, Sir Cassie Holden and Lord Harlech) were appointed to replace Sadd as vice-chairman. The three new deputies gave Linlithgow access to wide experience in industrial and political affairs. However, with the possible exception of Sir Cassie's expertise in company law, their qualifications included little direct experience of banking, in strong contrast to Sadd's executive banking role.

Under this regime the new orthodoxy on the relations between the board and management took root. Rouse, in the most fully-stated version of the new ground-rules, explained in 1949 that the general managers' relationships with their directors were the legacy of the country banks:

> the proprietors of the small banking houses from which the Midland Bank grew were themselves also occupied in other professions and trades. Because of their varying interests in those days they were often in competition with their banking customers and it suited both the banker and his customer that there should be an official who could stand between them when matters concerning the financial problems of the latter were under consideration. The early managers employed by private bankers were consequently vested with unusually wide powers and were given authority even to withhold details of customers' individual affairs from their principals; indeed, in our case the original deed of settlement specifically provided for this. Thus, in our own bank, a Mr Charles Geach, managing the Birmingham and Midland Bank over a century ago, was empowered

to exercise very wide discretion in the conduct of the bank's business and his status appears to have set a precedent which is still to be seen in the special responsibilities attaching to a 'top management' divorced from the immediate interests of ownership.[1]

Rouse's historical illustrations were not really appropriate—Geach had been a major shareholder and customer as well as Midland's first manager—but his comments certainly described the importance of independent professionalism in banking since the amalgamation period. The counterpart to this relationship between management and ownership, in Rouse's view, was the link between the general managers at head office and the branches of the bank under their control. Each branch was 'a microcosm of the whole bank in which all services of the Bank are available—the most junior manager speaks with the authority of the bank'. This microcosmic role of the branches left little room for independence of action. Rouse, as might have been expected from a graduate of the Holden and Hyde school of banking, was loyal to the concept of centralization. He argued that the general managers and the head office departments provided a 'reservoir' of information and advice available to branches at short notice.[2]

At branch level, the triumph of the Rouse/Edington version of the bank's structure confirmed that most of the brave new ideas submitted to the postwar planning committee had been either vetoed or indefinitely shelved. Branch managers, many of them in isolated country branches, were now stranded without the authority to lend even the smallest sum without reference to head office. During the war they had enjoyed the advantages of regional decentralization, and in many cases they would have welcomed the prolongation of the experiment in peacetime. Rouse dismissed this alternative as not more than a wartime necessity: 'we were glad to revert to our normal arrangements'. By that time, nonetheless, when Rouse and Edington were framing their new rules for the government of the bank, many managers were already looking enviously at Barclays Bank's system of local head offices.[3]

By 1951 Rouse and Edington's view of the bank's organizational structure had been accepted without challenge from either the board or the senior management. After Rouse's retirement in 1951 the mood became even more conservative and inward-looking. This outcome was partly the reflection of the personalities most involved and partly the result of the pressures on the bank's competitive position. Edington, who served as sole chief general manager between 1951 and 1956, was greatly influenced by his first-hand knowledge of the interwar depression in Lancashire and the north-west. In 1911 he had entered the bank at its Dale Street, Liverpool branch (the breeding ground of many a future general manager) and he had become a specialist in the lending facilities available to the cotton trade. In the 1930s, as manager of Oldham branch, he dealt with the consequences of many business failures caused by the slump in cotton manufacturing, and his experience undoubtedly shaped his later reputation as a cautious lender with a somewhat narrow outlook. Severely wounded in the 1914–18 war, he had called on enormous reserves of courage and determination to advance so far in his career, but having reached the top of his profession he proved to be insensitive to argument and unswerving in his convictions. His ability was undoubted ('he thinks three times and speaks twice as quickly as poor Londoners'), but his character and his experiences as a banker made it difficult for him to recognize the challenges and the opportunities of the early 1950s.

The importance of Edington's outlook as an influence on Midland's performance in the early 1950s should not be underestimated. Both by accident and by choice he was the 'strong man' in the bank's senior management. He had no obvious rivals when he emerged as sole chief general manager after Rouse's retirement. Moreover, because Rouse was essentially a great administrator rather than a lending banker, it could be argued that Edington's domination of Midland's banking business had dated from the moment of Sadd's retirement in 1948.

This primacy was underlined by a further unexpected break in the continuity of the bank's chairmanship. Linlithgow died suddenly in January 1952, at a time when his contributions to Midland's development were becoming increasingly effective and authoritative. The bank's directors had probably anticipated that Linlithgow would continue in office for at least ten years, perhaps for as long as McKenna had held the chairmanship. His death at the age of only sixty-four did not leave the same yawning gap which had appeared after McKenna's death, but the loss of such a statesmanlike chairman was nonetheless a serious blow to morale. The *Financial Times* believed that Linlithgow 'would have laughed at the suggestion that he was skilled in banking' but pointed out that 'his services to the bank were not nominal. To matters of high policy he contributed much and he was an ideal representative of the bank.'[4] His replacement, Lord Harlech, had served as deputy chairman since 1948. Although Harlech's family had long and close associations with the bank (his great-grandfather William Ormsby-Gore had been one of the founders of the London Joint Stock Bank in 1836), his own career was dominated by public and political service; he had been Postmaster-General and Commissioner of Works in the 1931 National Government and was Colonial

Secretary between 1936 and 1938. With this background and with continuing interests in the world of scholarship, he followed Linlithgow in his reluctance to take on any executive commitments. As a result Edington was incontestably the senior partner in the relationship between chairman and chief general manager during Harlech's chairmanship.

In the early 1950s Edington's dominant influence was evident when Midland attempted to reduce its commitments to inter-bank organizations and cooperative ventures. In September 1953, for example, he strongly opposed the Industrial and Commercial Finance Corporation's plans to open provincial branches: 'instead of being content to fulfil its original purpose, [ICFC] were taking active steps to create a demand for their services and attract business to themselves' (p 210). Two years later, he also flatly refused to join or subscribe to the new Banking Information Service (this decision was reversed in 1958). A larger and more painful decision was the withdrawal from the bank's long-standing shareholding in the Yorkshire Penny Bank. In 1951 this bank, which had been rescued by the clearing banks under Holden's leadership in 1911, appealed to the shareholding banks for further support of £1 million to cover the depreciation of its gilt-edged securities. Midland, as the largest shareholder, made the largest contribution, but it refused to subscribe to the issue of a further £1 million in new capital and argued in favour of a thorough review of the Penny Bank's affairs. These differences came to a head when the Penny Bank decided to reduce their shareholding banks' representation to one director per bank. Midland had until then nominated two directors, reflecting the size of its shareholdings. Rather than persevere with the Midland's case, however, Harlech and Edington recommended a disengagement. The bank's shares in the Penny Bank were sold early in 1953, thereby ending an association of over forty years in which Midland had been the largest shareholder and probably the greatest influence on the fortunes of the Yorkshire Penny Bank.

These decisions, even if they were justified in the circumstances of the bank's own business interests, confirmed that under Edington Midland's attitude was less flexible than that of Barclays, its principal rival. At the same time the bank was operating in an environment where even an ambitious and highly imaginative leader would have been forced to take a cautious attitude. A series of balance of payments crises and the additional burdens of the Korean war and the Suez débâcle forced on successive governments a policy of stop-go and credit restriction, which frustrated all attempts to plan for the increase in lending sought by banks and their customers. No bank could plan its affairs constructively in the face of the many overnight changes of government policy. It was particularly inhibiting to have 75 per cent of all deposits still lent to the government in one form or another compared with the prewar position when over 40 per cent was lent to customers at a much better rate of return (Appendix 2.2, p 325).

For the clearing banks these external pressures posed new problems over the management of their investments. The end of cheap money came in 1951, when the Conservative government decided to use Bank Rate as an instrument of monetary policy for the first time in almost twenty years. By March 1952 Bank Rate had doubled to 4 per cent and from then on the trend was generally upwards to counteract the continuing weakness of sterling abroad. Inevitably there was a substantial fall in the value of government securities. For the first time Midland reconsidered its traditional policy of revaluing investments to reflect their market price at each balance sheet date, and absorbing any investment losses in internal contingent funds. Edington and his colleagues asked themselves whether they should persist with the bank's established practice in view of the dramatic fall in market value of gilt-edged securities and bearing in mind that the majority of Midland's investments were in dated stocks maturing at par within ten years. There was no prospect of real loss (except by sale within the period) yet a change of policy could cause a loss of confidence by depositors and investors and certain major firms of auditors had reservations about such a change. In the event Midland (and three of the other clearers) decided to use cost as the valuation basis in the year ended December 1952 and to show the current market value only by a note to the accounts. The new procedure was accepted philosophically enough by the public and by investors. Inside the bank the residual question was whether it would have been possible at that time to follow the old practice of writing off losses to inner reserves. The losses were substantial; were the reserves adequate? If the answer was 'no' it could do much to explain the bank's conservative and sometimes inflexible outlook in the early 1950s. For the moment, there was a clear case for rebuilding the reserves to such a size that they could absorb any similar shocks in the future.

This factor, inextricably linked with the frustrating trading conditions of the late 1940s, almost certainly played a part in the collapse of the bank's old-established understandings with its staff representatives. The Midland Bank Staff Association had been launched in 1919 as the 'internalist' alternative to the Bank Officers' Guild, and for thirty years the bank had recognized and supported the Association as the sole channel for negotiation on salaries and conditions. By 1950 this arrangement had given the Association a membership strength of 10,200, or 63 per cent of the total staff (including the Executor and Trustee Company). The relationship between the bank and the Association owed much to the deferential and almost ritualistic style in which the bank's management and the Association's 'Grand Committee' consulted each other. In February 1950, for example, Lord Alanbrooke (deputizing for Linlithgow at the bank's general meeting) paid the customary tribute to the Staff Association:

> It is through the untiring efforts of that devoted band of men and women, coupled with the benevolent co-operation of the management, that many problems are smoothed out which might otherwise clog the wheels of this great undertaking. It is in no small part due to their untiring efforts that it has been justly stated that this bank is not merely a commercial undertaking, but is also a great family united by brotherly bonds.

Ironically the relationship between the bank and the Association was already crumbling. In the previous year the Association's claim for a cash payment of 10 per cent had been rejected on the grounds that the bank's staff could not expect immunity from 'considerations of national interest and government policy'. The Association protested, warning the bank that an accelerating decline in the staff's standard of living was leading to 'despondency and unrest'. Edington and Rouse had been adamant, and at a meeting with the staff representatives in May 1950 they refused to increase the cash payment offer to more than 7.5 per cent of salary (2.5 per cent less than the award to the staff of other banks). The Association declined to sign the announcement of the award in the usual way, and when its representatives sought an interview with the bank's directors their request was turned down. Thrown off balance, the Association asked for a referendum vote on whether the Association should continue, and early in 1951 the members voted by 5459 to 3055 votes to dissolve the Association. It was not until 1953 that, with Edington's encouragement, a new Staff Association was formed, but in contrast to its predecessor the new Association represented less than 50 per cent of the bank's employees. At a time when the National Union of Bank Employees (formerly the Bank Officers' Guild) had not yet won negotiating rights, the dissolution of the original Staff Association left a sudden vacuum in the relationship between the bank's management and its staff.

The dispute between the bank and the old Staff Association was a considerable blow to staff morale. Managers and senior clerical staff were clearly affected, as they had seen differentials eroded since the Second World War. Clerical scales had been revised in 1946 (when London allowances were introduced to help meet the high cost of living in the capital) and again in 1952. These revisions had more than doubled the salaries of junior clerks, and in 1952 a junior earned £150 per annum after one year compared with the equivalent £80 in 1939. Senior clerical staff only achieved a 60–65 per cent increase in the same period, with the result that an accountant in a country branch was unlikely to earn more than about £850 annually in the early 1950s. It was not until the middle of the decade that basic salaries were adjusted to make up lost ground in these appointments.

From the point of view of the bank's general managers, the dissolution of the old Staff Association had been surprising and regrettable. It left the bank without an established channel for communicating with its employees. This isolation was bound to affect the style of leadership within the bank, and in Edington's case the débâcle left him even more inclined towards caution. His reluctance to join inter-bank ventures was a sign of this introversion, while his own office diaries give the impression that he was more influenced by the possibility of recession than by any indications of postwar economic recovery.

Understandable as Edington's caution may have been, this attitude pervaded the bank's leadership at a time of renewed challenge to its competitive position. Throughout the early 1950s Barclays had vigorously extended its branch representation and at the end of 1958 its 2228 offices just outnumbered Midland's 2221. In March 1957 its total deposits of £1346 million had also taken it ahead of Midland's monthly total of £1342 million in deposits in England and Wales. A W Tuke, chairman of Barclays throughout this period, was convinced that 'fortune favours the bigger battalions; more precisely I should say that the more branches you have the more deposits you will get'.[5]

Midland's response to this sustained challenge was delayed until after Edington's retirement in 1956. After a period of five years in which the bank's management had been dominated by a single personality, the board again chose to divide the chief executive's responsibilities, and O E Wood and J Fitton were appointed chief general managers in April 1956. Fitton, a highly popular and rapidly-promoted member of the management committee, died suddenly only a few weeks later. His successor, F E G Hayward, had spent his entire career in London, thus breaking a succession of northern chiefs who had learned their trade in the hard, industrial school of banking. It was perhaps significant that Hayward was also much more involved in staff activities and welfare than many of his predecessors. O E Wood, the other new chief general manager, had also taken an unusual career path; with a double first in history and law from Cambridge University, he had been called to the Bar immediately before joining Midland in 1921. He was one of the handful of the bank's staff who had been recruited in response to Reginald McKenna's call for more graduate entrants. A man of wide cultural interests, the originality of his approach was an important ingredient in the bank's leadership over the next six years.

Wood and Hayward did not linger long before reviewing Midland's competitive capacity. The challenge from the other clearing banks (particularly Barclays) persuaded Hayward to establish a 'Business Development Committee' in October 1956, with the task of identifying and exploring opportunities for expansion. The new committee, under Hayward's chairmanship, threw itself into the discussion and analysis of competitors' activities.

As in every other phase of the bank's expansion, the strengthening of the branch network was an obvious priority. It was in this area that Barclays had made its largest gains, yet by 1956 (two years after the ending of official building controls) Midland had done no more than restore the number of branches to its prewar level. More alarming still, Hayward's committee learned that Midland had opened fewer branches between 1952 and 1957 than any of the other 'Big Five' clearing banks. In an attempt to recapture lost ground the committee recommended a major programme of extension and rebuilding. By 1960 a total of 150 new branches had been opened in four years. These offices were concentrated in the new towns, industrial estates and the government-assisted development areas. There was also a serious attempt to attract new personal accounts by opening branches on the campuses of universities and colleges. In most cases the new offices were extremely simple in style and open in layout in order to dispel the traditional image of the heavy woodwork and brass fittings of the old-established branch banks. Other specialist branches were established at the principal airports in England and Wales and at permanent exhibition centres, supported by temporary branches at exhibitions and shows, and mobile caravan branches for installation at exhibitions and agricultural shows. Although the amount of business acquired at the temporary branches was sometimes in inverse proportion to the hospitality dispensed, these measures were a conscious effort by the bank to show its face to new and potential customers.

The counterpart to the extension programme was the renovation or replacement of branches in the existing network. By 1960, for example, approximately one in every five of the bank's 2273 branches was undergoing major alterations. City centre branches were especially in need of extra space and facilities, while in other areas the changing character of a district made it essential to find new sites. Branches in areas where property was being run down or was falling under the shadow of redevelopment and road-widening schemes were an obvious problem, and efforts were made to relocate these branches in growing residential or shopping areas. The bank's premises department was greatly reinforced to cope with the administration of hundreds of such projects, while the design of new or rebuilt branches (previously the work of premises department and two or three firms of architects) was transferred to local architects. Over sixty local architects' firms were at work on Midland branches by 1961. Their efforts were in contrast with the craftsmanship in brick, stone and mahogany in branch building before 1939, but the new arrangements did offer the advantage of speedy distribution and completion of building work. Valuable as these developments were in the late 1950s, they were adaptations of a familiar theme: the expansion of the branch network as a response to competition. In that one respect, the business development committee bore a resemblance to Holden's branch extension committee in the 1890s. In other areas, however, the committee broke fresh ground by making adjustments to the bank's structure and by adding new 'products' to the services offered by Midland Bank.

The committee's innovation in the organization of the bank was small but potentially important. Greatly impressed by the success of the district head offices of Barclays Bank, Hayward and his colleagues looked for means of decentralizing Midland's management communications and responsibilities. Their first objective was the appointment of advisers at regional level, acting as intermediaries between head office and the branch managers and providing a channel for advice and ideas about business opportunities. To this end, in June 1957 a number of area representatives (later known as regional managers) were selected with the specific tasks of developing new connections, pooling information about local developments and new prospects for growth, and acting as the personal representatives of the general managers in their region. While in no way removing Midland's long-held preference for centralized control, it was a development which recognized the gap in communication and advice between a strong head office and the branch network in the regions.

The committee's contribution to the development of banking services was equally important. The bank's only recent experience of developing a new product had been the introduction of the United Kingdom's first 'gift cheques' during 1955. Designed and colour-printed for use by personal customers, the cheques were available for use as gifts at birthdays, weddings and at Christmas. They had been launched with the support of a major advertising effort, including the use of full-page colour advertisements. In December 1956 the gift cheques had also featured in the first use of television advertising by a British bank.

The introduction of gift cheques taught helpful lessons about the development and marketing of new services. In the event the success of the experiment owed more to its popularity amongst the bank's existing customers than to outside support. The next task, Hayward's committee believed, was to identify services which might attract new personal customers to the bank or recapture the personal account business lost to the other clearers. Consequently, during 1957 the committee made a close study of the activities of the American and Australian banks in their home markets. Hayward and his colleagues were especially impressed by the personal loans offered by the American banks and by the Bank of Australasia (since 1938) and the Bank of New South Wales (since 1943).[6] In all these cases banks were able to offer customers small loans without security, in stark contrast to British banking traditions.

When the long period of official credit restrictions was lifted in 1958, it was Midland's 'personal loans' which took pride of place in the bank's new services. This innovation, based on the committee's research and launched in September 1958, was tailored to assist personal customers in dealing with exceptional purchases, particularly in the burgeoning market for consumer durables. Loans under the scheme were available on a different basis from ordinary bank borrowing, with the customer's ability to repay acting as the sole criterion for accepting a credit risk. The scheme also met borrowers' long-felt preference for person-to-person negotiations with a bank manager rather than the clinical assessment required by hire purchase companies, the main alternative source of asset finance. The rate of interest was nevertheless high enough, from the bank's point of view, to cover the additional risk of bad debts.

Midland's personal loan service had been carefully planned well in advance of the ending of the credit squeeze, and it came as a considerable surprise to the financial world. 'You certainly put the cat among the banking pigeons', Harold Macmillan, the Prime Minister,

# FOREIGN AFFAIRS:
# ORIGINS AND LANDMARKS OF
# MIDLAND'S INTERNATIONAL BUSINESS

**5.1** *The London Joint Stock Bank, Princes Street, in 1850. This bank acted as the London agent for many leading foreign and colonial banks from the 1830s onwards, and when it became part of Midland in 1918 it was operating no less than 70 of these agencies*

DINNER given by THE CHAIRMAN & DIRECTORS of THE LONDON & MIDLAND BANK, Limited, to THE DIRECTORS of THE CITY BANK, Limited.

SAVOY HOTEL, LONDON, THURSDAY, NOVEMBER, 3RD 1898.

*5.2 Dinner card published to celebrate Midland's merger with the City Bank in 1898. The City Bank had an exceptionally large foreign business, which formed the nucleus of Midland's foreign banks department in the early years of this century*

*5.3 Caricature of Midland's new foreign banks department, drawn by a member of staff in about 1902*

*5.4 Broadway and Fifth Avenue, New York, showing the Fuller 'Flatiron' Building in the early 1900s. Edward Holden was greatly impressed by his first visit to the United States in 1904, and he returned to London with new contacts with American banks and with new ideas for Midland's own development.* BBC Hulton Picture Library

**5.5** *A £500 bond of the Armavir–Touapsé Railway in the Russian Caucasus, 1909. Midland handled the issue of £5.8 million of* these bonds—the bank's first involvement in the foreign issue market. *Stock Exchange Archives, Guildhall Library*

**5.6** *Russian steam: a class Yᵗʰ locomotive of the Armavir–Touapsé Railway, for which Midland had acted as London financial agent in 1909. This photograph was taken in 1913. By 1916 the railway was operating total rail lines of 293 kilometres.* Lomonossoff collection, Leeds Russian Archive

**5.7** *Letterhead of Midland's Petrograd office, 1917. The bank's connections with Russia led to the appointment of Frederick Bunker as representative in Petrograd (now Leningrad) in 1916. The office remained open until the spring of 1918. Bunker later became chief manager of Midland's overseas branch*

F. J. BUNKER,
Representative of
The London City & Midland Bank, Lᵀᴰ,
London.

Ф. И. БУНКЕРъ,
ПРЕДСТАВИТЕЛЬ
Лондонъ Сити и Мидландъ Банка
въ Лондонъ.

PETROGRAD,
Moika 42 (Temporary Office). Telephone № 1-73-25.

ПЕТРОГРАДЪ,
Мойка 42 (Временная контора). Тел. № 1-73-25.

21 March/4 April 1917

Sir E.H.Holden, Bt.,
Chairman
The London City & Midland Bank, Ltd..
5 Threadneedle Street,

London, E.C.

**5.8** *Advertisement featuring Midland's 'Atlantic offices' on the Cunard liners. These branches were inaugurated in 1920 to meet the burgeoning demand for international travel*

**5.9** *The Cunard liner Aquitania, where Midland opened one of its 'Atlantic offices' in 1920. The Aquitania, 'the grand old lady' of the Atlantic, eventually completed over 35 years of service*

**5.10** *A foreign exchange dealer's desk in about 1930. Midland's foreign exchange department was opened in 1905, and was the first of its kind amongst the clearing banks*

**5.11** *Midland's overseas branch in Gracechurch Street, London, the headquarters of the bank's international business between 1962 and 1983*

**5.13** *The dealing room of Midland Bank group treasury, which by the mid 1980s was handling transactions valued at between US$10 billion and US$15 billion each day*

**5.12** *H H Thackstone* (right) *and E J W Hellmuth* (left) *with L C Mather. Thackstone and Hellmuth were key figures in the development of Midland's overseas business after the Second World War. Thackstone was Midland's chief general manager between 1962 and 1968 and Hellmuth was deputy chief general manager from 1964 until 1968*

**5.14** *The headquarters of Midland Bank SA in Rue Piccini, Paris. Midland Bank SA is one of the principal international subsidiaries in the Midland Bank Group*

wrote to the bank's chairman, 'but I must congratulate you on your initiative . . . . I shall send my application in due course.'[7] The bank's current account business quickly benefited, and within two months of the announcement of the service over 45,000 personal loans—with a total value of £7 million and an average amount of just over £150— were agreed. Over half of this total was provided for the purchase of cars and motorcycles. This number more than doubled in the next twelve months and by 1963 over 450,000 personal loans, with a total value of £73 million, had been arranged.

A few days after personal loans had been launched on the British market, Midland stepped up the response to its competitors by introducing a 'personal cheque account' service. This initiative, which had also been devised by Hayward's committee, offered a streamlined current account without access to lending or any of the other services available at higher cost to the holder of a normal current account. Cheques were available at a fixed cost of 6d each including stamp duty, thus bringing the use of cheque payments within reach of the mass market and introducing new customers to the advantages of a bank account. The move was successful and in many cases led to transfers from personal cheque accounts to normal current accounts. Some years later the service was judged to have achieved its purpose and was withdrawn, but its early impact can be gauged from the growth of the number of customers' accounts. Accounts of all kinds increased in number by 14 per cent between September 1958 and December 1959, in comparison with only 5.5 per cent between January 1956 and August 1958. The largest part of the increase derived from personal cheque accounts and ordinary current accounts.

As the business development committee had always intended, these innovations were supported by a planned programme of advertise- ments, special booklets and in-branch displays. Hayward and his colleagues recognized that this type of campaign was essential to the success of the new services. In contrast to Barclays' preference for additional branches (which could be advertised and promoted through the local press), Midland's emphasis on new banking products relied upon advertising in the mass market. This more deliberate approach to capturing new business was marked by the appointment, in 1958, of the bank's first full-time public relations officer, and at the height of the competition in banking in the late 1950s Midland Bank's advertising expenditure was larger than that of any other bank. In the three years from 1957 to 1959, for example, Midland's spending of £519,054 was no less than 37 per cent of the clearers' total bill for advertising in the press, television, and in cinemas.[8]

This experience in the development and marketing of non-traditional services was of considerable tactical value to the bank when the Committee on the Working of the Monetary System, under the chairmanship of Lord Radcliffe, reported to Parliament in August 1959. The committee, appointed in May 1957, had produced the first thoroughgoing review of the banking industry since the Macmillan Report of 1931. Its recommendations revolved around the important principle that, instead of considering the monetary base alone, the actions of the government and the Bank of England should be influenced by the liquidity of the economy as a whole. Although not all its conclusions were immediately adopted, they were to have far-reaching consequences, especially in the controversial 'special deposits' method of controlling the banks' ability to lend. This device had been made available when credit restrictions were reduced in 1958, and it allowed the Bank of England to call for cash deposits from the clearing banks as a means of damping down temporary surges in the demand for credit. By a twist of irony the committee did not specifically support a special deposit scheme, but the new approach to financial liquidity made this method one of the principal control mechanisms of the next few years (the first call for special deposits was made in 1960). Noting the stability of the majority of bank deposits (even those expressed to be repayable on demand), the committee recommended that farmers and small businesses should be provided with facilities to borrow from banks *via* 'term loans', repayable over periods of up to ten years.

With its new-found preference for developing additional services, Midland gave an immediate response to the Radcliffe recommendations. In August 1959 the bank announced the introduction of loans of up to twenty years' duration to enable farmers to buy land or carry out farm improvements. The new service tied in well with plans which were already being developed by the business development committee, and in this sense the Radcliffe recommendations could not have come at a better time for the bank. In 1958 a special agricultural department had been established under Adrian Collingwood (an assistant general manager with a wide knowledge of farming) in an attempt to build up a reputation as the 'farmer's bank'. The expertise of Collingwood and his team soon became known and very significant numbers of farmers transferred their accounts to Midland. It was some years before the other banks responded by setting up their own agricultural departments, and in the interval Midland's initiative had given it a clear lead in an industry enjoying a new era of prosperity.

Within two months of the announcement of the new services to agriculture the influence of the Radcliffe Report was again evident in the introduction of term loans for small businesses. The service developed the bank's facilities for loans of fixed amounts (normally with a minimum of £600 and a maximum of £12,000), repayable by regular instalments over periods of up to ten years. This, together with the new agricultural loans, represented a major change in thinking. For the first time a bank had formally and publicly recognized that many of its advances to customers, though in theory repayable on demand, were in reality of a long-term nature, renewed year after year. Advances were increasingly expressed not as 'repayable on demand' but in accordance with formal loan documents with conditions and rates agreed at the outset of the loans.

Even in the context of the other new ideas of the late 1950s, these innovations were a courageous response to the Radcliffe Committee's lead. However, while these services and the other business development committee ideas were being developed, changes in the bank's group structure could also be used to broaden the range of its income and activities. It was this route which Midland chose when it entered the hire purchase market by acquiring, in 1958, a new subsidiary, Forward Trust.

For some time the banks had been looking enviously at the growth and profits of the hire purchase companies, especially as these companies were using funds borrowed from the banks which they could re-lend at much higher rates of interest. Most of the hire purchase concerns in the United Kingdom had been established in the 1920s, with a marked American influence on their organization and operations, and by the 1930s they held a firm foothold in the market for loans for purchasing cars and other major consumer products. Many of them had obtained exclusive financial agreements with manufacturers and agents. The growth of hire purchase business after the Second World War had been greatly hampered by official controls on credit. As soon as the restrictions were lifted in 1954 the Scottish banks seized the opportunity to share in this lucrative business. In the first instance, when John Campbell of the Clydesdale Bank proposed to form a Clydesdale-owned hire purchase company, Cameron Cobbold, the governor of the Bank of England, refused to give his approval; at that time it was argued that hire purchase was not the proper business of a bank. Campbell's second proposal, for a new company jointly owned by the Scottish banks, did not meet with the approval of the other Scottish general managers. As an alternative to the formation of a new company, however, the Commercial Bank of Scotland pushed ahead with its own scheme for buying an existing hire purchase concern, and in November 1954 the Commercial Bank announced its purchase of the Scottish Midland Guarantee Trust and the Second Scottish Midland Guarantee Trust.[9]

Banks both in Scotland and in England were now keen to take similar interests in hire purchase concerns. The governor of the Bank of England remained adamant in his disapproval, and in December 1954 the 'Big Five' banks were required to give an assurance that they would not attempt to enter hire purchase business while the period of tight credit continued. Understandably the banks maintained their close watch over the performance of hire purchase business, and in 1957 there were even rumours that the proposed merger of the Commercial Bank of Scotland and the National Bank of Scotland was being engineered by a London clearing bank which wished to have an indirect share in hire purchase. Campbell, reporting this to Hayward in November, pointed out that 'the hire purchase companies were attracting much lending business which might otherwise have come to the banks ... he felt it very unlikely that the other Scottish banks would be content to stand aside indefinitely and leave the amalgamated Commercial and National the only participants in the hire purchase field.'

Hayward and his colleagues on the business development committee shared this impatience, but the suspense was not broken until the governor of the Bank of England released the clearing banks from their agreement in 1958. All the banks rushed in to buy. Early in 1958 Barclays took a 25 per cent stake in United Dominions Trust, National Provincial acquired North Central Wagon and Finance and in August 1958 the Clydesdale at last fulfilled its ambitions by the purchase of Forward Trust in a joint move with Midland Bank. It was a different form of entry from that of the other banks. Forward Trust was relatively small, with only six branches in the Birmingham area and clearly its operations under Midland's banner would need to be expanded rapidly to enable it to compete with its larger rivals. But it had several advantages. Midland had been its banker since 1931 (three years after the company had been formed by Edgar Hounsell) and knew that it was well managed and profitable. Profits had advanced from £33,000 in 1950 to over £109,000 in 1958 and new branches had been opened in Glasgow and London. On the date of acquisition it had net assets of £935,000 and hirers' balances (and other advances) of £6.2 million. Midland and the Clydesdale paid £2.7 million, sharing the cost on a 60:40 basis. 'We have been impressed', Midland's chairman confirmed in his 1958 report, 'by the possibilities of fruitful development among other things through branches to be opened in major cities of both England and Scotland.' Accordingly, about 40 new branches were opened in 1959 and 1960, and the company's staff was expanded from only 70 in 1958 to 550 in 1962. In support of this commitment, Midland's managers were instructed to refer to Forward Trust 'whenever your customers are concerned with the sale or purchase of plant, machinery, motor vehicles and so on'.

The acquisition of Forward Trust, like the bank's affiliation with its Irish and Scottish banking subsidiaries forty years earlier, showed that growth could often be more rapidly achieved by the purchase of existing businesses rather than through the creation of new units. Equally by retaining the existing business identity and expertise of its subsidiaries, Midland was stating a preference for a group of companies rather than a single, multi-divisional monolith. Admittedly other banks had followed Midland's example of setting up or acquiring subsidiary companies (for instance, Westminster Bank's affiliation with the Ulster Bank and National Provincial's ownership of North Central Wagon and Finance), but the number and scale of Midland's affiliations was already distinctive. When combined with the new banking services introduced between 1957 and 1959, this approach confirmed that the bank was making a serious and creative attempt to recover from the frustrations and disappointments of the late 1940s and early 1950s.

These positive developments—the activities of Hayward's committee, the introduction of innovative services, and the purchase of Forward Trust—brought a greater degree of motivation into the bank in the late 1950s, giving the opportunity to exploit the new services and the enlarged branch network in the next decade. Part of that extra motivation came from the knowledge that Midland was taking a wider view of its business functions. At the end of the 1940s the bank's perception of its work had been limited to its traditional narrow range of banking services at home and abroad; the legacy of wartime cooperation with the other clearing banks and with the Bank of England was maintained, but contact with other sections of the financial community was kept to a minimum. By the end of the 1950s, in contrast, Midland's senior managers saw banking as a more pervasive business, available to customers through a multiplicity of brand-name services. Services could even be distributed through companies with separate names, images and branch offices, as the acquisition of Forward Trust had shown.

Leadership was a large influence on this changed outlook and potential. Wood and Hayward had brought to their task a refreshing willingness to plan ahead and compete with the bank's rivals in situations where their predecessors would almost certainly have drawn back. The new mood within the bank also owed much to the arrival of Lord Monckton, who succeeded Harlech as chairman in July 1957. Monckton, after a distinguished career as a barrister and as aide to the future Edward VIII, had held a succession of ministerial appointments, culminating in service as Minister of Labour and, briefly, Minister of Defence in the 1951–56 Churchill government. Although like Linlithgow and Harlech he could not claim to be a banker or a businessman, he was an outstanding manager and negotiator. He was immediately popular with Midland's staff, and his concern for their welfare and morale was the best-remembered feature of his chairmanship. His expertise in dealing with Whitehall and the press was also a major asset when Midland was introducing its new services and when it was under scrutiny in the 'Radcliffe period'. This change in the public face of the bank's operations, mixed with the statesmanlike prestige which Monckton brought to its affairs, could not be expected to overcome the many challenges to the bank's business and the organization. On the other hand, at a time of hectic competition in banking, the new leadership helped to dispel the public and private impression that Midland had been outpaced by its rivals in the postwar period.

# CHAPTER TEN

# MIXING NEW INGREDIENTS
## 1959–1971

The British banking community, stimulated by the lifting of credit restrictions in 1958 and urged on by the Radcliffe Report in 1959, entered a period of increasingly fierce competition in the 1960s. Freedom in lending proved short-lived. Throughout the decade controls of varying severity were re-applied by the Bank of England in response to renewed pressure on sterling and other economic uncertainties. In addition to traditional monetary control, the Bank's 'letters of guidance' (directives in all but name) established priority categories for bankers' support, especially in the manufacturing and export sectors. Nevertheless the struggle for new business was now being fought not only between the clearing banks but between the banks and a host of new financial institutions free from official controls and only too eager to tap new sources of funds with which to meet borrowing demand from 'non priority' categories of business.

Rival banks were competing in a market which was undergoing a strong surge of expansion. The total deposits of the London clearing banks increased from £6935 million in 1959 to £10,626 in 1969 (a 53 per cent increase).[1] Net bank deposits in the whole of the United Kingdom were lifted by 43 per cent from £8215 million to £11,748 million in the same period, but this excluded the fast growth of the resources of new finance houses and foreign banks in London. By these measures the banking market was growing faster than the rate of inflation; only in the two world wars had banks seen such a vigorous expansion of their total business.

The market for banking services in the 1960s was not only a much larger cake. It also contained entirely new ingredients. Variations on traditional banking services were an important part of the recipe. By the end of the 1960s the clearing banks were also operating in areas of the market previously confined to specialist firms or were active in entirely new types of finance. Midland's response was distinctive. If the bank was to keep or increase its portion of the available business, it needed to identify and then refine the new ingredients in banking. The acquisition of Forward Trust in 1958 had widened Midland's alliance of companies by adding near-banking business to its range of services; the scope offered by clearing banking, overseas business, and trustee work was no longer sufficient. In the 1960s this process was maintained and accelerated with several major acquisitions at home and new alliances abroad, and towards the end of the decade Midland had emerged as the most ambitious example of diversification in British banking. It was an approach which helped to raise the group's deposits to £2974 million in 1969 (no less than 55 per cent more than in 1959) while the bank's deposits grew by only 29 per cent to £2185 million. At the end of the 1960s and in the early 1970s, however, despite this strong and often imaginative response, Midland was to see some of its immediate competitors take even larger slices of banking business.

Amongst the major British banks, the time-honoured response to new competitive pressures was the extension of their branch bank networks either by merger or by finding new sites for branches and sub-branches. The late 1950s and early 1960s saw a rapid increase in the number of new, purpose-built banks throughout the United Kingdom, lifting the total number of branches in England and Wales from 10,645 in 1958 to 11,804 in 1964.[2] Midland took its full share in this expansion. Over 500 new offices were opened between 1957 and 1965, taking the bank's total representation to 2600 branches in England and Wales by 1965. This programme had been drawn up after a rather belated start in 1957, but five years later Midland's annual report could claim an average of one new branch per week and 'a larger number of units than is operated by any other financial institution in this country and the biggest branch system among the commercial banks of the western world'. In 1964, when the number of new branches opened reached a postwar peak of 93, the bank was gaining an average of 600 new accounts a day, reaching a total of 6.25 million by the end of that year. At the same time, the Clydesdale's network had grown to 347 branches, the Belfast Bank's to 96 and the Executor and Trustee Company had 35 offices. Forward Trust was fulfilling its planned expansion programme with 53 branches giving representation in every major city and town in the country.

By the mid-1960s Midland's branches not only were more numerous but also were visually more obvious in the high streets of England and Wales. The Clydesdale had been one of the first banks to adopt a corporate design policy in 1963, and Midland itself appointed a design panel in 1964. The panel produced an entirely new style of lettering and presentation for the bank, in which the type face of folio extra bold and the house colours of black and chrome yellow were standardized. In 1965 this was adopted for all branches, stationery, advertising and publications, replacing the rather scrappy mixture of styles which had been used for buildings and presentation in the 1950s. As its centrepiece the new image featured the griffin symbol, a simplified version of part of the bank's coat of arms, and this highly successful design was subsequently adopted for other subsidiary companies in the Midland group.

Impressive as the recovery of branch representation was, by the early years of the 1960s there were significant shifts in the boundaries of banking competition. Since the First World War the banks in London and the provinces had maintained their deposit rates on a uniform basis, offering 2 per cent less than Bank Rate on deposit and nil on current accounts. This arrangement, Midland shareholders were told in 1964, 'stemmed from an official request and the banks continue to believe that it contributes to orderliness in monetary arrangements, assists in the financial policy of the authorities and keeps down the rates charged to borrowers'. There is little doubt that at that time the authorities would not have permitted any change, but meanwhile local authorities, company treasurers and other holders of large, short-term funds were looking for better rates. There was also a substantial, unsatisfied demand from would-be borrowers in non-priority categories (particularly in the property market), who were denied access to clearing bank money. The clearing banks were, as they had been since the financial upheavals of the First World War, the main instrument of official controls on lending. Since 1958 their liquidity was also severely affected by the requirement that they should place special deposits at the Bank of England, rising to 3 per cent of total deposits in 1963. In Midland's own case the imposition meant that it could not make any banking use of no less than £66 million of its 1963 resources.

New markets grew at an astonishing rate to meet the demand for funds outside the clearing system. The deposits controlled by the accepting houses, overseas and other banks trebled between 1965 and 1969 to a total of £4600 million in sterling and £14,500 million in foreign currencies; these funds could be lent at good margins to local authorities and hire purchase finance houses or to multinational companies and overseas borrowers of currency.[3] The clearing banks, prevented by official controls from competing directly, were left with the alternative of forming their own subsidiaries to operate in the same markets. It was a form of diversification which was in effect thrust upon them rather than the outcome of a carefully-planned strategy.

With evidence all around of the development of new markets and new institutions to use them, there was no lack of advice to the banks on how to run their business and how to respond to the opportunities now offered. In May 1967 the Prices and Incomes Board, under the chairmanship of the Rt Hon Aubrey Jones, published its report on bank charges and came to the somewhat ungracious conclusion that 'it does not seem that the actual level of charges could be described as unreasonable'.[4] Characteristically, however, Jones' Board decided to extend its mandate beyond a mere examination of charges to a consideration of the way in which banks ran their businesses. It criticized their failure to participate directly in other financial activities and called on them to 'emerge as commercial undertakings', an exhortation greeted with some annoyance by the banks. Midland's response to this 'brave call' was summarized in 1967 by Sir Archibald Forbes, who had succeeded to the chairmanship when Lord Monckton had become seriously ill in 1964 (p 235). Sir Archibald found it particularly hard to reconcile the Prices and Incomes Board's criticisms with its 'acceptance of the existing cash and liquidity ratios in the interest of monetary regulations'. In an important statement of Midland's thinking, which held good until the new system of monetary regulation in 1971, Sir Archibald argued that

> the benefits of specialisation in production and commerce have long been recognized but the method varies, and when a bank, like any other business undertaking, wishes to expand its interests, it is likely to follow one of three courses. It may graft the new services on to its existing organisation; it may establish a fresh company to provide the new services; or it may purchase or secure an interest in an existing business. . . . The acquisition of an established company has the advantages of the existing premises, equipment, staff, expertise and customers and these provide a firm basis for further expansion. . . . In other circumstances, it has been considered more appropriate to follow the course of diversification through participation. . . . When the proposed venture enters quite new fields, however, we have followed the second method of development, that is by the formation of a new unit. . . . To try to provide the whole range of these more specialised activities through the bank's own branch system, employing staff whose training and experience have been differently directed, would present exceptional difficulties and would bring few, if any, benefits. . . . In activities more distant from our central effort, we have no doubt that in practice our expansion through subsidiaries or participations offers the real advantages of specialisation.

In pursuit of this strategy the appointment of H H Thackstone as chief general manager in 1962 and Sir Archibald Forbes as chairman two years later cleared the way for new initiatives. Both had backgrounds and experience quite different from any of their predecessors. O E Wood, a well-liked and respected chief general manager, retired and took a seat on the board in 1962. Wood's period in office had seen the acquisition of Forward Trust and the introduction of personal loans, and these initiatives in domestic banking had done much to restore both the competitive position and the morale of the bank. The arrival of Howard Thackstone, however, immediately gave a wider horizon to the expansion of Midland's interests.

Thackstone's career in the bank had begun in November 1920, when a few days after his fifteenth birthday he had begun work at Barnsley branch. He experienced all the usual routine duties of a junior clerk and was even allowed a taste of the securities department, a rare privilege for a young man at that time. Having completed his Institute of Bankers examinations, he learned shorthand and typing, a qualification which earned him a transfer to head office in 1929 as personal clerk to Frederick Hyde and a view of banking at the highest level. Hyde had owed his own early promotion to his success as Holden's 'office boy', and was now impressed by the hard work, personality and dapper appearance of Thackstone. In 1933 Hyde sent him to the overseas branch and then appointed him assistant secretary of the bank in 1934. Thereafter his career followed a broadly based path to the top. Short spells as an assistant manager at Threadneedle Street branch and assistant chief accountant of the bank preceded a return to overseas banking in 1944. He soon succeeded the veteran Frederick Bunker as chief foreign manager and then presided over the rapid rebuilding of the bank's international business during the immediate postwar years. His seven years as chief foreign manager, allied to the insight gained in the variety of his earlier appointments, convinced him that overseas business would have a much larger part to play in the affairs of the expanding bank. In this view he was encouraged and supported by his new chairman, Sir Archibald Forbes.

In 1964 Lord Monckton, now aged seventy-four and in failing health, retired from the chairmanship and died shortly afterwards. In the tradition of his three predecessors he had not seen his role as that of an executive chairman, but his personal standing and popularity both inside and outside the bank were instrumental in creating a good public image while the still powerful management committee got on with the business of banking. He had brought to his duties qualities of warmth and understanding, perhaps best remembered by his assiduous support for staff social and sports events. Sir Archibald Forbes' career had been equally distinguished but in a totally different sphere. Whereas Monckton had been the lawyer and mediator, Forbes was the administrator and business executive. Having qualified as a Scottish chartered accountant, and gained invaluable experience as an assistant to Sir William McLintock during the reconstruction of the Royal Mail group in the 1930s (p 185), he subsequently held appointments of increasing importance with the Ministries of Agriculture and Aircraft Production during the war and became chairman of the first Iron and Steel Board and of its successor until 1959. Among his directorships he numbered Dunlop, Spillers, and Shell Transport and Trading; he also enjoyed a two-year term as president of the Federation of British Industries. This combination of industrial and financial experience, allied to an enquiring approach, fitted him to play a different role from that of his predecessors. He quickly saw the need to bring the directors into closer touch with the executive of the bank—in effect to close the gap which had existed since 1948. In 1966 he appointed as directors the three senior executives: Thackstone, the chief general manager, E J W Hellmuth (Thackstone's deputy on the international side) and Bernard Clarke, who had recently retired as deputy chief general manager but had been retained as an executive for special duties.

This alteration in the relationship between the board and executive was paralleled by the reappraisal of strategy. The new chairman saw an urgent need to extend and speed up the process of diversification at home and to replace the somewhat isolationist policy which hitherto had governed the direction of the bank's overseas business. Forbes saw that correspondent banking, while still bringing substantial business to the overseas branch in London as the 'bankers' bank', could not be the only plank in the bank's strategy. Alternatives were needed for the growing demands of multinational companies such as those on whose boards he served. He accepted Thackstone's arguments that the friendly relations with overseas banks which had served Midland so well in the past could be taken a stage further by forming alliances to finance large-scale development projects too large for one bank to handle. This concept became the cornerstone of Midland's international plans until 1974 (Chapter Eleven).

At home, Midland turned its attention to representation in Northern Ireland. The merger of the Clydesdale and North of Scotland banks in 1950, which had been hinted at by McKenna as early as 1924, had rationalized Midland's alliances in Scotland and offered more effective competition to the much larger units which had emerged in Scottish banking. By 1972 the Clydesdale was one of only three Scottish-based banks, compared with a total of eight in 1946.[5] A similar trend towards rationalization and the reduction of the number of banks was emerging in Ireland. The old alliance with the Belfast Bank enabled Midland to share in the recovery of Irish banking in the 1950s and early 1960s. Nevertheless, a further alliance with one of the independent Irish banks would obviously create wider opportunities for expansion, particularly if it was linked with representation in Eire. In April 1965 Midland announced a £7.4 million offer for the shares of the Northern Bank, Belfast. Formed in 1824, the Northern was one of the pioneers of joint stock banking in the United Kingdom. It had been the subject of several previous merger negotiations (with Munster and Leinster Bank in 1917–18) and affiliation schemes (with Barclays Bank in 1919–20 and Lloyds Bank in 1926), but for various reasons these had been inconclusive. Subsequently, the Northern was approached by the Bank of Ireland in 1931 and the National Bank in 1960, and, when these negotiations also failed to produce agreement, it was left as the last independent bank in Northern Ireland. Discussions with Midland were opened in September 1964 and, when the offer was made in April 1965, both sides had accepted the mutual advantages of a merger. In keeping with Midland's long-established and successful policy in other similar alliances, it was agreed that 'the Northern Bank will continue to operate as a separate company'. The offer was approved by the Northern shareholders, but the agreement begged the question of how long Midland's two subsidiary companies would operate in overlapping territory, competing with each other and with the other Irish banks. Rival banks were in no doubt about the answer. News of Midland's offer was rapidly followed by the Bank of Ireland's acquisition of the National Bank's Irish branches in December 1965 and, nine months later, the creation of Allied Irish Banks, a merger of the Munster and Leinster, Provincial, and Royal banks. This sudden increase in the size of the competing banks ended Midland's initial hesitation over the merging of its Irish subsidiaries. In 1968 a new company, United Northern Banks, was formed as the holding company for the Northern and the Belfast Bank. The union was completed by statute in 1970, when the merged bank adopted the operating title of the Northern Bank. Inevitably, there was regret at the disappearance of the Belfast Bank's name from the banking scene, but in every other way the union was the most practicable response to the changing structure of Irish banking; the Northern's note issue was retained, and the combined bank inherited 238 offices in Northern Ireland and 54 branches in Eire.[6] The deposits of the enlarged bank,

**Table 10.1**

Midland Bank, principal subsidiaries in the United Kingdom, 1909–68

| Date | Acquisition of existing company | Formation of new company |
|------|---------------------------------|--------------------------|
| 1909 | | London City and Midland Executor and Trustee Co |
| 1917 | Belfast Banking Co | |
| 1920 | Clydesdale Bank | |
| 1924 | North of Scotland Bank | |
| 1958 | Forward Trust | |
| 1965 | Northern Bank | |
| 1967 | Montagu Trust (33 per cent) | Midland Bank Finance Corporation |
| 1968 | | Midland Montagu Industrial Finance |

at £163 million, could not be compared with the total Irish business of the Bank of Ireland and Allied Irish Banks, but nevertheless the Northern emerged by some margin as the largest banking unit in Northern Ireland.

By 1965 Midland was able to list nine subsidiary and sub-subsidiary companies (excluding the associated Midland and International Banks (p 253). The following year, 'in order to give proper emphasis to the profits and activities of the Group', the decision was taken to cease production of a separate profit and loss account for Midland Bank Limited and to publish in future only consolidated group results. Further opportunity for expansion came in 1967 following an approach to Sir Archibald Forbes from Louis Franck, chairman of Montagu Trust. The Trust was a holding company established in 1963, and its principal subsidiaries were Samuel Montagu and Co, Guyerzeller Zurmont Bank (in Switzerland) and two important insurance broking companies, E W Payne and Bland Welch. As its name suggested, the most important component in the Trust was Samuel Montagu and Co, a merchant bank founded in 1853 and carrying on business at 114 Old Broad Street. Its early business was based on foreign exchange, foreign loans and credit and bullion dealing, and over the years it had come to be recognized as one of the leading merchant banks in the City, with membership of the influential Accepting Houses Committee, the Issuing Houses Association and the

London Gold and Silver Markets. An alliance between Montagu and Midland had been contemplated for some time. The two banks had cooperated in financing sales of British turbo-prop aircraft in the late 1950s, when one of Montagu's senior directors had told E J W Hellmuth (then assistant chief general manager of Midland) that the merchant bank and the clearing bank would be 'an ideal joint operation'. The idea was put aside in 1960 but seven years later it was taken up in earnest. The discussions between Forbes and Franck rapidly bore fruit and in September 1967 it was announced that Midland would pay £8.7 million for a one third share in the Trust. 'The clearing banks will have to get their breath back. Midland took them completely by surprise', reported the *Observer*, which saw Samuel Montagu as 'a commercially orientated merchant bank rather than a glamorous takeover battler, with strong overseas connections'.[7]

The news of the agreement was undoubtedly a surprise to the City, as the functions of a clearing bank and a merchant bank had always been regarded as quite different. In the past any cooperation had taken the form of joint ventures: National Commercial Bank of Scotland and Schroders had formed a Scottish-based merchant bank in 1964 and Westminster Bank and Hambros had recently launched a joint unit trust. Midland's directors, persuaded and perhaps cajoled by Forbes and Thackstone, accepted the need for a gradual removal of some of the traditional demarcation lines between the two types of institutions. The bank would thereby gain a foothold in a highly profitable type of City business with opportunities for cooperation in the field of corporate finance, international services and foreign exchange. On the other side, Montagu would gain from introductions to Midland customers requiring the services of a merchant bank for capital issues, takeovers and mergers—and from access to the much larger resources of a clearing bank. One thing was clear from the outset: Montagu would retain the complete operational independence essential to membership of the Accepting Houses Committee, some of whose other members were uneasy about the new alliance. One senior figure in merchant banking declared his bank's intention to scale down its activities with Midland, adding 'I've always thought that merchant banking and clearing banking were different businesses'.[8] But the way was open for the two banks to begin to cooperate in joint ventures within the now much wider horizons of the group. In anticipation of this type of collaboration, Thackstone joined the board of Montagu Trust and E J W Hellmuth became a director of Samuel Montagu; David Graham, chairman of Samuel Montagu, joined Midland's board.

Because Midland had continued to follow its traditional practice of granting to its trading subsidiaries a large degree of autonomy, the expansion of group activities into fields outside those of a clearing bank posed problems of management and control. In November 1967 Thackstone and his colleagues decided to coordinate the activities of the newer group companies (except those associated directly with international affairs). This control would be provided by a new company, Midland Bank Finance Corporation (MBFC), operating from 30 St Swithins Lane in the City. The new company was formed with banking status (under section 123 of the Companies Act 1967) to enable it to fulfil its second main purpose of operating in the wholesale markets for deposits, in competition with the multitude of other financial institutions entering those markets. Forward Trust Finance was already active in this area, but MBFC had the advantage of the name of Midland Bank in its title, enabling it to attract large deposits at the finest rates. MBFC therefore assumed responsibility for financing the growing needs of Forward Trust, except for deposits from the public of £25,000 and under. In order to take ownership of Forward Trust, its opening issued capital of £4 million was quickly increased to £10 million, subscribed by Midland (£9 million) and by the Clydesdale (£1 million). At the same time the Clydesdale formed its own company, Clydesdale Bank Finance Corporation, with similar objectives. Two years later the Northern Bank Finance Corporation was launched as a parallel company in Ireland.

A third objective of MBFC was the provision of medium-term advances of large amounts for purposes not considered suitable for a clearing bank. In this respect the timing of its formation could hardly have been more unfortunate. The sterling crisis of 1967 and subsequent devaluation led to further lending restrictions by the Bank of England, which ruled that each bank's ceiling for advances was to be the amount outstanding on 31 October 1967, the day before MBFC opened its doors for business. Deposits began to flow in rapidly from customers seeking a better rate for short-term monies than a clearing bank could offer—£200 million by the end of 1968, £350 million the following year and no less than £600 million by 1971 (including those in foreign currency)—but the Bank of England would not agree to permit lending of more than £2.5 million. Midland pleaded that there should be some flexibility to cover the special circumstances (and in recognition that MBFC had a paid-up capital of £10 million). The appeal was in vain, and even by the end of 1971 MBFC was allowed a lending ceiling of only £10 million. Consequently the new company was restricted to placing its deposits in the short-term inter-bank market, at very small margins of profit.

From the outset, Midland recognized that MBFC would have an important role to play in the management and coordination of the growing number of related services as well as its deposit-taking and money market operations. Its board included Sir Archibald Forbes (as chairman), Howard Thackstone and Bernard Clarke with Malcolm Wilcox as managing director and Geoffrey Taylor as general manager. Frustrated by the ceiling on lending, the executive turned its main attention towards the coordinating task. In 1968 Taylor was seconded to Samuel Montagu to explore ways in which the new alliance could be used to advantage. It was also his task to allay fears on the part of Samuel Montagu that MBFC would be in competition with it in the provision of traditional merchant banking services—a purpose for which the new company had certainly not been formed. He was able to assure the Montagu executive that, though there could be areas in which the two banks might overlap, MBFC was principally a deposit-taking and lending organization. It recognized that it could not in many other respects match the expertise of a merchant bank. In September 1968, the association between the two banks gave birth to a new company, Midland Montagu Industrial Finance (MMIF), in which the experience of each had a part to play. For some time it had been obvious that progressive small and medium sized companies with ambitions to grow large enough to obtain a stock exchange quotation needed help in the run up to public status. MMIF came into being to provide term loans and equity capital to bridge the need for finance and, again, introductions flowed from Midland's branch network (*via* MBFC) with Montagu available to advise on the details and timing of any public issue. The new company created within the Midland group an organization prepared to assess and accept the greater risks and rewards in the provision of share capital. In the next decade, this type of facility was further extended to suitable small companies which were not aiming at a public flotation.

The new ventures, allied to the recovery of its lead in the number of branches in England and Wales in 1959, enabled Midland to maintain its deposits position as the second largest clearing bank in the United Kingdom. Its principal rivals were also set on a course of growth, although none could match the pace of Barclays. By the end of 1967 Barclays, with deposits of £2529 million compared with Midland's £2316 million, had extended the lead over Midland first established ten years before. Nevertheless, at almost exactly the moment when Midland's strategy of group diversification gave hope of reclaiming the initiative in a rapidly changing financial environment, it lost its ranking as Barclays' chief rival. Ironically, this change in status did not stem from institutional failure or lack of effort in developing the bank's services. Instead it was the old-established device of banking amalgamations—the weapon which Holden had used to bring Midland to pre-eminence up to 1918—which now pushed the bank from its place as the second largest bank in the United Kingdom.

To the surprise of other banks, National Provincial Bank had acquired the District Bank in 1962. The purchase had the consent of the Bank of England but the combined resources of the two were still well below those of Midland and Barclays. The matter of bank mergers was a sensitive one: ever since the Colwyn Committee of 1918 reported on the subject, it had been accepted that all such proposals would be subject to approval by the Bank of England in consultation with the Treasury (p 130). The essential criterion was that merging banks should be complementary rather than overlapping and this test was applied in the favourable decision regarding National Provincial and District. In 1967, however, the Prices and Incomes Board's report on bank charges shed light on a new official attitude by stating that 'the Bank of England and the Treasury have made it plain to us that they would not obstruct some further bank mergers'.[9]

The first bank to react to the Bank of England's signal was Martins, the largest of the banks based in the north of England and the sixth largest clearing bank. Rather than attempt a merger with one of the Scottish banks, as had been mooted, the Martins directors made it clear that they would welcome bids from the London clearers. The governor of the Bank of England, Leslie O'Brien, decided that in preference to allowing rival suitors to bid for Martins in the normal way the Bank would invite tenders. The Bank would then select the three highest bids and give interested parties the opportunity to revise their offers. In January 1968, before these arrangements could be settled, it became known that Westminster and National Provincial were not in the contest for Martins but that these two banks, the smallest of the 'Big Five', had obtained official approval for a merger with each other. This in turn caused Barclays and Lloyds to announce that they too proposed to merge and that the combined bank would bid for Martins; all three boards of directors had already agreed the scheme in principle. This was all too much for the Treasury and the Bank of England, who confirmed their approval for the Westminster/ National Provincial merger but referred the Barclays/Lloyds/Martins proposal to the Monopolies Commission. After a lengthy delay, the Commission rejected the proposal by six votes to four. Barclays then acquired Martins as the higher of the only two bidders (the other being Lloyds).[10]

**Table 10.2**

Clearing banks in mergers in England and Wales, 1968

| *31 December 1968* | *Balance sheet totals (£ million)\** | *Number of branches* | *Number of staff* |
|---|---|---|---|
| **Barclays Bank** | **3539** | **3397** | **44,900** |
| Comprising: Barclays | 2959 | 2660 | 37,000 |
| Martins | 580 | 737 | 7900 |
| **National Westminster Bank** | **3418** | **3661** | **47,900** |
| Comprising: National | | | |
| Provincial | 1362 | 1631 | 20,200 |
| Westminster | 1662 | 1441 | 22,400 |
| District | 394 | 589 | 5300 |
| **Coutts Bank** | **79** | **9** | **1150** |
| **Williams and Glyn's Bank** | **345** | **319** | **4250** |
| Comprising    Williams | | | |
| on 30 Sept    Deacons | 195 | 280 | 2500 |
| 1968:    Glyn Mills | 93 | 4 | 1100 |
| National Bank | 57 | 35 | 650 |
| **Lloyds Bank** | **2285** | **2217** | **29,700** |
| **Midland Bank** | **2459** | **2712** | **31,700** |

*Note* \*Parent bank only (excluding contra items)

*Source:* Evidence by the Committee of London Clearing Bankers to the Committee to Review the Functioning of Financial Institutions, November 1977, p 22

Midland's decision to stay out of the contest for Martins and, indeed, out of the pattern of mergers in general, was explained by Sir Archibald Forbes in his 1968 report to shareholders. He argued that Martins was strongest in Merseyside and surrounding areas where Midland was particularly well represented (unlike Barclays) and a merger would not have made commercial sense. On the general question of mergers, 'further increases in size and position in a "league table" would, of itself, give no assurance of superior service, improved efficiency or greater profitability'. In fact late in January 1968, immediately after the announcement of the National Provincial/ Westminster Bank merger, Sir Archibald had called on the chairman of Lloyds Bank and suggested an association (not necessarily a formal amalgamation) between the two banks. However 'the idea was not very warmly received' by Lloyds,[11] with the result that Midland took no further part in the reshuffle in British banking in 1968. Hence, by the end of the year the two major amalgamations had dramatically altered the 'league table' and left Midland and Lloyds well behind the two new groups of Barclays and National Westminster (Table 10.2).

An assessment of the relative strengths of the clearing bank groups was further assisted in early 1970. The Companies Act of 1948 had given the banks statutory permission not to publish full profits and reserves. The exemption made it possible for the banks to continue their tradition of allocating an unspecified proportion of profits to a reserve hidden in their 'current, deposit and other accounts'. Twenty years later, however, both the Prices and Incomes Board and the Monopolies Commission reported in favour of disclosure of these allocations. In this changed climate, and with a real prospect of government intervention, the banks announced in September 1969 their common agreement to disclose true profits in their 1969 accounts and to reveal the strength of the inner reserves. They also agreed to adopt common practices in assessing bad debt provisions. Both inside and outside the banks, the figures were awaited with great interest and there was much speculation in the press. Obviously the 1968 merger would have ensured for Barclays and National Westminster a lead over Midland and Lloyds. Nevertheless it came as a genuine shock to Midland's directors, managers, staff and shareholders that Lloyds, at that time regarded as the smallest of the big four, was really in a stronger capital position than Midland (Table 10.3).

For Midland, the results of disclosure demanded that operating methods, profit per branch and profit per member of staff should be closely reviewed in comparison with the other banks. By these measures Midland's performance was distinctly weak. Profits as a proportion of capital held up well—as might be expected with a relatively small capital, but the productivity position was discouraging. The bank's domestic branches were generating an average of only £6969 in profits in comparison with the average of £9794 for the three other major banks. Profits of £609 for each member of staff were also below the other three banks' average of £762. Midland's salaries, ranging from £400 for junior clerks to £1200 for country managers to £2500 for city branch managers in the mid 1960s, were closely comparable with those paid by the other major banks. The implication was that the bank had either taken on too many staff or that its overheads were

**Table 10.3**

Capital position of the major clearing banks after disclosure, 31 December 1969

| Group figures ($£$ million) | Midland Bank | Barclays Bank | Lloyds Bank | National Westminster Bank |
|---|---|---|---|---|
| Capital and reserves, 1968 | 121.9 | 172.8 | 140.8 | 208.2 |
| Retained profits, 1969 | 9.4 | 15.5 | 17.6 | 20.1 |
| Sundry adjustments | 1.3 | 39.1 | 9.1 | −1.5 |
| Inner reserves transferred | 60.2 | 137.4 | 98.0 | 118.1 |
| TOTAL SHAREHOLDERS' FUNDS, 1969 | **192.8** | **364.8** | **265.5** | **344.9** |

*Note:* the sundry adjustments by Barclays Bank included revaluation of premises by $£45.4$ million

unusually large. Perhaps for the first time, Midland's management began to consider whether it had too many branches, manned by too many staff. Could the hitherto unchallenged policy of expanding the branch network have been pursued at too great a cost? The banking mergers would enable Barclays and National Westminster to take advantage of economies of scale and to close branches in overlapping areas (between 1970 and 1977, National Westminster closed 400 and Barclays 150 without any obvious loss of business). Midland would need to experiment with alternative cost-effective methods of using its extensive network. In the meantime, since the object was to present a true picture of the value of the business, a decision was taken to revalue premises in 1970, adding a further £63 million to group reserves. Thus between 1950 and 1970 the net disclosed worth of the group rose from £31 million to £258 million, an increase achieved almost entirely in the last ten years (Table 10.4).

The task of reorganizing the bank's branch network and systems in the aftermath of the 1968 mergers fell to Leonard Mather, one of the most experienced and popular figures in British banking. In March 1968 Howard Thackstone had retired as chief general manager and his untimely death only ten months later deprived the board of the services of a fine banker who had made an outstanding contribution at a time of major expansion and innovation. Mather, the natural choice as his successor, had served as assistant and later deputy chief

**Table 10.4**

Growth of disclosed shareholders' funds of Midland Bank Group, 1950–70

| Date | Source of funds | £ million |
|------|-----------------|-----------|
| 1950 | Shareholders' funds in hand | 31 |
| 1959 | New cash capital by rights issue | 5 |
| 1959 | Transfer from inner reserves | 5 |
| 1961 | New cash capital by rights issue | 24 |
| 1964 | New capital issued for holding by Midland and International Banks | 4 |
| 1964 | Transfer from inner reserves | 11 |
| 1965 | New capital for Northern Bank acquisition | 3 |
| 1968 | Transfer from inner reserves of subsidiaries | 7 |
| 1969 | Transfer from inner reserves on disclosure | 60 |
| 1970 | Revaluation of properties | 63 |
| 1950–70 | Retained earnings and sundry adjustments | 35 |
| 1970 | Shareholders' funds in hand | 258 |

general manager since 1964. His formidable claims as a practical banker were enhanced by a degree in commerce and fellowship of the Chartered Institute of Secretaries—qualifications which were unusual amongst his generation of bankers. A master of both the spoken and written word, he lectured extensively for the Institute of Bankers and earned its premier award for one of his several textbooks on banking which still remains as a definitive work. On his way to the top, he took in the specialist appointments of principal of legal department (1948–50) and general manager of the Executor and Trustee Company (1956–58). His claim to succeed Thackstone as chief general manager was thus undeniable. With an extrovert personality, he was regarded with admiration and affection by those with whom he came into contact; his brief spell as manager of Bolton branch in the late 1940s was still remembered by a certain customer who complained to a general manager visiting the branch twenty years later to view its overcrowded conditions: 'Fancy letting this happen to Mr Mather's branch'. This reputation in many ways reflected Mather's own belief, based on a long tradition, that a bank's success could be earned only by the services provided in its branches and the standing and influence of its men on the spot. Yet the time had clearly arrived for fundamental changes both in operating methods and in strategy to meet the challenge of the other clearing banks.

The bank's management hierarchy was certainly due for review.

The centralized structure of command was in effect unchanged since the late 1920s (Fig 7.1) and in many ways it was the direct successor to Holden's regime in the 1890s and early 1900s (Fig 4.1). For years Mather and Bernard Clarke (deputy chief general manager between 1964 and 1966 and subsequently a director) had argued for decentralized control of the branch network. They had been greatly impressed by the regional organization of Barclays and, more recently, Lloyds[12] and it was their powerful advocacy which eventually persuaded Howard Thackstone and the directors to create a regional structure. Mather addressed enthusiastic managers' meetings up and down the country to introduce the concept and there were few who returned to their branches without the firm belief that a period of renewal in branch banking was about to begin. The decision to decentralize came not a moment too soon; Midland had enlarged its branch network but Barclays was maintaining and extending its lead in total deposits. The area representatives (subsequently known as regional managers, p 223), appointed by Midland ten years earlier, were never more than advisers without any executive authority and certainly proved no counter to the influence of the semi-autonomous local boards of Barclays. Even as early as 1960 the business development committee, looking for reasons why Midland was losing corporate customers as a result of the spate of industrial mergers, believed that a larger and more influential regional operation was needed if the bank was to regain these business customers. The first of Midland's new regional head offices opened in Preston in January 1968, headed by Colin Parmley as regional director. Parmley had the local knowledge and background typical of the qualities required of the new regional directors, each of whom was given a wide measure of authority over the branches under his control in matters of lending, staff, and the marketing of new services. By the end of 1969, 17 of the intended 20 regional offices were in operation and in the following year, the pattern was widened to include four new offices covering London and its suburbs.

This rearrangement could not be expected to answer all the questions posed by Midland's situation after disclosure. Remarkably, the bank's branches were left relatively undisturbed by decentralization and in most respects their staff structure, their work and their methods were little changed since the 1920s. The volume of work had certainly increased, and many branches designed for the quieter business conditions at the beginning of the century were now overcrowded with staff, machinery and records. Perhaps the biggest change in the routine life of the branches had been the decision of the clearing banks to close their branches on Saturdays as from July 1969. This decision, which was accompanied by an extension of weekday opening from 10am–3pm to 9.30am–3.30pm, actually increased the workload of the branches rather than changed their business in any way. The traditional configuration of branch manager, accountant, security clerks, cashiers and clerks was still firmly in place, even though their main point of contact had been moved from London to the new regional head offices. Similarly there had not been any fundamental changes in systems. Mechanization of branch book-keeping—a process which had begun in the late 1920s (p 173)—was not completed throughout Midland's branch network until 1959. Head office accounting had been computerized since 1962 but as yet there was no form of electronic processing for the bulky cheque-handling and accounting jobs in the branches. Clearly these conditions needed searching examination if the bank's efficiency and overhead costs were to be brought back to competitive levels.

Midland had not been the only clearing bank to embark on a programme of diversification in the 1960s, although the scale of its commitment to a 'group' of non-traditional services was greater than that of its main rivals. No other clearer sought an interest in an existing merchant bank, preferring to form their own and start from scratch. But the banking mergers in 1968, allied to the growth of the new financial markets and general expansion of international business, had set them on a course of fierce competition not only with each other but also with the growing number of foreign banks and intermediaries operating in the wholesale markets for money. Two formidable obstacles stood in their path—the management of interest rates and the official restrictions on lending. It was the reform of both these procedures in October 1971 that now set the stage for a period of accelerated growth and structural change unprecedented in the history of the clearing banks.

# CHAPTER ELEVEN

# INTERNATIONAL BANKING AND THE 'GRAND DESIGN'
## 1945–1975

> We now think that our attitude to participation in activities abroad should be changed so that we could present a positive and viable approach to overseas problems. . . . This 'Grand Design' would unquestionably enhance our image at home, and give us a valuable growth factor so essential to the expansion of our domestic business.
>
> Howard Thackstone, chief general manager of Midland Bank, report to the board, February 1963

In the period immediately before the Second World War Midland Bank's general management viewed their overseas branch with satisfaction and perhaps complacency. In the circumstances the satisfaction was justified. Midland had escaped the misfortunes of its rivals in their experiments in overseas branch representation; by relying on its correspondent banking connections and its strong foreign exchange business, even the troubles over the German standstill arrangements had made little impact on the good profitability record of overseas business (p 165). Complacency was not so justifiable. By refusing to operate overseas in its own name, Midland was left with little experience of direct international banking. More seriously, the success of the bank's approach between the wars rested on the strength and attraction of sterling for overseas banks. Any deterioration in sterling would immediately weaken the bank's international position. This vulnerability did not become obvious until the late 1950s, forcing Midland to devise a new strategy in which its lack of experience in direct representation was not a serious disadvantage.

The inevitable decline in foreign business during the 1939–45 war had forced a reduction in the staff of Midland's overseas branch from a peak of 750 in 1939 to no more than 260 by 1945. This position was soon transformed by the upsurge in activity after the war. Within months 1000 staff were working at the overseas branch in Old Broad

Street, with a further 80 in the provincial foreign branches in Bradford, Liverpool and Manchester. Three years later Howard Thackstone, then chief foreign manager, was confident that Midland continued to enjoy the lion's share of all foreign business handled by the London banks. A staff of 160 was dealing with a weekly average of 1000 documentary credits paying out 'several million pounds'. Telegraphic and mail transfers abroad were handled at the rate of scores of thousands annually, and inland payments amounting to millions of pounds ran to an average of 1500 every working day. The bank was the custodian of 30,000 securities held for customers abroad which involved the collection of over 3 million coupons and dividend warrants; with the added complication of exchange control restrictions, this work engaged the full time services of 100 staff. The exchange control department alone employed 60 people processing, 'at times frantically', hundreds of thousands of forms a year flowing in from the bank's 1950 branches. Dealings in foreign currency and the provision of forward currency contracts, both important features of the bank's overseas business before the war, were still severely restricted. Official controls were one obstacle to the recovery of this side of the business, but the stability of exchange rates was also inhibiting.

Thackstone's assessment, given in a lecture to the Institute of Bankers' international summer school in September 1948,[1] was a testament of faith in the policies which had served Midland so well for the past 30 years. It was the rationale for the use of correspondent relationships with overseas banks as a means of satisfying the needs of each others' customers. Describing the network of 16,000 correspondents, he explained:

> my own bank has no branches in any other country, for we have no desire to compete on their own ground with the banks of other countries. What business we have to transact abroad we send to our banking friends in that particular country, and in the same way we trust that what business *they* have in the United Kingdom, they will pass on to us.

This orthodoxy in Midland's overseas policy can be traced back to the abandonment of the experiments in overseas representation during the First World War (Chapter Five). If Midland subsequently needed justification for its conservatism, it was to be found in some of the setbacks in foreign banking suffered by the four other major London clearers (pp 164–5). By the end of the 1939–45 war, however, the ground rules for overseas banking business were changing radically. The threat of a severe shortage of foreign exchange prolonged the life of the strict exchange control regulations well beyond the end of the war, and saw the temporary abandonment of sterling's role as an international currency. The existence of the sterling area centred in London reduced the attractions to British banks of opening up elsewhere within the area. Outside the sterling area the shortage of foreign exchange (especially dollars) for many years made investment by British companies often impossible and always difficult and expensive. Immediately after the war efforts to re-establish the convertibility of sterling diverted attention from the long-term implications of sterling's eclipse by the dollar as a world currency.[2]

In these conditions the threat to Midland's foreign business posed by the decline of sterling was not fully perceived. The bank's management committee flirted with the possibility of acquiring a British or Dutch overseas bank in the late 1940s but this notion made little progress in the face of the old orthodoxy. For correspondent banking still provided reasonable profits and, as long as broader factors made direct representation overseas relatively unattractive, there was little positive incentive to change course. The growth of business in the immediate postwar years was continuing at an ever-increasing pace. The rise in value of documentary credits, for example, was 400 per cent between 1938 and 1948. The trend continued into the 1950s when the value of foreign exchange transactions handled rose from under £27 million in 1949 to over £135 million by 1954. As a measure of volume alone, payments made or received on the instructions of overseas banks each year doubled within ten years to reach 1.23 million transactions by 1962. The original overseas branch premises at 112 Old Broad Street, London became inadequate to deal with this volume of business and in 1962 the branch was transferred to a new purpose-built office on the corner of Gracechurch Street and Fenchurch Street.

By the early 1960s major changes in the international business climate were challenging Midland to modify its original stance. An important constraint on earnings from correspondent banking had been introduced when, in response to the sterling crisis of 1957, the British authorities imposed restrictions on the use of sterling to finance trade between third countries. Convertibility of non-resident sterling was restored in 1958, but by then the crisis had severely disrupted the settled routines of correspondent banking. The signing of the Treaty of Rome in 1957, by setting the scene for closer political and economic ties in Europe, indicated that banking relationships would also face structural change. At this stage, moreover, the world economy was beginning to recover from the ravages of war, entering a prolonged period of relative peace and strong growth. Within this environment the market in foreign currency deposits and loans, mainly in US dollars, was set for a rapid and sustained expansion. London, by virtue of its large banking establishment, the strength of its infrastructure and the liberal policy of the Bank of England in the regulation of overseas banks, was uniquely fitted to play the role of leading centre in the 'Euromarkets' for dollar transactions. American banks were arriving in London in force to take advantage of the new markets; as one observer declared:

> for sheer concentration in terms of power, pace and time, the recent expansion of American banks outside the United States is one of the wonders of the economic world. It has compressed in little more than a decade, the kind of coverage which a more leisurely British banking system achieved in more than a century.[3]

By 1958 Lord Monckton, Midland's chairman, was ready to acknowledge that events in Europe would call for some new thinking. Referring to Midland's large share of overseas business passing through London, 'thanks no doubt to its consistent policy of refraining from opening branches abroad or operating through subsidiaries overseas', he promised that 'we are giving close attention to possible effects on our business of the inauguration and development of the European Common market'. It was the first hint of a major reappraisal of the bank's overseas policy, the blueprint of which was to be the so-called 'grand design' policy which emerged in 1962–63. Two main avenues of deeper international involvement were envisaged. The first was to seek greater cooperation with certain major European banks, leading eventually to a unified European bank; the second was to establish close links with banking partners to increase Midland's share of Commonwealth business. It was appreciated that some of the old relationships might suffer as a result but the bank's senior managers still hoped to retain the long-established goodwill created by its reciprocal policies as well as taking advantage of the opportunities arising from European cooperation and the revival of international trade.

Both strategies became practical possibilities when Howard Thackstone was appointed chief general manager in 1962, bringing to the appointment his seven years' experience as chief foreign manager at the overseas branch and many friendships formed with overseas bankers during that period. Thackstone was a truly international banker who saw overseas business as an integral part of the total operations of a major clearing bank and not just as a convenient service for domestic customers. In this he had the support of an old friend and colleague from the overseas branch, E J W Hellmuth, who was then assistant chief general manager. Tony Hellmuth was widely travelled and experienced in overseas business, and, indirectly, his remarkable wartime record also had an important influence on some of the bank's overseas alliances. Rising to the rank of colonel on the staff of the Second Canadian Corps, Hellmuth took part in the D-day landings at Caen, being awarded the Croix de Guerre for his part in the operations. His banking experience was later recognized when he was appointed a member of the Control Commission for Germany, with special responsibilities for the banking section of the British military government. In this capacity he met Hermann Abs. A director of some 45 German industrial companies, Abs was also on the managing board of the powerful Deutsche Bank, one of Midland's long-standing correspondent bank partners. Abs subsequently became one of the men behind the remarkable recovery of the German economy in the 1950s.[4] In December 1962, by then chairman of Deutsche Bank, Abs contacted Hellmuth. He recalled their meeting in 1945 and invited Midland to join the 'Club de Célibataires'.

Deutsche Bank was one of the three existing members of the Club, a loose association of banks, of which the others were Société Générale de Banque of Belgium and Amsterdam Rotterdam Bank. Midland accepted the invitation and the four banks formed the European Advisory Committee (EAC) for the purpose of cooperating in joint ventures and the exchange of ideas, an enterprise which was entirely in the spirit of the 'grand design' policy of cooperation developed through correspondent relationships. The principle of not competing by direct operational representation was adhered to among the original EAC members, none of which operated in the territory of the other three; the only exception to this pattern was the presence in London of Banque Belge (a subsidiary of Société Générale de Banque), a connection which dated back to 1909. The concept of an eventual integrated European bank, dovetailing with broader economic and political aspirations in Europe, was seen as an incentive to cooperation among the EAC members.

The second part of the 'grand design' was activated shortly afterwards when it was decided to establish a new London-based bank in conjunction with the Commercial Bank of Australia, Standard Bank and Toronto-Dominion Bank. Midland and International Banks (MAIBL) was incorporated in 1964, the first of a number of consortium banks which appeared in London in the 1960s and 1970s.[5] From its premises at 36 Throgmorton Street, MAIBL made steady progress and on its tenth anniversary in March 1974 was showing assets of £587 million and a pre-tax profit of over £4 million. The strength of its partners enabled it to attract deposits in the wholesale market at fine rates, thereby fulfilling its objective of providing funds for large scale development projects worldwide. As an indirect outcome of the formation of MAIBL, the association with Standard Bank moved closer in 1965 when Midland paid £1.45 million for a 5 per cent share in Standard Bank. This share was originally part of Lloyds Bank's holding in the Bank of West Africa, which had merged with Standard Bank in March of that year.[6]

The purpose of these two major steps in the 'grand design' was comparable with the international objectives maintained by Barclays Bank. Geographically Barclays and then Midland saw scope for expansion in Europe, while Midland's interest in Commonwealth business had an earlier parallel in Barclays' Dominion Colonial and Overseas subsidiary. Lloyds Bank had set itself rather different horizons, with special emphasis on South America. However, the major difference between Midland on the one hand and Barclays and Lloyds on the other lay in attitudes to overseas indigenous banks. Barclays and Lloyds sought active competition by takeover and shareholdings; Midland's emphasis was on agreement and cooperation, even if the new consortium arrangements gave a more direct presence than some of the old correspondent links.

Within the EAC complex the original concept was soon developed and transformed. The regular meetings of the partners led to a number of substantial joint ventures. In September 1967 the four banks, joined by Samuel Montagu, formed the Banque Européenne de Crédit à Moyen Terme (BEC), a new Brussels-based bank with the object of developing facilities in Europe for medium term loans of substantial amounts for major industrial projects. In December of that year Banca Commerciale Italiana, Crédit Lyonnais and Société Générale (France) joined BEC, as did Creditanstalt-Bankverein in 1970.[7] Then in May 1968 the partners set their sights on horizons beyond Europe when, by agreement with Société Générale de Banque, they jointly acquired its former subsidiary the Belgium American Banking Corporation of New York. This concern immediately became the vehicle for the formation of the European American Banking Corporation (EAB) and its associated European-American Bank and Trust Company. The two banks were to specialize in the finance of international trade (especially in Europe) and in commercial banking services in the United States. Midland decided, in the spirit of its original consortium agreements, that it would close its New York office at 44 Wall Street

## Table 11.1

Midland Bank, consortium links in international banking, 1963–73

| Date | Consortia and joint ventures via European Advisory Committee | Other consortia and joint ventures |
|---|---|---|
| 1963 | European Advisory Committee (EAC) | |
| 1964 | | Midland and International Banks (MAIBL) |
| 1967 | Banque Européenne de Crédit à Moyen Terme (BEC) | |
| 1968 | European-American Banking Corporation (EAB) | |
| 1970 | Euro-Pacific Finance Corporation European Banks International Company (EBIC) | |
| 1972 | European Asian Bank (EURAS) | Union de Banques Arabes et Françaises (UBAF) |
| 1973 | European Banking Co (EBC) | Iran Overseas Investment Bank |

(first opened as a representative office in 1945) and steer future business towards EAB.

The impact of the EAB scheme was encouraging and opened the way for new cooperative ventures (Table 11.1). In July 1970, for example, the four partners joined with American, Australian and Japanese banks in founding the Euro-Pacific Finance Corporation based in Melbourne. This progress persuaded the four banks to formalize their 1963 agreement by establishing, later in 1970, the European Banks International Company (EBIC). The new company, based in Brussels, was designed essentially to coordinate and promote the partners' interests and, thereafter, the various joint ventures were referred to under the general classification of 'EBIC companies'. Between 1971 and 1973, the EBIC group was strengthened by the admission of three other major European banks to the original four shareholders; Société Générale of France, Creditanstalt-Bankverein of Austria and Banca Commerciale Italiana added their names to the 1963 agreement for cooperation. By 1973 the combined assets of the seven, allied to a network of some 9000 branches, enabled the group to initiate and participate in the financing of major international projects undertaken by government agencies and multinational companies, almost irrespective of size.

The partners continued to seek new cooperative ventures in the early 1970s. Their initiatives included the European Banking Company (EBC), established in London in July 1973 to operate in the field of international merchant and investment banking, and European-Asian Bank (EURAS) which commenced business in November 1972 by taking over the existing operations of the Deutsch-Asiatische Bank, Hamburg, as a stepping-stone to a major banking presence in the rapidly developing economies of South-East Asia. Outside the EBIC complex, Midland's extensions included a shareholding in UBAF Bank (a consortium of banks in France and the Arab world) and the sponsorship of the Iran Overseas Bank. These moves confirmed that participation in joint ventures had become the main thrust of Midland's international development in the framework of its 'grand design'.

At first sight the development arising from the concept of EAC during the first ten years of its life followed the principle of co-operation rather than competition. In fact, the original outlines of the 'grand design' approach had become somewhat blurred at the edges. The advent of the three new partners from France, Austria and Italy admitted nationalized banks for the first time. Société Générale's presence in London was also a break with the original formula that member banks would not be active in their own names in another partner's country. Some of the initiatives, for example BEC in Brussels and EBC in London, had been established to provide specialist services within the domestic areas of operation of an EAC member: others had led the EAC members into direct competition with indigenous banks in third countries, as for example in New York. Furthermore the goal of a unified European bank had receded further into the distance when progress towards a federated political structure in Europe came to a halt.

By the end of 1974 the joint ventures arising from the EAC and EBIC club had given Midland a lead in cooperative banking over the other London clearers. Only Barclays had embraced a parallel approach to overseas representation, through the Associated Banks of Europe Corporation (ABECOR), a somewhat looser form of association than EBIC. Yet both Barclays and Lloyds also had long-established networks of branches overseas and both had been concentrating on a programme of branch expansion since 1945. By the end of 1974, when the consolidated overseas interests of Barclays had been merged into Barclays Bank International, there were some 1700 Barclays offices in nearly 70 countries. Lloyds obtained a controlling interest in a new bank when in 1971 it merged its wholly-owned subsidiary, Lloyds Bank Europe, with the Bank of London and South America; having bought out the minority interests in 1973, Lloyds renamed the merged bank Lloyds Bank International. National Westminster set out to expand the representation of the former Westminster Foreign Bank, both by opening branches and acquiring control of local banks in the world's important financial centres. It was also a shareholder in Orion Bank, which rivalled MAIBL as one of the largest and most influential consortium banks in London.[8] Midland alone had no direct banking branches abroad, relying on its EBIC and other joint ventures and representative offices in Brussels, Frankfurt, Zurich, Teheran, Tokyo, Johannesburg and Toronto.

Even if sterling had not weakened and lost its attraction to international banks, Midland sooner or later would have been forced to consider alternative overseas strategies. The methods used to fulfil the 'grand design' had been carefully planned so as not to tread upon the bank's traditional correspondent relationships. The extensive use of joint ventures had also had the advantage of not exposing Midland's comparative lack of experience and expertise in direct international business. By the early 1970s, nevertheless, these determined efforts to 'protect the bank's traditional relationships' were being sidestepped by the massive increase in foreign banks' representation in the United Kingdom.[9] The old unwritten rules about not competing with banking friends in their own countries were steadily being discarded, often to Midland's disadvantage. In this changed atmosphere, it was essential for Midland to reconsider its reluctance to seek international representation. The bank's international position, and the overseas services which it could offer its customers, were bound to be eroded if it did not review both the direction and organization of its overseas activities, preferably in the context of diversification of the Midland group.

The first sign of response to these conditions was a major change in the structure and image of Midland's international business; the coordination of strategy was delayed until reorganization was complete. In May 1974 Midland's board received and approved a management report on group planning in which it was declared that 'special priority will be given to developing international banking activities with particular emphasis on increasing the long term profit contribution from international investments'. This was only possible by recognizing that international banking differed fundamentally in scope, risk and experience from that on the domestic front. Midland Bank International Division was created on that basis in July 1974. The new division was invested with a wide measure of autonomy, its own credit committee and a mandate to fulfil the objectives set out in the group planning document. There was a general acceptance within the plan that, in future, overseas affairs would need at least as much direction and management as domestic. That commitment was reflected in June 1974 in the appointment of two chief general managers, of whom Stuart Graham became responsible for domestic banking and Malcolm Wilcox for related services and international banking (pp 286–7).

Wilcox lost no time in defining the role and objectives of the new International Division. For this purpose he called in Stanford Research Institute to undertake a thorough review of international banking and to recommend alternative strategies for Midland to pursue. There was a pressing need for such a review. The period of twelve years since the 'grand design' plan was launched had seen fundamental shifts in the world economy and in the structure of banking. A decade of rapid growth culminated in the boom of 1971–73 with inflation remaining at a high rate. Floating exchange rates had replaced the Bretton Woods structure in 1973 and the oil price increases of 1973–74 had brought about a dramatic shift in incomes and in relative prospects for economic growth. Competition between British banks had intensified, while the flood of new overseas banks' offices in London was stimulated by the continued growth of the market in foreign currency deposits and loans. In terms of gross deposits alone, the size of this market had increased on estimate from around $50 billion in 1958 to $425 billion in 1976. Above all, the rising importance of the multinational corporation, not only in international trade but in meeting demand in local markets, had acted as a catalyst to the expansion of international banking.

Armed with the results of the five months' work of Stanford, Wilcox called his international general managers to a weekend conference at the bank's staff college at Betchworth in November 1974 to consider the recommendations and to formulate plans to meet them. The studies included a survey of the strategies, organization and management principles of 15 major international banks as well as an analysis of the current international activities of Midland, taking into account the impact of the EBIC relationship and the group's recent acquisitions of Samuel Montagu and other major subsidiaries. Midland had a long way to travel to match the truly international banks in both earnings and representation. Table 11.2 tends to understate the size of the problem as First National City Bank was only one representative of 30 American banks which operated 650 overseas branches at that time.

The Stanford report's succinct presentation of the strengths of the opposition now made it clear that a change of direction was essential, even if that meant breaking with the traditions which had served the

**Table 11.2**

International earnings and facilities of selected banks, 1973

| Earnings and facilities | First National City Bank | Banque Nationale de Paris | Barclays Bank Inter- national | National Westminster Bank | Lloyds Bank | Midland Bank |
|---|---|---|---|---|---|---|
| *Financial position, 1973 ($ million)* | | | | | | |
| (a) Total parent bank assets | 44,000 | 33,000 | 31,000 | 28,000 | 18,000 | 19,000 |
| (b) Earnings after tax | 252 | 53 | 227 | 232 | 154 | 146 |
| (c) International earnings after tax | 151 | 16 | 59 | 40 | 46 | 31 |
|    (c) as percentage of (b) | 60 | 30 | 26 | 17 | 30 | 21 |
| *Number of international facilities, 1973* | | | | | | |
| (a) branches | 242 | 65 | 428 | 7 | — | — |
| (b) office of subsidiaries | 99 | 143 | 1222 | 59 | 464 | — |
| (c) representative offices | — | 16 | 17 | 5 | 4 | 5 |
| (d) principal subsidiaries | 32 | 11 | 26 | 8 | 6 | 1 |
| (e) principal affiliates | 20 | 23 | 10 | 5 | 1 | 7 |

*Source:* FNCB and BBI published accounts (estimates only for other banks)

bank so well in the past. The conference formally recognized three important corporate objectives against which the new policy would be established. First, the bank should be, and be recognized as, a major international banking group with the range of services and geographical spread implied by such recognition. The second objective was to ensure that international business made a greater contribution to bank profits in future. Thirdly, it was essential to diversify the source of group earnings so that a greater proportion originated from outside the United Kingdom. This strategy implied both a widening and deepening of Midland's present international capacity and, in particular, the bank needed to seek representation in major overseas banking centres without upsetting the EBIC arrangements or the relationship with some 20,000 correspondent banks. As many of the main correspondent banks had already opened offices in London, they could have little cause for complaint if Midland chose to operate in their own territories. The EBIC ventures had been a successful outcome of the 1963 agreement for cooperation, but the time had come when any major bank could insist on promoting its own name in foreign business centres in addition to participation in joint ventures. The growing number of Midland's own multinational customers made this essential. The objective was now to supplement and in some cases replace its existing overseas links with extensive direct representation. It was a task with obvious long-term benefits, but in the near future (certainly for the remainder of the 1970s) it was a search which proved to be a heavy consumer of time and expertise at the highest levels of the bank's management.

❁

# CHAPTER TWELVE

# WILL YOU WALK A LITTLE FASTER? THE DOMESTIC BANKING SCENE

## 1971–1975

In the late 1960s British bankers had been understandably preoccupied with the huge merger negotiations of 1968 and the preparations for 'disclosure' in 1970. The size and complexity of these issues obscured from view other fundamental changes in the financial community. The London clearing banks' maintenance of common rates for deposits, allied to continuing official restrictions on lending, had brought about a rapid growth in parallel markets for money and an unsatisfied demand for credit for property development and other non-industrial categories of business. This was a climate in which 'secondary' banks could flourish, free from supervision and lending restrictions. By 1970 it was evident that the incoming Conservative government's policy of giving some stimulus to growth in the economy was incomplete without a new look at the way in which credit was made available.

In September 1971 the Bank of England's discussion paper 'Competition and Credit Control' (ccc) was adopted as the new control mechanism. All lending restrictions were removed and banks were set free to compete for deposits (thereby allowing the clearers to operate in their own names in the wholesale money markets). The old liquidity ratios which had governed them were replaced by a system of reserve assets which allowed much greater room for manoeuvre. To the clearers, it was as if the Bank of England had assumed the role of the whiting in *Alice in Wonderland*, exhorting them to walk a little faster because the porpoise close behind them, in the guise of the secondary banks, was treading on the official tail. It marked the beginning of a new wonderland in which, for a time, nothing was quite as it seemed. For a time too, it was possible to walk much faster. Then the porpoise found the pace too much for its limited reserves of strength and it needed to be carried or even abandoned.

The authorities believed that the introduction of CCC in 1971 would remedy the distortions in the old control system. The operations of the secondary banks would be curtailed as the clearing banks made use of their new ability to compete on equal terms. Industry would benefit from the extra credit available. However, they had not reckoned with the effect of the new forces unleashed in the CCC doctrine which actually allowed the secondary banks to expand dramatically. In a special paper submitted in 1978 at the request of the Wilson Committee, which had been formed in 1977 to review the functioning of financial institutions, the Bank of England affirmed that 'the expectation was, perhaps not immediately but in a short while, the fringe would contract to a level of comparative unimportance'.[1]

The overall thrust of economic policy in 1971 and 1972 was towards expansion, and the main stimulus to investment by industry was to be provided by a more freely available supply of credit. Nevertheless, demand for money from manufacturing industry remained low in 1972 and early 1973. In the industrial sector the rates of return in a still rather stagnant economy were unattractive; businesses were reluctant to embark on capital expenditure programmes until confidence returned. Most of the new money available went to finance a boom in consumer goods and, in particular, into the property market. There was no other general area of economic activity that seemed to offer as good a rate of return to an entrepreneur as property development, held back in the late 1960s by both planning and financial restrictions. By 1971 there was a large demand for office property, which brought about a sharp increase in rentals when they could be freely negotiated. Prices of all types of property, especially land with planning permission, rose rapidly and lent support to the widely held view that property was the only real hedge against the inflation which seemed to be a permanent feature of the postwar economy.

The finance of property development by the banks had been officially discouraged throughout the 1960s. Again, in August 1972, concern was expressed about the banks' capacity to meet the expected upturn in demand from industry. In any case, banks were traditionally cautious about becoming too heavily involved in property commitments, having learned from experience that builders and developers were top of the list of customers whose activities could lead to bad debts. Nevertheless, some banks began to believe that their own prudence had allowed the secondary institutions too much of the seemingly profitable business of financing the development of offices and residential blocks of property for ultimate sale to pension funds or

**Figure 12.1**  *Midland Bank advances, growth and distribution chart, 1968–73*

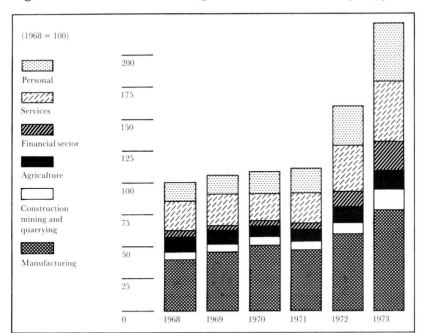

insurance companies. Midland retained a cautious view. Although from time to time there were discussions in the bank's management committee as to whether a more adventurous attitude was called for, in August 1972 the authorities officially discouraged banks from financing 'speculative developments'.[2]

The effect on Midland's advances of the new freedom to lend is shown in Figure 12.1. Sir Archibald Forbes pointed out, early in 1974, that 'the increased lending to the financial sector (including property development) reflected on the one hand, a modest extension of lending to instalment credit finance companies and an increase in demand . . . from investment trusts and other funds; and, on the other, a growth in ordinary business activity including the building of residential and industrial premises. Moreover, the proportion made available to property development companies as such has remained fairly stable over the period shown and is minimal when set against the totality of our advances.'

Not all the clearers had been so circumspect in their lending to the secondary banks and associated property developers. The clearing banks had unwittingly become the source of funds for the secondary banks and other institutions less inhibited by official exhortations or

**Table 12.1**

Inter-bank sterling borrowing and inter-bank borrowing on Certificates of Deposit (CDs), 1971–3

| Date | All banks (£ million) | | | London clearing banks | | |
|------|-----------|-----|-------|-----------|-----|--------|
|      | Interbank | CDs | Total | Interbank | CDs | Total* |
| Oct 1971  | 2004 | 1863 | 3867  | 183 | 83   | 266  |
| June 1972 | 3295 | 3595 | 6890  | 498 | 564  | 1062 |
| Dec 1972  | 4573 | 4926 | 9499  | 592 | 1292 | 1884 |
| June 1973 | 6134 | 5088 | 11222 | 967 | 1745 | 2712 |

*Note* * Figures for parent banks only. On a group basis, the clearing bank total for June 1973 was £5633 million, some 50 per cent of the total for all banks.

*Source: Midland Bank Review*, August 1973.

the classic dangers of borrowing short and lending long. With the slow pick-up of demand from industry the banks generally had more lendable funds than they were finding traditional opportunities to lend and were therefore increasingly prepared to on-lend their surplus resources through the medium of the money markets. Fringe institutions found that they could attract deposits through brokers, mainly at short term, by offering only modestly higher rates than the banks. Much of the money was employed in property development; the expectation that such deposits would continue to be renewed at maturity further encouraged several of the secondary banks to lend short-term money for long-term development, disregarding the risk of becoming locked in.

The markets for inter-bank and sterling certificates of deposit grew at an astonishing rate, and borrowing approximately trebled in the period between October 1971 and June 1973 (Table 12.1).

The clearing banks were able to operate in these markets as both lenders and borrowers; they could issue CDs to meet their own needs at the same time as being net lenders in the market. The amount of reserve assets required was calculated only on the basis of a bank's *net* position. Commenting in the August 1973 issue, the *Midland Bank Review* argued that 'more generally, the banking system does not appear to be taking on any additional risk, since inter-bank borrowing and lending must net out'.[3]

With a readily available supply of funds and an almost insatiable demand from developers, the price of land and property of all descriptions rose and continued to rise throughout 1972 and 1973. The money market was also fuelled by the sterling money brokers. As a consequence of the disparity in commission structures between authorized and secondary banks, coupled with the brokers' total lack of credit review facilities, funds tended to be deliberately channelled towards the poorest commercial risks. The inter-bank market therefore represented a chain-letter mechanism; it transferred cash deposits from individuals and corporations into the primary banking system (via the clearers, leading accepting houses and foreign banks) to secondary banks. Ultimately, many of these deposits were transferred to what were often disparagingly referred to as the 'bucket shops', which would lend them on for highly speculative property ventures.[4]

These developments affected the banking system in the context of a generally deteriorating economy. With the terms of trade moving against the United Kingdom, sterling began to depreciate rapidly and the rate of $2.6057 established against the United States dollar in December 1971 was clearly impossible to sustain without a substantial increase in minimum lending rate. In preference to this, the authorities decided to allow the pound to float and find its own level. As pressure of demand for money market funds continued throughout 1973, however, interest rates rose steadily, with the key three months' inter-bank rate up from 9 per cent in mid-July to 16 per cent in December. In the same period, clearing bank minimum lending rates were forced up from 7.5 per cent to 13 per cent, causing the Bank of England to deploy the whole armoury of defensive measures available under the ccc rules. Supplementary special deposits (popularly known as 'the corset') were called for monthly, based on the level of each bank's interest bearing deposits, accompanied by further qualitative guidance on lending priorities.

These combined measures constituted a new credit squeeze of unprecedented severity and changed the economics of borrowing for property development. Long-term loans made by fringe banks earlier in the year, based on short-term money borrowed at 7 per cent, suddenly began to look like bad deals as interest rates for roll-over funds rose. Moreover, because developers' ability to cover interest payments out of cash flow was now jeopardized, property began to look like dubious security for outstanding loans.[5]

In this overheated situation, it required only a spark to ignite the whole structure and destroy the confidence which is an essential ingredient of banking. The City was already becoming nervous about the deposit structure of the fringe banks. When, in November 1973, Donald Bardsley, a respected City banker, resigned from the board of

London and County Securities after only five months, its share price collapsed in panic selling, accompanied by a major run on the bank by depositors. In a chain reaction, several other similar companies found themselves unable to renew the short-term deposits on which their lending operations depended. A rapidly escalating crisis of confidence threatened the collapse of many other deposit-taking institutions with the danger that it could quickly work its way through to parts of the banking system proper.

The case of Cedar Holdings, as well as illustrating the mushroom growth and subsequent downfall of some of the fringe banks, brought the crisis onto a wider stage. Incorporated as a private company in 1958, Cedar was floated as a public company in January 1971 when its business was described as 'second mortgages and banking facilities'. The banking connotation was its registration under Section 123 of the 1967 Companies Act, which had the effect of affording protection from the terms of the Money-lenders Act of 1900 but left the company free from banking supervision by the authorities. Hence, in contrast to the traditional banking system, it operated without any official judgement of the quality of its management. Its second mortgage activities, in company with those of certain other fringe institutions, took advantage of the fact that many householders found themselves with large equities in their houses following the rapid rise in values in the 1960s, against which the clearing banks and building societies were unwilling to provide long-term loans at the owners' option. In this field of lending some of the fringe banks were beginning to attract unfavourable publicity from the exorbitant rates of interest charged, from the penalties for early termination of the contract, and from methods of enforcing collection of repayments. Their activities were, nonetheless, profitable and expanding rapidly. At the date of its flotation as a public company in 1971, Cedar Holdings had an asset base of £11 million. By June 1972, this had risen to over £37 million financed by loans and short-term deposits of over £31 million against share capital and reserves of only £6 million. The company sought to lengthen its deposit book by offering gifts to those who were prepared to commit funds for three years and by advertising its interest-rate advantage over the clearing banks. In November 1973, for example, when the clearers were officially restricted to a rate of 9.5 per cent for deposits of less than £10,000, it proclaimed that 'Cedar Holdings is not a listed bank and prides itself on the fair deal it offers to depositors ... it will pay 7 per cent on large current account deposits ... deposit account holders earn 11 per cent'. One business commentator noted that Cedar was calling itself a bank while not entitled to; it 'looks like a case of trying to have it both ways'.[6] Yet institutions which had been sufficiently impressed to supply capital and loans to the group included Phoenix Assurance and the pension funds of the electricity supply industry, the National Coal Board and Unilever. Barclays were the main bankers.

In June 1973 Cedar diversified, moving directly into property development by an agreed merger with Amalgamated Securities. Many of its short-term deposits were already deployed in financing loans of up to fifteen years, and by June 1973 a continuation of trading depended entirely on the ability to renew the deposits as they fell due. Undeterred, Cedar took over Alexanders Stores three months later for £7 million in cash. This was not the limit of the company's ambitions. Towards the end of the year, negotiations were opened with a view to acquiring the Chester National Bank of New York State. The deal was frustrated by the delay required to secure the approval of the United States Federal Authority, during which Cedar was overtaken by the arrival of the fringe bank crisis and the bid lapsed.

When the London and County crash became public, there was an immediate reaction from depositors in Cedar Holdings. As monies flowed out, the share price fell dramatically. After a long meeting at the Bank of England on the night of 19–20 December 1973, the four investing institutions were persuaded by the Bank to put together a rescue package of £50 million, accompanied by loans of £22 million from Barclays.[7] On the following day, 20 December, Cedar's Stock Exchange quotation was suspended, when the market capitalization was a mere £7.6 million against over £54 million earlier in the year. Cedar's current liabilities stood at £70 million, against liquid assets of only £15 million. The institutions took over voting control in April 1974 and began the difficult process of running down the company by the realization of assets. The auditors' report subsequently revealed that certain directors' loans, following the merger with Amalgamated Securities, 'may have been in contravention of Section 190 of the Companies Act 1948' and that the value of certain assets 'is dependent on the resumption of borrowing and banking operations'. Accounts to 30 June 1974 revealed a loss of £5 million for the year and a deficit of £6.3 million in shareholders' funds. As an example of the way in which the value of some of the balance sheet assets had collapsed, an uncompleted block of property at Buckingham Gate, London, valued in the accounts at £9 million, was offered for sale at £1.5 million. Samuel Montagu and Co, brought in as the company's merchant bank advisers, put together reconstruction proposals in March 1975, including a drastic reduction in the interest of ordinary shareholders and a sale to institutions of the bulk of the group's property portfolio at 90 per cent of its April 1974 valuation. Thus shorn of its prime assets, the company continued to trade on a much restricted scale until it was sold to Lloyds and Scottish Finance for £9.6 million in 1978.[8]

The collapse of London and County and Cedar Holdings made the Bank of England realize that, in the face of a possible loss of confidence in the banking system itself, it had to take prompt and decisive action. In the first instance the London and County problem had been seen as essentially one of recycling deposits withdrawn in the panic atmosphere of the time; the Bank therefore called together National Westminster Bank, London and County's main clearing bank, Eagle Star Insurance Company (a major shareholder) and other interested parties. On 3 December 1973 a consortium was formed headed by First National Finance Corporation (FNFC) to lead a £30 million rescue operation. The Bank joined with FNFC in a joint company to take over London and County's banking operations, and thereafter in March 1975 the company's banking subsidiary was placed in liquidation. This first individual response to the crisis suggested that the Bank had not at that time foreseen the extent of the problem. Moreover, the selection of FNFC as leader of the rescue is difficult to defend in the light of subsequent events, during which it became one of the largest passengers in the 'lifeboat' operation.

After having to take similar steps to deal with the Cedar Holdings problem, the Bank of England now became conscious that it had a full-scale crisis on its hands and urgently called together the clearing banks to prepare its defence against further collapse in the secondary banking system. Meetings were held throughout December 1973, leading to the announcement later in the month that the Bank and the clearers were acting together to protect depositors in secondary banks threatened with liquidity problems. The 'lifeboat' had been launched.

The controlling committee of the rescue operation formally met for the first time on 28 December 1973. The names of twenty passengers and potential passenger banks were listed, with £100 million already advanced to them and an estimated further exposure of £160 million. The chairman of the committee was Jasper (later Sir Jasper) Hollom, deputy governor of the Bank of England, supported by a senior banker from each of the English and Scottish clearing banks.

Stuart Graham, assistant chief general manager, was Midland's representative at that first meeting, though subsequently John Cave, assistant chief general manager, and Dennis Kitching, a general manager, attended many of the meetings in the early days. The bankers identified each deposit-taking company with known or anticipated liquidity difficulties; the clearing bank with the closest connection was appointed as the 'related bank' to that company, responsible for a rapid assessment on which the committee could make a decision on whether or not to give support. The criteria were:

1  that the company was solvent and likely to remain so if it was supported by recycled deposits;

2  that it 'exhibited sufficient banking characteristics' for inclusion in the scheme, with deposits from the public;

3  that it did not possess any institutional shareholders who might properly be expected to provide the required support.

Most cases were accepted by the committee and the risk was shared between all members *pro rata* to the size of their deposits, although in some cases a related bank would continue to handle a case as its sole risk. The Bank of England's share was agreed at 10 per cent and, based on the deposit formula, Midland's risk was fixed at 17.1 per cent and Clydesdale's at 1.7 per cent. Interest on support loans by all the participating banks was charged at a commercial rate, typically 1.5 to 2 per cent over inter-bank rate in the market.

In the early stages of the operation, from December 1973 to March 1974, 21 institutions were supported with total loans of just under £400 million. During the remainder of 1974 the economic situation of the country deteriorated and confidence in the fringe banking operations showed no sign of returning. The miners' strike, the three day week, the general election and a tough March budget combined to sap business confidence, already undermined by the four-fold increase in oil prices at the end of 1973. The value of commercial property tumbled and the underlying assets of some companies in receipt of lifeboat support began to look vulnerable. Even the larger deposit-taking institutions, especially those known to have substantial property portfolios, found it impossible to maintain their deposits. United Dominions Trust and FNFC made large calls on the support operation which, by the end of December 1974, was committed to loans of almost £1200 million. This represented some two-fifths of the capital and reserves of the English and Scottish clearing banks, and by August 1974 the Bank of England accepted the force of their argument that this must be the limit of their exposure. At the peak, Midland's share of the amounts advanced was just over £219 million and Clydesdale's almost £22 million. An exposure of over 50 per cent of shareholders' funds of £474 million was clearly a cause for concern.

When these new levels of vulnerability were reached, the Bank of

England's attitude was obviously crucial. The governor and his colleagues confirmed that, if necessary, support in excess of the £1200 million figure would be undertaken at its own risk. The fear was that if any further deposit-taking institution was refused help, the restoration of confidence engendered by the lifeboat operations so far would be lost and the whole banking system would remain in danger of collapse. The international financial community noted with approval the closing of ranks and the steps taken to protect depositors in the United Kingdom, but suddenly a series of international banking failures took place. In the autumn of 1973 Franklin National Bank in New York had failed and in Germany Bankhaus Herstatt closed its doors following massive foreign exchange losses. The Israel-British Bank of Tel Aviv failed in the following year, in conjunction with its London subsidiary. Lloyds Bank International suffered losses on exchange dealings at its Lugano branch in Switzerland. Such was the crisis of confidence that even National Westminster, the bank most involved in financing the fringe banks and their associated property ventures, found it necessary to publish a statement by its chairman in December 1974 that it was not receiving any support and remained both sound and liquid.

In the event the need for additional support over and above the £1200 million in the shared operation proved to be modest and short-lived, amounting to only £85 million by March 1975. Later in 1975, however, the Bank of England itself moved in to rescue Slater Walker and, shortly afterwards, Edward Bates and Sons, where there were ramifications beyond those of 'normal' United Kingdom banking.[9] After March 1975, the total amount of support began to decline as companies re-established themselves or were taken over by stronger ones. It was by now evident that far from a simple recycling of deposits until confidence could be restored, the lifeboat operation would be a long-term commitment. The fall in property values made it impossible to reduce borrowing by the sale of assets except over an extended period. The existing management of the fringe banks, seemingly so enterprising and innovative in the boom conditions of 1972 and early 1973, was in many cases quite inadequate to cope with hard times. The clearers not only supplied funds through the lifeboat but in several cases provided senior executives to take control, including Derek Wilde from Barclays (to Keyser Ullmann) and Len Mather from Midland (to the chairmanship of United Dominions Trust). The lifeboat controlling committee eventually gave support to 26 companies in all, of which eight were placed in receivership or liquidation between May 1974 and May 1975. (The eight companies were: Audley Holdings, Boston Finance, Cannon Street Acceptances, First Maryland, Guardian Properties (Holdings), London and County Securities, David Samuel Trust, and Triumph Investment Trust.) All had originally been seen as solvent and capable of being rescued in accordance with the agreed criteria, and their failure was indicative of the escalation of the crisis over the twelve months. At the date of their last balance sheets in 1973, the eight companies were showing total assets of almost £650 million, a figure grossly in excess of realizable values. When each collapsed into liquidation, the way in which those assets had been financed became all too obvious.

By December 1975 the lifeboat's total commitment had fallen to £913 million as assets were realized, schemes of reconstruction completed and refinancing arranged, and to £782 million in 1976 and £676 million by the end of 1977. The largest amount of support was provided to United Dominions Trust, but under the direction of Len Mather, assets were realized over a period of years until, in 1981, a successful sale of the company to the central Trustees Savings Bank allowed all support loans to be repaid. By the end of 1981, the only active company in receipt of support was FNFC.

Each passenger in the lifeboat had been linked with a 'related' bank, and although not an accurate barometer of the policy of each of the clearers before December 1973, Table 12.2 gives some indication of their attitudes. Midland's conservatism stands out; the two Midland 'related' companies, both quite small, disembarked from the lifeboat in 1975 and their solvency was never in question. Midland's share of the total lending at its peak in December 1974 was just over £200 million, of which it was considered unnecessary to provide for more than £26 million as 'doubtful'; most of the provisions were recovered in due course.

Reviewing the crisis in his 1974 report to Midland's shareholders, Sir Archibald Forbes referred to the 'fitful fever' of the previous year. It was an appropriate description of twelve months during which the reputation, perhaps even the survival, of the United Kingdom's banking system had been in jeopardy. The affair led directly to the 1976 Banking Act which not only gave the Bank of England additional powers of surveillance but created a fund for the protection of depositors.[10]

The dramatic events of 1973–5 were the most obvious outcome of CCC. At Midland the first response to CCC had been to create a new money market division in the bank itself to handle all the wholesale deposit-taking functions of the group, operate its money 'book' and be responsible for the maintenance of the required level of reserve assets.

**Table 12.2**

'Lifeboat' loan support provided by the London clearing banks, 1974–75

| Bank | Number of related companies | Maximum amount of support provided (£ million) |
| --- | --- | --- |
| Barclays | 4 | 487 |
| Lloyds | 3 | 146 |
| Midland | 2 | 8 |
| National Westminster | 8 | 607 |
| Williams and Glyn's | 2 | 13 |

At the same time, the steadily increasing flow of applications from branches for medium-term lending on behalf of customers was channelled through a new term loan division. This centralization of money market operations and term lending deprived MBFC of two of its principal activities and gave rise to major considerations of what its new role should be. Samuel Montagu, in which the Midland then had only a 33 per cent interest, continued to operate with complete independence in both deposit-taking and lending activities. MBFC had quickly established a leading position in the market for deposits and the issue of sterling CDs and at the end of October 1971, when Midland's money market division opened for business, MBFC held deposits of £390 million in sterling and £130 million in currency alongside CDs of £193 million. Its lending had been severely limited by the credit restrictions which came into force at the time of its incorporation, and the main part of its funds had therefore been redeployed in the market at very small margins of profit. For the moment, it continued to take deposits with which to undertake lending activities considered unsuitable for Midland itself, mainly in respect of property development. Looking further ahead, the decision was taken to develop and expand MBFC's function as the management vehicle for the growing number of related service companies. In the four years up to 1971, however, MBFC had built up a fund of experience in deposit-taking and term lending; this benefit passed to the bank when Geoffrey Taylor, then MBFC's assistant managing director, acted as group treasurer in the establishment of the bank's new money market division. Most of MBFC's executives and staff concerned with lending were transferred to the bank's term loan division. Staff concerned with currency activities were transferred to the overseas branch, and others went to Samuel Montagu. Thereafter, Midland's

**Table 12.3**

Midland Bank, numbers of current accounts, cheques and cash handled, 1960–75

| Million | 1960 | 1970 | 1975 |
|---|---|---|---|
| Number of current accounts | 1.9 | 3.2 | 3.9 |
| Number of cheques handled | 275 | 490 | 645 |
| Cash handled | £4300 | £8000 | £16,000 |

money market operations were placed on an altogether larger scale than those previously conducted by MBFC: under the guidance of K B Cox, the general manager appointed to head the new division, this involvement was rapidly expanded.

By 1975, long-term and significant changes were beginning to take place in the pattern of banking itself. The demand for advances began to rise steeply in the mid-1970s. With the Stock Exchange effectively out of action as a source of new money, owing to a lack of investor confidence and the competing claims of attractive government stocks on issue, bank money was for the time the only alternative for a company wishing to expand. Traditionally banks had been able to finance their lending by using funds flowing over branch counters into current and deposit accounts (the 'retail' part of the business). The evolution of the wholesale markets for money had now introduced an entirely new element. Certain large deposits were now tending to by-pass the clearing bank system and find their way directly into the inter-bank wholesale markets. As a result, the clearers needed to take deposits from those markets in order to meet heavy demands for advances (subsequently Midland's inter-bank deposits rose to some 40 per cent of the total of all sterling deposits in 1980, when they were greater than the amounts lodged on either current or deposit accounts). These funds had to be bought at market rates and were therefore more expensive than retail deposits, while competition ensured that lending margins were fine. At the same time the clearers were allowed to participate in currency lending as from 1975, which permitted an enormous expansion in deposit and lending totals; within five years one third of all Midland's deposits were in currency and deployed in currency lending. The growth in deposits and advances between 1970 and 1975 was accompanied by increases of major proportions in the number of current accounts, the number of cheques handled annually and the amount of cash passing over branch counters (Table 12.3).

In the 1970s this rapid growth was challenging Midland's

management to examine the efficiency of operations in its branch network. Another even more urgent problem was that of dealing with the competition from the many foreign banks in London in the handling of accounts of major multinational company customers. At Midland, it had long been almost a tenet of faith that the branch manager should be the first point of contact for customers, large or small. Simple matters would be dealt with locally, more complex ones referred up through the chain of command and, if necessary, to head office in London, until the appropriate sanctioning authority had been reached. The system involved only a slight delay covering papers in transit and had worked well ever since Midland first became a nationwide bank. The basic assumption was that, if a customer wanted anything, he would ask for it. But the American banks were now competing in the form of 'cold calling': not just a polite approach on the 'can we do anything for you' basis, but a formal offer of facilities based on a careful study of the target company's products, markets, ambitions and financial requirements. The offers were followed up with skill and patience and many finance directors began to be impressed by such a positive approach, comparing it favourably with the passive, wait-till-asked attitude of the British banks.

There was another reason for taking a new look at the way in which large accounts were handled. Since the war, industry had enjoyed a period of relative stability and prosperity and it was rare to hear of a large company in trouble. When difficulties did occur, however, neither Midland nor its competitors had separate departments affording special care and attention, using staff experienced in the particular problems of receivership and liquidation. It was not only when a crash came that something more was needed. As later experience proved, there was much that could be done when difficulties first came to notice, and often a company could be nursed back to financial health. Ideally, such a department would be charged with the sole responsibility for these accounts, as the normal chain of line management had neither the time nor special experience to handle the often complex issues. The problem was brought sharply into focus in 1970 and 1971 by the crisis in the affairs of one of the great engineering companies, Rolls-Royce, where the position of principal banker to the company was shared by Midland and Lloyds.

Since it first opened an account at Derby branch in 1908, Rolls-Royce had become one of Midland's most important customers. By long tradition its affairs were dealt with at regular meetings in the bank's head office between a general manager and senior company officials. At the end of the 1960s, Rolls-Royce's business included important government defence contracts and the manufacture of engines for the Anglo-French supersonic airliner, Concorde. Additionally, in March 1968 it had entered into a large contract with the Lockheed Aircraft Corporation in the United States to supply 450 engines for the proposed new wide-bodied civil aircraft, the Tri-Star. The engine, the RB 211, was designed using the most advanced technology and new materials; development costs at the time of signing the contract were estimated at £65 million, of which the government promised to find a maximum of £47 million in exchange for royalties. Under the contract, Rolls-Royce was bound to commence delivery to Lockheed in 1971 and a fixed price of £354,000 was agreed for each engine.

Unfortunately, certain technical problems remained to be solved and the company seriously underestimated both the cost of the development expenditure and the time it would take to perfect the engine. At a succession of meetings with its bankers in 1970 the directors repeatedly revised their estimates upwards, and both Midland and Lloyds began to be concerned at the extent of the company's borrowing, actual and potential. They were then providing overdraft facilities of £25 million each, while a consortium of merchant banks led by Lazards covered an acceptance credit of £20 million; the company itself had £55 million of quoted debenture stock in issue. With further funds needed, the company had requested from the government-sponsored Industrial Reorganization Corporation a further loan of £20 million, and soon there were rumours in the City that Rolls-Royce was in financial difficulties.

At Midland, the company's affairs were being handled by John Cave, general manager of the bank's Midlands division, but because of the size of the problem and of the government's involvement, the chairman was kept closely informed. In September 1970 Sir Archibald Forbes, with Sir Eric Faulkner, chairman of Lloyds Bank, asked for a meeting with Sir Denning Pearson, the Rolls-Royce chairman. It was disclosed that further talks were in progress with the government because the estimated development costs of the RB 211 had now risen to £140 million; meanwhile Rolls-Royce acknowledged some pressure from creditors, though the directors remained optimistic about the course of its affairs. Not surprisingly, in view of past estimates, neither the government nor the banks were ready to put up any more money without some reliable financial information and in November, Sir Henry Benson of Cooper Brothers was called in to prepare a report on the company's estimates and general financial position. Before this could be completed, it was overtaken by events and in January 1971, a critical reassessment of the RB 211 project disclosed that the existing programme of development and production could not be met. If the company ceased production, there would be substantial penalties under the contract; if it managed to negotiate a postponement, substantial additional borrowing would be necessary.

At this stage, the affairs of Rolls-Royce had reached a crisis point. If the banks and the government were not prepared to put up any further funds, there was no alternative to calling in a receiver and manager, but in view of the interest of the United States authorities in the affairs of Lockheed, normal remedies could not be applied without first dealing with the political implications. It was left to the Prime Minister, Edward Heath, to telephone the President, Richard Nixon, with the news that a decision had been taken to let the receivership take its course.

As protection for national defence contracts, the government took steps to form a separate company, Rolls-Royce (1971) Ltd, which purchased the trading assets and patents of the four gas-turbine divisions, leaving the question of price to be negotiated later. The receiver appointed was E R Nicholson of Peat Marwick Mitchell and Co, who conducted the affairs of the troubled company with such skill and determination—including his negotiations with the government about the amount to be paid for assets taken over by the new company—that in due course the banks and other unsecured creditors were paid in full.[11]

From Midland's point of view, the size and importance of the Rolls-Royce problems brought about a complete departure from normal banking practice. The seriousness with which the bank regarded the company's affairs in the autumn of 1970 was reflected in the direct intervention of Sir Archibald Forbes in an issue which would normally have been left to the executive. Recourse to normal banking remedies had to be subordinated to the national interest and other parties had to be consulted (for example the consortium of accepting houses and the debenture holders). For a long period early in the crisis nobody was ready to believe that the government would allow Rolls-Royce to fail. Fortunately, Midland had in John Cave a banker who proved equal to the situation; in recognition of the firmness and ability he showed in the long negotiations, he was able to play a leading part and, frequently, to represent the other lenders (he later became deputy chief general manager, chairman of MBFC and a director of the bank). Nevertheless, there would not always be a John Cave to handle problems of this size and complexity, and the case for some new treatment was firmly established.

When Stuart Graham was appointed to control the affairs of the domestic bank in 1974 (p 286), one of his first moves was to establish a corporate finance division to assume responsibility for the affairs of major corporate customers, including a 'special situations' unit to deal with problem accounts. In this, he had the enthusiastic support of Dennis Kitching, the general manager in charge of the new division, whose experience included senior appointments in Forward Trust and in the bank's money market operations as well as in more conventional domestic banking. The division was staffed by a small number of experienced senior bankers, each of whose sole responsibility was to look after the affairs of a dozen or so large customers. The division set out to study the needs of its customers and, by maintaining regular contact through visits at home and abroad, to establish a relationship which would ensure that Midland became the first and most obvious choice for their banking needs. In addition, Kitching was anxious that his new team should market the whole range of the bank's services to businesses which had not hitherto been customers, act as a forum for the discussion of new ideas and take part in syndicated loans for the finance of major projects.

Inevitably the new concept met with some initial opposition from managers and regional directors who had spent much time in building up good relationships with their major customers and found it difficult to believe that some hitherto unknown official in London could do better. Then gradually it came to be accepted that corporate finance directors had the advantage of being specially trained to be able to offer any group service and were free from the distractions of other duties with which managers were faced. Managers still had an important part to play in dealing with their larger customers in the provision of local services, including money transmission facilities. As they became increasingly aware of the nature of the competition from overseas banks, they were glad to turn to specialists for support. The other clearing banks watched Midland's new approach to corporate business with interest and by the late 1970s they had all taken similar measures, though none settled for so complete a break from the branch concept of handling business.

Having set up a new mechanism for major corporate business, Graham next turned his attention to the position of the personal customer and smaller businesses and the way in which their requirements were being catered for in the network of branches. The problem needed a different emphasis from that of the corporate customer. Personal customers ordinarily had little cause for complaint, except perhaps in the matter of opening hours and the lack of Saturday morning banking which was proving an intractable problem in the face of determined opposition from the staff unions. At the end of 1975, the bank itself was employing 42,000 people in its 2600 branches and direct staff costs constituted 60 per cent of the bank's expenses; on cost grounds alone, the question arose as to whether the system of hundreds of small branches, each with a manager and full support staff, was an effective way of operating a bank in the latter half of the century. The development of central computer accounting had taken care of much of the routine drudgery and enabled the servicing of far more accounts per member of staff than ever before. Bank branches were inevitably situated in prime positions in the centre of towns and cities, yet much of the space at the back of the counter was still being used for routine duties, often at the expense of inadequate accommodation in the banking hall. In very small branches, managers were having to do their own typing as the services of a full-time secretary could not be justified; at best they were required to spend much of their time in routine duties performed by clerical staff in larger branch banks.

In 1975, this problem was examined by a newly established strategic services department. It recommended setting up operations centres in the regions to handle further routine branch operations—for example, the processing of the thousands of cheques paid in by customers each day. Consideration was also given to the setting up of central management teams operating from area offices, leaving the remaining offices to become 'service branches' dealing with day-to-day customer affairs requiring little or no banking judgement. These concepts were pursued in the following year by the setting up of a branch network reorganization department leading, in the latter half of the 1970s, to a major reshaping of Midland's network.

Fundamental to the problem of reorganizing the branch network was a recognition that the bank was competing in an increasing number of markets outside those of traditional banking. In whatever form it eventually emerged, the network of branches had to be made to earn its keep by selling new services alongside the more familiar activities of a clearing bank. Insurance was one field in which branches had a marketing role to play. Until the early 1960s, it had been accepted that insurance commissions should be the personal earnings of branch managers: in some country branches (in Lincolnshire, in particular), a manager's insurance commission might exceed his salary from the bank. In the 1960s the bank purchased these insurance agencies from managers and in May 1971 formed a central insurance agency with regional advisers. In 1972, Midland Bank Insurance

Services was incorporated under the supervision of Randle Manwaring, an experienced broker, to formalize insurance as an important source of additional earnings. In conjunction with leading insurance companies, a series of specialized packages was devised, including household insurance, life insurance, assistance with school fees, personal accident and house purchase insurance backed with life cover.

The use of credit cards had become an accepted and almost essential part of everyday life in the United States during the 1960s but in Britain it was still considered somewhat radical as a method of paying for goods and services. As a different approach, Midland's business development committee examined the alternative of issuing cards which would guarantee its customers' cheques up to a maximum of £30. Midland's cheque cards, the first of their kind in British banking, had been introduced on these lines in March 1966. Within two years 500,000 customers were using the service. In June the same year, however, Barclays introduced their own credit card, Barclaycard. The new card was modelled on American practice, eliminating the link with a cheque-based current account. It enjoyed instant popularity and within three years a million cardholders were using the Barclays service; it was clear that the initiative would be fully justified once the high start-up expenses had been recovered.

The other clearers now recognized that they would have to compete and decided that in view of the cost of setting up the service, it would be preferable to do so jointly, though each would maintain its own cardholders and the profit on the lending. Early in 1971 Midland, Lloyds and National Westminster formed the Joint Credit Card Company with a mandate to devise a cooperative credit card service. At the first meeting of the new company, Stuart Graham from Midland was elected chairman, and H G Cameron was seconded by National Westminster as chief executive. Suitable premises were found at Southend-on-Sea and the new credit card was launched in October 1972 under the name of Access (Williams and Glyn's Bank and the Royal Bank of Scotland joined the venture immediately before the launch). The new name came at the suggestion of J Walter Thompson, appointed as agents to market the service, after the member banks had sought in vain for inspiration. Earlier suggestions for the credit card's brand name included 'Omnicard', 'Supercharge' and 'Three-in-One'.

The introduction of Barclaycard had proved that a demand existed for a credit card and there was little doubt that Access would meet the challenge. As interest rates fluctuated with the cost of funds taken from the money market, the service was soon profitable. During the high interest rate era of the late 1970s, even a *monthly* rate on outstanding balances of as much as 2.5 per cent did not deter customers. The convenience of easy credit outweighed the cost, and outstanding balances continued to rise each year.

Midland Bank's response to the upheavals in its home market in the 1970s was essentially structural. The more competitive conditions ushered in by ccc in 1971 and the crisis in British banking in 1974 had been answered with major organizational changes. In branch banking this transformation presaged an even more dramatic change in the concept and use of the branch network. The guiding principle of those changes in domestic banking after 1974 was to combine business expansion with efficient and productive systems at head office and at the branches, but the forthcoming restructuring of Midland's operations in England and Wales had to be attempted before any reassessment could be made of the bank's range of services. This applied particularly to the retail end of the banking market for, despite the proliferation of new services in the late 1950s and 1960s (up to and including the introduction of insurance services and the Access credit card in 1971), relatively few new *types* of banking products had been made available across Midland's branch counters in the early 1970s. This was partly due to the 'corset' system of official controls over credit expansion from 1973, but it was also the result of the bank's preoccupation with its domestic systems and its international banking ambitions. A review of the bank's functions and targets in its home market was necessary if the new branch and corporate finance facilities, backed up with fast-changing and increasingly sophisticated computerization, were to be fully exploited. This task was inextricably linked with appraising the relative importance of the different activities of the Midland group as a whole. If these interests were to be brought into a realistic balance, the bank's domestic services now needed a new focus and even a new identity—a need which was to be imaginatively fulfilled by the new services and marketing efforts of the late 1970s and early 1980s.

# CHAPTER THIRTEEN

# UNDER NEW ORDERS MIDLAND AS A BANKING GROUP
## 1971–1975

The disclosure of Midland's relatively weak capital position in 1970 came as a genuine shock to the bank's senior management. They had barely accustomed themselves to the emergence of two much larger rivals as a result of the 1968 mergers, only to learn that Midland had lost its position in terms of capital as well as deposits. Rapid adjustment was needed to show that the bank's customers would be given the same range and depth of services offered by its larger rivals. There was now a new determination to change the pace of the bank's development, and, in a remarkable period in which British banking changed beyond recognition, Midland's progress was distinctive. The major changes in the domestic financial scene produced innovative responses from the bank, especially in the restructuring of its corporate and personal banking services. Perhaps the largest opportunity, however, was to diversify the business and to develop Midland's potential as a group of companies. This chance could only be taken by overhauling the bank's organization as well as its strategic ambitions.

In the early 1970s the organization of Midland Bank at board and top management level was very much as it had been for the previous 50 years. The traditional pattern of a non-banking chairman, supported by a largely non-executive board of senior figures from industry, the professions and public life, left operations and decision-taking heavily centralized in the hands of a chief general manager, assisted by an executive team of joint general managers, each responsible for a geographical division. Other general managers were concerned with service functions, such as personnel, administration and special services such as the Executor and Trustee Company, but they were not members of the ruling management committee of the bank, so long the main channel for assessments and decisions on Midland's lending and the deployment of surplus funds. It was a pattern quite suitable for an old-style, traditional clearing bank but clearly inadequate to provide the drive and planning necessary to meet the agreed strategy of diversification at home and abroad. In fact, the need for organizational change was common to all the clearers. There was special urgency at Barclays and National Westminster, as the mergers of 1968 called for the consolidation into a unified whole of the different systems of the individual banks. Both banks sought the aid of management consultants. In 1970, impressed by the advice given to National Westminster, Midland called on the same consultants to advise them—McKinsey and Co of New York, an international firm with a major reputation for advice on the management problems of large companies.

In February 1971, McKinsey and Co's report, 'Strengthening Midland's ability to grow profitably', was delivered direct to the bank's chairman. It was a thorough review of the needs of the organization based on discussions with senior officials, after some time spent at branches and regional head offices in order to gain experience of the problems and possibilities. The tenor of the report was reflected in a call for a more systematic and disciplined approach by all levels of management to an increase in earnings; the consultants also stressed the need to exploit all the possibilities of the subsidiary companies and permit the overseas side of the bank a measure of independence. This last factor was seen as essential for rapid growth. With these objectives in mind, the organizational changes recommended came under four main headings:

1 To allocate responsibility for the group's operations among five executives reporting to the chief general manager as group chief executive. The group chief executive would, in future, delegate day-to-day management of the branch banking network to a deputy, who would be the second ranking executive in the group. The four other executives reporting to him would be those responsible for domestic financial subsidiaries, international, Clydesdale and Northern Banks.

2 To strengthen the chief executive's staff support. McKinsey and Co saw the role of chief executive under four principal headings: allocating resources, planning strategy, challenging proposals put forward by operating management and controlling performances to ensure that plans were achieved. It was obvious that he would need support, to be provided by a new chief of staff, heading a planning and financial team.

3 To reorganize the branch banking function. A new head of branch

banking would assume responsibility over all departments involved with or affecting the profitability of branch banking; for example, the organization and methods and premises departments, which reported at the time to the general manager (administration), would be brought under this umbrella.

4 To discontinue the management committee as a level of authority and responsibility. In future the lending function should be assumed by a loans committee, leaving matters of policy to the chief executive and his team and freeing the joint general managers to control the profit performance of their respective divisions.

Outside the proposed organization changes the recommendations for change in management processes were concerned mainly with the development of formal planning as a discipline at all levels, aided by a better management information base and a system of performance appraisal. Figures 13.1 and 13.2 provide comparisons of the existing and recommended structures.

The McKinsey report was never formally adopted by the bank, although its recommendations were to have an important influence on changes in top management in 1972 and 1974. There were two main objections to the proposals. The first was that the creation of a group chief executive inferred that the chairman would continue to fulfil the traditional non-executive role in relation to the general management. Sir Archibald Forbes had never accepted this interpretation of the passive nature of a chairman's duties. He saw that there was a need for attitudes to change if Midland was to make progress through diversification, and he believed that the best interests of the bank would be served if he assumed a more active role, leaving the senior bankers to concentrate on pushing for growth at home, in overseas banking and in related services. The second objection lay in the radical nature of some of the proposals (although they were perceived by some senior general managers as little more than tinkering with something that was already working well—change for change's sake). Perhaps the recommendation which most offended traditional susceptibilities was the proposal to relegate the management committee to the duty of credit control and no more. Since 1929 it had been the seat of all major decision-taking, the pivot of an establishment in which a place at the round table in the small room on the fourth floor at Poultry was regarded as the supreme achievement of the most able and ambitious members of the staff.

If the McKinsey plan was not to be adopted, there was the need to find an alternative way to coordinate group policy, particularly in the

**Figure 13.1** *Midland Bank Group organization, February 1971*

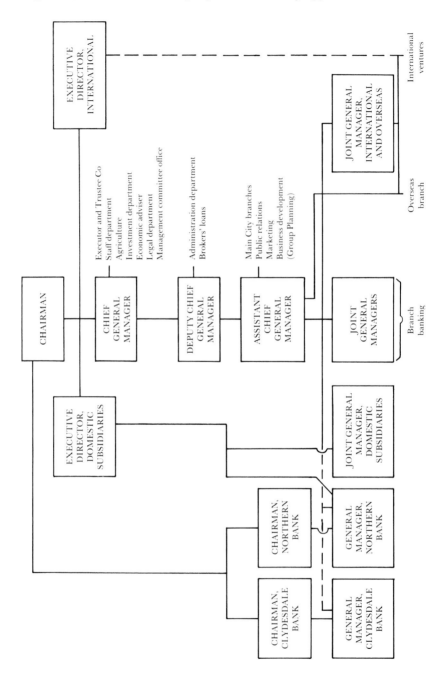

**Figure 13.2** *Midland Bank Group, McKinsey and Co's proposals for reorganization, February 1971–73*

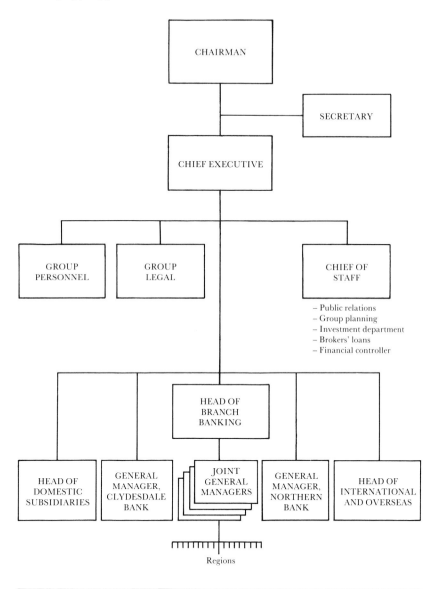

*Note:* The McKinsey report recommended that the head of branch
banking should be the most senior executive below chief executive
level, deputizing for the chief executive in his absence.

relationship with the subsidiaries in the United Kingdom. Initially, the bank appeared to have settled for an *ad hoc* arrangement. In February 1972, Len Mather, then 61, ended his four-year term as chief general manager, when he was appointed vice-chairman of the bank with special responsibilities for overseas affairs and related services. For the first time since 1948, the bank had as vice-chairman a man who had risen from the ranks, and many saw it as a fitting tribute to a banker unrivalled in knowledge of the principles and practice of lending.

Although the vice-chairmanship experiment owed little to McKinsey's review, other appointments in 1972 suggested that the consultants' preference for clearer functional responsibilities was gradually being accepted. Mather was succeeded as chief general manager by his deputy, Charles Trott, who was then 59 and could look forward to only a relatively short term of office. Two new assistant chief general managers were also appointed: John Cave to support Trott on the domestic side, and Malcolm Wilcox to be responsible for related services. Trott remained in office for two eventful years, covering the fringe bank crisis and lifeboat operation, the acquisition of Thomas Cook and the consolidation of the bank's interests in merchant banking (pp 290-1). But with the additional burden of two years as chairman of the chief executive officers' committee of the London clearing banks, he was in no position to undertake the type of enlarged role for the chief executive which had been recommended in the McKinsey report. Consequently, when Trott retired in June 1974, the need for a division of executive responsibility was formally recognized. Two chief general managers of equal rank were appointed to succeed him, both in their early fifties and available for a longer term of office than had been possible in recent appointments. This left the way clear for Mather to respond to the request of the Bank of England and the other clearing banks to take on the difficult assignment, in October 1974, of chairman of the troubled finance house United Dominions Trust, in the aftermath of the fringe banks crisis (p 271).

The two new chief general managers, Stuart Graham and Malcolm Wilcox, had both enjoyed ranges of experience different from the usual paths of promotion. Selected early in his career for accelerated promotion, Graham spent only a short spell in branch management in the provinces before returning to head office in 1962 as a general manager's assistant with responsibilities for planning, which hitherto had not been treated as a separate and specific discipline in banking. By 1970, at the age of 49 and still continuing with responsibility for planning, he had become assistant chief general manager with additional duties in the supervision of the main City branches. Wilcox had also been selected for rapid promotion. After a series of managerial appointments, including that of the important City Square branch, Leeds, he returned to head office as an assistant general manager in 1965, shortly afterwards becoming managing director of Forward Trust. He was appointed the first managing director of MBFC on its formation in 1967 and a joint general manager of Midland in the same year. In 1972 his appointment as assistant chief general manager was combined with the vice-chairmanship of MBFC.

The appointment of two chief general managers was clearly a watershed in the structural development of Midland. When Edington and Rouse held similar appointments in the 1950s, they were jointly responsible for all the operations of the bank and any division of responsibilities was purely a matter of convenience. Graham and Wilcox, however, though jointly responsible for central services and major policy issues, were each undertaking separate responsibilities— Graham for the operations of the clearing bank, and Wilcox for the newly formed International Division and the related services under the management of MBFC. In addition to a division of interests, it marked the end of the era of the 'lending banker'; in effect the board recognized that the ability to lend safely and profitably was by then only one of the virtues necessary for success as a top clearing banker. The challenge to the two chief general managers was to plan new enterprises, move the group into new markets and, above all, to assess and match the competition offered not only by the other clearers but by foreign banks operating in London in ever-increasing numbers. Both had been involved at different times in planning aspects of the bank's future at home and abroad, and both accepted the need for International Division to be expanded until the bank was represented in its own right in the major financial centres of the world. Wilcox believed that the related services could be harnessed for major expansion and a much larger contribution to group earnings; Graham had already determined that there had to be changes in the organization and efficiency of the branch network to cope with ever-rising costs and the volume of business handled.

In framing their recommendations, McKinsey and Co had recognized the need for a new structure and approach which would have placed an altogether wider range of duties on the chief executive's shoulders. There were clear indications, for example in the creation of a corporate planning department in September 1971 and the use of budgeting, that the need for the more disciplined approach had already been accepted. Yet the bank had chosen not to channel the task of chief executive through the hands of one man; the creation of two top posts, each with separate responsibilities, had distanced the bank from the McKinsey concept. The chairman decided to deal with the problem by the formation of a group co-ordinating committee, on which he would be joined by the two deputy chairmen and the two chief executives, meeting weekly to discuss policy matters and the allocation of resources. The creation of this body no doubt owed much to the influence of Lord Armstrong, then a deputy chairman and destined shortly to succeed Sir Archibald Forbes as chairman (p 298). His long career in the Civil Service had accustomed him to such committees, a form of decision-taking perhaps less familiar to a commercial enterprise such as the bank. The new committee acted as the channel for the bank's business at the highest level and at least followed McKinsey in the formal removal of executive decision-taking from the management committee. General managers lost the prefix 'joint' and the old committee became concerned only with credit control.

This series of structural modifications within the bank, particularly the emphasis on group coordination, was dominated by the diversification theme. The new organization and appointments were designed to cope with recent group acquisitions as well as to pursue further diversification at home and overseas. For while the structure of the bank was being reviewed by McKinsey in 1970–71, the commitment to spreading the bank's interests was already emerging; by 1974, when Graham and Wilcox took on their appointments, that commitment was being converted into a distinctive assortment of acquisitions and new activities.

Midland's diversification in the 1960s had been confined largely to the activities of MBFC in deposit taking (including new companies in the Channel Islands) and an expansion and enlargement of the activities of Forward Trust. By 1970 associated company interests included Montagu Trust (33 per cent), MAIBL (45 per cent) and, on the international front, the early fruits of the joint ventures of the European Advisory Committee, Banque Européenne de Crédit à Moyen Terme and the European-American Banking Corporation. At that point the diversified interests were still tiny in comparison with the bank's traditional function as a clearing bank. For example, although separate figures were not given for overseas business, the group's profits of £36.4 million in 1969 included only £2.75 million from MBFC and Forward Trust. The remainder came from the domestic bank, the Trust Company and the Scottish and Irish subsidiaries.

Of Midland's main rivals, Barclays and National Westminster had an unassailable lead in deposits as a result of the 1968 mergers. Lloyds was still behind but it had a powerful overseas business and, with a high proportion of large branches in its network, its overhead expenses were relatively lower than Midland's. It was clear to Sir Archibald Forbes and his board that Midland needed the stimulus of new initiatives to counter the advantages enjoyed by its competitors. The bank needed to show that it had not lost its taste for adventure, that it retained its ambitions in international banking, offering services beyond those of a mere domestic financial institution. The chosen path was an expansion of the range of related services and a new concept of representation abroad.

The first chance for a major diversification came in 1971 when the Thomas Cook group, the largest travel company in the world, came on offer for sale. Its share capital had been acquired in the early 1940s by the Hay's Wharf Cartage Company, in which the four mainline railway companies held a controlling interest. When the railways were nationalized in 1948, the government thus indirectly acquired control of the travel agency. The accession of a Conservative government in 1970 brought about a change of policy. Thomas Cook and the other travel concerns were put up for an auction sale. 'I have come to the conclusion', John Peyton, the Minister of Transport reported, 'that there is no reason why the government should continue to be involved in the travel business'.[1] At first sight it might not have seemed obvious why a bank should wish to become involved either, but Sir Archibald Forbes explained in 1972, 'we have been providing financial services for travellers for many years and have wide international connections; our branch system has a distinct resemblance to the travel agency business in that we provide a personal service through a retail network'. Thomas Cook, whose origins dated back almost as far as those of the bank, had a long and colourful history in the course of which it had become a household word for travel facilities, including its own travellers' cheques of worldwide acceptance. Midland saw that, with an injection of both management and capital for expansion, the substantial credit balance arising from the sale of both travel facilities and travellers' cheques could be used to advantage within the group. They were not alone in this view and various consortia with a bank as member were assembled to bid. Midland, in partnership with Trust House Forte and the Automobile Association, submitted a tender of £22.5 million. In May 1972 this bid was declared successful, above rival bids from consortia led by Barclays and Trafalgar House. It was arranged that Midland would provide some 78 per cent, with the proviso that Trust House Forte would acquire a further 8 per cent from Midland in due course.

It soon became apparent that during the years of nationalization the Thomas Cook business had stagnated and the new owners found that the problems were even more deep-rooted than they had estimated. In 1973 organizational changes were put in hand with a new managing director from outside the bank and a new chief executive for the North American business, where the main troubles lay. Though recorded profits improved from £800,000 in 1972 to £1.9 million in 1973, the improvement was illusory. In the following years the travel industry suffered from the failure of several major tour operators and other adverse factors from which Thomas Cook was not immune. Despite an increased volume of business, losses of £1.6 and £3.3 million were suffered in successive years. The main problem was that the new management, preoccupied with marketing, failed to understand that increased sales without fundamental changes in the structure of the business would never enable its undoubted potential to be realized. In 1975 Sir Alan Walker, from Midland's board, was appointed chairman and T E Fisher became vice-chairman and chief executive.

Tom Fisher was no stranger to the problems of a group company needing a facelift. He had been transferred from a senior management position in the domestic bank a few years before to steer through a similar programme of reorganization and expansion of Forward Trust, leading to a substantial increase in productivity and profits. It took him only a short time to realize that, to achieve the expected results with Thomas Cook, sweeping changes were necessary. His planned programme involved the systematic dismantling of previous structures, the rebuilding of the headquarters operation and the restaffing and re-equipping of the operating divisions. Such fundamental changes needed time to become effective and the problems proved deep-seated, but the Fisher reforms were to lead over the next few years to the emergence of Thomas Cook as an essential and profitable arm of the diversified Midland Bank Group.

As a second major step in widening the related services activities of the bank, in 1973 Midland made an offer for the outstanding share capital of Montagu Trust. This offer, made with the agreement of the Montagu board, converted a minority interest into a wholly owned subsidiary through the issue of £70 million 7.5 per cent loan stock and £23.5 million 10.75 per cent loan stock, the former with conversion rights. When the cost of acquiring the minority stake in 1967 was added, Midland had paid a total of £105 million for Montagu Trust.

Its ambitions did not stop there. In a surprise move a few months later, the bank also bought the share capital of the Drayton Group for £21 million cash and convertible loan stock. In the period between 1943 and 1966, under the leadership of Harley Drayton,[2] this group had established a high reputation for its corporate finance and investment management services which it continued to enjoy under Philip Shelbourne, its chief executive at the time of the Midland offer. These two acquisitions were designed to give the Midland group a sophisticated range of merchant banking services to compare with any in the City. By merging their activities under the chairmanship of Shelbourne, the group would be in a position to provide a type of financial service not offered by any other clearing bank. Barclays and National Westminster had taken a different path by starting their own merchant banking subsidiaries from scratch; in Samuel Montagu and Co, Midland had a proven member of the Accepting Houses Committee with executives experienced in investment management, lending in both sterling and currency, bullion dealing, insurance broking and including some specialized overseas banking activities through its subsidiary, Guyerzeller Zurmont Bank of Zurich.

One further diversification was made before the division of executive responsibility in Midland in 1974. In the United States, factoring (providing customers with sales accounting services and protection against bad debts) had already become big business, though its acceptance in the United Kingdom was considerably slower. Midland tested this market by forming an association with First National City Bank through a joint company, Midland-Citibank Factors, founded in 1970. Three years later, the bank bought a 50 per cent interest in Shield Factors, merging the two businesses and buying out the minority interest in 1974; the resulting concern was renamed Griffin Factors and became a wholly owned subsidiary of MBFC.

As a result of these acquisitions and diversifications, and following the 1974 division of executive responsibility (p 286), Malcolm Wilcox was appointed chief general manager in charge of an assortment of companies under the general heading of related services. He was given a mandate for further expansion of these operations. Before this could become part of any formal plan, however, there was a major task of regrouping and reorganizing the parallel elements resulting from the recent takeover of Montagu and Drayton and the transfer of the trading activities of MBFC. In the field of investment management, insurance, leasing and certain merchant banking functions, there was overlapping to a greater or lesser degree. Taking an even wider view, Midland, Montagu and Thomas Cook each had international activities. When in 1975 Midland acquired a majority stake in London American Finance Corporation export and confirming house, it was clear that competition between the various companies should be prevented by a process of consolidation. Here the division of executive responsibility at the top of the bank militated against a full acceptance of the group concept. Companies under the related services banner, even when consolidated and reorganized, continued to enjoy the traditional independence accorded to Midland subsidiaries over the years. The consolidation process represented, in effect, a 'grouping within groups' of related companies and it was not until 1981, when the management structure was completely revised under a single chief executive, that the group concept was made fully effective. It was, nevertheless, a vital exercise and Wilcox brought to it a talent for reorganization, allied to a recognition of the potential of the new parts of the group.

Although related services still earned only a small part of the group's profit, they could be developed and used as a buffer against the years when the domestic element of the clearing bank might meet a combination of unfavourable factors. Since its formation in 1967, MBFC had undertaken several different roles, including that of holding company for group members engaged in asset finance (Forward Trust, Forward Leasing and Griffin Factors). After CCC in 1971, its deposit-taking and lending functions had been largely assumed by the bank, but in order to finance its specialized lending it had continued to take funds from the wholesale markets. At the end of 1973 its total assets of some £230 million included loans to local authorities of £107 million and commercial advances of £72 million. MBFC's trading activities were transferred to the combined Montagu/Drayton enterprise in 1974, and a new company, Midland Montagu Leasing, was created to bring the leasing activities of the enlarged group into a unified operation. These allocations left MBFC acting solely as a governing company for the group's specialist financial services in the areas of instalment finance, leasing, factoring and offshore trust and finance business. The reorganization was effected by winding up the original MBFC and creating a new company under the same name in June 1974. (The new company was a reconstruction of Midfin Ltd, which had been formed as a nominee company late in 1973.) On completion of this complex restructuring, John Cave was appointed chairman of MBFC (and of its principal subsidiary Forward Trust) when he retired from his position as deputy chief general manager of the bank in February 1975.

Forward Trust, the oldest company in the MBFC stable, had made substantial progress since it was acquired in 1958. Having been granted the status of a bank in 1973 under the Protection of Depositors Act (1963), its scope and range of services widened. Operating through some 80 branches it earned a profit of £7.5 million in 1973. Hire purchase control orders and restrictions on the level of permitted deposits throughout the 1970s were a discouragement, but the company·continued to prosper, achieving major increases in new business and profits year by year.

As with Thomas Cook a few years later, the business judgement of Tom Fisher played a major role in the improved fortunes of the company. Fisher had been appointed general manager in 1967 (shortly afterwards becoming managing director) and his first task had been to modernize the company's book-keeping and systems and to seek new methods for the consideration of applications for facilities. In the past, applications had been judged mainly on the nature of the asset to be acquired with the company's funds, on the basis that in case of default that asset could be realized to repay the advance. The large number of accounts in default convinced Fisher that it would be more logical to assess the creditworthiness of the borrower, stressing ability to pay rather than the value of the asset. After visits to Holland and the United States to study the techniques employed there, he was the first to introduce into the United Kingdom the practice of credit-scoring. The technique listed a number of personal factors in each case and gave them a 'weighting' in accordance with past experience. Only those proposals achieving a minimum credit-score were approved. The innovation was immediately effective, so much so that the number of default cases fell sharply, and in due course the same sort of system was adopted by the bank in assessing the creditworthiness of customers applying for personal loans. One of the side benefits was that the majority of proposals could be dealt with by less senior members of the staff, and only those in the 'grey' areas had to be referred to a manager. By the 1970s Forward Trust was geared for expansion both at home and abroad, and there were imaginative joint ventures with the National Coal Board, companies such as Avis, Fiat and J Hepworth, and with the Oversea Chinese Banking Corporation in Singapore, Banco Hispano Americano in Spain and Banco Bamerindus in Brazil.

Insurance was also emerging as a significant group activity in the 1970s but in this case there was a divergence of activity between Midland and Samuel Montagu. The bank's own insurance subsidiary, MBIS, had evolved from the largely domestic business taken over from the managers' agencies, and throughout the 1970s the business developed into an essential part of the marketing plans of each region and branch. In the Montagu camp, however, the insurance group was of a very different nature, comprising the two large Lloyd's broking firms of Bland Welch and Co and E W Payne and Co, responsible in 1973 for some £3 million of the Montagu Trust profits. Bland Welch, founded in 1895, had become one of the leading international insurance and reinsurance broking houses, placing business at Lloyds as well as in international company markets, with subsidiary and associated companies in Europe, Canada, South America, South Africa and the Far East. E W Payne, founded in 1919, carried on business as Lloyd's brokers, handling marine, fire and accident, aviation and reinsurance business. Its subsidiaries included Wallace Shipping, brokers for the sale, purchase, charter and construction of ships and for ship finance. Other companies handled life, mortgage and employee benefits and in general the group could cover almost any type of domestic and international insurance.

Soon after Midland's full acquisition of Montagu Trust the Bland Welch and Payne insurance interests were merged into a unified company, Bland Payne. The new concern's progress was spectacular. As new business flowed in from all parts of the world and new overseas companies were formed in conjunction with indigenous partners, profits rose to £8.6 million by 1975 (and to almost £22 million in 1978). If Midland needed justification for its purchase of the Montagu interests at over £100 million, the results of the insurance group alone provided an answer, even if it is unlikely that this outcome was foreseen at the time. No other clearing bank could point to an established merchant bank within its group; certainly none owned such a comprehensive and profitable insurance business. In this sense, ambitious ideas for the group's diversification had become reality— related services were beginning to provide a real contribution to group profits. With the Midland branch network available to provide the marketing support, it was expected that insurance would play an even larger part in future.

Whilst sweeping changes were being made to the organization of the more recent related service companies, the oldest of them all had been largely undisturbed. The Executor and Trustee Company formed in 1909 remained under the control of its own board of directors, of whom the chairman was a member of the main board of the bank. It had taken some time for the public to become accustomed to the idea of a limited company performing the functions of an executor or trustee, hitherto regarded as the most personal of duties. In its early years, progress was steady rather than spectacular. By 1926, branches had been opened in Liverpool, Manchester and Birmingham and as these proved their worth, representation was steadily widened until, in its jubilee year of 1959, there were 32 branches holding a total of 87,000 will appointments. Twenty years later business had grown rapidly and as well as almost 250,000 will appointments, the company was managing 7500 investment portfolios and 25,000 personal income tax assessments. In parallel with the growth of personal business, the postwar years saw a major expansion by the company in the field of corporate trusteeship leading to a substantial increase in assets held in its name. In January 1973 the company's name was changed to Midland Bank Trust Company to reflect the variation and changing nature of its services. The company had become a market leader in the trusteeship of unit trust investments and when in 1975 the bank decided to establish its own range of unit trusts, the Trust Company joined with the investment division of Samuel Montagu to form a management company under the name of Midland Bank Group Unit Trust Managers. The five initial units were developed from the existing Drayton Unit Trusts to become Midland Drayton Units, offered to the public by advertisement and through the branch network of the bank. Both to outsiders and within Midland, the initiative was a useful example of how the bank made use of the combined skills of two members of the enlarged group to offer a new service.

The postwar years had seen a considerable extension of the range of services provided by the Trust Company. As well as those traditionally associated with executors and trusteeship, new facilities included portfolio management, custodianship of investments, including those of pension funds, and the functional management of the bank's registrar's department, stock office and new issues department. Table 13.1 shows how the company grew from an ancillary service in its early days to an essential part of the group structure, earning profits both from the fees charged to its customers and from the deployment of the substantial credit balances arising as a result of its operations.

Midland's formation of a separate International Division in 1974 had been greatly influenced by the main corporate objectives at the time: to be recognized as a major international bank and to improve the proportion and geographical spread of group earnings. There were many difficulties. The formation of a wholly-owned enterprise in banking or financial services was often impossible due to local restrictions on foreign investment. A stake in an existing retail bank would be extremely expensive. Whereas it had been hoped that joint ventures could be undertaken with associated banks—such as Standard Chartered—in the field of financial services, little progress was evident.

**Table 13.1**

Midland Bank Trust Company, summary of progress, 1909–79

| Date | Net profit (£000) | Shareholders' funds (£000) | Assets in name of company (£ million) | Number of staff | Number of branches |
|------|-------------------|----------------------------|---------------------------------------|-----------------|--------------------|
| 1909 | 0.1  | 150  | 0.87 | 6    | 1  |
| 1919 | 18   | 168  | 4    | 17   | 1  |
| 1929 | 78   | 376  | 30   | 81   | 6  |
| 1939 | 70   | 445  | 92   | 297  | 20 |
| 1949 | 87   | 492  | 164  | 635  | 24 |
| 1959 | 99   | 899  | 195  | 841  | 32 |
| 1969 | 185  | 1305 | 411  | 1295 | 38 |
| 1979 | 2073 | 2277 | 4448 | 1160 | 40 |

Doubts also arose as to whether further cooperation with the EBIC partners was compatible with the bank's new objectives as compared with the establishment of offices abroad in the bank's own name. Some of the EBIC partners had already been active in pursuit of their own lines by opening offices abroad and Midland could therefore feel free to do likewise if it suited.

When in 1975 Midland increased its stake in Standard Chartered Bank to some 16 per cent by purchasing Chase Manhattan's former holding, it seemed that some part of its corporate objectives had been realized by acquiring an indirect interest in Africa and the Far East. At that time, the ambitions of Midland for direct representation overseas seemed complementary to those of Standard Chartered which lacked a United Kingdom domestic branch network to supplement its overseas coverage. Some form of merger, similar to that of Lloyds Bank and the Bank of London and South America in 1971, was obviously one possibility to be considered by the boards of both banks, but Midland's directors were sensitive to the political and economic implications of a direct association with a bank conducting a large part of its business in South Africa and preferred to follow an independent course (Midland's shares in Standard Chartered were sold for £65 million in 1978–79[3]).

On the formation of International Division in 1974, Midland had no branches or subsidiary companies outside the United Kingdom and only four representative offices (in Brussels, Frankfurt, Tokyo and Zurich). In effect, this represented an almost clean slate, considering the limited banking capacity of a representative office, and the first problem was to define the priorities on a geographical basis. Europe was an obvious early target, followed by the United States and the Far East, but questions also arose of the relative advantage or disadvantage in each target area of a branch, subsidiary company or representative office. And was it preferable, in any particular country, to seek to acquire an existing bank or to start from cold, in retail or wholesale banking or even in the related services field?

To Wilcox and his colleagues in International Division, these problems were an immense challenge which was to occupy much of their time and energy in the latter half of the seventies. It was a challenge demanding patience and banking judgement as well as capital resources. Expansion on the scale contemplated would also call for the recruitment of additional senior management from outside the bank to bring in experience of direct international banking and an altogether wider concept of the scope and demands of an overseas network.

Not least it was a task which needed conviction and strong nerves. For the banking world of the 1970s was more in the public eye than ever before; the banks were exposed to an unprecedented volume of analysis, debate and opinion, all of which could affect share prices, planning and morale. The increasing quantity and sophistication of investment analysis by stockbrokers had transformed the City's knowledge of banking since the 1960s, especially after 'disclosure' in 1970. Meanwhile a growing army of financial journalists provided their readers with significantly more news and rumour of banking developments, and consumer magazines and broadcasters were ever-ready to investigate the business behaviour of the big banks. Official enquiries (notably the Wilson Committee, which was appointed to survey the role of financial institutions in 1977) kept the clearing banks firmly in the spotlight. As a new dimension to their external relations, British banks found themselves under extremely close official and public scrutiny whenever they wished to enter or expand their business in the other major Western economies. In these respects every move which Midland made in attempting to fulfil its ambitions was to be examined and publicized in a way which would have been inconceivable to bankers twenty or even ten years earlier.

The chairmanship of Midland would clearly have a big influence on the consolidation and presentation of developments in the group. Sir Archibald Forbes, who retired in 1975 after eleven years as chairman, had been the catalyst at a time when rapid change was essential to counter the challenge of Midland's clearing bank rivals and the foreign bank invasion. From the outset he had been unwilling to accept the figurehead role of many of his predecessors. His questioning and challenging of established assumptions within the bank were necessary ingredients for survival in a period of intense competition. He had led the bank in the purchase of Montagu Trust and Thomas Cook, in support of his strongly held view that Midland needed the stimulus of ambitious new acquisitions. In a fruitful partnership with Howard Thackstone, chief general manager at the beginning of his term of office as chairman, he had supported the need to alter the course of the bank's overseas policy without destroying the valuable correspondent relationships; one result was the beginning of the EBIC partnership. During his term as chairman of the Committee of London Clearing Bankers he also spoke up strongly in defence of the interests of the clearing banks in general. When he retired in 1975, Midland's board recognized his services by appointing him president, the first such appointment in the bank's history.

Sir Archibald was succeeded as chairman by Lord Armstrong of Sanderstead, the recently retired Head of the Civil Service and formerly Permanent Secretary of the Treasury. His new role was certainly not as straightforward as commentators assumed. At the top of the bank, as in other clearing banks since the 1968 mergers, the relationships between chairmen, board and senior management were far from settled. In the complex and entrepreneurial business world of the 1970s, the allocation of responsibility for major corporate developments was becoming less clear cut. The division of executive responsibility between Graham and Wilcox was no more than a partial response to this problem. In the domestic bank, which would always be the mainstay of the group, the great enlargement of activities in the last few years had left many branch managers somewhat confused and unsure of the role they needed to play in conducting the affairs of their branches under the new circumstances. In the great efforts to achieve new status as an international group, communications down to middle management level had not always been as good as they should have been. There was need for a programme of re-education, emphasizing the bank's future status as a multi-disciplinary financial body, needing to exploit the power of its branch network to sell every available service at every possible opportunity. It was not enough merely to change the emphasis on management training at Oxted and Betchworth colleges (though this was done): the real need was to make managers more conscious of the part they had to play in supplying the new services as well as practising the old virtues of the deposit-taking and lending banker. They had to be convinced that they were still as important a link in a financial group as they had always been in traditional branch banking.

One of Lord Armstrong's first priorities was to tackle the communications problem and for this purpose he set himself a formidable programme of visits to managers' meetings up and down the country, as well as to branches, departments and computer centres. Both as a speaker and listener, he had exceptional qualities. Frequently, in replying to the toast of 'the bank' at a dinner, he would put aside his prepared script and respond in an impromptu speech, in the course of which he never failed to pay tribute to the vital role of local managers, regional head office officials and regional achievements. These occasions were in every sense *tours de force* and managers returned to their branches with more awareness of the achievements of the bank and more confidence in their own ability and performance. The chairman's influence was in this way essential in persuading the bank's middle management of the need for change and preparing them for the quite fundamental alterations in branch network operating procedures that were just around the corner. Similarly, as soon as he came into office, the new chairman was ready to play an active part in the public promotion of the group and in the presentation of the clearing banks as a whole. This leadership was soon valuable during the debate over nationalization of banking and insurance in 1975-76, when Lord Armstrong headed the clearing banks' campaign against a Labour Party conference resolution in favour of nationalization.

Sixty years earlier, the role of Midland's chairmen had been crucial in drawing the disparate elements of the enlarged bank into a single workable structure. Holden and then McKenna had differed from many of their predecessors and contemporaries by insisting on proper communications within the bank and by projecting the bank into a more public role. This type of leadership would be equally important when Midland was transforming itself from bank to group in the mid-1970s. Clearly Midland was crossing a major strategic frontier. In 1975, when Lord Armstrong was elected chairman, Midland was leaving behind the familiar ground of acting as a single bank with a confederation of allied subsidiaries; instead it was entering the new territory of coordinated group banking, supplying any type of financial service at home and abroad. The framework for this new existence was already in place in 1975, providing the base for a massive growth in business and services throughout the group over the next ten years.

# MIDLAND'S MODERN CALENDAR

## Key Events in the Group, 1976–1986

**1976**

February — Completion of Midland's issue of $100 million in floating rate capital notes—the bank's first *loan capital* in a non-sterling currency.

December — *Loan capital* of $75 million in guaranteed bonds issued by Midland International Financial Services BV (MIFSBV).

December — Midland, with the British Gas pension funds and Prudential Assurance, forms *Moracrest Investments Limited*, providing equity finance for small to medium sized businesses.

**1977**

March — Announcement of *branch network reorganization* for streamlining the role of branch banking. This plan, which was to be tested in the Newcastle and Southampton areas in 1978, featured the grouping of management at new area offices and the formation of operations centres.

March — Staff *profit sharing scheme* announced. The first payments under arrangements were made in 1978 after declaration of Midland's 1977 results.

March — Midland acquires remaining minority holdings in *The Thomas Cook Group Limited*.

April — *Loan capital* of $50 million in floating rate notes issued by MIFSBV.

April — Equity investments by Midland and its subsidiaries grouped under the control of *Midland Bank Equity Holdings Limited*.

August — *Loan capital* of $75 million in guaranteed bonds issued by MIFSBV.

September — Midland's share in *London American Finance Corporation Limited* increased from 52 per cent to 75 per cent.

**1978**

January — *Rights issue* of 30 million new shares to increase Midland's shareholders' funds by approximately £96.4 million.

| March | Midland becomes first United Kingdom clearing bank to appoint a *woman director* by inviting Dame Rosemary Murray to join its board. |
| July | *Loan capital* of $125 million in floating rate notes issued by MIFSBV. |
| October | *Midland Bank France SA* established in Paris. |

**1979**

| February | Merger of *Bland Payne Group* with Sedgwick Forbes. Midland retained a 10 per cent share holding in the combined group. |
| April | Midland enrolled as founder member of *London Enterprise Agency*, founded to promote the regeneration of business in inner London. |
| June | Midland's entry into house loan business through the *Midland Bank House Mortgage Scheme*. |
| June | Acquisition by Midland of a majority share in Banque de la Construction et des Travaux Publics SA, France, subsequently renamed *BCT Midland Bank*. |
| July | Acquisition in Australia of Associated Securities Finance Limited, renamed *Associated Midland Corporation Limited*. |
| September | Formation of *Meritor Investments Limited* by Midland and Rolls-Royce Pension Trust for investment in private limited companies. |
| October | *Midland Bank Venture Capital Limited* established for investments in small businesses and 'start up' finance for new companies. |
| October | Reduction of Midland's shareholding in *Standard Chartered Bank* from 16 per cent to 4.3 per cent. |
| December | *Loan capital* of $125 million in floating rate notes issued by MIFSBV. |
| December | Formation of *Midland Bank Insurance Brokers Limited*. |

**1980**

| January | Sale of Midland's remaining shares in *Standard Chartered Bank* and *Sedgwick Forbes Bland Payne Group*. |
| May | *Business development division* established with responsibility for Midland's branch planning, strategic services and market planning. |

| | |
|---|---|
| May | Midland's first *'listening bank'* advertising campaign launched. |
| June | *Loan capital* of $150 million in floating rate notes issued by MIFSBV. |
| July | Death of *Lord Armstrong of Sanderstead* and election of *Sir David Barran* as Midland's chairman. |
| July | Preliminary agreement announced for Midland's acquisition of majority interests in *Crocker National Corporation* of California and *Trinkaus & Burkhardt* of West Germany. |
| October | *Loan capital* of 180 million *Deutsche Marks* bonds issued by MIFSBV. |

## 1981

| | |
|---|---|
| March | *Forward Trust Group* established, drawing together the business of Forward Trust, Midland Montagu Leasing and Griffin Factors. |
| March | Imposition by Chancellor of the Exchequer of *capital levy* on clearing banks (the 'windfall profits tax'), adding £65 million to Midland's taxation costs in 1981. |
| April | *Loan capital* of $150 million in floating rate notes issued by MIFSBV. |
| May | Midland Bank shares quoted on *Paris bourse*—the first overseas stock market listing for Midland shares. |
| July | Further *loan capital* of $75 million in floating rate notes issued by MIFSBV. |
| September | *Midland Bank Canada* (established as Midland Financial Services in 1975) awarded chartered bank status in Canada. |
| October | Midland Bank's acquisition of majority interest in *Crocker National Corporation*. |

## 1982

| | |
|---|---|
| January | Formation of *group treasury* for controlling money market business, foreign exchange currency, and financial future activities of Midland and its subsidiaries. |
| February | Midland Bank Limited reregistered and renamed *Midland Bank plc*. |

| April | *Midland Bank Group International Trade Services Limited* formed as a wholly-owned subsidiary to bring together the export and trade finance activities of the London American group and other Midland interests. |
|---|---|
| April | *Midland gold card* introduced in association with MasterCard International. |
| May | Election of *Sir Donald Barron* as chairman and appointment of *G W Taylor* as group chief executive and *J A Brooks* as deputy group chief executive. |
| June | *Loan stock* of £100 million issued by Midland Bank. |
| July | Introduction of *'branch controller'* micro-computers in Midland's branch banks. |
| July | Acquisition by Aetna Life & Casualty Company of 40 per cent stake in *Samuel Montagu* group. |
| September | *'Save and borrow'* accounts introduced for monthly savings linked to overdraft facilities. |
| September | Agreement by Midland Bank and National Westminster Bank to provide reciprocal facilities for the use of *Autobanks* and National Westminster's cash dispensers. |
| September | Acquisition by Midland of majority share in Handelsfinanz Bank—later renamed *Handelsfinanz Midland Bank*—in Switzerland. |
| December | *Loan capital* of $150 million in guaranteed bonds issued by MIFSBV. |

---

## 1983

| January | Formation of *UK banking division*, responsible for Midland's branch and corporate finance business. |
|---|---|
| February | Sale of Midland's 45 per cent share in *Midland and International Banks*. |
| April | Midland's *'shoppers' branch'* opened at Leamington Spa, the forerunner for major branch development and refurbishment throughout England and Wales. |
| April | Midland becomes first United Kingdom clearing bank to issue *Eurocheques*, a uniform system for payments in most European countries. |
| June | Restructuring of group interests in France as *Midland Bank SA*. |

| | |
|---|---|
| July | Appointment of M F Julien as *group finance director*—the first appointment of its kind by a major clearing bank. |
| July | *'Shelf registration'* obtained by Midland for capital issues in the United States of America. |
| August | *Rights issue* of 45.7 million new shares to increase shareholders' funds by £155 million. |
| October | *Group risk management* established with responsibility for all aspects of customer risk. |
| November | *Loan capital* of $150 million in guaranteed notes issued by Midland American Capital Corporation. |
| December | Heavy losses at *Crocker National Corporation* led to revocation of Crocker's operational autonomy and major changes in its senior management, including appointment of F V Cahouet as chairman and chief executive officer of Crocker and a director of Midland. Review of Crocker's loan portfolio and large additional provisions resulted in further trading losses at Crocker in the first and fourth quarters of 1984. |

## 1984

| | |
|---|---|
| February | Introduction of *Clearing House automated payments system* (CHAPS) by the clearing banks for improving the speed and efficiency of inter-bank sterling payments. |
| February | Midland's *high interest cheque account* introduced to provide chequebook facilities linked to high interest earnings. |
| March | *Loan capital* of $200 million in floating rate notes issued by MIFSBV. |
| March | Acquisition by Samuel Montagu and Co of a 29.9 per cent interest in *W Greenwell and Co*, the leading stockbrokers, with agreement to take full ownership after deregulation of the London securities market in 1986. |
| March | As a result of the 1984 budget, *tax allowance on capital equipment* phased out, requiring clearing banks to make large transfers from reserves for deferred taxation (£228 million in Midland's case). |
| April | *Group management services* division formed with overall responsibilities for group administration and computer operations. |

| | |
|---|---|
| May | Midland named as a member of the *Franco–British Channel Link Financing Group*. Proposals for the design and construction of a fixed Channel Link by the *Channel Tunnel Group*, of which Midland was a founder, were selected by the British and French governments in January 1986. |
| July | Formation of *group executive committee* comprising representatives of all major group functions and business sectors. |
| August | '*Griffin Saver*' accounts introduced for 7 to 16 year olds. |
| September | Introduction of '*Saver Plus*' accounts with graded levels of interest and cash cards for withdrawals. |
| October | Formation of *UK business sector* to bring together into a single management grouping the United Kingdom activities of Midland, Clydesdale, Northern, Forward Trust and Thomas Cook. |
| October | *Retirement service* launched by Midland for advice and banking facilities for retired people. |
| November | '*Free-if-in-credit*' terms announced, the first major initiative by a clearing bank to provide free banking facilities. Within a year the service had attracted over 450,000 new personal accounts. |
| November | Installation of MIDNET telecommunications system within the group. |

---

**1985**

| | |
|---|---|
| January | 'Free banking' terms made available to *new businesses* operating under the government's Enterprise Allowance Scheme and (in May 1985) introduction of '*small business loans*' for amounts of £1000 to £15,000 and '*business development loans*' for amounts of above £15,000. |
| March | Pilot scheme for personal *in-store banking* services at Tesco superstores launched by Midland and Tesco. |
| May | *Loan capital* of $500 million issued in floating rate notes. |
| May | Midland's acquisition of full ownership of *Crocker National Corporation* completed. Subsequent restructuring of Midland Group's interests in the United States included the purchase of some $3.1 billion of Crocker's assets by Midland. A separate 'workout' company was established to acquire up to $500 million of Crocker's domestic assets. |

| | |
|---|---|
| July | Midland's acquisition of minority interests in *Samuel Montagu* group from Aetna Life & Casualty Company and sale of *Midland Investment Management* (Samuel Montagu's investment management company) to Aetna. |
| July | Thomas Cook's acquisition of the retail travel business of *Frames Travel Agencies* and *Blue Sky Travel Agencies*. |
| August | *Loan capital* of $500 million issued in floating rate notes. |
| October | Introduction of a *common retirement age* of 60 and improvement in pension benefits for Midland staff as from January 1986. |
| October | *Trinkaus & Burkhardt* obtains Stock Exchange quotation in Germany, with Midland retaining 70 per cent ownership. |
| November | Midland Bank *Finance for Export* scheme launched, providing export services and finance in replacement of facilities formerly available under Export Credits Guarantee Department arrangements. |

## 1986

| | |
|---|---|
| January | Programme of events for *Midland's 150th anniversary* included a £1 million fund for charity work initiated by the bank's staff, and business and community projects in Birmingham, the bank's birthplace. |
| January | Announcement of formation of *Northern Bank (Ireland)*, a subsidiary of Northern Bank, to consolidate the group's interests in the Republic of Ireland. |
| February | *Homeowner Plus* introduced, offering a series of financial incentives to applicants for Midland house mortgages. |
| February | Agreement reached for sale of *Crocker National Corporation* to *Wells Fargo and Company*. |
| February | Adoption of *group strategic plan*, involving division of Midland Bank Group business into retail, corporate, investment and international banking sectors. |
| February | Midland's '*Speedline*' service in electronic shopping launched in Milton Keynes as the first full-scale experiment in electronic funds transfer (EFT-POS) in England. |

| | |
|---|---|
| March | *Saturday service* introduced at selected Midland branches in England and Wales. |
| April | *C W McMahon* joins Midland from Bank of England as deputy chairman and as chairman and group chief executive-designate. |
| April | '*Midland Business Banking*' campaign launched to attract corporate customers. |

# REFERENCES

Unless otherwise stated all quotations, statistics and other information have been extracted from the archives of Midland Bank plc. These archives, which include the records of the constituent banks as well as those of Midland itself, are listed in L S Pressnell and M J Orbell, *A Guide to the Historical Records of British Banking* (Aldershot: Gower, 1985). Enquiries about specific quotations or statistics without references should be addressed to the Archivist, Midland Bank plc, Poultry, London EC2P 2BX.

## Introduction (*pages 1–5*)
1 L S Pressnell, *Country Banking in the Industrial Revolution* (Oxford University Press, 1956), ch 9
2 W F Crick & J E Wadsworth, *A Hundred Years of Joint Stock Banking* (Hodder & Stoughton, 1936, and new editions 1938, 1958 and 1964)
3 E.g. C A E Goodhart, *The Business of Banking 1891–1914* (Weidenfeld & Nicolson, 1972); P L Cottrell, *Industrial Finance, 1830–1914. The Finance and Organization of English Manufacturing Industry* (Methuen, 1979), ch 7
4 E.g. N Simpson, *The Belfast Bank, 1827–1970* (Belfast: Blackstaff Press, 1975); E Swinglehurst, *The Romantic Journey. The Story of Thomas Cook and Victorian Travel* (Pica Editions, 1974). In addition a new history of Clydesdale Bank is in preparation

## 1 Setting up in banking, 1836–1851 (*pages 7–34*)
1 B L Anderson & P L Cottrell, *Money and Banking in England. The Development of the Banking System, 1694–1914* (Newton Abbot: David & Charles, 1974), p 240
2 Ibid, p 244
3 Crick & Wadsworth, pp 15–21; C W Munn, *The Scottish Provincial Banking Companies, 1747–1864* (Edinburgh: John Donald, 1981), pp 220–1
4 *Banking Almanac,* passim
5 Crick & Wadsworth, pp 49–52

6  R S Sayers, *Lloyds Bank in the History of English Banking* (Oxford University Press, 1957), pp 5–7, 47n; Pressnell, pp 27–8; E Edwards, *Personal Recollections of Birmingham and Birmingham Men* (Birmingham: Midland Educational, 1877), p 49

7  Quoted in D J Moss 'The private banks of Birmingham, 1800–1827', *Business History*, 24 (1982), p 86

8  Pressnell, pp 41–4

9  Crick & Wadsworth, pp 51–3

10  R E Cameron, *Banking in the Early Stages of Industrialization* (Oxford University Press, 1967), p 26

11  Pressnell, p 488

12  D J Moss, 'The Bank of England and the country banks: Birmingham, 1827–33', *Economic History Review*, 2nd series, 34 (1981), p 546

13  National Westminster Bank Archives, District Bank board minutes, 16–23 July 1829. Gibbins was also a promoter of the Gloucestershire Banking Company in 1831. Sayers, *Lloyds Bank*, p 144

14  Edwards, p 14

15  Ibid, p 130

16  Crick & Wadsworth, p 419; Bank of England Archives, branch banks committee minutes, 5 Oct 1831; *Bankers' Magazine* (Dec 1854), p 419

17  *Birmingham Post*, 31 Jan 1930. The Birmingham Town and District Bank, after a complex series of amalgamations, eventually became part of Barclays Bank in 1916.

18  Bank of England Archives, court of directors minutes, 25 July 1836; Birmingham private letter books, vol 6, 23 July 1836

19  Ibid, Birmingham private letter books, vol 6, 17 Aug 1836

20  Secret Committee on Joint Stock Banks, 1836, quoted in Anderson & Cottrell, pp 298–9

21  Crick & Wadsworth, p 223

22  Bank of England Archives, branch index refs Ab239 & 259, Bb349; J H Clapham, *The Bank of England. A History*, 2 (Cambridge University Press, 1944), pp 115, 140–2

23  S E Thomas, *The Rise and Growth of Joint Stock Banking*, 1 (Pitman, 1934), pp 281–94

24  Anderson & Cottrell, p 245

25  Bank of England Archives, quarterly analysis of circulation of accounts at Birmingham, 28 Dec 1840

26  Ibid, Birmingham agent's letter books, vol 6, 12 Apr 1845

27  Ibid, vol 5, 14 Oct 1844; vol 6, 7 Aug 1845 and vol 7, 9 Sept 1846; Birmingham private letter books, vol 8, 15 Oct 1844

28  Crick & Wadsworth, p 62

29  M Collins, 'The business of banking: English bank balance sheets, 1840–80', *Business History*, 26 (1984), p 46

30  Ibid, p 54

31  Edwards, p 24; Moss, 'Private banks', p 83

32  M Collins & P Hudson, 'Provincial Bank Lending: Yorkshire and

Merseyside, 1825–60', University of Leeds, School of Economics Discussion Paper 51 (1977), p 4

33 Collins & Hudson, p 13

34 Edwards, p 62

35 Ibid, pp 127–8; Bank of England Archives, Birmingham agent's letter books, vol 7, 9 Oct 1846; R Davenport-Hines, *Dudley Docker, The Life and Times of a Trade Warrior* (Cambridge University Press, 1985), p 27

36 Edwards, pp 126–7

37 Bank of England Archives, Birmingham agent's letter books, vol 7, 9 Oct 1846

38 *Times*, 2 Jan 1854; *Bankers' Magazine* (Dec 1854), p 419

39 Crick & Wadsworth, p 421

## 2 Midland banking, 1851–1874 (*pages 35–56*)

1 Crick & Wadsworth, p 78; J F Ashby, *The Story of the Banks* (Hutchinson, 1934), pp 109–10

2 Bank of England Archives, Birmingham agent's letter books, vol 5, 18 Jan 1844

3 Collins, 'Balance sheets', p 47, table 3

4 M Collins, 'Long-term growth of the English banking sector and money stock, 1844–80', *Economic History Review*, 2nd series, 36 (1983), p 376

5 M Collins, *Money and Banking in Britain since 1826* (Croom Helm, forthcoming), ch 3, table 4

6 Bank of England Archives, Birmingham agent's letter books, vol 11, 10 Feb 1855

7 Ibid, vol 12, 8 Feb and 15 Dec 1856

8 Ibid, vol 12, Nov and Dec 1857

9 Ibid, vol 14, 9 June 1862

10 Collins, *Money and Banking*, ch 5

11 Edwards, pp 51–2

12 Ibid, pp 66–7

13 Bank of England Archives, Birmingham agent's letter books, vol 15, 29 May 1865

14 Crick & Wadsworth, p 188

15 *Times*, 11 May 1866

16 *Bankers' Magazine* (May 1860), pp 283–7

17 E Jones, *Accountancy and the British Economy 1840–1980. The Evolution of Ernst and Whinney* (Batsford, 1981), p 43

18 See also Sayers, *Lloyds Bank*, pp 180–2; S G Checkland, *Scottish Banking. A History, 1695–1973* (Collins, 1975), p 470; G A Fletcher, *The Discount Houses in London. Principles, Operations and Change* (Macmillan, 1976), p 24

19 Crick & Wadsworth, p 151; Cottrell, *Industrial Finance*, pp 217–9

20 Bank of England Archives, Birmingham agent's letter books, vol 15, 11 May 1866

21 Ibid, 4 July 1866

22 Ibid, 12–13 July 1866
23 Edwards, p 59
24 *Bankers' Magazine* (Oct 1866), p 1177
25 Bank of England Archives, Birmingham agent's letter books, vol 15, 14 July 1866
26 Crick & Wadsworth, pp 183, 186, 226–7
27 B Supple, *The Royal Exchange Assurance. A History of British Insurance, 1720–1970* (Cambridge University Press, 1970), pp 327–8; G Hurren, *Phoenix Renascent* (Phoenix Assurance, 1973), p 65
28 G Rae, *The Country Banker. His Clients, Cares and Work* (Murray, 1885), letter 29
29 *Banking Almanac*, passim; Crick & Wadsworth, pp 32, 299
30 Collins, *Money and Banking*, ch 3 table 4
31 Bank of England Archives, Birmingham agent's letter books, vol 16, 17 Nov 1868
32 Crick & Wadsworth, p 78
33 Edwards, p 68

### 3 Amber: Birmingham to London, 1874–1891 (*pages 57–87*)

1 Cottrell, *Industrial Finance*, p 197
2 Edwards, p 64
3 Crick & Wadsworth, p 33
4 Ibid, p 74
5 Bank of England Archives, Birmingham agent's letter books, vol 18, 19 Dec 1878
6 Ibid, vol 18, 16 Oct 1877
7 E Green, *Debtors to their Profession. A History of The Institute of Bankers 1879–1979* (Methuen, 1979), p 50
8 Bank of England Archives, Birmingham agent's letter books, vol 18, 4 Oct 1878
9 Ibid, vol 11, 13 Oct 1855; vol 14, 29 Jan 1863; vol 15, 18 Oct 1867; R Hay, 'Frederick Buck Goodman' in D J Jeremy (ed), *Dictionary of Business Biography*, 2 (Butterworth, 1984), pp 609–11
10 E Jones, 'Arthur Keen', in D J Jeremy (ed), *Dictionary of Business Biography*, 3 (Butterworth, 1985), pp 570–4
11 Cottrell, *Industrial Finance*, pp 87–8
12 Ibid, p 196
13 Bank of England Archives, Birmingham agent's letter books, vol 19, 21 Sept 1883
14 Ibid, vol 19, 24 Sept 1883
15 Crick & Wadsworth, pp 94–5
16 E.g. Crick & Wadsworth, pp 35–7
17 Cottrell, *Industrial Finance*, pp 223–8
18 Ibid, pp 152, 240–1
19 Checkland, *Scottish Banking*, pp 481–6

20  E Green, 'Sir Edward Holden', in *Dictionary of Business Biography*, 3, pp 290–8
21  *Financial News*, 24 July 1919
22  Ibid


## 4 Campaigns and conquests, 1891–1908 (*pages 89–119*)

1  Crick & Wadsworth, p 106
2  Green, *Debtors to their Profession*, pp 72–3
3  F Capie & A Webber, *A Monetary History of the United Kingdom, 1870–1982*, 1 (Allen & Unwin, 1985), table 111(3)
4  E Green, 'Sir Charles Sikes' in D J Jeremy (ed), *Dictionary of Business Biography*, 5 (Butterworth, 1986), pp 162–4
5  Crick & Wadsworth, pp 163–4
6  *Financial News*, 24 July 1919; Crick & Wadsworth, p 317
7  Goodhart, ch 12
8  See also Goodhart, p 180n
9  Ibid, pp 172, 448–9
10  Crick & Wadsworth, p 333
11  Goodhart, p 53
12  Green, 'Holden', *Dictionary of Business Biography*, 3, p 297
13  Y Cassis, 'Management and strategy in the English joint stock banks, 1890–1914', *Business History*, 27 (1985), pp 304–5
14  *Bankers' Magazine* (May 1909), p 736
15  Ibid, pp 736–7
16  L Joseph, *Industrial Finance. A Comparison between Home and Foreign Developments* (1911) quoted in Cottrell, *Industrial Finance*, p 237
17  Cottrell, *Industrial Finance*, p 237
18  *Leeds Mercury*, 9 Nov 1901
19  G H Pownall, 'The interdependence of trade and banking', *Journal of the Institute of Bankers* (April 1900), p 199
20  Goodhart, appendix IVB
21  *Banking Almanac*, passim


## 5 Colossus, 1908–1919 (*pages 121–151*)

1  F Capie & Ghila Rodrik-Bali, 'Concentration in British banking, 1870–1920', *Business History*, 24 (1982), p 287
2  Crick & Wadsworth, p 42; Green, *Debtors to their Profession*, pp 60–2
3  *Bankers' Magazine* (Sept 1919); *Times*, 24 July 1919
4  Crick & Wadsworth, p 448; Goodhart, p 7
5  Clapham, 2, p 388
6  Crick & Wadsworth, pp 40–1
7  Cottrell & Anderson, pp 316–25
8  *Morning Post*, 18 Dec 1926
9  Capie & Rodrik-Bali, p 287
10  Ibid, p 297

11  *Toronto News*, 24 Sept 1904

12  Green, *Debtors to their Profession*, pp 89–90

13  See also *Bankers' Magazine* (Oct 1920) pp 411–2

14  Crick & Wadsworth, p 308

15  Goodhart, pp 136–7; obituary of A A Shand, *Morning Post*, 16 April 1930

16  See also R Davenport-Hines, 'Charles Birch Crisp', in D J Jeremy (ed), *Dictionary of Business Biography*, 1 (Butterworth, 1984), pp 822–6

17  Olga Crisp, 'Russia' in Cameron, *Banking in the Early Stages of Industrialization*, pp 225–7

18  Baring Brothers & Co Ltd Archives, COF/05/6/9

19  G Jones, 'Lombard Street on the Riviera: the British clearing banks and Europe, 1900–1960', *Business History*, 24 (1982), p 187

20  Goodhart, pp 131, 134

21  *Financier*, 24 July 1919

22  *Bankers' Magazine* (April 1907), p 591

23  Clapham, 2, pp 414–5

24  *Financial News*, 24 July 1919

25  Clapham, 2, p 412

26  R Jenkins, *Asquith* (Collins, 1964, revised edition 1978), p 540; *Financial News*, 24 July 1919

27  Public Record Office, T170/55–6, conference on wartime banking, 4–5 August 1914

28  Kathleen Burk, *Britain, America and the Sinews of War, 1914–1918* (Allen & Unwin, 1985), pp 71–2; *Forbes Magazine*, 9 Aug 1919

29  R S Sayers, *The Bank of England 1891–1944*, 1 (Cambridge University Press, 1976), pp 89–90

30  *Wall Street Journal*, 29 April 1919

31  *Times, Trade Supplement*, 2 Aug 1919

## 6 Holden's legacy, 1919–1929 (*pages 153–174*)

1  L Hannah, *The Rise of the Corporate Economy* (Methuen, 1976), ch 6

2  J F Darling remained a director until his death in 1938. Darling's pamphlet publications included *Empire Consols* (1922), *Currency Co-operation in the British Empire* (1922), *The Rex. A New Money to Unify The Empire* (1930)

3  Appreciation of Reginald McKenna by 'K' (J M Keynes), *Times*, 15 Sept 1943

4  *Bankers' Magazine* (Oct 1920), pp 414–6

5  J S Boswell and B R Johns, 'Patriots or profiteers? British businessmen and the First World War', *Journal of European Economic History*, 11 (1982)

6  Public Record Office, CAB 63/31 (The authors are grateful to Dr Richard Davenport-Hines for pointing out this reference)

7  Cottrell, *Industrial Finance*, pp 168–9

8  Simpson, *Belfast Bank*, p 219

9  *Times*, 20 June 1917

10 Checkland, *Scottish Banking*, pp 562–3, 576–8

11 J M Reid, *The History of the Clydesdale Bank 1838–1938* (Blackie, 1938); Checkland, *Scottish Banking*, pp 481–5; M Kita, 'The Scottish banking invasion of England 1874–1882', *Soka Economic Studies Quarterly* (1977)

12 *Glasgow Herald*, 25 Nov 1920

13 A Keith, *The North of Scotland Bank* (Aberdeen Journals, 1936), pp 168–71

14 Ibid, pp 153–4

15 E.g. R E Muirhead in *Scotsman* and *Daily Record and Mail*, 29 Dec 1923

16 *Journal of the Institute of Bankers*, summaries of bank accounts (1924–1929)

17 B R Mitchell, *Abstract of British Historical Statistics* (Cambridge University Press, 1962), p 284

18 Jones, 'Lombard Street on the Riviera': p 188

19 *Journal of the Institute of Bankers* (1925), p 417

20 Sayers, *Bank of England*, 2, pp 243–8

21 Jones, 'Lombard Street on the Riviera', pp 192–6

22 Ibid, p 194

23 *Bankers' Magazine* (July 1927), pp 85–7

24 *Journal of the Institute of Bankers* (1920–1930) passim

25 R S Sayers, 'The springs of technical progress in Britain, 1919–1939', *Economic Journal*, 60 (1950); J Foreman–Peck, 'Seedcorn or chaff? New firm formation and the performance of the interwar economy', *Economic History Review*, 2nd series, 38 (1985), pp 402–22

26 F Capie & A Webber, 'Profits and profitability in British banking', City University Monetary History Discussion Paper, 18 (1985), pp 8–27

27 *Catalogue of the Drawings Collection of the RIBA. Edwin Lutyens*, ed M Richardson (Gregg, 1973), pp 34–36, 40

28 *Journal of the Institute of Bankers* (Dec 1933), p 483

29 Ibid (May 1920), pp 154–5

30 Crick & Wadsworth, p 341

## 7 Opposite the Bank of England, 1929–1939 (*pages 175–196*)

1 A S G Butler, *The Architecture of Sir Edwin Lutyens* (Country Life, 1950), vol 3, p 27

2 D E Moggridge, *British Monetary Policy 1924–1931. The Norman Conquest of $4.86* (Cambridge University Press, 1972), pp 42–4

3 *East Anglian Times*, 24 Aug 1928

4 Sayers, *Bank of England*, 2, p 553

5 E.g. *Midland Bank Monthly Review* (Jan–Feb 1927)

6 J R Hume and M S Moss, *Beardmore: The History of a Scottish Industrial Giant* (Heinemann, 1979), pp 212–4; Sayers, *Bank of England*, 1, p 363

7 Sayers, *Bank of England*, 1, p 366

8 *Minutes of Evidence taken before the Committee on Finance and Industry* [Macmillan Evidence] (HMSO, 1931), 1, pp 56–69

9 A Boyle, *Montagu Norman* (Cassell, 1967), pp 165, 255–9

10 M S Moss, 'Montagu Collet Norman', in D J Jeremy (ed), *Dictionary of*

*Business Biography*, 4 (Butterworth, 1985), pp 447–58

11 K Middlemas, *Politics in Industrial Society. The Experience of the British System since 1911* (Deutsch, 1979), pp 178–80

12 Hannah, p 73; Middlemas, p 206; Sayers, *Bank of England*, 1, ch 14

13 J D Scott, *Vickers. A History* (Weidenfeld & Nicolson, 1962), pp 156–9; R Church, *Herbert Austin: The British Motor Car Industry to 1941* (Europa, 1979), pp 18–19, 55–6, 146–7

14 W A Thomas, *The Finance of British Industry, 1918–1976* (Methuen, 1978), pp 76–9

15 J Foreman-Peck, 'Exit, voice and loyalty as responses to decline. The Rover Company in the inter-war years', *Business History*, 23 (1981), pp 191–204

16 Middlemas, p 180n

17 Macmillan Evidence, questions 1017–9, 1038

18 *Report of Committee on Finance and Industry* [Macmillan Report], Cmnd 3897 (HMSO, 1931), pp 160, 169; Thomas, *Finance of British Industry*, pp 117–9

19 Sayers, *Bank of England*, 1, pp 325–7

20 Hannah, p 74. See also J H Bamberg, *The Government, the Banks and the Lancashire Cotton Industry, 1918–1939* (Cambridge University, unpublished PhD thesis, 1984)

21 See also L Dennett, *The Charterhouse Group, 1925–1979. A History* (Gentry Books, 1979), ch 3. The Industrial Mortgage Corporation plan had first been mooted by Sir Otto Niemeyer in October 1933.

22 See also Thomas, *Finance of British Industry*, pp 119–20

23 Sayers, *Bank of England*, 1, pp 321–3; Hume & Moss, *Beardmore*, ch 7

24 E Green & M S Moss, *A Business of National Importance. The Royal Mail Shipping Group, 1902–1937* (Methuen, 1982), chs 7 & 8

25 D Joslin, *A Century of Banking in Latin America* (Oxford University Press, 1963), ch 14; Sayers, *Bank of England* 1, p 263–7

26 E.g. E Rosenbaum & A J Sherman, *M M Warburg & Co, 1798–1938, Merchant Bankers of Hamburg* (Hurst, 1979), pp 147–50

27 Sayers, *Bank of England*, 2, p 508

28 Ibid, pp 493–4, 585, 590

29 Macmillan Evidence, question 408; *Financial News*, 11 April 1944, appreciation by 'HBD'

30 A H Allman, *Williams Deacon's 1771–1970* (Williams Deacon's, 1970), pp 157–9

31 Capie & Webber, 'Profits and profitability', p 15

32 *The Banker* (May & June 1935), pp 96–9, 205–6

33 *Journal of the Institute of Bankers* (Nov 1935), p 421

34 *The Banker* (Dec 1933), pp 238–44

35 Green, *Debtors to their Profession*, pp 120, 123–5

36 Sayers, *Bank of England*, 2, pp 544–6

37 *Times*, 10 July 1935

38 Westminster Bank's share of deposits and advances remained stable at

15.5–16 per cent and 14.5 per cent respectively. Lloyds Bank's deposits declined from about 19.5 per cent to 18.5 per cent and its advances from about 20 per cent to 18 per cent. National Provincial Bank's share of deposits slackened from about 15 per cent to 14.5 per cent and its advances fell from about 16 per cent to 14.5 per cent.

## 8 Banking on the defensive, 1939–1948 (*pages 197–212*)

1 J E Wadsworth, *Counter Defensive, Being the Story of a Bank in Battle* (Hodder & Stoughton, 1946), pp 15, 23
2 See also A W Tuke and R J H Gillman, *Barclays Bank Limited 1926–1964* (Barclays Bank, 1972), pp 4–5, 48
3 Wadsworth, pp 63–6
4 Crick & Wadsworth, p 192
5 Wadsworth, pp 66–7
6 Ibid, appendix D
7 *The Banker* (Dec 1942), pp 99–101; *Bankers' Magazine* (Aug 1942), p 82
8 *The Banker* (Sept 1948), p 160
9 Appreciation of Reginald McKenna by 'K' (J M Keynes), *Times*, 15 Sept 1943; E Green, 'Reginald McKenna', in *Dictionary of Business Biography*, 4, pp 33–7
10 Sadd's knighthood ·was awarded for services to the Lawn Tennis Association, of which he was treasurer for many years
11 *Times*, 3 Oct 1962
12 R Harrod, *The Life of John Maynard Keynes* (Macmillan, 1951), ch 14
13 J Glyn, 'AMC A Jubilee Year', *Bankers' Magazine* (May 1978), pp 11–15
14 Thomas, *Finance of British Industry*, pp 119–22
15 R G Garnett, *A Century of Co-operative Insurance. The Co-operative Insurance Society 1867–1967: A Business History* (Allen & Unwin, 1968), pp 232–66

## 9 Burdens of leadership, 1948–1959 (*pages 213–230*)

1 H L Rouse, 'Midland Bank Limited' in G E Milward (ed), *Large-Scale Organisation* (Macdonald & Evans, 1950), p 192
2 Ibid, pp 192–3
3 Tuke and Gillman, *Barclays*, pp 78–80
4 *Financial Times*, 7 Jan 1952
5 Tuke & Gillman, *Barclays*, pp 20–4
6 R F Holder, *Bank of New South Wales. A History* (Sydney: Angus & Robertson, 1970), 2, pp 836, 870
7 Lord Birkenhead, *Walter Monckton. The Life of Viscount Monckton of Brenchley* (Weidenfeld & Nicolson, 1969), p 319
8 *Statistical Review of Press Advertising and Statistical Review of Independent TV Advertising* (Legion Publishing, 1957–60)
9 Checkland, *Scottish Banking*, pp 644–5

## 10 Mixing new ingredients, 1959–1971 (*pages 231–248*)

1  Capie & Webber, *Monetary History*, 1, tables 11(1) and 111(4)
2  *The London Clearing Banks. Evidence by the Committee of London Clearing Bankers to the Committee to Review the Functioning of Financial Institutions* (CLCB, 1977), p 161
3  *Midland Bank Review* (Nov 1969), p 3
4  National Board for Prices and Incomes, *Bank Charges*, Report 34, Cmnd 3292 (HMSO, 1967)
5  Checkland, *Scottish Banking*, p 702
6  Simpson, *Belfast Bank*, pp 330–1, 340–3
7  *Observer*, 24 Sept 1967
8  *Financial Times*, 20 Sept 1967
9  *Bank Charges*, p 53
10  *London Clearing Banks*, pp 22–3; Tuke and Gillman, *Barclays*, pp 16–18
11  J R Winton, *Lloyds Bank, 1918–1969* (Oxford University Press, 1982), p 196
12  Ibid, pp 171–6

## 11 International banking and the 'grand design', 1945–1975 (*pages 249–260*)

1  H H Thackstone, 'The work of the foreign branch of a commercial bank', paper given to Institute of Bankers' international summer school, Oxford (1948)
2  A Cairncross & B Eichengreen, *Sterling in Decline. The Devaluations of 1931, 1949 and 1967* (Oxford: Blackwell, 1983), ch 4
3  D F Channon, *British Banking Strategy and the International Challenge* (Macmillan, 1977), p 153
4  E.g. F Seidenzahl, *100 Jahre Deutsche Bank, 1870–1970* (Deutsche Bank, Frankfurt, 1970), pp 389–90
5  *London Clearing Banks*, pp 26, 143–4
6  R Fry, *Bankers in West Africa. The Story of the Bank of British West Africa Limited* (Hutchinson, 1978), pp 252
7  Channon, pp 130–1
8  *London Clearing Banks*, pp 143–4
9  R Pringle, *Banking in Britain* (Methuen edition, 1975), pp 80–90

## 12 Will you walk a little faster? The domestic banking scene, 1971–1975 (*pages 261–280*)

1  *Bank of England Quarterly Bulletin* (June 1978), pp 231–2
2  Ibid, p 232
3  *Midland Bank Review* (Aug 1973)
4  Channon, p 43
5  Ibid, p 96
6  *Times*, 23 Nov 1973

7 In the case of the Unilever pension fund, Unilever itself contributed to the rescue in place of the pension fund. J Plender, *That's the Way the Money Goes. The Financial Institutions and the Nation's Savings* (Deutsch, 1982), pp 110–1; 'A lifeboat for the banks', BBC Radio 4, 19 Dec 1983

8 Plender, pp 105–16; Margaret Reid, *The Secondary Banking Crisis, 1973–75* (Macmillan, 1982), pp 129–30

9 *Bank of England Quarterly Bulletin* (June 1978), p 235

10 Margaret Reid, pp 192–8; *The Banker* (Dec 1978)

11 *Rolls-Royce Limited and the RB 211 Aero-engine*, Cmnd 4860 (HMSO 1972); *Rolls-Royce Limited, Investigation under Section 165a(i) of the Companies Act 1948* (HMSO, 1973)

## 13 Under new orders. Midland as a banking group, 1971–1975 *(pages 281–299)*

1 *Hansard*, 27 Jan 1971

2 J Hibbs, 'Harold Charles Gilbert Drayton' in *Dictionary of Business Biography*, 2, pp 173–6

3 *Standard Chartered Bank. A Story Brought up to Date* (Standard Chartered, 1980), p 22; Channon, p 131

# APPENDIX I

## Midland Bank, deposit accounts and estimates of total deposits and advances, 1838–1870

| Date | Deposit accounts (£) | Estimated total deposit accounts (£) | Estimated total deposits (£) | Estimated total advances (£) |
|------|------|------|------|------|
| Dec 1838 | | 33,550 | 76,250 | |
| 1839 | | 44,000 | 100,000 | |
| 1840 | 53,722 | | 122,095 | |
| 1841 | | 61,000 | 138,636 | |
| 1842 | | 66,000 | 150,000 | |
| 1843 | | 75,350 | 171,250 | |
| 1844 | 79,702 | | 181,141 | |
| 1845 | | 100,650 | 228,750 | |
| 1846 | | 107,250 | 243,750 | |
| June 1847 | 139,249 | | 316,475 | 155,354 |
| 1848 | 101,059 | | 229,679 | 190,114 |
| 1849 | 72,139 | | 163,952 | 104,608 |
| 1850 | 86,275 | | 196,079 | 155,124 |
| 1851 | 120,237 | | 273,266 | 196,265 |
| 1852 | HO 137,073 (S 120,000) | 257,073 | 584,257 | 391,563 |
| 1853 | HO 240,005 (S 120,000) | 360,005 | 818,193 | 469,508 |
| 1854 | HO 163,868 (S 120,000) | 283,868 | 645,154 | 429,193 |
| 1855 | HO 171,343 (S 120,000) | 291,343 | 662,143 | 432,842 |
| 1856 | HO 209,501 (S 120,000) | 329,501 | 748,866 | 440,444 |
| 1857 | HO 209,011 (S 120,000) | 329,011 | 747,752 | 441,447 |
| 1858 | HO 218,079 (S 120,000) | 338,079 | 768,361 | 570,780 |
| 1859 | HO 243,453 (S 120,000) | 363,453 | 826,029 | 561,025 |

| Date | Deposit accounts (£) | Estimated total deposit accounts (£) | Estimated total deposits (£) | Estimated total advances (£) |
|---|---|---|---|---|
| June 1860 | HO 252,418 (S 120,000) | 372,418 | 846,404 | 516,267 |
| 1861 | HO 262,714 (S 120,000) | 382,714 | 869,804 | 565,476 |
| 1862 | HO 301,630 (S 120,000) B 53,204 | 474,834 | 1,079,168 | 698,573 |
| 1863 | HO 299,437 S 116,673 (B 53,000) | 469,110 | 1,066,159 | 737,413 |
| 1864 | HO 329,399 S 107,686 (B 53,000) | 490,085 | 1,113,829 | 674,778 |
| 1865 | HO 372,230 S 136,004 (B 53,000) | 561,234 | 1,275,531 | 1,032,802 |
| 1866 | HO 503,349 S 127,010 (B 55,820) | 686,179 | 1,559,497 | 1,233,249 |
| 1867 | HO 560,098 S 111,381 (B 64,267) | 735,746 | 1,672,150 | 910,433 |
| 1868 | HO 610,287 S 101,589 (B 75,318) | 787,194 | 1,789,077 | 1,106,326 |
| 1869 | HO 556,406 S 99,281 (B 67,731) | 723,418 | 1,644,131 | 1,154,314 |
| 1870 | HO 610,288 (S 99,739) (B 83,261) | 793,288 | 1,802,927 | 957,103 |

*Notes*

*Deposit accounts*
1840 & 1844:   totals of all individual credit balances in deposit
account ledger, 1838–46

1847–1851:            deposits entered in stock accounts, 1847–1851

1852–1870 'HO':       deposits entered in stock accounts re head office deposit
                      accounts only, 1852–1870

1852–1862 'S':        estimates for deposit accounts at Stourbridge branch,
                      based on actual deposit accounts in 1851 and 1863

1862–1869 'S':        deposit accounts at Stourbridge branch, abstracted
                      from Stourbridge general ledger

1862 'B':             deposit accounts at Bewdley branch listed in acquisition
                      agreement

1863–1865 'B':        estimates for deposit accounts at Bewdley branch based
                      on actual deposits in 1862

1866–70 'B' ⎫        estimates of deposit accounts at Bewdley and
1870    'S' ⎬ :      Stourbridge branches based on return of interest paid
                      on deposits in stock accounts, 1866–1870

*Estimated total deposit accounts*

1838–1839 ⎫          estimates for deposit accounts based on yearly numbers
1841–1843 ⎬ :        of deposit accounts and average account balance for
1845–1846 ⎭          1840 and 1844 of £550 for each account

1847–1870:            totals of actual and estimated deposit accounts

*Estimated total deposits*

1838–1870:            estimates have been based on deposit accounts
                      averaging 44 per cent of total deposits (the actual
                      average percentage in 1871–73). The ratio of deposit
                      accounts to total deposits is certain to have fluctuated
                      significantly between 1838 and 1870, but this average
                      has been adopted to give a conservative estimate of
                      total deposits

*Estimated total advances*

1847–1870:            estimates of loans and overdrafts on current accounts
                      by deduction of deposit accounts from estimated total
                      deposits with adjustments for 'customer accounts'
                      entries in stock accounts 1847–1870

# APPENDIX 2.1

## Midland Bank, deposits, advances and total assets
## 1871–1918

| Date | Deposit, current and other accounts (£000) | Advances (£000) | Total assets (£000) |
|------|------|------|------|
| 1871 June | 1799 | 1064 | 2298 |
| 1872 | 1953 | 1095 | 2465 |
| 1873 | 2204 | 1109 | 2731 |
| 1874 | 2565 | 1252 | 3116 |
| 1875 | 2686 | 1430 | 3247 |
| 1876 | 2592 | 1622 | 3181 |
| 1877 | 2509 | 1758 | 3073 |
| 1878 | 2364 | 1947 | 2934 |
| 1879 | 2187 | 1441 | 2750 |
| 1880 | 2015 | 1327 | 2590 |
| 1881 | 1973 | 1192 | 2558 |
| 1882 | 2168 | 1337 | 2765 |
| 1883 | 2127 | 1358 | 2729 |
| 1884 | 2454 | 1525 | 3078 |
| 1885 | 2541 | 1559 | 3180 |
| 1886 Dec | 2640 | 1841 | 3237 |
| 1887 | 2545 | 1546 | 3125 |
| 1888 | 2703 | 1671 | 3299 |
| 1889 | 3481 | 2208 | 4215 |
| 1890 | 5616 | 3502 | 6811 |
| 1891 | 8119 | 4232 | 9527 |
| 1892 | 8871 | 4792 | 10,377 |
| 1893 | 9160 | 4878 | 10,665 |
| 1894 | 12,167 | 6606 | 13,948 |
| 1895 | 13,221 | 6918 | 15,005 |
| 1896 | 15,757 | 8670 | 17,873 |
| 1897 | 21,725 | 11,567 | 25,248 |
| 1898 | 31,888 | 16,409 | 38,997 |
| 1899 | 33,818 | 18,278 | 40,723 |
| 1900 | 37,845 | 19,774 | 45,327 |
| 1901 | 44,780 | 23,215 | 53,264 |
| 1902 | 46,748 | 23,393 | 55,412 |

| Date | Deposit, current and other accounts (£000) | Advances (£000) | Total assets (£000) |
|------|-------------------------------------------|-----------------|---------------------|
| 1903 | 45,423 | 24,554 | 53,859 |
| 1904 | 47,672 | 24,750 | 56,205 |
| 1905 | 50,259 | 27,402 | 61,063 |
| 1906 | 52,224 | 28,040 | 63,543 |
| 1907 | 53,282 | 28,992 | 63,985 |
| 1908 | 66,974 | 34,002 | 79,815 |
| 1909 | 69,645 | 36,897 | 82,513 |
| 1910 | 73,415 | 41,088 | 87,917 |
| 1911 | 77,708 | 43,435 | 91,606 |
| 1912 | 83,664 | 46,442 | 98,277 |
| 1913 | 93,834 | 51,310 | 108,584 |
| 1914 | 125,733 | 62,425 | 142,540 |
| 1915 | 147,751 | 65,922 | 166,163 |
| 1916 | 174,621 | 63,869 | 191,189 |
| 1917 | 220,552 | 81,156 | 239,994 |
| 1918 | 334,898 | 113,432 | 363,517 |

*Note* Total assets between 1871 and 1878 exclude any valuation of premises (which were valued at £60,000 in 1879)

# APPENDIX 2.2

## Midland Bank, deposits, advances and total assets
## 1919–1985

| Date | Deposits (£ million) | Advances (£ million) | Total assets (£ million) | Group total assets (£ million) |
|---|---|---|---|---|
| 1919 | 372 | 179 | 419 | |
| 1920 | 372 | 190 | 423 | |
| 1921 | 375 | 177 | 418 | |
| 1922 | 354 | 182 | 404 | |
| 1923 | 360 | 189 | 420 | |
| 1924 | 356 | 191 | 421 | |
| 1925 | 349 | 197 | 411 | |
| 1926 | 366 | 200 | 431 | |
| 1927 | 374 | 206 | 438 | |
| 1928 | 395 | 214 | 498 | |
| 1929 | 380 | 210 | 446 | 511 |
| 1930 | 400 | 204 | 455 | 521 |
| 1931 | 360 | 198 | 407 | 471 |
| 1932 | 419 | 170 | 462 | 533 |
| 1933 | 414 | 164 | 457 | 527 |
| 1934 | 419 | 164 | 462 | 532 |
| 1935 | 442 | 177 | 487 | 564 |
| 1936 | 487 | 189 | 533 | 610 |
| 1937 | 496 | 210 | 546 | 626 |
| 1938 | 463 | 209 | 509 | 587 |
| 1939 | 496 | 221 | 543 | 621 |
| 1940 | 577 | 188 | 620 | 702 |
| 1941 | 686 | 170 | 729 | 830 |
| 1942 | 759 | 159 | 801 | 907 |
| 1943 | 860 | 157 | 903 | 1022 |
| 1944 | 1003 | 168 | 1048 | 1180 |
| 1945 | 1060 | 176 | 1115 | 1261 |
| 1946 | 1241 | 220 | 1326 | 1495 |
| 1947 | 1279 | 269 | 1368 | 1546 |
| 1948 | 1349 | 310 | 1444 | 1635 |
| 1949 | 1351 | 331 | 1440 | 1631 |
| 1950 | 1392 | 344 | 1502 | 1698 |
| 1951 | 1347 | 394 | 1468 | 1661 |
| 1952 | 1368 | 364 | 1454 | 1653 |

| Date | Deposits (£ million) | Advances (£ million) | Total assets (£ million) | Group total assets (£ million) |
|------|---------|---------|-------------|-------------------|
| 1953 | 1443 | 344 | 1517 | 1730 |
| 1954 | 1488 | 398 | 1575 | 1802 |
| 1955 | 1460 | 386 | 1540 | 1759 |
| 1956 | 1473 | 398 | 1559 | 1780 |
| 1957 | 1506 | 398 | 1603 | 1829 |
| 1958 | 1579 | 473 | 1674 | 1906 |
| 1959 | 1697 | 622 | 1804 | 2055 |
| 1960 | 1709 | 759 | 1816 | 2097 |
| 1961 | 1698 | 754 | 1834 | 2135 |
| 1962 | 1742 | 788 | 1882 | 2195 |
| 1963 | 1899 | 918 | 2046 | 2393 |
| 1964 | 1955 | 1025 | 2132 | 2519 |
| 1965 | 2111 | 1065 | 2309 | 2819 |
| 1966 | 2157 | 1107 | 2388 | 2909 |
| 1967 | 2316 | 1226 | 2549 | 3084 |
| 1968 | 2348 | 1133 | 2603 | 3356 |
| 1969 | 2185 | 1125 | 2372 | 3248 |
| 1970 | 2299 | 1235 | 2556 | 3690 |
| 1971 | 3175 | 1593 | 3449 | 4468 |
| 1972 | 4544 | 2859 | 4843 | 5897 |
| 1973 | 5860 | 3766 | 6314 | 8215 |
| 1974 | 7188 | 4727 | 7772 | 9940 |
| 1975 | 7355 | 5095 | 8008 | 10,365 |
| 1976 | 8338 | 5872 | 9068 | 11,843 |
| 1977 | 9335 | 6604 | 10,080 | 13,383 |
| 1978 | 10,744 | 7752 | 11,621 | 15,550 |
| 1979 | 13,255 | 9386 | 14,337 | 20,205 |
| 1980 | 16,493 | 12,034 | 17,595 | 25,343 |
| 1981 | 20,158 | 14,964 | 21,272 | 41,014 |
| 1982 | 22,403 | 17,652 | 23,633 | 47,999 |
| 1983 | 24,631 | 20,012 | 26,801 | 52,613 |
| 1984 | 29,003 | 22,231 | 31,027 | 61,483 |
| 1985 | 30,264 | 23,679 | 33,118 | 58,074 |

*Notes*

*Deposits* comprise current, deposit and other accounts and balances due to subsidiaries

*Advances* comprise advances and balances due by subsidiaries

*Group total assets* were not computed or published until 1929

# APPENDIX 3

## Midland Bank, analysis of shareholdings, 1837–1888

| Category | Number of shareholders | | | | Paid-up value of shares (£) | | | | Mean average paid-up value per shareholder (£) | | | | Paid-up value as % of total paid-up value | | | |
|---|---|---|---|---|---|---|---|---|---|---|---|---|---|---|---|---|
| | 1837 | 1859 | 1874 | 1888A–F | 1837 | 1859 | 1874 | 1888A–F | 1837 | 1859 | 1874 | 1888A–F | 1837 | 1859 | 1874 | 1888A–F |
| All shareholdings | 199 | 111 | 258 | (905) | 33,500 | 165,400 | 302,000 | (336,687) | 168 | 1490 | 1163 | (369) | 100.0 | 100.0 | 100.0 | (100.0) |
| Shareholdings A–F | | | | 289 | | | | 121,625 | | | | 421 | | | | 36.1 |
| Holdings of £3000+ | 0 | 17 | 24 | 8 | 0 | 94,800 | 178,000 | 46,750 | 0 | 5576 | 7417 | 5844 | 0 | 57.3 | 58.9 | 38.4 |
| Holdings outside Birmingham | 10 | 15 | 50 | 66 | 3400 | 12,700 | 76,450 | 36,400 | 340 | 847 | 1529 | 551 | 10.1 | 7.7 | 25.3 | 29.9 |
| Occupations Executors & trustees | 0 | 16 | 18 | 10 | 0 | 21,650 | 17,150 | 18,700 | 0 | 1353 | 953 | 1870 | 0 | 13.1 | 5.7 | 15.4 |
| Gentlemen | 13 | 11 | 68 | 61 | 3400 | 31,250 | 147,600 | 38,275 | 262 | 2841 | 2171 | 627 | 10.1 | 18.9 | 48.9 | 31.5 |
| Manufacturers | 55 | 21 | 37 | 46 | 9900 | 39,200 | 31,300 | 8362 | 180 | 1867 | 846 | 182 | 29.6 | 23.7 | 10.4 | 6.9 |
| Merchants | 34 | 15 | 17 | 21 | 7075 | 28,500 | 28,550 | 20,625 | 208 | 1900 | 1679 | 982 | 21.1 | 17.2 | 9.4 | 17.0 |
| Other commercial | 5 | 1 | 13 | 13 | 550 | 400 | 5350 | 1787 | 110 | 400 | 411 | 137 | 1.6 | 0.2 | 1.8 | 1.5 |
| Metalcrafts & jewellers | 16 | 1 | 17 | 25 | 2150 | 900 | 7400 | 4250 | 134 | 900 | 435 | 170 | 6.4 | 0.5 | 2.4 | 3.5 |
| Professional & clerical | 29 | 19 | 30 | 50 | 4275 | 28,250 | 32,950 | 12,800 | 147 | 1487 | 1098 | 256 | 12.8 | 17.1 | 10.9 | 10.5 |
| Shopkeepers & retailers | 38 | 8 | 3 | 31 | 4350 | 3300 | 500 | 3575 | 114 | 412 | 167 | 115 | 13.0 | 2.0 | 0.2 | 2.9 |
| Widows & spinsters | 0 | 13 | 48 | 19 | 0 | 9750 | 27,700 | 6962 | 0 | 750 | 577 | 366 | 0 | 5.9 | 9.2 | 5.7 |
| Others | 9 | 6 | 7 | 13 | 1800 | 2200 | 3500 | 6287 | 200 | 367 | 500 | 484 | 5.4 | 1.3 | 1.1 | 5.2 |

*Notes*

*Holdings outside Birmingham* Shareholders located within approximately 5 miles of Birmingham centre (i.e. excluding residents of Brierley Hill, Coventry, Dudley, Kidderminster, Stourbridge, Walsall and Wolverhampton)

*Occupations* *Other commercial* Factors, agents and travellers

*Others* Occupations include builders, farmers, millers, printers, trustees of bank's shares, and occupations not known

# APPENDIX 4

## Midland Bank, shareholders' funds, profits and dividends, 1836–1985

This appendix provides details of Midland Bank's share capital, reserves and profits since 1836. The bank's long history as a shareholders' company has meant that these details form an unusually long series of statistics of banking performance. We have also included a profile of actual and published net profits between 1879 and 1968— the first occasion on which a major British bank has made this information available.

Before 1969 the London clearing banks, including Midland, used exemptions under a series of companies acts which allowed banks not to publish details of their full total profits. This practice and its sanction by the authorities had its origins in the mid-Victorian economy. It was rooted in the belief that banks needed to provide for contingencies such as exceptional bad debts in severe commercial crises. Bankers created special contingent funds for this purpose, but treated them as part of their deposit liabilities rather than as part of their published reserves. These contingent funds were supplied by payments from annual net profits, and in exceptional circumstances they were used to meet actual contingencies. In Midland's case, this inner contingent fund was established as early as 1866, although we have not been able to trace the dates and values of payments into the fund before 1879.

For the banks, an important advantage of these unpublished transfers to and from contingent funds was the ability to dampen any big fluctuations in their published net profits. Stability of performance had become a special preoccupation of bankers, particularly after the collapse of the City of Glasgow Bank in 1878. Stability and steady returns were perceived as essential parts of confidence in the banking system, parallel to the regular yields of government stock; it was also important that profits should not fluctuate in such a way as to attract speculative trading in bank shares.

By the 1960s the banks' privileges in not disclosing their full profits had lost some of their relevance. The stability of the banking system was no longer the sensitive issue which it had been in the late nineteenth century. Official attitudes towards profits and dividends were also changing. In these circumstances the London clearing banks abandoned their exemptions and published their full profits from 1969 onwards. In the meantime the level of the banks' actual profits had become the subject of serious interest and research, especially amongst stockbrokers and the financial press. By the mid-1960s the estimation of bank profits had become a familiar part of the investment scene, especially during the banks' annual 'reporting season'. Analysts calculated that the actual profits of the banks were as much as three times the published figures, and they also doubted whether the published results were a true reflection of trends in performance.

The outside estimates were never challenged while the banks continued to use their exemptions from full disclosure. In some cases, however, those calculations strayed far from their target, often because analysts continued to underestimate the high overhead costs of running a large bank. For example, 'Phaedra' in the *Bankers' Magazine* (July 1966) estimated Midland's 1965 profits at £31.3 million whereas its actual profits were £16.8 million. In the following year stockbrokers' estimates of the Midland group's profits ranged up to £38 million at a time when the bank's profits were £17.3 million. In this appendix we have placed on record a comparison of the bank's published and actual net profits in the years before disclosure. This new material suggests that actual profits were lower, and closer to the published trend of earnings, than previous estimates have allowed.

In the following appendix the statistics of shareholders' funds and profits refer to Midland Bank rather than to the entire group of subsidiaries and associated companies. The only exception is Appendix 4.3, which provides the group's consolidated results since 1969 (the practice of publishing separate profit and loss accounts for Midland Bank had ended in 1965).

The statistics for the bank's *capital* relate to paid-up or issued amounts rather than to nominal or authorized values. *Published reserves* denote the main reserve funds of the bank, excluding internal contingent funds and share premiums. Since 1965 these published figures have included each year's balance of profit and loss. The *total shareholders' funds* in Appendix 4.2 and 4.3 comprise paid-up capital, published reserves, balances of profit and loss, and share premiums, which since 1948 have been specified in the published accounts as a requirement of the 1948 Companies Act. The *actual net profits* between 1879 and 1968 are essentially the published net profits correlated with payments to or from the bank's contingent funds and, between 1946 and 1950 only, payments to an investment reserve fund. The *published profits* listed in Appendix 4.1 and 4.2 are the net published profits after taxation. In the years since disclosure in 1969, the focus has moved to the pre-tax level of the bank's profits, but for comparison Appendix 4.3 reproduces both the published pre-tax group profits and the published profits attributable to shareholders after tax. Finally, *dividends* are quoted as a percentage of the bank's paid-up or issued capital. Before December 1914 the full value of the dividend was paid to shareholders, and the bank met any income tax due on those payments. Between December 1914 and December 1965 income tax was deducted from dividends before payments, although the published dividends continued to be quoted at a pre-tax rate. Changes in taxation in 1966 required the bank to account for the income tax due on dividends, and as a result dividend rates since 1966 have reflected their full costs to the bank.

# APPENDIX 4.1

## Midland Bank, capital and reserves, profits and dividends 1836–1918

| Date | Paid-up capital (£000) | Published reserves (£000) | Paid-up capital and reserves (£000) | Actual net profits (from 1879) (£000) | Published net profits (£000) | Dividend (%) |
|---|---|---|---|---|---|---|
| 1836 Dec | 28 | | 28 | | | |
| 1837 May | 33 | | 33 | | | |
| 1838 June | 44 | 4 | 48 | | 5 | 6 |
| 1839 | 50 | 10 | 60 | | 7 | 8 |
| 1840 | 50 | 13 | 63 | | 7 | 8 |
| 1841 | 50 | 17 | 67 | | 8 | 8 |
| 1842 | 50 | 23 | 73 | | 8 | 8 |
| 1843 | 50 | 24 | 74 | | 5 | 8 |
| 1844 | 50 | 30 | 80 | | 7 | 8 |
| 1845 | 50 | 35 | 85 | | 9 | 9 |
| 1846 | 90 | 23 | 113 | | 13 | 10 |
| 1847 | 90 | 30 | 120 | | 15 | 10 |
| 1848 | 90 | 38 | 128 | | 16 | 10 |
| 1849 | 90 | 43 | 133 | | 13 | 10 |
| 1850 | 120 | 18 | 138 | | 13 | 10 |
| 1851 | 120 | 23 | 143 | | 15 | 9 |
| 1852 | 129 | 33 | 162 | | 17 | 10 |
| 1853 | 129 | 39 | 168 | | 18 | 10 |
| 1854 | 130 | 50 | 180 | | 22 | 10 |
| 1855 | 130 | 62 | 192 | | 27 | 12 |
| 1856 | 130 | 76 | 206 | | 30 | 14 |
| 1857 | 150 | 108 | 258 | | 31 | 15 |
| 1858 | 150 | 117 | 267 | | 30 | 16 |
| 1859 | 165 | 109 | 274 | | 29 | 16 |
| 1860 | 165 | 118 | 283 | | 32 | 16 |
| 1861 | 165 | 136 | 301 | | 40 | 16 |
| 1862 | 200 | 113 | 313 | | 35 | 16 |
| 1863 | 200 | 126 | 326 | | 37 | 16 |
| 1864 | 200 | 147 | 347 | | 47 | 18 |
| 1865 | 249 | 179 | 428 | | 53 | 19 |
| 1866 | 250 | 200 | 450 | | 63 | 20 |
| 1867 | 275 | 215 | 490 | | 59 | 20 |
| 1868 | 275 | 200 | 475 | | 53 | 20 |
| 1869 | 275 | 206 | 481 | | 56 | 20 |

| Date | Paid-up capital (£000) | Published reserves (£000) | Paid-up capital and reserves (£000) | Actual net profits (from 1879) (£000) | Published net profits (£000) | Dividend (%) |
|---|---|---|---|---|---|---|
| 1870 June | 275 | 212 | 487 | | 55 | 20 |
| 1871 | 275 | 219 | 494 | | 55 | 20 |
| 1872 | 275 | 225 | 500 | | 57 | 20 |
| 1873 | 275 | 232 | 507 | | 61 | 20 |
| 1874 | 300 | 240 | 540 | | 64 | 20 |
| 1875 | 300 | 250 | 550 | | 63 | 20 |
| 1876 | 300 | 260 | 560 | | 65 | 22 |
| 1877 | 300 | 270 | 570 | | 71 | 22 |
| 1878 | 300 | 270 | 570 | | 67 | 22 |
| 1879 | 300 | 210 | 510 | 71 | 61 | 19 |
| 1880 | 300 | 210 | 510 | 61 | 53 | 16 |
| 1881 | 300 | 210 | 510 | 57 | 49 | 16 |
| 1882 | 300 | 210 | 510 | 61 | 50 | 16 |
| 1883 | 300 | 210 | 510 | 58 | 49 | 16 |
| 1884 | 334 | 220 | 554 | 62 | 55 | 16 |
| 1885 | 334 | 220 | 554 | 60 | 56 | 16 |
| 1886 | 334 | 220 | 554 | 60 | 55 | 16 |
| 1886 Dec | 334 | 220 | 554 | 33 | 27 | 16 |
| 1887 | 334 | 220 | 554 | 51 | 51 | 15 |
| 1888 | 334 | 230 | 564 | 66 | 57 | 15 |
| 1889 | 410 | 290 | 700 | 92 | 79 | 15 |
| 1890 | 637 | 500 | 1137 | 136 | 116 | 15 |
| 1891 | 761 | 575 | 1336 | 129 | 125 | 15 |
| 1892 | 818 | 600 | 1418 | 148 | 134 | 15 |
| 1893 | 818 | 600 | 1418 | 148 | 140 | 15 |
| 1894 | 983 | 700 | 1683 | 171 | 154 | 15 |
| 1895 | 983 | 700 | 1683 | 183 | 170 | 15 |
| 1896 | 1055 | 750 | 1805 | 237 | 210 | 15 |
| 1897 | 1468 | 1251 | 2719 | 329 | 298 | 17 |
| 1898 | 2202 | 2202 | 4404 | 478 | 456 | 18 |
| 1899 | 2202 | 2202 | 4404 | 553 | 531 | 17 |
| 1900 | 2523 | 2523 | 5046 | 583 | 569 | 18.5 |
| 1901 | 3000 | 3000 | 6000 | 630 | 610 | 18.5 |
| 1902 | 3000 | 3000 | 6000 | 634 | 618 | 18.5 |
| 1903 | 3000 | 3000 | 6000 | 664 | 623 | 18 |
| 1904 | 3000 | 3000 | 6000 | 586 | 576 | 18 |
| 1905 | 3143 | 3143 | 6286 | 649 | 612 | 18 |
| 1906 | 3143 | 3143 | 6286 | 788 | 668 | 18 |
| 1907 | 3143 | 3143 | 6286 | 785 | 686 | 18 |

| Date | Paid-up capital | Published reserves | Paid-up capital and reserves | Actual net profits | Published net profits | Dividend |
|------|------|------|------|------|------|------|
| | (£000) | (£000) | (£000) | (£000) | (£000) | (%) |
| 1908 | 3799 | 3419 | 7218 | 679 | 679 | 18 |
| 1909 | 3799 | 3419 | 7218 | 763 | 737 | 18 |
| 1910 | 3989 | 3590 | 7579 | 892 | 802 | 18 |
| 1911 | 3989 | 3390 | 7379 | 891 | 789 | 18 |
| 1912 | 3989 | 3390 | 7379 | 1077 | 1010 | 18 |
| 1913 | 4349 | 3700 | 8049 | 1311 | 1235 | 18 |
| 1914 | 4781 | 4000 | 8781 | 1192 | 1107 | 18 |
| 1915 | 4781 | 4000 | 8781 | 1211 | 1131 | 18 |
| 1916 | 4781 | 4000 | 8781 | 1637 | 1637 | 18 |
| 1917 | 5189 | 4343 | 9532 | 1968 | 1968 | 18 |
| 1918 | 7173 | 7173 | 14,346 | 3314 | 2700 | 18 |

# APPENDIX 4.2

## Midland Bank, shareholders' funds, profits and dividends 1919–1968

| Date | Paid-up capital (£ million) | Published reserves (£ million) | Total shareholders' funds (£ million) | Actual net profits (£ million) | Published net profits (£ million) | Dividend (%) |
|---|---|---|---|---|---|---|
| 1919 | 8.4 | 8.4 | 17.6 | 3.8 | 3.1 | 18 |
| 1920 | 10.9 | 10.9 | 22.5 | 4.2 | 2.8 | 18 |
| 1921 | 10.9 | 10.9 | 22.5 | 2.8 | 2.5 | 18 |
| 1922 | 10.9 | 10.9 | 22.5 | 2.7 | 2.3 | 18 |
| 1923 | 10.9 | 10.9 | 22.5 | 2.2 | 2.2 | 18 |
| 1924 | 12.0 | 12.0 | 24.7 | 2.8 | 2.4 | 18 |
| 1925 | 12.7 | 12.7 | 26.1 | 3.2 | 2.5 | 18 |
| 1926 | 12.7 | 12.7 | 26.2 | 3.3 | 2.5 | 18 |
| 1927 | 12.7 | 12.7 | 26.2 | 3.1 | 2.6 | 18 |
| 1928 | 13.4 | 13.4 | 27.7 | 3.1 | 2.7 | 18 |
| 1929 | 13.4 | 13.4 | 27.7 | 3.7 | 2.7 | 18 |
| 1930 | 14.2 | 14.2 | 29.3 | 2.1 | 2.3 | 18 |
| 1931 | 14.2 | 11.5 | 26.6 | 2.5 | 2.1 | 16 |
| 1932 | 14.2 | 11.5 | 26.6 | 2.4 | 2.0 | 16 |
| 1933 | 14.2 | 11.5 | 26.6 | 2.8 | 2.3 | 16 |
| 1934 | 14.2 | 11.5 | 26.6 | 3.0 | 2.3 | 16 |
| 1935 | 14.2 | 11.5 | 26.2 | 3.4 | 2.4 | 16 |
| 1936 | 14.2 | 11.5 | 26.3 | 3.2 | 2.5 | 16 |
| 1937 | 15.2 | 12.4 | 28.1 | 3.7 | 2.5 | 16 |
| 1938 | 15.2 | 12.4 | 28.2 | 3.2 | 2.4 | 16 |
| 1939 | 15.2 | 12.4 | 28.2 | 2.8 | 2.2 | 16 |
| 1940 | 15.2 | 12.4 | 28.2 | 2.7 | 1.9 | 16 |
| 1941 | 15.2 | 12.4 | 28.2 | 2.3 | 2.0 | 16 |
| 1942 | 15.2 | 12.9 | 28.7 | 2.1 | 2.0 | 16 |
| 1943 | 15.2 | 13.4 | 29.3 | 2.0 | 2.0 | 16 |
| 1944 | 15.2 | 14.1 | 30.0 | 2.1 | 2.0 | 16 |
| 1945 | 15.2 | 15.2 | 31.1 | 2.2 | 2.1 | 16 |
| 1946 | 15.2 | 15.2 | 31.1 | 2.3 | 2.0 | 16 |
| 1947 | 15.2 | 15.2 | 31.1 | 3.3 | 2.0 | 16 |
| 1948 | 15.2 | 12.3 | 31.1 | 3.1 | 2.0 | 16 |
| 1949 | 15.2 | 12.3 | 31.1 | 2.5 | 2.0 | 16 |
| 1950 | 15.2 | 12.3 | 31.1 | 2.7 | 2.0 | 16 |
| 1951 | 15.2 | 12.3 | 31.1 | 3.2 | 1.9 | 16 |
| 1952 | 15.2 | 12.3 | 31.1 | 4.0 | 2.0 | 16 |

| Date | Paid-up capital (£ million) | Published reserves (£ million) | Total shareholders' funds (£ million) | Actual net profits (£ million) | Published net profits (£ million) | Dividend (%) |
|------|------|------|------|------|------|------|
| 1953 | 15.2 | 12.3 | 31.2 | 4.5 | 2.1 | 16 |
| 1954 | 15.2 | 12.3 | 31.2 | 7.2 | 2.4 | 18 |
| 1955 | 15.2 | 12.3 | 31.2 | 6.1 | 2.7 | 18 |
| 1956 | 15.2 | 12.3 | 31.2 | 6.9 | 2.9 | 18 |
| 1957 | 16.2 | 14.3 | 33.2 | 5.9 | 2.8 | 18 |
| 1958 | 16.2 | 14.3 | 33.2 | 6.3 | 2.9 | 18 |
| 1959 | 24.2 | 14.6 | 43.6 | 7.3 | 3.8 | 17 |
| 1960 | 24.2 | 15.6 | 44.6 | 8.3 | 4.5 | 19 |
| 1961 | 40.3 | 8.5 | 69.7 | 9.7 | 5.0 | 17 |
| 1962 | 40.3 | 10.0 | 71.0 | 8.8 | 5.0 | 15 |
| 1963 | 40.3 | 11.5 | 72.6 | 9.1 | 5.3 | 15 |
| 1964 | 61.8 | 25.6 | 89.6 | 11.0 | 6.5 | 15 |
| 1965 | 64.7 | 31.1 | 97.9 | 16.8 | 10.8 | 14 |
| 1966 | 64.7 | 32.2 | 101.2 | 17.3 | 11.1 | 14 |
| 1967 | 64.7 | 35.6 | 102.5 | 13.9 | 10.4 | 14 |
| 1968 | 64.7 | 39.2 | 106.0 | 17.9 | 12.9 | 14.5 |

## APPENDIX 4.3

### Midland Bank, shareholders' funds, group profits and dividends, 1969–1985

| Date | Issued capital (£ million) | Reserves (£ million) | Total shareholders' funds (£ million) | Group shareholders' funds (£ million) | Group net pre-tax profits (£ million) | Group net profits attributable after tax (£ million) | Dividend (% of issued capital) |
|---|---|---|---|---|---|---|---|
| 1969 | 64.7 | 90.0 | 156.8 | 192.8 | 36.4 | 19.1 | 15.0 |
| 1970 | 64.7 | 145.4 | 212.2 | 257.8 | 45.4 | 25.2 | 16.0 |
| 1971 | 64.7 | 158.7 | 225.5 | 279.3 | 52.0 | 30.5 | 17.5 |
| 1972 | 97.0 | 149.2 | 246.2 | 314.1 | 72.1 | 42.7 | 13.6 |
| 1973 | 97.0 | 182.5 | 279.6 | 367.1 | 113.4 | 65.5 | 10.0 |
| 1974 | 97.0 | 276.9 | 373.9 | 474.0 | 96.2 | 42.2 | 10.8 |
| 1975 | 132.5 | 285.3 | 448.6 | 563.4 | 82.4 | 32.7 | 11.5 |
| 1976 | 132.5 | 317.2 | 479.9 | 622.4 | 166.4 | 71.7 | 12.6 |
| 1977 | 132.5 | 346.5 | 509.2 | 688.3 | 192.8 | 82.5 | 15.1 |
| 1978 | 162.5 | 388.3 | 647.4 | 953.6 | 231.4 | 118.8 | 16.4 |
| 1979 | 163.3 | 552.3 | 814.7 | 1219.8 | 315.5 | 166.2 | 20.0 |
| 1980 | 164.3 | 590.5 | 856.3 | 1348.6 | 231.8 | 168.9 | 21.5 |
| 1981 | 165.2 | 579.9 | 848.7 | 1448.3 | 232.2 | 123.9 | 24.0 |
| 1982 | 171.0 | 641.9 | 935.0 | 1561.7 | 251.4 | 144.6 | 25.5 |
| 1983 | 229.0 | 1396.0 | 1899.0 | 1899.0 | 225.0 | 114.0 | 25.5 |
| 1984 | 230.0 | 1178.0 | 1685.0 | 1685.0 | 135.0 | 45.0 | 25.5 |
| 1985 | 231.0 | 1341.0 | 1847.0 | 1847.0 | 351.0 | 122.0 | 25.5 |

APPENDIX 4.4

**Midland Bank, actual and published net profits, 1880–1968**

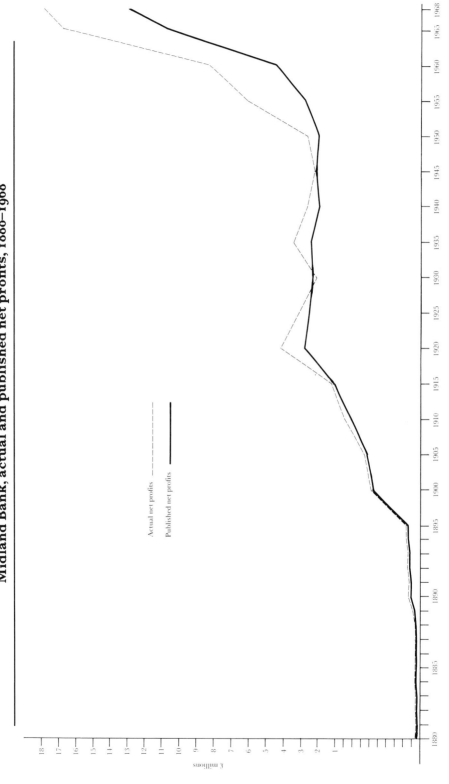

# APPENDIX 5

## Midland Bank, classification of advances, 1929–1980 (percentages)

| # | | 1929 | 1933 | 1945 | 1950 | 1955 | 1960 | 1965 | 1970 | 1975 | 1980 | 1985 |
|---|---|---|---|---|---|---|---|---|---|---|---|---|
| 1 | Coal mining | 1.7 | 1.1 | 0.3 | 0.01 | | 0.01 | 0.01 | 0.3 | 0.5 | 1.3 | 2.7 |
| 2 | Quarrying | 0.3 | 0.4 | 0.2 | 0.2 | 0.2 | 0.2 | 0.3 | | | | |
| 3 | Iron, steel | 6.1 | 6.1 | 1.6 | 0.9 | 1.5 | 2.0 | 3.3 | 2.9 | 1.4 | 2.0 | 1.4 |
| 4 | Non-ferrous | | | | 0.2 | 0.3 | 0.2 | 0.8 | | | | |
| 5 | Engineering | | | 9.1 | 5.5 | 10.0 | 18.5 | 18.8 | 25.4 | 18.4 | 12.5 | 6.9 |
| 6 | Shipping and shipbuilding | 4.3 | 3.3 | 0.9 | 0.7 | 0.9 | 0.7 | 0.9 | 2.4 | 4.2 | 0.2 | |
| 7 | Transport and communications | 0.8 | 1.1 | 0.7 | 0.7 | 0.8 | 0.9 | 1.2 | 1.8 | 3.0 | 2.8 | 2.0 |
| 8 | Cotton | 10.1 | 7.1 | 0.8 | 0.2 | 0.5 | 0.3 | 0.3 | 3.8 | 1.9 | 7.9 | 5.8 |
| 9 | Wool | | | 0.6 | 1.4 | 1.3 | 1.8 | 1.2 | | | | |
| 10 | Other textiles | | | 0.8 | 1.6 | 1.9 | 1.9 | 1.7 | | | | |
| 11 | Leather and rubber | | | 0.6 | 0.8 | 0.9 | 0.8 | 1.2 | | | | |
| 12 | Chemicals | 3.4 | 2.8 | 1.5 | 1.2 | 1.9 | 1.8 | 2.2 | 2.6 | 1.4 | 4.4 | 0.8 |
| 13 | Agriculture and fishing | 6.0 | 7.8 | 7.2 | 8.8 | 9.0 | 9.9 | 11.8 | 9.2 | 4.2 | 7.4 | 6.8 |
| 14 | Food, drink and tobacco | 5.6 | 6.9 | 3.6 | 4.9 | 6.8 | 3.7 | 4.7 | 4.7 | 3.6 | 4.4 | 1.9 |
| 15 | Retail trade | 6.5 | 8.1 | 7.6 | 12.1 | 9.0 | 9.8 | 10.8 | 12.0 | 8.4 | 12.0 | 10.7 |
| 16 | Entertainment | 0.8 | 1.3 | 1.1 | 0.8 | 0.5 | 0.4 | 0.3 | — | — | — | — |
| 17 | Builders and contractors | 6.8 | 9.0 | 5.5 | 4.3 | 4.1 | 4.2 | 4.3 | 5.0 | 5.1 | 5.0 | 4.3 |
| 18 | Building materials | | | 0.7 | 1.0 | 1.0 | 0.7 | 1.0 | | | | |
| 19 | Unclassified | 6.2 | 6.0 | 3.7 | 6.9 | 8.2 | 7.0 | 8.7 | 5.2 | 3.3 | 0.1 | |
| 20 | Local government | 3.9 | 3.0 | 22.1 | 13.9 | 11.7 | 5.2 | 1.5 | 0.3 | 0.5 | 0.3 | 0.6 |
| 21 | Public utilities | | | 2.0 | 5.2 | 6.8 | 3.4 | 0.7 | 0.7 | 3.9 | 2.5 | |
| 22 | Churches, charities and hospitals | 1.7 | 2.2 | 1.4 | 0.9 | 0.9 | 0.7 | 0.9 | — | — | — | — |
| 23 | Stockbrokers | 4.0 | 1.8 | 0.2 | 0.1 | 0.1 | 0.1 | 0.05 | — | — | — | — |
| 24 | Hire purchase companies | — | — | — | — | 1.3 | 2.3 | 1.4 | 0.7 | 0.5 | 0.8 | 15.8 |
| 25 | Other financial | 25.5 | 23.7 | 5.9 | 8.9 | 7.3 | 6.6 | 6.4 | 3.6 | 11.4 | 6.7 | |
| 26 | Personal and professional | 6.3 | 8.3 | 21.8 | 18.7 | 13.1 | 16.8 | 15.5 | 19.4 | 28.3 | 29.5 | 40.3 |

*Notes:* Classification numbers and descriptions are those adopted after the Macmillan Committee report of 1931. (Category 24 was not classified separately before 1955, and categories 16, 22 and 23 were not classified separately from 1970.)

# APPENDIX 6

## Midland Bank, numbers of branches and staff at five year intervals, 1885–1985

| Date | Number of branches and sub-branches | Number of staff (including Trust Company from 1910) |
|---|---|---|
| 1885 | 10 | 80 estimated |
| 1890 | 45 | 350 estimated |
| 1895 | 147 | 735 |
| 1900 | 314 | 1500 estimated |
| 1905 | 481 | 2705 in 1906 |
| 1910 | 689 | 3691 |
| 1915 | 1087 | 7086 including 1424 with HM Forces |
| 1920 | 1497 | 10,697 |
| 1925 | 1850 | 12,058 |
| 1930 | 2100 | 13,192 |
| 1935 | 2140 | 13,070 |
| 1940 | 2031 | 15,687 including 2139 with HM Forces |
| 1945 | 1805 | 19,941 including 7845 with HM Forces |
| 1950 | 2118 | 16,091 including 443 with HM Forces |
| 1955 | 2123 | 16,506 including 450 with HM Forces |
| 1960 | 2273 | 21,970 |
| 1965 | 2599 | 28,418 in 1966 |
| 1970 | 2663 | 34,927 |
| 1975 | 2624 | 41,717 |
| 1980 | 2462 | 52,609 in Group total of 77,900 |
| 1985 | 2220 | 45,435 in Group total of 78,590 |

# APPENDIX 7

## Chairmen and chief executives of Midland Bank, 1836–1986

*Chairmen*

1880–1898 John D Goodman
1898–1908 Arthur Keen
1908–1919 Sir Edward Holden
1919–1943 The Right Hon Reginald McKenna
1943–1945 Stanley Christopherson, JP
1945–1952 The Most Hon The Marquis of Linlithgow, KG, KT
1952–1957 The Right Hon Lord Harlech, KG, PC, GCMG
1957–1964 The Right Hon The Viscount Monckton of Brenchley,
           PC, KCMG, KCVO, MC, QC
1964–1975 Sir Archibald Forbes, GBE
1975–1980 The Right Hon Lord Armstrong of Sanderstead, PC, GCB, MVO
1980–1982 Sir David Barran
1982–     Sir Donald Barron, DL

*Chief executives*

1836–1846 Charles Geach, manager
1846–1854 Charles Geach, managing director
1847–1867 Henry Edmunds, manager
1867–1874 Henry Edmunds, managing director
1875–1878 William Goode, manager
1878–1887 G F Bolding, manager
1887–1891 John A Christie, manager
1891–1897 John A Christie, joint general manager
1891–1897 Edward H Holden, joint general manager
1898–1919 Edward H Holden, managing director
1919–1922 Samuel B Murray, joint managing director
1919–1929 Frederick Hyde, joint managing director
1919–1920 John F Darling, CBE, joint managing director
1920–1929 Edgar W Woolley, joint managing director
1929–1938 Frederick Hyde, managing director
1938–1943 Herbert A Astbury, chief general manager
1943–1948 Clarence Sadd, CBE, JP, DL, chief of executive
1943–1946 G P A Lederer, MC, chief general manager
1946–1951 Harold L Rouse, chief general manager
1946–1956 William G Edington, chief general manager
1956–1962 Oswald E Wood, chief general manager
1956      Joseph Fitton, chief general manager
1956–1958 Frederick E G Hayward, chief general manager
1962–1968 Howard H Thackstone, chief general manager
1968–1972 Leonard C Mather, chief general manager

| 1972–1974 | Charles E Trott, MBE, chief general manager |
| 1974–1981 | Stuart T Graham, CBE, DFC, chief general manager |
| 1981–1982 | Stuart T Graham, CBE, DFC, group chief executive |
| 1974–1981 | Malcolm G Wilcox, MBE, chief general manager |
| 1982– | Geoffrey W Taylor, group chief executive |

# APPENDIX 8

## Midland Bank Group principal subsidiaries, 1985–6

| Company | Country of incorporation and operation |
| --- | --- |
| Clydesdale Bank PLC | Great Britain |
| Crocker National Corporation | USA |
| Forward Trust Limited | Great Britain |
| Griffin Factors Limited | Great Britain |
| Handelsfinanz Midland Bank | Switzerland |
| Midland Bank Canada | Canada |
| Midland Bank Equity Holdings Limited | Great Britain |
| Midland Bank Group International Trade Services Limited | Great Britain |
| Midland Bank Insurance Services Limited | Great Britain |
| Midland Bank International Financial Services Limited | Great Britain |
| Midland Bank SA | France |
| Midland Bank (Singapore) Limited | Singapore |
| Midland Bank Trust Company Limited | Great Britain |
| Midland Finance (HK) Limited | Hong Kong |
| Midland International Australia Limited | Australia |
| Midland International Financial Services BV | The Netherlands |
| Midland Montagu Leasing Limited | Great Britain |
| Northern Bank Limited | Northern Ireland |
| Samuel Montagu & Co Limited | Great Britain |
| The Thomas Cook Group Limited | Great Britain |
| Trinkaus & Burkhardt | West Germany |

# INDEX

Aberdeen Town & County Bank 162
Abs, Hermann 253
Accepting Houses Committee 238–9, 291
Access credit card 279–80
Addison, Samuel, banker 38
Adkins, Thomas 29–30
Aetna Life & Casualty Co 303, 306
Agricultural & Commercial Bank of Ireland
20
Agricultural Mortgage Corporation 209–10
Alanbrooke, Lord 220
Alexanders Stores 267
Alliance Bank of London & Liverpool 82
Allied Irish Banks 237–8
Amalgamated Securities 267
amalgamations in banking 91, 98, 104, 113,
121, 124, 126, 128, 132, 156, 162, 242–3, 261;
see also Midland Bank, amalgamations and
affiliations
Amery, John 14, 26, 28, 41
Amsterdam Rotterdam Bank 253
Anderson, Alexander 162
Anderson, Sir John 206
Anderson, L D 166
Anglo-Russian Trust 136–7
Anglo-South American Bank 186
Armavir-Touapsé Railway 135–6
Armstrong & Co, bankers 139
Armstrong of Sanderstead, Lord 288, 298–9,
302, 340
Armstrong, Whitworth & Co, shipbuilders
and engineers 183
Ashby & Co, bankers 105
Asquith, Herbert H 144, 147, 149, 155
Associated Banks of Europe (ABECOR) 256
Associated Midland Corporation 301
Association of English Country Bankers 90
Astbury, Herbert A 194, 207, 340
Attwood, Spooner & Co, bankers 10, 42–3, 52
Austin Motor Co 179
Automobile Association 289
Avis Rentacar 293

Bacchus, George 14–15
Baldwin, Stanley 156
Balfour, Jabez 144
Banca Commerciale Italiana 254–5
Banco Bamerindus 293
Banco Hispano Americano 293
bank failures 3, 18, 20, 40, 42–3, 46, 60–1, 90,
144, 145, 270
bank hours 16–17, 54, 198, 248, 278
bank notes see note issue
Bank of Australasia 224
Bank of Birmingham 12, 13, 36, 58
Bank of England
    Birmingham branch 11, 12, 14, 20, 26, 70;
    building 175; 'Competition and Credit
    Control' 261; gold reserves 142–3; indus-
    trial reorganization 181–4; London Ex-
    change Committee 150; Midland Bank,
    relationship with 18–21, 24–6, 39, 81, 134,
    176; nationalization 210; privileges 2–3,
    7–8; regulatory role 209–11, 227–8, 231,
    240, 248; special deposits 226, 233, 265,
    280; support operations 20, 45, 90, 119,
    122, 147, 268–70; see also Norman, Mon-
    tagu
Bank of Ireland 237–8
Bank of London & South America 186, 256,
296
Bank of New South Wales 224
Bank of West Africa 254
Bank of Westmorland 91–2, 99
Bank of Whitehaven 26
Bank Officers' Guild 172, 192, 219–20
Bankers' Guarantee & Trust Fund 65
Bankers Industrial Development Co (BIDC)
181–2, 210
Bankhaus Herstatt 270
Banking Information Service 218
Banque Belge 253
Banque Européenne de Crédit à Moyen
Terme (BEC) 254–6, 288
Banque Nationale de Paris 259

Barclays Bank
    acquisitions 53, 100, 129, 159, 163, 228, 237, 243–4; Barclaycard 279; inter-bank cooperation 145, 186; international business 164–5, 254, 256, 259; management structure 216, 218, 223, 247, 282; merchant banking 291; origins 9, 57; ranking 118, 167, 169, 196, 221–2, 241, 245, 288–9; secondary banking crisis 267, 272
Bardsley, Donald 265–6
Barham, F 61, 72
Baring Brothers, bankers 89, 122, 135, 138–9, 183
Barnett Hoare & Co, bankers 100
Barran, Sir David 302, 340
Barron, Sir Donald 303, 340
Barton, J A 50
Bate & Robins, bankers 39
Bates & Sons, Edward, bankers 270
Bates, Sir Percy 155
BCT Midland Bank 301
Beale, Charles 63–4, 67, 81
Beale, Samuel 37, 47, 76
Beale, William 37, 76
Beardmore & Co, shipbuilders and engineers 176, 183
Beazley, Robert 155
Beckett & Co, bankers 101
Bedworth Coal & Iron Co 59–60
Belfast Banking Co 158–9, 162, 163, 165, 185, 232, 237–8
Belgium American Banking Corporation 254
Bell, Henry 159
Bell, Sir James 161
Belsize Motors 179
Benson, Sir Henry 276
Bevin, Ernest 176
bills of exchange see discount business
Birkbeck Bank 90, 144
Birmingham 7, 11, 27–8, 30–1, 36, 48, 59, 79, 87
Birmingham & Midland Bank see Midland Bank
Birmingham Assay Office 54
Birmingham Banking Co (Metropolitan Bank of England and Wales from 1893) 12–14, 16, 18–20, 25–6, 32–3, 38, 51, 58–9, 69, 71, 73, 75, 82, 86, 90, 102
    amalgamated with Midland 125, 126–7, 169; stoppage and reconstruction 46–8, 52; transferred to London 83
Birmingham banks 10–17, 19, 27, 38, 42–3, 46–7, 52, 59, 69, 118
Birmingham Canal Navigation Co 50–1
Birmingham District & Counties Bank see Birmingham Town & District Bank
Birmingham Dudley & District Bank see Birmingham Town & District Bank
Birmingham Exchange Bank see Midland Bank

Birmingham Joint Stock Bank 43, 55, 59, 69, 71, 73, 75
Birmingham Small Arms Co 68, 72, 80, 155
Birmingham Town & District Bank (Birmingham Dudley & District Banking Co from 1874) 15, 16, 19, 26, 38, 59, 69, 71, 73, 75, 83, 104
Birmingham Water Works 51
Blackett, Sir Basil 178–9
Bland, F L 172
Bland Payne Group, insurance brokers 294, 301
Bland Welch & Co, insurance brokers 238, 294
Boer War 105, 144
Bolckow Vaughan & Co, steelmakers 106
Bolding, G F 58, 61, 63, 64, 65, 81–2, 83, 340
Bolton & Co, merchants 28
Bolton, F S 67–8
Bolton, Thomas 15, 16, 37
Boulton & Watt, engineers 10
Bowater's Bush Farm Iron Works 59
Bradford Banking Co 17, 41, 123–5, 136
Bradford Dyers' Association 116, 117
Bradshaw, William G 91, 94, 109
branch banking 38, 41, 115, 232; see also Midland Bank, branches
Brand, R H 176, 187
British Bankers' Association 90, 187, 199
British Gas pension funds 300
British Linen Bank 159, 163
British Trade Corporation 164
Brown Marshall & Co, engineers 68
Bruce-Gardner, Charles 181
Buchanan, J G 166
Bunker, Frederick 139–41, 166, 235
Burdett, Sir Henry 137
Burgan, John 70
Burgess, Henry 8

Caledonian Banking Co 60
Cahouet, Frank V 304
Cameron, H G 279
Campbell, John 227–8
Canada 133, 166
Capital & Counties Bank 82, 91, 126, 129
Carlisle City & District Banking Co 92, 99
Carnock, Lord 155
Catto, Lord 210
Cave, John 268, 275–7, 286, 292
Cedar Holdings 266–8
Central Association of Bankers 90, 101
Central Bank of London 84–6, 91
Central Electricity Board 181
Certificates of deposit (CDs) 264
Chamberlain, Joseph 59
Channel Islands Bank, Jersey 94, 99, 109
Channel Tunnel Group 305
Charing Cross Bank 144
Charterhouse Industrial Development Co 182–3

Charterhouse Investment Trust 182
Chase Manhattan Bank 296
Chester National Bank, New York 267
Chesterfield Gas & Water Board 116
Chippindale, W 46, 47, 54
Christie, John A 63, 70, 73–6, 83–4, 87, 91, 93–4, 340
Christopherson, Stanley 206–7, 340
Churchill, Winston, 168, 230
*Circular to Bankers* 7, 8
City Bank 93, 95, 96, 99, 105, 109, 113, 116, 117, 123, 132
City of Birmingham Bank 98, 99, 104
City of Glasgow Bank 46, 60–2, 65
City of London College 193
Clapham, Sir John 123
Clarke, Bernard F 236, 241, 247
Clauson, A C 158
Clay, Prof Henry 181
Clay, William 22
clearing banks, 'Big Five' 121, 132, 167, 196, 222, 228, 242; *see also* Barclays, Lloyds, Midland, National Provincial and Westminster banks
Clearing House, London Bankers' 79, 84, 90, 198
    Clearing House automated payments system (CHAPS) 304
Clydesdale Bank 26, 82, 232, 236–7, 240, 269, 282, 341
    affiliation with Midland 159–62, 163, 238; Forward Trust 227–8
Clydesdale Bank Finance Corporation 240
Cobbold, Cameron 227
Cochrane & Co, ironfounders 48
Collingwood, Adrian 226
Colville & Sons, David, steelmakers 184
Colwyn Committee, Treasury Committee on Bank Amalgamations 129–32, 156–7, 180, 189, 242
Commercial Bank of Australia 253
Commercial Bank of England 14
Commercial Bank of Scotland 227–8; *see also* National Commercial Bank of Scotland
Committee of London Clearing Bankers 183, 187, 199, 205, 298
'Competition and Credit Control' (CCC) 261–2, 271, 280, 292
Cook, Thomas *see* Thomas Cook Group
Cooper & Co, J R, gunmakers 65
Cooper, Colin 200–1
Cotton Fine Spinners' Association 116
Cousins, Allen & Co, bankers 76
Coutts & Co, bankers 243
Coventry Union Banking Co 75, 85
Craven Banking Co 104
Credit for Industry 183
Crédit Lyonnais 82, 134, 166, 254
Creditanstalt-Bankverein 254–5
Crick, Wilfrid F 3, 154, 187, 205
Crisp, C Birch 136–7, 139

Crocker National Corporation 302, 304–6, 341
Cumberland Union Banking Co 45, 80, 117
Cunard Steam-Ship Co 155, 167, 185
Cunliffe, Lord 144, 180

Darling, John F 154, 160, 340
Davidoff, L 137–8
Derby Commercial Bank 76, 85, 123
Desreaux, W T 203
Deutsch-Asiatische Bank 256
Deutsche Bank 82, 187, 253
Dimsdale, Fowler, Barnard & Dimsdale, bankers 93; *see also* Prescott, Dimsdale, Cave, Tugwell & Co
'Disclosure' 244–5, 261, 297, 328–30
discount business 2, 42–4; *see also* Midland Bank, discount business
District Bank 12, 242, 243
Dixon, Dalton & Co, bankers 19
Dixon-Hartland, Sir Frederick 84–5, 109
Docker, F Dudley 115, 155, 195, 206
Drayton Group, investment bankers 291
Dresdner Bank 134, 187
Dudley & West Bromwich Banking Co 40
Dumbell's Banking Co 119

Eagle Star Insurance Co 268
East London Bank *see* Central Bank of London
Edington, William G 210, 214–17, 219–21, 287, 340
Edmunds, Henry 33, 35–6, 40, 42, 48, 55, 57–8, 67–8, 340
Edwards, E 35, 46
Elswick Cycle Co 117
English Joint Stock Bank 45
Esdaile & Co, bankers 25
'Euromarkets' 252
Euro-Pacific Finance Corporation 255
European Advisory Committee (EAC) 253–6, 288
European-American Banking Corporation (EAB) 254–5, 288
European Asian Bank (EURAS) 255–6
European Bank 43, 46
European Banking Co (EBC) 255–6
European Banks International Co (EBIC) 255–6, 258–60, 296, 298
European Economic Community (EEC) 251–3
Exchange & Discount Bank 76, 78, 85
exchange controls 197, 208–9, 250

Faber, Beckett 101
Faringdon Committee on Financial Facilities for Trade 164
Farley, Lavender & Co, bankers 40
Farley, Turner & Co, bankers 40
Faulkner, Sir Eric 275
Fenton & Sons, bankers 60
Fiat 293
Fidgeon, William 101

financial crises 3, 119, 142, 147–9, 175, 266–71; *see also* bank failures
Finch, Francis 15, 17
First National Bank of Chicago 149
First National City Bank 258–9, 291
First National Finance Corporation (FNFC) 268–9, 271
Fish, H M 203
Fisher, T E 290, 293
Fitton, Joseph 221, 340
Fleetwood-Wilson, Sir Guy 155
Fontaine, Edward 134
Forbes, Sir Archibald 234–6, 238–9, 241, 243, 263, 275–6, 283, 288–9, 297, 340
foreign exchange *see* Midland Bank, international business
Forgan, J B 149
Forward Trust 227–9, 232, 235, 238, 240, 277, 287–8, 290, 292–3, 302, 341
Foster & Bolitho, bankers 14
Francis, John 15, 16, 37
Franck, Louis 238–9
Franco-Prussian war 59, 135
Franklin National Bank 270
Fraser, Kirkpatrick & Smith, stockbrokers 81
Freshfield, J W 14

Galton & James, bankers 10–14
Gammon, William 15, 16
Geach, Charles
   Bank of England, career with 14, 16; dealings with 19–21, 24–26, 33; Bate & Robins, negotiations with 39; business interests 30–1, 47, 68, 76; manager 16–17, 32, 215–16, 340; Midland Bank, formation of 15; personality and reputation 14, 19, 32–3, 35; public duties 31–2
Geach, Edward 17
Geach, George 14
Gee, H Simpson 155
German 'standstill' agreement 186–7, 249
Gibbins & Lovell, bankers 12, 13
Gibbins, Joseph junior 12, 15
Gibbins, Joseph senior 10, 12
Gibbins, Smith & Goode, bankers 11–14, 15, 36
Gibson-Jarvie, John 183
Gladstone, William E 45
Glasbrook, John 155
Glyn, George C 8
Glyn Mills & Co, bankers 8, 49, 135, 185
Goddard, Samuel 31
gold standard 142–3, 175, 177
Goode, William 36, 58, 63, 64, 67, 340
Goodman, J D 65–6, 68–9, 70, 72, 82–3, 86–7, 91–3, 340
Gordon, W B 45
Goschen, Viscount 99
Gotch & Saunders, architects 171
government, banks' relationship with 23–4, 45, 122, 143, 147–50, 156, 211, 219, 248; *see*

*also* Treasury, HM
Graham, David 239
Graham, Stuart T 258, 268, 277, 279, 286–8, 341
Granet, Sir Guy 181
Great North of Scotland Railway 162
Greenway, Smith & Greenway, bankers 75
Greenwell & Co, W, stockbrokers 304
Gregory, T E 176
Griffin Factors 291–2, 341
Guest Keen & Co (Guest Keen & Nettlefolds from 1902) 67, 115, 181
Guinness, Arthur, brewers 157
Guyerzeller Zurmont Bank 238, 291

Haes & Co, stockbrokers 137–8
Halifax Joint Stock Bank 105
Hambro & Son, C J, bankers 139, 239
Handelsfinanz Midland Bank 303, 341
Hankey, Sir Maurice 156
Hardy & Wright, ironmasters 30, 31
Harland & Wolff, shipbuilders 115, 155, 157, 160, 184–5
Harlech, Lord 215, 217–18, 230, 340
Harvey & Son, Charles, bankers 46
Harvey, Sir Ernest 188
Hay's Wharf Cartage Co 289
Hayward, Frederick E G 221–3, 228–9, 340
Head, George 45
Heath, Edward 276
Heaton, Henry 84
Hellmuth, E J W 236, 239, 253
Henderson, John 160
Hepworth & Son, J, multiple tailors 293
Higginson & Co, bankers 181
Hill, Rowland 23
Hillman, W H 123
hire purchase 227–8, 233; *see also* Forward Trust
Hodges, Frank 181
Holden, Sir Cassie 158, 195, 215
Holden, Edward H
   acquisitions, role in Midland Bank 74–6, 83–7, 92–9, 104–9, 124, 126–7, 129–31, 157–9, 242; chairman 117, 340; early career 70, 73, 83–4; gold reserves, views on 142–3; influence 153–4, 166, 171, 188, 299; international business, role in 131–41, 186; knighted 147; management style 89, 101, 105, 123, 153; parliamentary career 108, 147; personality and reputation 86, 89, 101, 122–3, 133–4, 142, 150–1; promotions 86–7, 91, 93–4, 123, 340; USA and Canada, visits to 133; war finance, role in 147–50; Yorkshire Penny Bank, rescue of 143–7
Holden, Norman 137–8
Hollams, Sir John 84–5
Hollom, Sir Jasper 268
Holmes, Edward 55
Hounsell, Edgar 228

Huddersfield Banking Co 8, 17, 29, 94–5, 99, 102

Hume, Nutcombe 183

Hunt & Sons, merchants 28

Hyde, Frederick 123, 154, 170–1, 173–4, 178, 180, 184–5, 187, 190, 194, 235, 340

Imperial Bank 82

Inchcape, Lord 131

Industrial & Commercial Finance Corporation (ICFC) 210, 218

Industrial Reorganization Corporation 275

industry and banking 113–17, 177–85, 210; see also Macmillan Committee; Midland Bank, business customers; Midland Bank, lending

Inland Revenue 54, 168

Institute of Bankers 64, 90, 112, 142, 172–3, 193, 207, 246

Institute of Bankers in Scotland 64

interest rates 79, 99–100, 177, 199, 208, 219, 261, 265

International Harvester Corporation 139

Iran Overseas Investment Bank 255–6

Israel-British Bank 270

Issuing Houses Association 238

Ivy House & Northwood Colliery 60

Jackson, A T 166, 173, 194

James & Shakspeare Ltd, commodity dealers 195

James, Paul 12, 15

Jekyll, Gertrude 171

Joint Credit Card Co 279

joint stock banks 2, 3, 7–10, 17, 22–3; Secret Committee on 17, 19

Jones, Aubrey 234

Joplin, Thomas 17, 23, 49

Joseph, L 113

Julien, Michael F 304

Keen, Arthur 67, 80, 84, 91, 94, 102, 115, 340

Kennet Committee on Post War Employment 203–4, 210

Keynes, John Maynard 176–8, 206, 213

Keyser Ullmann, bankers 270

Kidderminster, Worcestershire 40, 53, 54

Kinross, John 210

Kitching, Dennis W C 268–9, 277

Kitson, Arthur 150

Kitson, Sir James 106–7

Korean war 218

Kossuth, Louis 31

Kylsant, Lord 184–5

Lacy, Hartland, Woodbridge & Co, bankers 84–5

Lancashire
 banking 3, 11, 25, 95–6; cotton industry 45, 92, 174, 181–2, 217

Lancashire & Yorkshire Bank 107

Lancashire Cotton Corporation 181–2

Lancashire Steel Corporation 183

Laurie Milbank & Co, stockbrokers 81

Laycock, Samuel 17

Lazard Brothers, bankers 176, 187, 275

Le Masurier, A E 202–3

Leadenhall Securities Incorporation 183

Leamington Priors & Warwickshire Banking Co 75, 85

Lederer, G P A 182, 194, 207–8, 214, 340

Leeds & County Bank 76, 78, 85, 92, 98

Leeman, George 45

Legislation
 Bank Charter Act (1833) 8; Bank Charter Act (1844) 22–4, 45, 52; Bank Holidays Act (1871) 54; Banking Act (1976) 271; Banking Copartnerships Act (1826) 3, 7, 22; Bills of Exchange Act (1882) 64; Companies Act (1857–62) 52; Companies Act (1879) 62–3, 65, 70; Companies Act (1948) 244, 267; Companies Act (1967) 240, 266; Joint Stock Bank Act (1844) 22, 23, 52; Money-lenders Act (1900) 266; Protection of Depositors Act (1963) 293; Reform Act (1832) 10; Savings Bank Act (1863) 144

Leicestershire Banking Co 27, 33, 38, 105–7, 113, 117

Leigh, James 90

lending see Midland Bank, lending

Leverhulme, Lord 150

Leyland & Bullins, bankers 200

Liberator Building Society 144

limited liability 58, 62–3

Lincoln & Lindsey Banking Co 53, 104, 124–5

Lindner, Maximilian 75

Lings, Scott 116

Linlithgow, Marquess of 207–11, 217, 220, 230, 340

Liverpool banking 95, 107, 109, 112

Lloyd George, David 144, 147–9, 150, 156

Lloyd, Howard 107

Lloyds & Scottish Finance 268

Lloyds Bank
 acquisitions 43, 52, 75, 100, 107, 125, 128–9, 159, 163, 237, 242–5, 296; branches 38, 103, 125, 169–70; capital 36, 71, 93, 245; deposits 40, 59, 69, 86, 89, 91, 97, 118, 126, 167; dividends 73, 118; inter-bank cooperation 145, 182, 272, 274–5, 279; international business 139, 164–5, 254, 256, 259, 270, 289, 296; management structure 113, 247; origins 9–11; ranking 56, 97, 108, 118, 179, 289; transferred to London 57, 79, 82, 87

Lockheed Aircraft Corporation 275–6

London
 bank agencies 25, 50, 100; foreign banks in 82, 134–5, 257–8; influence of 57, 81–2, 87; joint stock banks 8, 21, 34, 52, 91, 96, 98; see also Central Bank of London; City

London (*cont.*)
Bank; London Joint Stock Bank; Midland
Bank transfer to 57, 87, 93, 96, 97
London American Finance Corporation 292,
300, 303
London & County Bank (London County &
Westminster Bank from 1909) 84, 91, 93, 97,
113, 126, 128–9, 139, 164; *see also* Westminster Bank
London & County Securities 266–8, 271
London & General Bank 90, 144
London & Midland Bank *see* Midland Bank
London & Provincial Bank 95, 103, 129
London & South Western Bank 91, 93, 95,
101, 129
London & Westminster Bank 8, 49, 84, 93,
96, 135
London Bankers' Clearing House *see* Clearing
House
London Birmingham & South Staffordshire
Banking Co 43
London City & Midland Bank *see* Midland
Bank
London City & Midland Bank Executor &
Trustee Co *see* Midland Bank Trust Co
London County & Westminster Bank *see*
London & County Bank
London Enterprise Agency 301
London Joint City & Midland Bank *see*
Midland Bank
London Joint Stock Bank
amalgamation with Midland Bank 125–6,
129–31, 156, 159, 169, 206; branches 102,
169; deposits 34, 86; inter-bank cooperation 145, 148; international business 135,
140; management structure 113, 173;
ranking 84, 96
Lorsignol, David 134
Lort, William 15, 16, 17, 37
Lovell, Goode & Stubbs, bankers 12, 13, 19
Lubbock, Sir John 142
Lutyens, Sir Edwin 171, 175

McDowell, Alexander 158
McKenna, Pamela 171
McKenna, Reginald
affiliations, role in Midland Bank 159–60;
banking and finance, views on 176–8, 188;
buildings, influence on Midland Bank 171–
2; chairman 154–6, 340; Chancellor of
Exchequer 146, 149; death 206–7; Home
Secretary 146; industrial reorganization,
role in 179, 182–3; international business,
role in 165–6, 187; Macmillan committee
member 177–8, 180; Norman, Montagu,
relationship with 177–8, 188, 206; outside
interests 195–6; personality and reputation
176–8, 190, 195, 206, 299; political career
159–60
McKinsey & Co, management consultants
282–8

McLintock, Sir William 180, 184–5, 236
McMahon, Christopher W 307
Macmillan Committee on Finance and Industry 176–83, 188, 189–90, 196, 226
Macmillan, Harold 224–5
Madders, John M 109, 123, 125–6
Manchester & County Bank 83
Manchester Joint Stock Bank 91, 99
Manchester & Liverpool District Banking Co
*see* District Bank
Manchester Sheffield & Lincolnshire Railway
31
Manwaring, Randle 279
Marshall, J G & E, engineers 48
Martin, Richard 101
Martins Bank 101, 179, 242–3
Maryport Haematite Iron Co 80
Mason, Josiah 47
Mather, Leonard C 245–7, 270–1, 286, 340
Maxwell, Brig-Gen Sir Arthur 184–5
mergers *see* amalgamations
Meritor Investments 301
Messel & Co, L, stockbrokers 139
Metropolitan Bank (of England & Wales) *see*
Birmingham Banking Co
Metropolitan Carriage Wagon & Finance Co
31, 155
Midland & International Banks (MAIBL) 238,
253–5, 257, 288, 303
Midland Bank
acquisitions 39–41, 70, 74–6, 78–9, 83, 84–
5, 91–9, 103–9, 124–7, 129–31
advertising and public relations 188–9,
207, 222, 224–5, 233, 302
affiliations 157–63, 174, 227, 237–40; *see
also* Midland Bank, subsidiaries
agencies with other banks 25–6, 100, 132;
*see also* Midland Bank, international business, correspondent banking
bad debts 26, 32, 61, 65, 68, 79, 174, 189–
90, 328
balance sheet 4–5, 27–8, 35–6, 57–8, 320–
36
Bank of England, discount account 18–21,
24–6, 39, 82
board of directors 16, 58, 61, 65–6, 110,
131, 155–6, 161, 211–12, 213–15, 236, 281,
284–5, 301
branches
administration 112, 216, 273–4; business
112, 127–8, 244–5, 248, 278; extension
69–70, 72–4, 77, 86, 102–3, 125, 169–72,
192, 222; numbers 89, 169, 232, 339;
proposed branches in Ireland and Scotland 157, 159; reorganization 273–4,
278, 282–3, 287, 299; wartime experience 199–204, 209
Aldershot 102; Bath 102–3; Bewdley
40–1, 53–4, 69, 72, 74, 321–2; Birmingham 70, 72, 74; Bolton 246; Brighton
102; Bristol 102–3, 192; Cardiff 102;

Channel Islands 201–3; Cheltenham
102; Cleobury Mortimer 40, 54; Coleshill 75; Derby 274; Ealing 102; Hastings 102; Huddersfield 103; Knowle
72; Leamington Spa 303; Leeds 103,
192, 287; Leicester 76; Leytonstone 102;
Liverpool 103, 200, 217; London (Camden Town 200; Chiswick 200; Grays Inn
200; Leadenhall Street 171; Monument
200; Peckham 200; Piccadilly 171;
Rotherhithe 102); Manchester 171;
Newcastle-upon-Tyne 102; Norbury
200; Northampton 76; Nottingham 102;
Oldham 182, 217; Preston 103; Sheffield
76, 200–1; Southampton 94; Southsea
200; Slough 192; Stourbridge 39–41, 48,
69, 74, 320–2; Torquay 102; Walsall 72;
Wednesbury 38, 59, 74
buildings 103, 126, 171–2, 223
business customers 28, 30–1, 59–60, 62, 67–
8, 80, 115–17, 133, 139, 157, 163–4, 174,
179–85, 247, 258, 273–4, 277
business development committee 222–6,
228–30, 247, 279
capital structure 15–16, 18, 32, 36–8, 58,
63, 78–9, 86, 95, 127, 131, 161, 244–6, 281,
300–6, 328–36
chairmen 16, 67, 83, 206–7, 283, 297–9,
340–1
computerization 248, 278, 303
contingent funds 52, 219
departments
    agriculture 226; Channel Islands 202;
    cheque clearing 190; corporate planning
    287; foreign banks 132; foreign ex-
    change 133–4; legal 246; new issues
    295; organization and methods 283;
    overseas see international business;
    premises 283; registrar 295; shipping
    134; stock office 295; strategic services
    278; see also Midland Bank divisions
deposits 2, 27–9, 37, 41, 47, 50, 57, 72, 78,
86, 97, 100, 118, 126, 157, 167, 196, 208,
232, 241, 273, 320–6
directors' committees 63, 65–6, 69, 108–10,
191, 223
discount business 26, 28, 41–2, 47, 61, 114–
16
diversification 227–9, 232, 234, 236–41,
248, 257, 281, 283, 286, 288–99
divisions
    business development 301; corporate fi-
    nance 277, 280; group risk management
    304; group treasury 302; international
    see Midland Bank International Divi-
    sion; money market 272–3; term loan
    272; UK banking 303; UK business 305
entry to London 57, 93, 96, 97
formation 1, 7, 9, 15, 17
gold dealings 143
griffin symbol 233

group development 1, 4, 238–41, 281–99,
300–6
group executive committee 305
headquarters
    Birmingham, New Street 55, 79; Bir-
    mingham, Union Street 16, 21, 55;
    London, Cornhill 84, 87, 93; London,
    Poultry 171, 175, 198; London, Thread-
    needle Street 96–7, 109, 143, 173
inter-bank cooperation 178–96, 199, 205,
218, 229, 233
international business
    Atlantic offices 167; Canada 133, 166;
    consortium banking 253–60; corre-
    spondent banking 132, 140, 165–6, 236,
    250–1, 260; foreign banks department
    132; foreign exchange 133–4, 251; Ger-
    man 'standstill' 186–7; 'grand design'
    policy 252–60; New York office 254–5;
    overseas branch 140–1, 165–6, 173, 208–
    9, 235, 249–51, 272; proposed overseas
    branches 133, 139; provincial branches
    250; representative offices 257, 297;
    Russia 135–41, 164; shipping 134;
    United States of America 133, 150, 166,
    254; see also Midland Bank International
    Division
investments 49–51, 80–1, 141, 149, 219
lending 2, 29, 42, 47–8, 63, 80–1, 113–17,
129–30, 161, 174, 179–80, 190–1, 196, 206,
213, 226–7, 263, 273, 320–6, 338
loan capital 300–6
management committee 190, 194, 214–15,
235, 251, 263, 281, 283, 288
management structure 41, 63–4, 66, 73–4,
83, 87, 94, 108–12, 123, 153–4, 161, 173–4,
190–1, 198, 205, 211–16, 236, 246–7, 274,
277, 280, 281–5, 287, 298
mechanization 173–4, 190–1, 193, 205, 248
MIDNET telecommunications 305
name changes 16
    London & Midland Bank 85; London
    City & Midland Bank 97; London Joint
    City & Midland Bank 131; Midland
    Bank Limited 157; Midland Bank plc
    302
new issues 116, 135
overseas branch see international business
postwar planning committee 205–6, 209,
216
profits 5, 32, 35, 51, 58, 61, 68, 69, 72, 74,
103, 126, 170, 189–90, 244, 328–37
ranking 33, 56, 69, 86, 117–18, 122, 127,
150, 156, 174, 213, 221, 241–2, 244, 289
regional head offices 223, 247
registration 58, 63
related services 241, 287, 289, 291–2
reserves 32, 35, 51–2, 244, 328–36
secondary banking crisis 269–72
services
    Access 279; Autobanks 303; cheque

Midland Bank, services (*cont.*)
cards 279; chequelets 168–9; Euro-cheques 303; factoring 291; 'Finance For Export' 306; 'free-if-in-credit' bank-ing 305; gift cheques 224; gold Master-Card 303; 'Griffin Savers' 305; high interest cheque accounts 304; home safes 168–9; 'Homeowner Plus' 306; in-store banking 305; insurance 277–80, 293–4; mortgages 306; personal cheques 225; personal loans 224–5, 235; retirement service 305; Saturday service 307; 'Save and Borrow' 303; 'Saver Plus' 305; small business loans 305; small deposits 168; 'Speedline' 306; term loans 227; unit trusts 295
share values and dividends 51, 63, 69, 73, 91, 93, 99, 118, 189–90, 328–36
shareholders 4, 28–9, 37–8, 70–1, 97, 98, 101, 118, 127, 130, 169, 316
staff 33, 53–4, 64–5, 111–12, 118, 172, 193, 199, 203–5, 220, 230, 244, 278, 298, 339
female staff 128, 172, 193, 204; pension funds 112, 161; salaries 64, 103, 112, 172–3, 192–3, 220–1, 244, 300; training 133, 193, 205, 298; war service 128, 199, 204
Stock Exchange quotation 98
subsidiaries 1, 238–41, 300–6; *see also* Mid-land Bank, affiliations
war damage 199–200
wartime arrangements 197–9, 201, 205
Midland Bank Canada 302, 341
Midland Bank Equity Holdings 300, 341
Midland Bank Finance Corporation (MBFC) 238, 240–1, 272–3, 277, 287–8, 291–2
Midland Bank France SA 301
Midland Bank Group International Trade Services 303, 341
Midland Bank Group Unit Trust Managers 295
Midland Bank Insurance Brokers 301
Midland Bank Insurance Services (MBIS) 279–80, 293–4, 341
Midland Bank International Division 257–9, 287, 295–6
*Midland Bank Review* 189, 211, 264
Midland Bank SA 303, 341
Midland Bank (Singapore) 341
Midland Bank Staff Association 161, 172–3, 213, 219–21
Midland Bank Trust Co 141–2, 232, 238, 246, 281, 294–6, 341
Midland Bank Venture Capital 301
Midland Banking Co 52–3
Midland-Citibank Factors 291
Midland Finance (HK) 341
Midland International Australia 341
Midland International Financial Services BV (MIFSBV) 300–3, 341
Midland Investment Management 306

Midland Land & Investment Corporation 60, 67, 79
Midland Montagu Industrial Finance 238, 241
Midland Montagu Leasing 292, 341
Midland Railway Co 48, 50, 51, 80
Miller, David 134, 136–9
Moilliet & Sons, bankers 10, 12, 43, 52
Monckton of Brenchley, Viscount 230, 234, 235–6, 252, 340
Monopolies Commission 242, 244
Montagu Trust 238–9, 288, 290–1, 294–5, 298; *see also* Samuel Montagu & Co
Moracrest Investments 300
Moreno, A 166
Morgan & Co, J P 149
Morris, Edward 64
Munster & Leinster Bank 237
Murray, Samuel B 109, 123–6, 136–9, 144–5, 148–9, 151, 153–4, 340

Nash, Frederick 155
National Bank 237, 243
National Bank of Scotland 82, 83, 159, 163, 228
National Bank of Wales 90, 102, 126
National Coal Board 293
National Commercial Bank of Scotland 239
National Penny Bank 145
National Provincial Bank 14, 33, 36, 82–3, 86, 89, 91, 97, 101, 128–9, 141, 164–5, 167, 169, 186, 228–9, 242–3
National Savings 208
National Westminster Bank 8, 242–5, 256–7, 259, 268, 270, 272, 279, 282, 288, 291
Naylor Vickers & Co, steel manufacturers *see* Vickers
Newman, Cardinal 72
Nichols, Baker & Crane, bankers 40, 50, 100
Nicholson, E R 276
Nicholson, Sir Arthur 138, 139
Nixon, Richard 276
Norman, Montagu 177–82, 184, 186–8
North & South Wales Bank 22, 44, 48, 49, 58, 61, 107–9, 113, 200
North Central Wagon & Finance 228–9
North of Scotland Bank 162–3, 236, 238
North of Scotland Insurance Co 162
North Western Bank, formerly Moss & Co, bankers 92, 93, 95, 99, 101
Northern & Central Bank of England 14, 18, 20, 46
Northern Bank 237–8, 282, 341
Northern Bank Finance Corporation 240
Northern Bank (Ireland) 306
note issue 2, 8, 18, 22
Nottingham & Nottinghamshire Banking Co 102
Nottingham Joint Stock Bank 104, 106, 107

O'Brien, Leslie 242
Oldham Joint Stock Bank 95–6, 99, 109
Oppenheimer brothers, merchants 28
Orion Bank 257
Ormsby-Gore, William 217; *see also* Harlech, Lord
Osterreichische Creditanstalt 186
Overend, Gurney & Co, bankers 43–5, 47, 49, 50
Oversea Chinese Banking Corporation 293

Panmure Gordon & Co, stockbrokers 139
Park Gate Iron Manufacturing Co 31
Parkes, Ebenezer T 182
Parmley, Colin 247
Parr's Bank 125–6, 128, 135, 139
Patent Nut & Bolt Co 67
Patent Shaft & Axle Tree Co 30, 31, 51, 60, 68, 72, 80
Patterson, William 158
Payne, E W, insurance brokers 238, 294
Pearson & Co, contractors 139
Pearson, James 12
Pearson, Sir Denning 275
Peel, Sir Robert 22
Pelican Life Assurance Co 49
pepper crisis 195
Petrograd *see* St Petersburg
Peyton, Abel 48
Peyton & Peyton, tubemakers 48, 62, 67, 79
Peyton, John 289
Pinches, Thomas 16
Pirrie, William, Lord 115, 155, 157–8, 160, 184
Poliakoff, L 137–8
Pollock, D G H 105, 109, 123
Ponting, F W 92, 96
Post Office Savings Bank 94, 100–1
Powell, Ellis 86, 144, 147
Pownall, George H 114
Prescott, Dimsdale, Cave, Tugwell & Co, bankers 95
Preston Banking Co 27, 45, 92, 99
Price, Joseph 63
Prices and Incomes Board 234, 242
Prudential Assurance Co 182, 300

Queensland National Bank 141

Radcliffe Committee on the Working of the Monetary System 226–7, 231
Rae, George 44, 50, 58, 64, 107
railway shares 50–1, 80, 141
Reading, Lord 149–50
Renouf, P H 203
reserved liability *see* limited liability
Revelstoke, Lord 139
Ridout, Jeremiah 16
Roberts, Skey & Kenrick, bankers 40
Robins, William 39
Rochdale Joint Stock Bank 95

Roger, Sir Alexander 215
Rolls-Royce Ltd 274–6
Rouse, H L 173–4, 193, 214–17, 220, 287, 340
Rover Co, motor manufacturers 179
Royal Bank of Liverpool 25
Royal Bank of Scotland 82, 279
Royal Exchange Assurance 49, 141
Royal Mail shipping group 184–5, 236
Royden, Sir Thomas 155, 195, 206
Runciman, Walter 164, 185
Russia 135–41, 164
Russian banks 136–9

Sadd, Clarence T A 194, 207–8, 211–14, 217, 340
St Petersburg (Petrograd) 136–9, 151, 164
Salt & Co, Titus 141
Salter, Sir Arthur 179
Samuel Montagu & Co, bankers 82, 238, 241, 254, 258, 267, 272–3, 291, 293–4, 303–6, 341; *see also* Montagu Trust
Scholefield & Sons, merchants 28, 47, 65
Scholefield, Joshua 28, 31, 47, 65, 76
Scholefield, William 28, 47, 65, 76
Schroder & Co, J Henry, bankers 139, 183, 239
Schuster, Sir Felix 122, 148, 150
Scottish banks 9, 159, 236; *see also* Clydesdale Bank; North of Scotland Bank
Scottish Midland Guarantee Trust 228
Scrimgeour, J & A, stockbrokers 81
Second Scottish Midland Guarantee Trust 228
secondary banks 233, 261, 263–9
'lifeboat' 268–72
Securities Management Trust (SMT) 181
Selfridge, Gordon 115, 150
Shand, Allan A 135
Sheffield & Hallamshire Bank 44, 49, 124–5
Sheffield Union Banking Co 106, 107, 173
Shelbourne, Philip 291
Shield Factors 291
Shrewsbury & Birmingham Railway 31
Sikes, Sir Charles 94
Slater Walker, bankers 270
Smith, Bassett 15
Société Générale 254–6
Société Générale de Banque, Belgium 253, 254
South Staffordshire Water Co 48
Standard Bank of South Africa (Standard Chartered Bank from 1970) 82, 253–4, 295–6, 301
Stanford Research Institute 258–9
Steel-Maitland, Sir Arthur 179
Stewarts & Lloyds, steelmakers 181
Stourbridge & Kidderminster Banking Co 14, 26, 28, 36, 38, 39, 41, 51
Stourbridge Railway Co 48
Stourbridge, Worcestershire 39, 52, 54, 59, 72

Stuckey's Banking Co Ltd 125
Suez crisis 218

Taylor & Lloyds, bankers *see* Lloyds Bank
Taylor, Geoffrey W 241, 272, 303, 341
Taylor, J Frater 176, 181
Taylor, John 16
Thackstone, Howard H 235, 239–41, 245–7, 249–50, 252, 298, 340
Thomas Cook Group, travel service company 286, 289–91, 293, 298, 300, 306, 341
Thompson, J Walter, advertising agents 279
Thornton, Samuel 62
Tindal, Charles 19, 20, 24, 26, 27, 36
Toronto-Dominion Bank 253
Trafalgar House 289
treasurerships 48, 54
Treasury, HM 130–1, 146, 148, 150, 159–60, 162–3, 166, 168, 174, 210, 242
Trinkaus & Burkhardt 302, 306, 341
Trott, Charles E 286, 341
Trust House Forte 289
Trustee and executorship service *see* Midland Bank Trust Co
Trustee savings banks 101
Tuke, A W 221
Tulloch, Anne 128

Ulster Bank 163, 229
Union Bank of Birmingham 57, 59, 70–2, 83, 85, 104, 127
Union Bank of London (Union of London & Smiths Bank from 1902) 25, 44, 48, 50, 81, 93, 100, 118, 122, 126, 128, 145, 148
Union Bank of Manchester 25, 104
Union Bank of Moscow 137–8
Union de Banques Arabes et Françaises (UBAF) 255–6
United Dominions Trust 183, 228, 269, 270–1, 286
United Northern Banks 237
United States of America 133, 150, 166

Van Beek, Herman 134
Vanner, James E 97, 109
Vickers Ltd, steel and arms manufacturers 106, 179

Wadsworth, John E 3
Walker, Sir Alan 29
Walker, Thomas 60, 68
Wallace Shipping 294
war loans 149, 175

Warburg & Co, S G (formerly New Trading Co), bankers 183
Watt, Alexander 137–8
Watt, Hugh 17
Webb, Robert 15, 16, 17, 19, 25, 67
Wells Fargo & Co, bankers 306
West Cumberland Iron & Steel Co 80
West of England & South Wales District Bank 60–1
West Riding Union Banking Co 29
West Yorkshire Bank 145
Western Bank of Scotland 40
Westminster Bank 164–5, 167, 170, 186, 229, 239, 242–3
Whinney, T B 103
Whinney Son & Austen Hall, architects 171
Whitehaven Joint Stock Banking Co 105
Whitehead & Coles, stockbrokers 81
Wilcox, Malcolm G 241, 258, 286–7, 288, 291–2, 297, 341
Wilde, Derek V 270
Williams & Glyn's Bank 243, 272, 279
Williams Deacon & Co, bankers 25, 45; *see also* Williams & Glyn's Bank
Wills, William 16
Wilson Committee to Review the Functioning of Financial Institutions 262, 297
Wilts & Dorset Banking Co 125–6
Wolverhampton & Staffordshire Banking Co 40
Wood & Co, James, bankers 55
Wood, Oswald E 221–2, 229, 235, 340
Woods, Alexander 205
Woolcombers' Association 181
Woolfall & Eccles, architects 171
Woolley, Edgar 154, 170–1, 174, 194, 340
Worcester City & County Banking Co 75
World War, First 121, 127–8, 147–50
World War, Second 198–205
  air raids 199–200, 203; banking arrangements 197–9, 250
Wurth, C A 166
Wyley, William F 109, 155

York City & County Banking Co 8, 33–4, 78, 106, 173
Yorkshire Agricultural & Commercial Bank 18
Yorkshire Banking Co 22, 27, 30, 45, 106, 113–14
Yorkshire banks 48, 76, 79, 82, 106
Yorkshire Penny Bank 100, 106, 143–7, 155, 168, 183, 218
Young, David 160